Introduction to Coding for Class VII

A Perfect Textbook to Learn Basics of Block Coding

S P Verma
M.Sc., M.Ed., PGCPM
Former Principal, KVS, New Delhi

www.bpbonline.com

FIRST EDITION 2022

ISBN: 978-93-5551-259-8

REPRINT 2025

Distributors:

BPB PUBLICATIONS
20, Ansari Road, Darya Ganj
New Delhi-110002
Ph: 23254990/23254991

DECCAN AGENCIES
4-3-329, Bank Street,
Hyderabad-500195
Ph: 24756967/24756400

MICRO MEDIA
Shop No. 5, Mahendra Chambers,
150 DN Rd. Next to Capital Cinema,
V.T. (C.S.T.) Station, MUMBAI-400 001
Ph: 22078296/22078297

BPB BOOK CENTRE
376 Old Lajpat Rai Market,
Delhi-110006
Ph: 23861747

To View Complete BPB Publications Catalogue Scan the QR Code:

Published by Manish Jain for BPB Publications, 20 Ansari Road, Darya Ganj, New Delhi-110002 and Printed by him at Manipal Technologies Limited, Manipal

www.bpbonline.com

Dedicated to

Late Mr Raj Bal Singh ji,

Late Mrs Santosh Kumari ji

and

All Lovely Learners

About the Author

S P Verma, M.Sc; M.Ed; PGCPM has been working in the field of education since last 35 years. As a seasoned educationist, teacher trainer, career counsellor, academic auditor, motivator, mentor, author and editor, he has authored 55 school books, 6 research papers, 10 research articles, more than 70 articles on careers and edited more than 200 educational products. More than 20k educators (teachers and principals) attended his training sessions across the country. More than 200k students were career counselled and inspired to take right career plan by him.

Formerly holding the positions of Principal, Kendriya Vidyalaya Sangathan, New Delhi; Regional Director, Teacher Sity, New Delhi; Regional Director, iDC, New Delhi; and Director (School Trg), Vidya Institute of Training and Development, VKP, Meerut; he is now associated as Director (Trg and Innovation) with GEM Foundations, Bengaluru. Besides **Associate Life Member** of Computer Society of India (CSI), he is associated with a number of professional bodies as **Life Member**, like Vigyan Parishad, Allahabad; Hindi Vigyan Sahitya Parishad, BARC, Mumbai; InSc, Bengaluru, PTAI, New Delhi, CSTA, etc.

The 35 years of dedicated services in the field of education of Mr S P Verma has been recognised by many organisations by conferring awards to him. He was presented the **Life Time Achievement Award (2021)** by Maharshi Uni. of Information Technology, Noida; **Life Time Achievement Award (2022)** by PAAI and KIET Group of Institutions; **KVS Incentive Award (2005)** Conferred By HRM Minister ; **Mrs Sarla Chopra Memeorial Award** (2008) Conferred By Vice Chancellor, MDS Uni., Ajmer ; **Paryavarna Dronacharya Award** (2008), **Guru Dronacharya Award** (2007), **Avantika National Humanity Award** (2003), etc. His services were also recognised by various organisations, like Lions Club, Rotary Club, PAC, Hindi Parishad, etc.

Acknowledgements

I would like to acknowledge the contributions of all the educationists (teachers and principals), professionals, and reviewers, who provided their feedback and suggestions on the MS of this book. Especially, I am grateful to **Mr. Pavnesh Kumar**, Former Controller of Examinations, CBSE; **Dr DK Sharma**, Dean (School of Engineering and Technolgy), IIMT University, Meerut; **Prof. RC Singh**, Controller of Examinations, Sharda University, Greater Noida; **Mr. Akshay Sharma**, B.Tech., ONGC, Mehsana, **Er Amit Kaushik, B.Tech., M.Tech., Founder CEO, Wisdom Space Labs; Mr Shubham Verma**, B.Tech., MBA and **Mrs. Shweta Agrawal**, MCA for their specific suggestions.

It's my proud privilege to put on record my sincere gratitude to my publisher **M/s BPB Publications**, New Delhi, for accepting my vision and plan of writing Coding books for classes VI to VIII and providing me the opportunity for the same. The initial interaction with **Mr. Manish Jain**, CEO, and **Mr. Varun Jain**, Director was fruitful in making a long-term association and bonding. I am grateful to them and the entire team of BPB Publications for bringing out these publications in a short span of time.

I am grateful to my well-wishers namely **Mr. RL Jamuda**, Former Commissioner KVS; **Dr. MM Swami**, Former Deputy Commisioner, KVS; **Mr VK Gupta**, Former Deputy Commissioner, KVS; **Mr. DK Saini**, Former Deputy Commissioner, KVS; **Mr AK Verma**, CEO, Eduwix, New Delhi; **Mr NK Verma**, AGM, BHEL HQ; **Mrs and Mr Sandesh Kumar, Pune; Mr AK Pattnaik**, SrGM (Academic), Kalorex Group of Institutions, Ahmedabad; **Mr YP Sharma, Mr Vipin Agrawal; Mr. Matin Ahmed, Mr. NK Giri, Mr NK Bansal** and **Mr SC Sharma** for their constant support, help and motivation to do something good to the society.

I am touched by the love, patience and tolerance shown, during the completion of this project, by my family members- **Mrs. Rekha Verma** (Life Partner), **Sqn Ldr Anuj Verma** (Son), Dearest **Atharv** (Grandson) and **Mrs. Shelja Sharma**, B.Tech., B.Ed., MBA (Daughter in Law). I am grateful to them as well as to all my friends and relatives supporting me in all the creative tasks.

While preparing the manuscript of this book, I have gone through a number of books and different websites. I am grateful to all those authors, contributors, editors, freelancers whose articles are read and used in one or another way in this book. And last but not least, I am indebted to God for keeping my brain alive and my health sound even at the time of the Covid Pandemic so that He could get completed this task through me.

— S P Verma

Preface

It gives me immense pleasure to put the first edition of "**Introduction to Coding (for class VII)**" before the enthusiastic learners. Coding and Artificial intelligence is getting more attention in the world day by day. Coding is touching almost all fields related to the development of the human-beings. AI based Technology using coding and it applications is changing at a very fast rate influencing day-to-day life positively. AI and coding are nowadays applied in almost all fields, be it education, transport management, air traffic control, medicine manufacturing, space research, customer care, pandemic control, or entertainment.

After understanding the importance and demand of Coding and AI, the Govt of India, through CBSE, has launched Skills Development subjects from class VI onwards, including Coding, Artificial Intelligence, etc. CBSE has introduced 'Coding' as a skill module of 12 hours duration in classes VI-VIII from the Session 2021-2022 onwards to simplify the coding learning experience. It is an attempt to nurture design thinking, logical flow of ideas and apply this across the disciplines.

This book is written according to the latest guidelines and syllabus of Coding issued by CBSE. The main objective of writing this series of books for classes VI to VIII is to provide technical knowledge with all practical aspects of Block Coding without the use of any programming language, like Python. Thus, the learners will become fully competent to face the challenges of living in an AI-based applications-equipped futuristic society. Moreover, emphasis on the development of 21st Century Life Skills through a variety of activities, practical and projects is laid down.

The book contains five chapters and two annexures. The salient features of the book are as follows:

- It is written after following the guidelines provided by CBSE.
- It explains the concepts of Coding with proper examples in lucid language.
- Simple, easy, and understandable language is used to clarify the content.
- It incorporates a pictorial setup in presenting the content by using tables, charts, graphs, pictures, photographs, etc.
- It illustrates a good number of '**Solved Examples on Block Coding**'.
- **Activities and Projects** have been incorporated for inculcating 21St Century Life Skills, including creativity, innovation, critical thinking, team work, working in a diverse environment, etc.
- Important concepts are provided as '***Summary***' at the end of each chapter.
- '**Coding Quiz**' section provide an opportunity for learners to test their knowledge in a fun way.
- '**Practice Time**' section contains all sorts of questions including HOTS.
- '**Factz Funda**' provides additional information related to the content of the chapter.
- **Some Unsolved Projects** are provided at the end of chapter to practice the concepts learned in the chapter.
- Two Annexures providing extra useful information are annexed at the end of the book.

I am sure that the sincere efforts put in by the author and publication team will be well received by the dynamic, dedicated and passionate teachers, and energetic learners. The author will appreciate all sorts of feedback from the readers to improve the quality of the content.

SP Verma
Email: spv1962@gmail.com

Coloured Images

Please follow the link to download the
Coloured Images of the book:

https://rebrand.ly/jx7j5rc

We have code bundles from our rich catalogue of books and videos available at **https://github.com/bpbpublications**. Check them out!

Errata

We take immense pride in our work at BPB Publications and follow best practices to ensure the accuracy of our content to provide with an indulging reading experience to our subscribers. Our readers are our mirrors, and we use their inputs to reflect and improve upon human errors, if any, that may have occurred during the publishing processes involved. To let us maintain the quality and help us reach out to any readers who might be having difficulties due to any unforeseen errors, please write to us at :

errata@bpbonline.com

Your support, suggestions and feedbacks are highly appreciated by the BPB Publications' Family.

Did you know that BPB offers eBook versions of every book published, with PDF and ePub files available? You can upgrade to the eBook version at www.bpbonline.com and as a print book customer, you are entitled to a discount on the eBook copy. Get in touch with us at :

business@bpbonline.com for more details.

At **www.bpbonline.com**, you can also read a collection of free technical articles, sign up for a range of free newsletters, and receive exclusive discounts and offers on BPB books and eBooks.

Piracy

If you come across any illegal copies of our works in any form on the internet, we would be grateful if you would provide us with the location address or website name. Please contact us at **business@bpbonline.com** with a link to the material.

If you are interested in becoming an author

If there is a topic that you have expertise in, and you are interested in either writing or contributing to a book, please visit **www.bpbonline.com**. We have worked with thousands of developers and tech professionals, just like you, to help them share their insights with the global tech community. You can make a general application, apply for a specific hot topic that we are recruiting an author for, or submit your own idea.

Reviews

Please leave a review. Once you have read and used this book, why not leave a review on the site that you purchased it from? Potential readers can then see and use your unbiased opinion to make purchase decisions. We at BPB can understand what you think about our products, and our authors can see your feedback on their book. Thank you!

For more information about BPB, please visit **www.bpbonline.com**.

Table of Contents

Ethical Approach in Coding

All the teachers and learners who have to build capabilities around coding, will be equipped, through the course on coding, to build software on your own. This will have an impact on society in general. Hence, it is crucial to follow ethical practices while building your own code.

Some ethical practices given as below are to be followed while learning to code:

❖ Contribute to society and human wellbeing.

❖ Limit negative results of software, including dangers to safety, health, personal security, and privacy.

❖ Limit the aftereffects of the software.

❖ Ensure your Code respects diversity and is utilized responsibly with social issues in mind.

❖ Promote environmental sustainability both locally and globally.

❖ Avoid harm to others.

❖ Avoid to become the cause of physical or mental injury, unjustified destruction to property or information.

❖ Avoid unjustified damage to environment.

Variables In Real Life

Structure

In this chapter, you will learn:

- How to use variables in real life.
- Learn how to initialize variables in programming.
- Learning how to validate user input.
- Performing mathematical operations of different data types.

INTRODUCTION

In the previous class, we have learned that coding/programming is affecting our lives positively. There are many appliances and devices that use coding to make our lives easier and comfortable. Variables play an important role in coding. Coding is defined as the way we communicate with the computer. Code tells a computer what actions are to be taken in a sequence.

Learning the process of coding is important for young guys as the process increases their thinking process in them. During the coding process, the learners are empowered with some life skills, like creativity, computational skills, problem-solving skills, working in a team, etc.

A variable is something that changes/varies. For example, age, income, and expenses, family size, capital expenditure, class/ grades, blood pressure readings, body temperature readings of a patient, eye colour, and vehicle type are all examples of variables. This is due to the fact that each of these properties varies or differs from one individual to another.

Figure 1.1

In this chapter, we will study the variables and their usage in real life, initialisation of variables, validation of user's input, data types, and performing mathematical operations in different data types.

Learning Objectives:

At the end of this chapter, you will be able to:

- have an understanding of variables.
- have an understanding of the initialization of variables.
- know how to apply different mathematical operations to different data types.
- know variables in Real Life.

Have your parents a bank account (saving or current) in any private or nationalised bank? If yes, then from their bank account, they may withdraw some amount either by using an ATM card or visiting the bank. Moreover, they may deposit some amount in their account too. So, the amount in saving accounts may vary during each bank transaction. Thus, the amount in a bank account is called a variable.

A variable is defined as a number that does not have a fixed value. In our daily lives, we use a good number of variables. The figures are given here, and the list below shows some real-life examples where the value of variable changes with the change in place and time.

- The height of a growing child changes with time.
- The weight of a growing child changes with time.
- The temperature in different places changes.
- The speed of a car passing through a market change with time.
- The age of people keeps on increasing year by year.

Figure 1.2

Figure 1.3

Activity 1.1

- Participate in the larger group activity on "**Examples of Variables in Real Life.**"
- The teacher will initiate the discussion on the topic in the class, and all students will provide their inputs in the form of examples of variables.
- A volunteer student will make a list of all such examples and will put them before the full class.

1.2 VARIABLE IN PROGRAMMING

A variable is defined as a named location that is used to store data in the memory of the computer. It is like that variable as a container (like envelope or bucket) holding data that can be changed later throughout programming. For example,

x = 34

y = 49

z =101

The above declarations make sure that the program reserves memory for three variables with the names x, y, and z. The variable names stand for the memory location. Thus, in programming, a variable is a packet that can store data. The packets can be named and referenced and can be used to perform various operations. To perform a mathematical operation, we can declare two or more variables and perform the operation on them.

Factz Funda

A variable is defined as a named unit of data that is assigned a value, and when the value is modified, the name does not change.

The name which is assigned to a variable acts as an identifier for that variable. Scope of a variable normally refers to the part of the code where the variable can be used. The scope or accessibility of the variables defined in a program depends on where you have declared it in each program. Any defined variable cannot be accessed beyond its scope.

Figure 1.4

Factz Funda

A Variable is an entity whose value can change during the execution of a program.

1.3 VARIABLE INITIALISATION

We need to create one or more variables for use in programming/coding and assign them a reference in computer memory. After creating a variable, we also need to assign it a value before it is used at all. The process of assigning a value to a variable is known as **"Variable Initialisation."**

A variable that is not initialised ever has an undefined value. Thus, a variable without assigning any value cannot be used till it is assigned with a certain value. When a variable is declared/created but is not initialized, we can assign it a value in later steps of programming using assignment operators.

In programming, a variable can be initialised using the below syntax:

Datatype VariableName = Value;

Example: Int (x) = 51

We cannot take any action on any variable till the time we initialize it. However, you can initialize the value of a variable to null. Do not confuse the value of null with a variable that is not initialized. "Null" is still a value; a variable that is not initialized does not hold any value, not even null.

Figure 1.5

It is interesting to note that in some programming languages like Python, there is no command to declare variables. A variable is created at the moment when we first assign a value to it.

Example of declaring variables in Python

```
a = 17
b = "Hello India"
c = 5.8
```

Activity 1.2

- Participate in the pair activity on **"Creating and Initialization of Variables."**
- The teacher will divide the class into pairs without gender bias.
- Each pair will complete the activity in Arcade.makecode.com to understand how variable initialization works in programming by following the steps given below:

Step 1: Setup Minecraft education edition by typing the following in the address bar of the computer having internet facility and clicking the link: https://arcade.makecode.com/

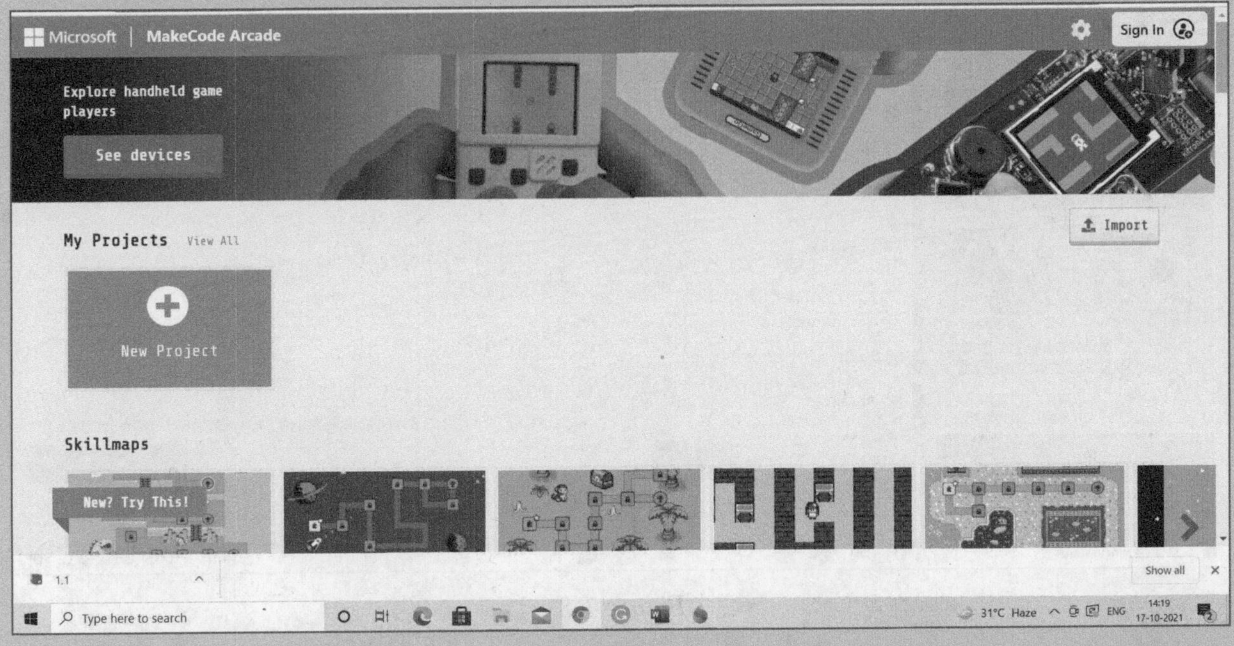

Figure 1.6

Step 2: Click the new project, and the following window will open. Write "Variables" as a new project.

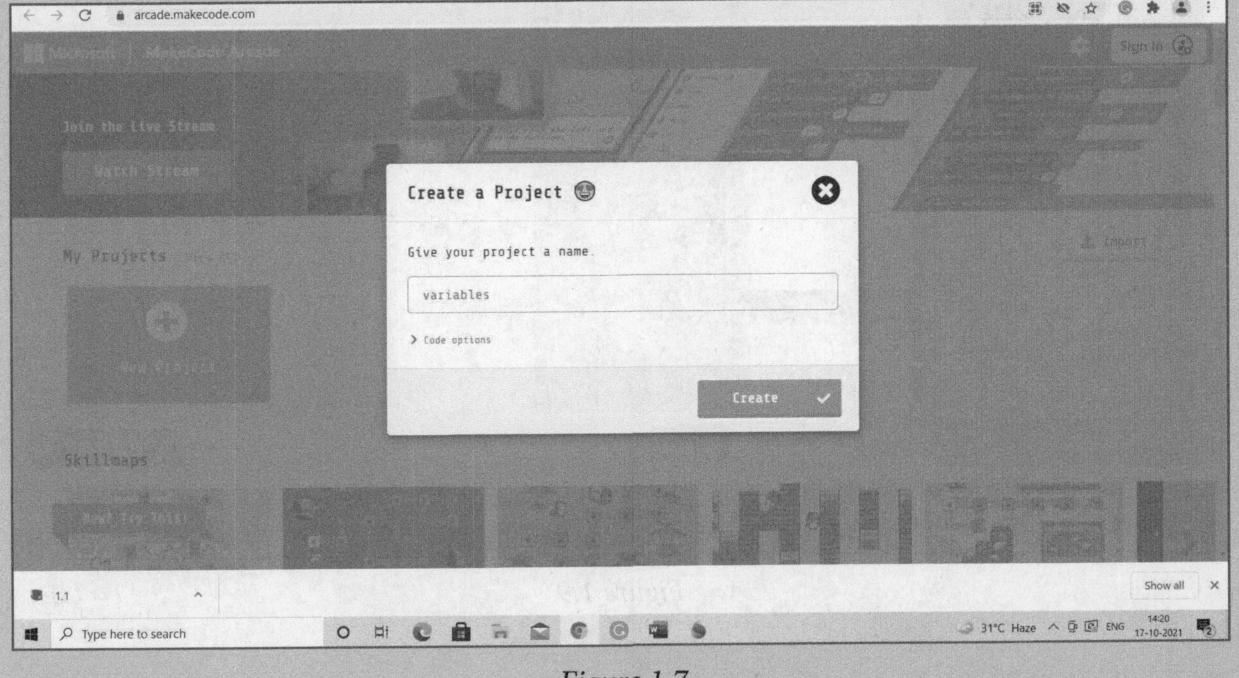

Figure 1.7

Step 3: On clicking the OK button, the following screen will appear.

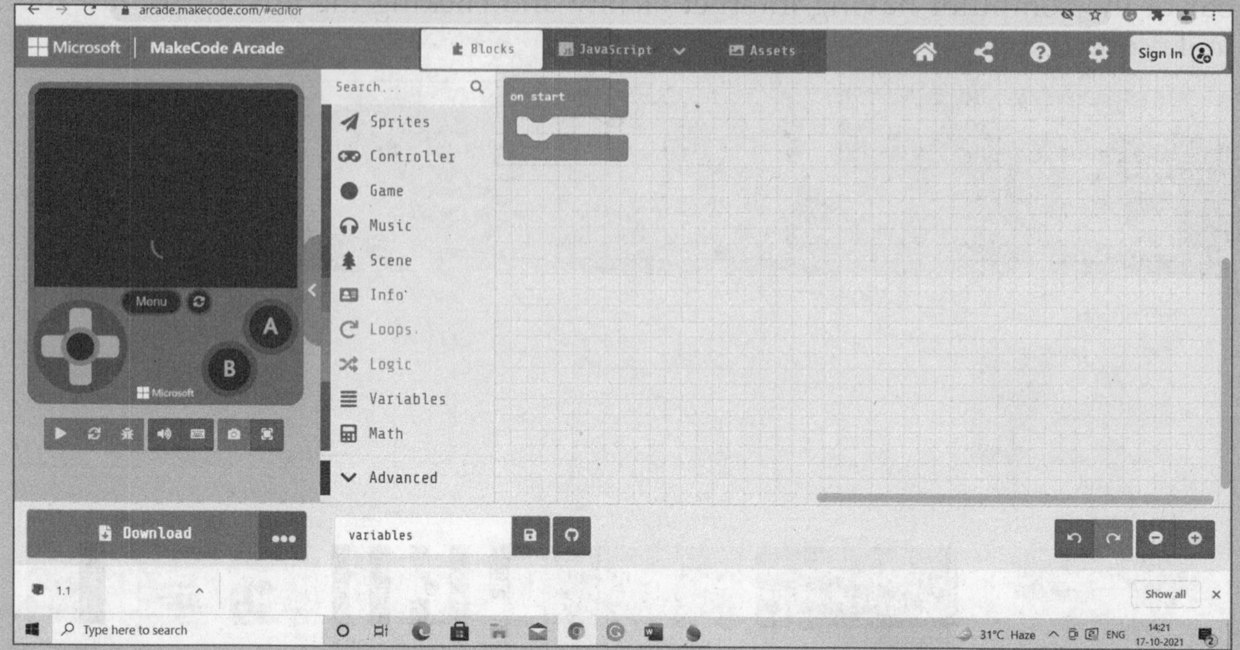

Figure 1.8

Step 4: Click on the 'Variables' link and then click on 'Make a Variable.'

Figure 1.9

Step 5: Write 'a' in the 'new Variable Name' text box that appears on the screen and click on the 'OK' button.

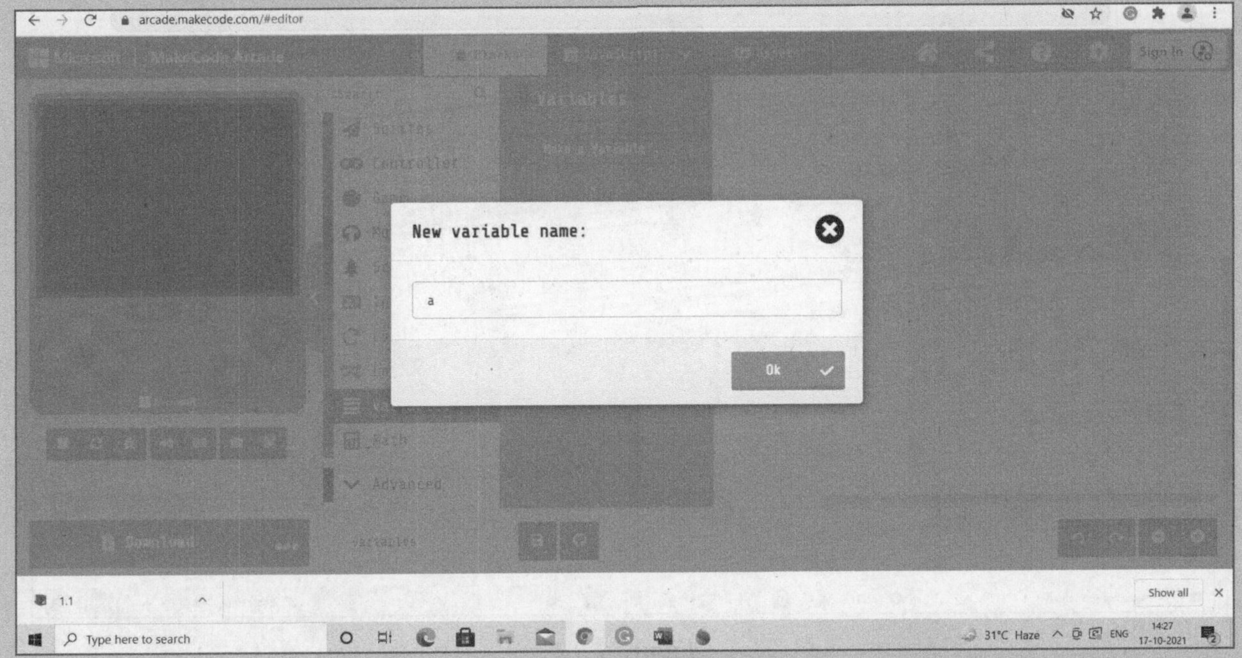

Figure 1.10

Step 6: The created variable does not hold any value. So, we will assign a value to this variable, and this step is called "initialiazing the variable." For this, click on the 'Variables' link again in the toolbox and then drag and drop the "set a to" block in the play area.

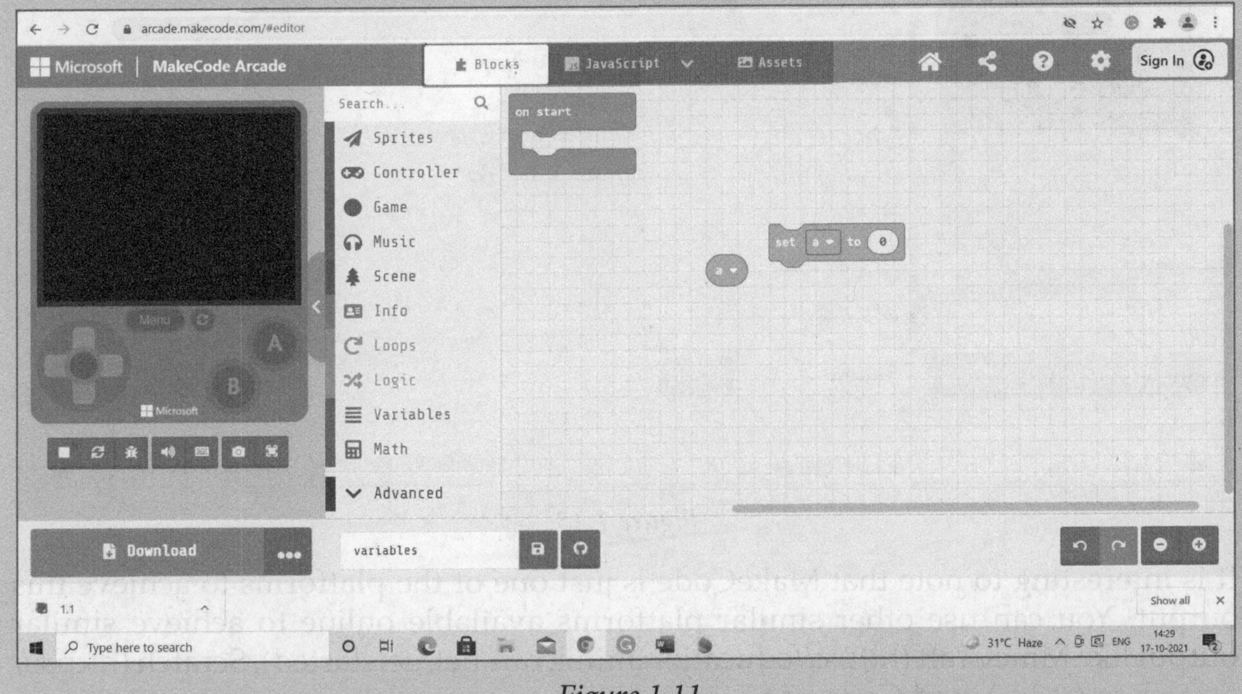

Figure 1.11

Step 7: In the "set" block, assign a value to the variable 'a' as 20, as shown here.

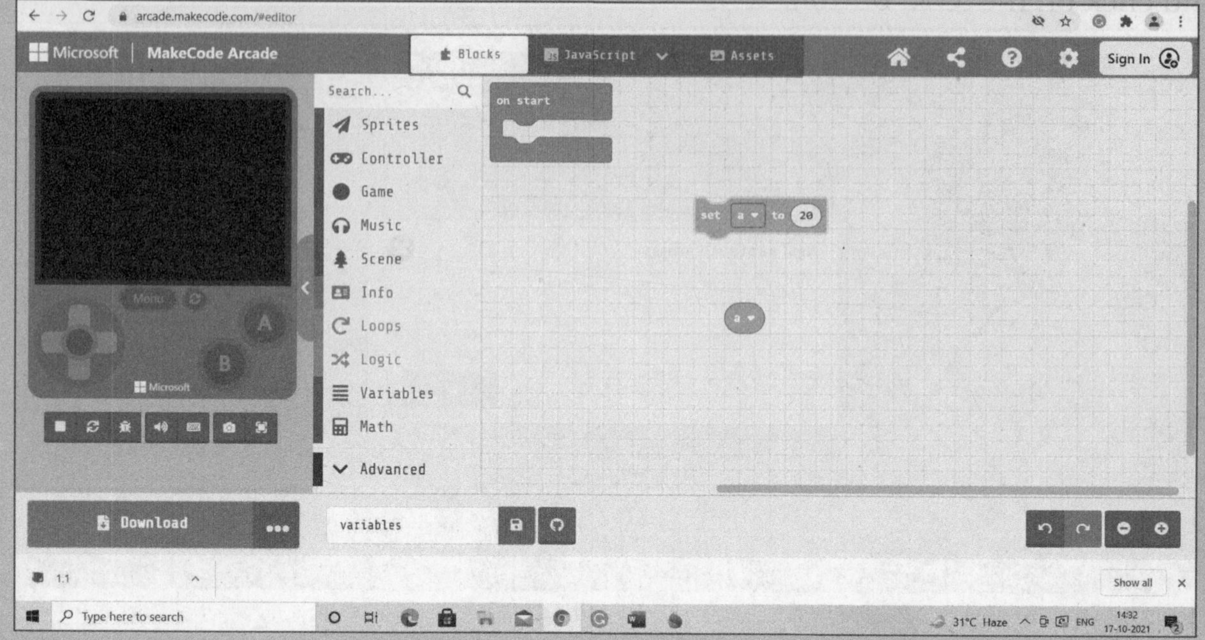

Figure 1.12

Step 8: Drag and drop set block into "on start" block.

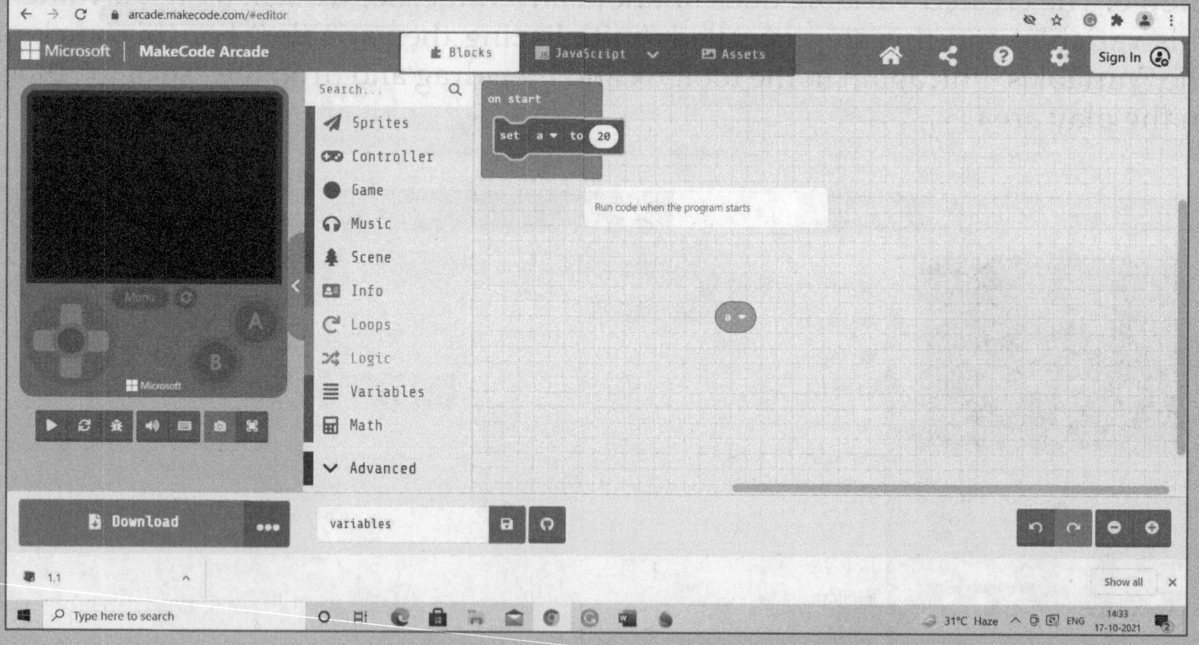

Figure 1.13

It is interesting to note that MakeCode is just one of the platforms to achieve this output. You can use other similar platforms available online to achieve similar output like MineCraft (https://education.minecraft.net/getstarted), Scratch (https://scratch.mit.edu/), and Code.org.

1.4 DATA TYPES IN PROGRAMMING

Variables are the values that are acted upon. Every value needs to be assigned to a specific data type to make the variable more readable by a computer. Data type identifies the type of data that the declared variable can hold. Thus, it indirectly helps the computer to understand what operations need to be performed on those variables. The declaration of a variable in a program contains two components: the name of the variable and its type.

Factz Funda

There are three types of variables in the Java programming language: Local variables, Instance variables, and Class/Static variables.

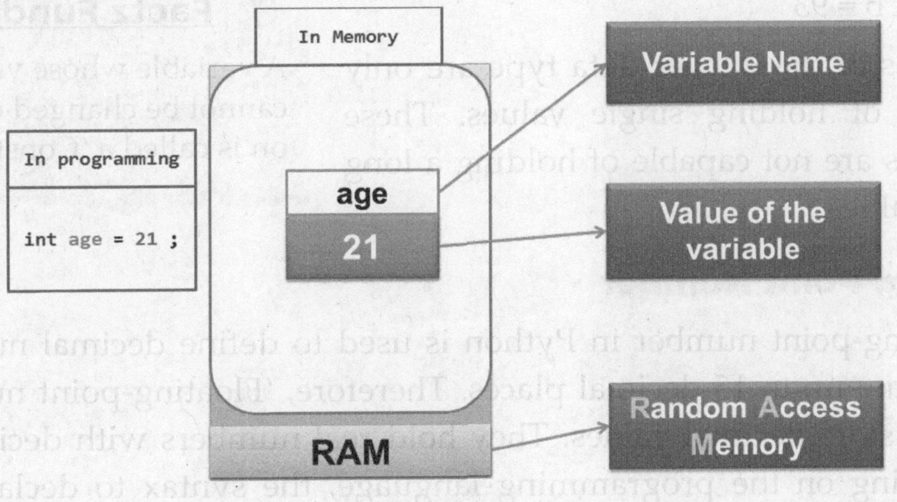

Figure 1.14

Let us now understand the common data types that we can use in programming that are given in Table 1.1.

Table 1.1 Common types in variables

- Integer
- Floating-point number
- Character
- String
- Boolean

Factz Funda

Some variables are mutable, which means that their values can change. Other variables are immutable, which means their value, once assigned, cannot be deleted or altered.

(i) Integer Data Type

Integer data type variables store integer values only. They store whole numbers which have zero, positive and negative values but not decimal values. Multiple programming languages support different syntax to declare an Integer variable. If a user tries to create an integer variable and assign it a non-integer value, the program returns an error.

Thus, the integer is a data type that is used to define integer variables. Integers can be of any length. They can be any positive or negative whole number.

Examples of declaring an integer variable:

```
int a = 7
int b = 93
```

Variables of the integer data type are only capable of holding single values. These variables are not capable of holding a long list of values.

Factz Funda

A variable whose value cannot be changed even later on is called a 'Constant.'

(ii) Floating Point Number

A floating-point number in Python is used to define decimal numbers and is accurate up to 15 decimal places. Therefore, 'Floating-point numbers' are used to store decimal values. They hold real numbers with decimal values. Depending on the programming language, the syntax to declare floating-point variable changes.

Examples of declaring a floating -point number variable:

```
float a = 1.4;
float b = 7.9;
float c = 172.8;
```

(iii) Character Data Type

Character type variables are used to store character values. Syntax of declaring a character variable is specific to the programming language that you are using. If a user tries to create a character variable and assign it with a non-character value, the program will throw an error. The character data type is the smallest data type in programming.

Examples of declaring a character variable:

char a = 'P';

char b = 'S';

char c = 'T'

Any character value can be declared as a char variable.

(iv) String

A string in Python is a sequence of Unicode characters. It is used to define any form of string. Examples: Text, Alphanumeric, etc. For example, in Python, we can use single quotes, double quotes, or triple quotes to define strings. Multi-line strings in Python can be represented using triple quotes.

To extend the character data type, a user may have a requirement to store and perform an operation on a sequence of characters. In such cases, the String data type is present to fit the gap. The String data type stores value in a sequence of characters, i.e., in String format. Any string value can be declared as a string variable.

Examples of declaring a string variable:

str a = "Shelja is my daughter";

str b = "Wonderful School";

str c = "MatinShaheen"

(v) Boolean

There is a subtype of Integer Data Type called "Boolean Data Type," which stores values in Boolean type only, i.e., "true" or "false." Users can choose between the data types for variables as per program needs and assign variables an appropriate data type.

Examples of declaring a boolean variable:

bool a = true;

bool b = false;

Boolean is a subtype of integer data type. It stores two values only: true and false, where true means non-zero and false means zero. Any Boolean variable holding Boolean value can be declared as Boolean.

Factz Funda

When a variable's value conforms to a specific data type, it is called a 'typed variable.'

It is interesting to note that in some programming languages like Python, there is no command to declare variables. A variable is created at the moment when the user first assigns a value to it.

Examples of declaring variables in Python:

```
a = 3;
b = "Wow";
c = 3.2
```

When we want to specify the data type of variable, then this can be done using casting.

Example: x = str("hello Satish"),

y = int(9),

z = float(2.7)

x will be saved as 'hello Satish'

y will be saved as 9

z will be saved as 2.7

Now, we will learn how to apply different data types in pseudocode. We will first declare different types of variables, followed by assigning them to appropriate values. Finally, we will use the variables by outputting their values.

Function Main

```
Declare
..........................................................................
    Declare Integer i
    Declare Float f
    Declare Char c
    Declare String s
    Declare Boolean b
Assign
..........................................................................
    Assign i = 237
    Assign f = 7.16
```

```
    Assign c = 'S'
    Assign s = "I love my India"
    Assign b = false
Use
.............................................................................
    Output "Integer i = " & i
    Output "Float f = " & f
    Output "Char c = " & c
    Output "String s = " & s
    Output "Boolean b = " & b
End
```

The output from the above pseudocode will be like as follows:

```
    Integer i = 237
    Float f = 7.16
    Char c = S
    String s = I love my India
    Boolean b = false
```

It is interesting to note that the syntax is different for different data types in different programming languages.

1.5 VALIDATION OF INPUT IN PROGRAMMING

It is important to ensure that the program works fine. For this purpose, we validate that the user enters valid values in the places where these are expected. For example, consider someone asking you a question, "Which game did you play today?". To answer this question, we should answer the person what game had been played. Imagine someone is answering back, "I have a blue coloured shirt." This is not an acceptable answer to the question that was asked and may confuse the person who asked the question. Similarly, validation of input by the user is required.

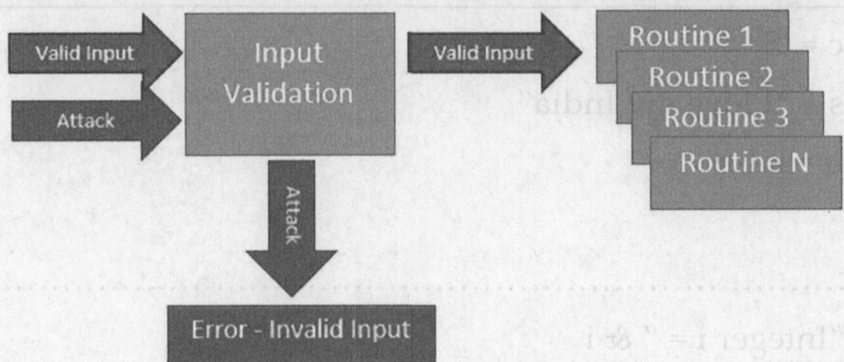

Figure 1.15

Factz Funda

Python allows validation of text fields to prevent invalid input from the user by allowing variable tracing using a callback function. This function is used whenever input is added/deleted to/from an Entry widget.

Now, in programming, whenever we create a variable with a specific data type, and we are expecting a user to enter some value in that data type, we have to make sure that the user enters the right type of value. Thus, it would not cause any error during program execution. This validation of input plays an important role while writing a code/program.

We have to remember that a computer program behaves exactly the way how a flowchart flow. Thus, any deviation of data type in the user's input will create an error by the program.

Flagging out the wrong input is a common method of validating a user's input. For doing this, common practice is to set a flag in a program that has a default value "false." If the user input matches the expected input, we will reset the flag to true and execute. If the user's value is set to false, we will stop the execution of the program by displaying an error message.

1.6 MATH OPERATIONS IN PROGRAMMING

Till now, we have understood how to declare and initiate a variable and how to validate the user's input. Now, we will try to understand how we can perform mathematical operations of these variables. An arithmetic operation combines two or more numeric expressions using the Arithmetic Operators to form a resulting numeric expression.

Operators are special symbols that represent computation. They are applied to operand(s), which can be values or variables. Operators, when applied to operands, form an expression.

The basic operators for performing arithmetic are the same in many computer languages:

- ❖ Addition
- ❖ Subtraction
- ❖ Multiplication
- ❖ Division
- ❖ Modulus (Remainder)

1.6.1 Addition

An addition operation is used to perform the mathematical addition of two or more variables. The addition arithmetic operation is used to add the values stored in one variable with another variable. Like the way we add values in mathematics, we can store values in different variables and perform addition operations. Additions of these variables are displayed as an output of the program.

In programming, we refer to "+" as a symbol of addition. Please note that Addition can only be carried out on Integer, Float, and String datatypes only. You can use this operator to concatenate two strings on either side of the operator.

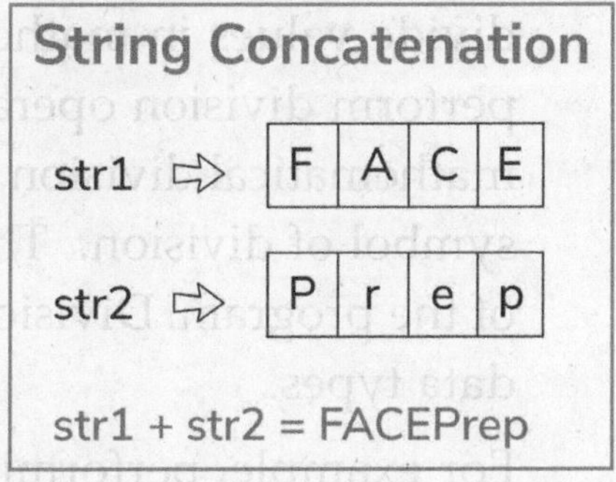

Figure 1.16

For example, if there are two float variables, "x" and "y" declared in the program; where x = 3.5, and y = 7.2. If we perform the 'addition' operation of these variables in programming, the result is going to be 10.7.

(b) Subtraction: The subtraction arithmetic operation is used to subtract the values stored in one variable from another variable. Like the way we subtract values in mathematics, we can store values in different variables and perform subtraction operations. In programming, we refer to "-" as a symbol of subtraction. Subtraction of these variables is displayed as an output of the program. Subtraction operation can only be carried out on Integer, Float, Double datatypes only.

For example, performing subtraction operation on a variable "a" holding value "87" and a variable "b" holding value "25" will give result an output "62".

(c) Multiplication: Multiplication arithmetic operation is used to multiply the values stored in two variables. Like the way we multiply values in mathematics, we can store values in different variables and perform multiplication operations. Thus, a multiplication operation is used to perform the mathematical multiplication of two variables. In programming, we refer to "*" as a symbol of multiplication. Multiplication can only be carried out on Integer, Float, and Double datatypes. Multiplication of these variables is displayed as an output of the program.

For example, performing multiply operation on a variable "a" holding value "5" and a variable "b" holding value "13" will result in an output "65."

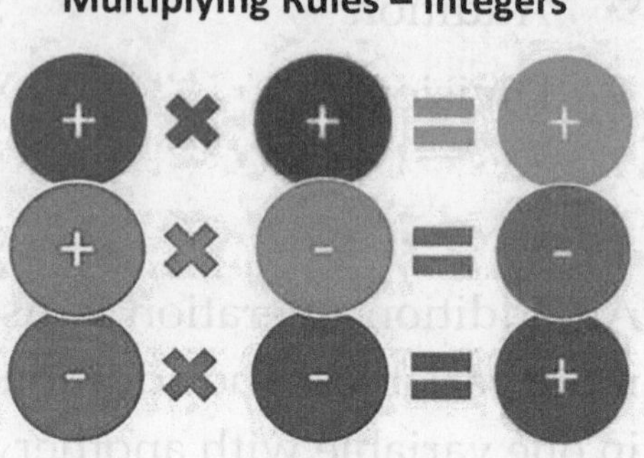

Figure 1.17

(d) Division: Division arithmetic operation is used to divide the value stored in one variable by the value stored in another variable. Like the way we divide values in mathematics, we can store values in different variables and perform division operations. Thus, division operation is used to perform the mathematical division of two variables. In programming, we refer to "/" as a symbol of division. The division of these variables is displayed as an output of the program. Division can only be carried out on Integer, Float, and Double data types.

For example, performing division operation on a variable "a" holding value "20" and a variable "b" holding value "4" will result in an output "5".

In a second case, performing division operation on a variable "x" holding value "37" and a variable "y" holding value "12" will result in an output "3".

Factz Funda

Google's Blockly is a platform that produces working code in a variety of conventional programming languages like JavaScript. Thus, it is possible to experiment with blocks and see the result in the desired programming language simultaneously.

(e) **Modulus (Remainder):** 'Modulus' operator (%) calculates the remainder when two variables are divided. It should be noted that this operation can only be performed on integer and float variables in Python. Thus, the 'Modulus' operation is used to perform the mathematical remainder of two variables. In programming, we refer to "%" as a symbol of modulus. Modulus operator divides variable on the left to the variable on the right and returns the remainder. Modulus can only be carried out on integer and float data types in Python.

For example, performing modulus operation on a variable "a" holding value "19" and variable "b" holding value "4" will result in an output "3" as there is 3 as remainder in this operation.

Project Time

Project 1.1

Aim: To perform a '**Division**' operation by using Block Coding.

Learning Outcome:

- To learn how to use a mathematical operator (division) in block coding.
- To learn how to use functions and variables.

Problem Statement: Using different mathematical functions is crucial during learning how to code. We will learn how to implement division operations using block coding.

Solution:

A division operation is used to divide the values stored into two variables. Like the way we divide values in mathematics, we can store values in different variables and perform a division operation. The division of these variables is displayed as an output of the program.

For example, performing division operation on a variable "a" holding value "35" and a variable "b" holding value "7" will result in an output "5". We will use variables to solve such types of problems.

Use the steps given here to solve the problem:

Step1: Open the MakeCode arcade home screen.

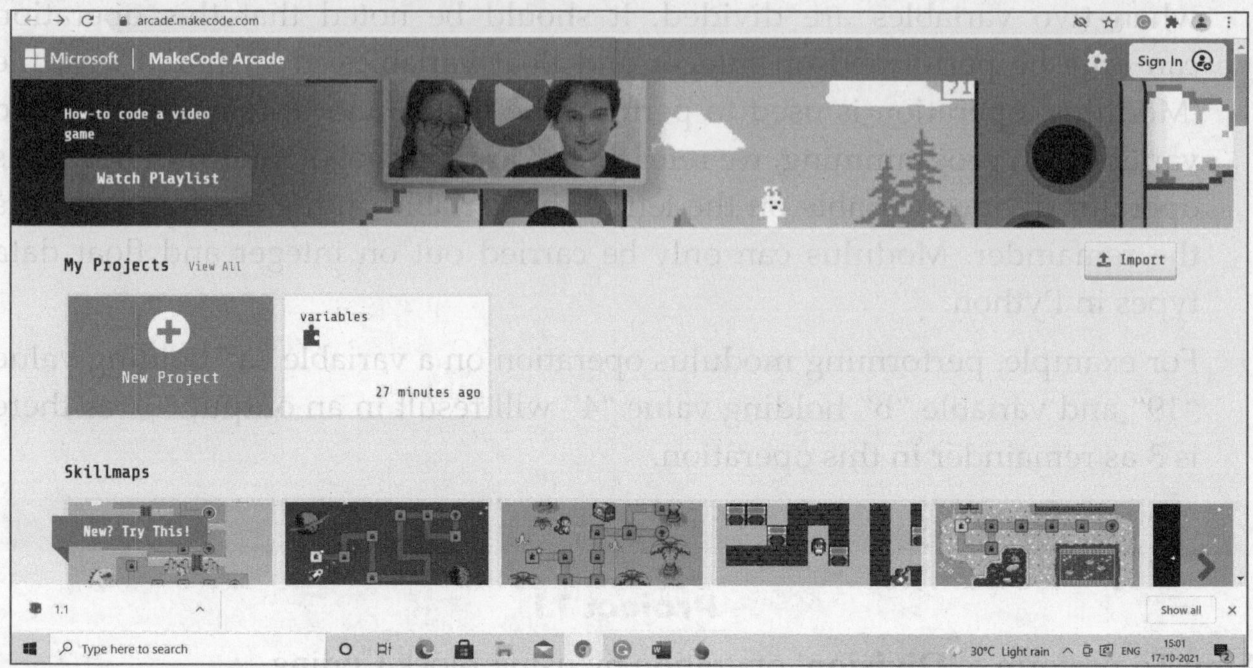

Figure 1.18

Step 2: Click on "New Project," give a name to the project "Arithmetic Operations," and click on the "'create" button.

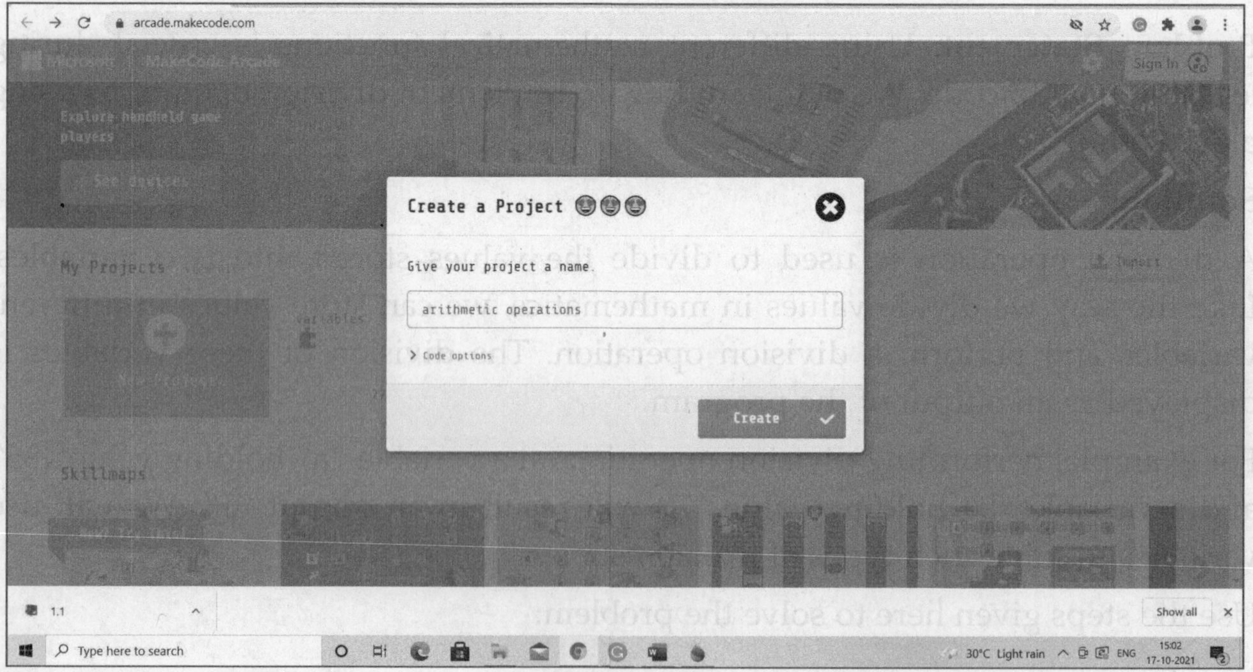

Figure 1.19

Step 3: From the list in the centre of the page, click on "Variables" and then click on "Make a Variable."

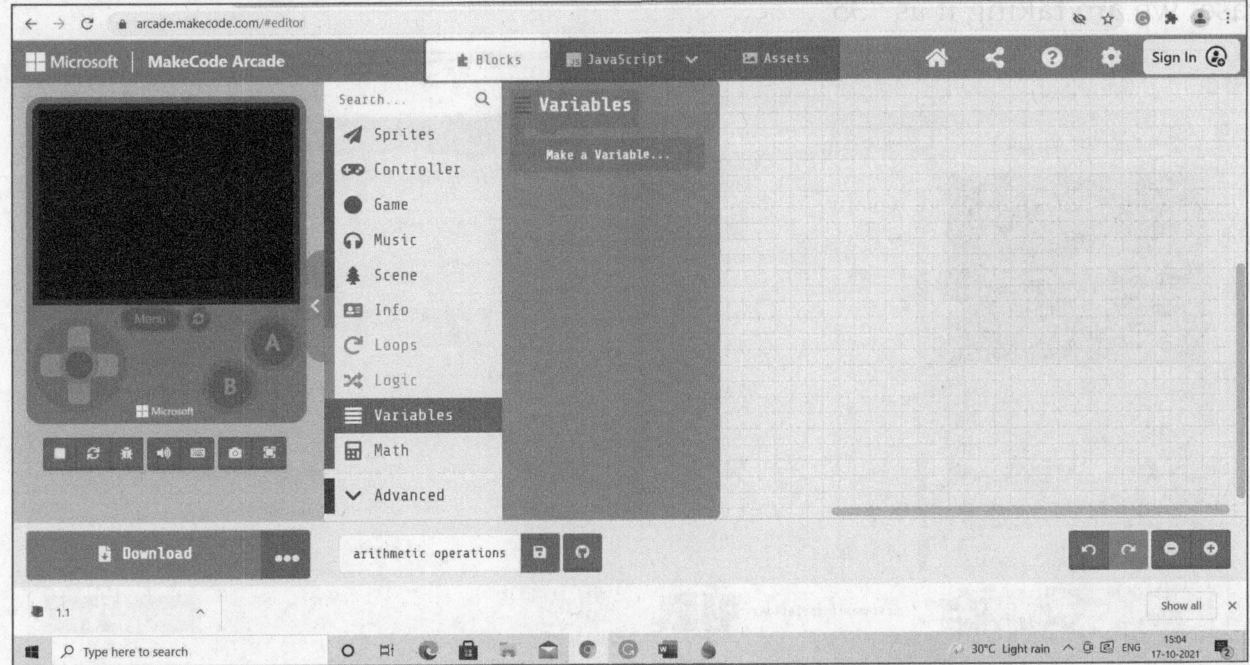

Figure 1.20

Step 4: Name the new variable as "a" and click on the "OK" button.

Figure 1.21

Step 5: Click "Variables" and select "set a to " block for drag and drop in the main play area. Click on the value of "a" and change to the desired value. In this case, we are taking it as "35".

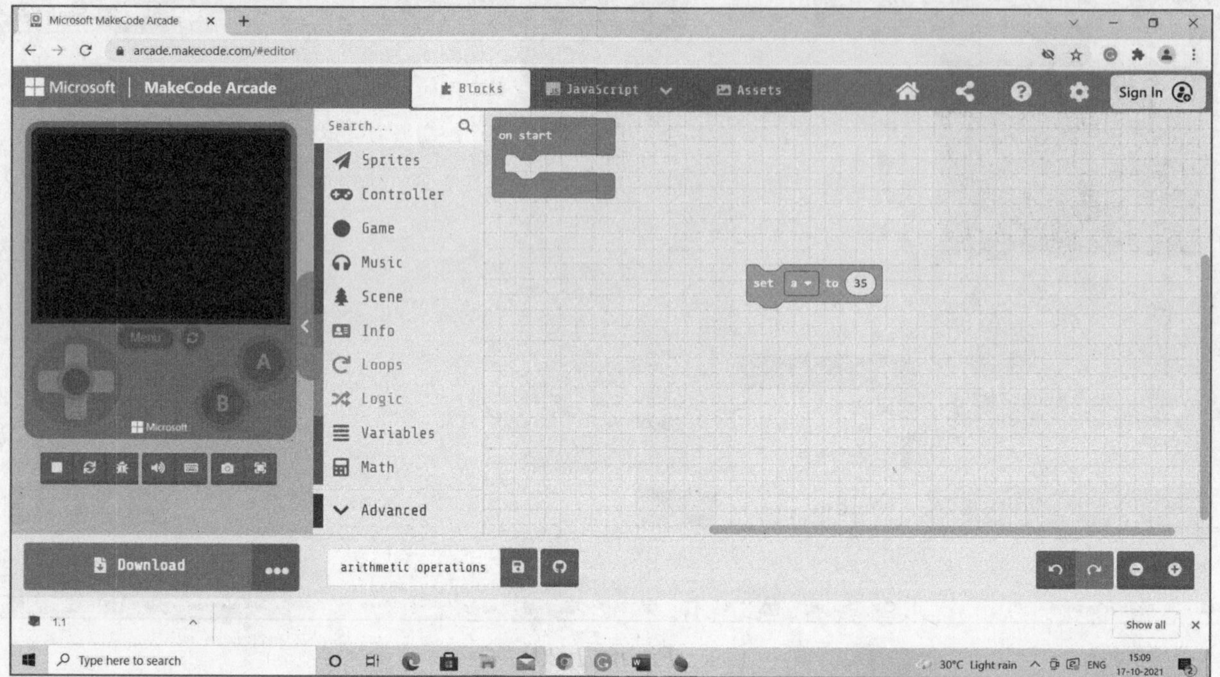

Figure 1.22

Step 6: Drag and drop "a" to the green block.

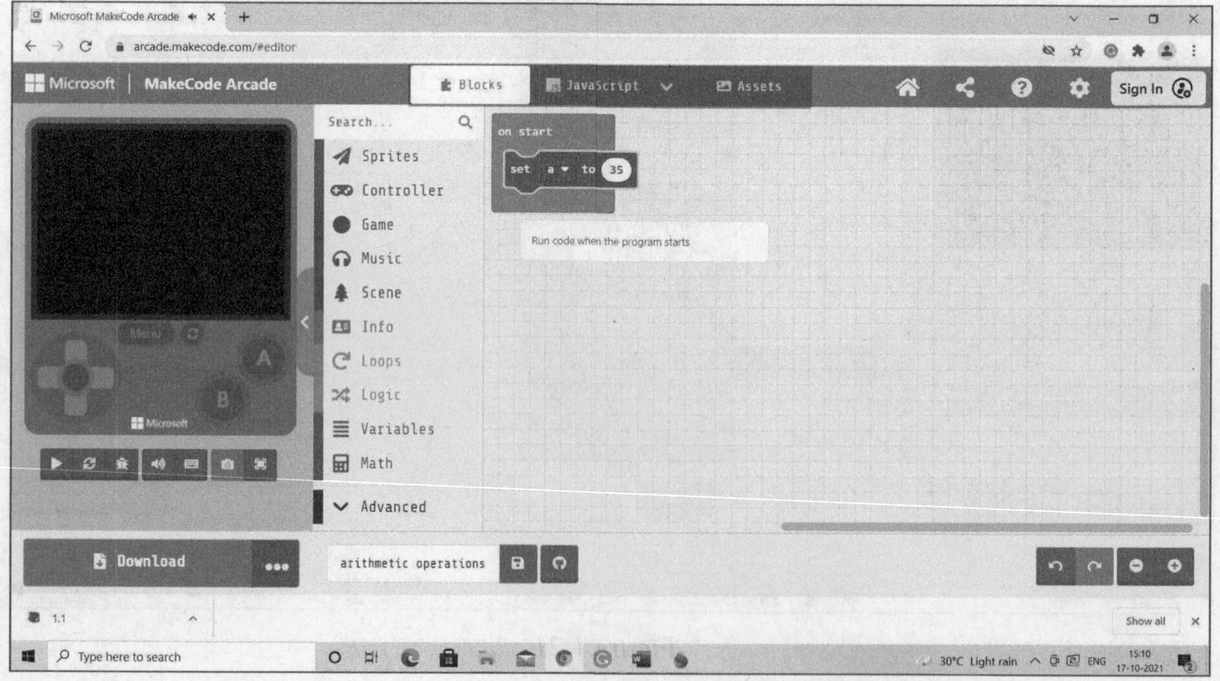

Figure 1.23

Step 7: Similarly, make another variable "b" and assign it a value "7," and drag and drop it on the green block.

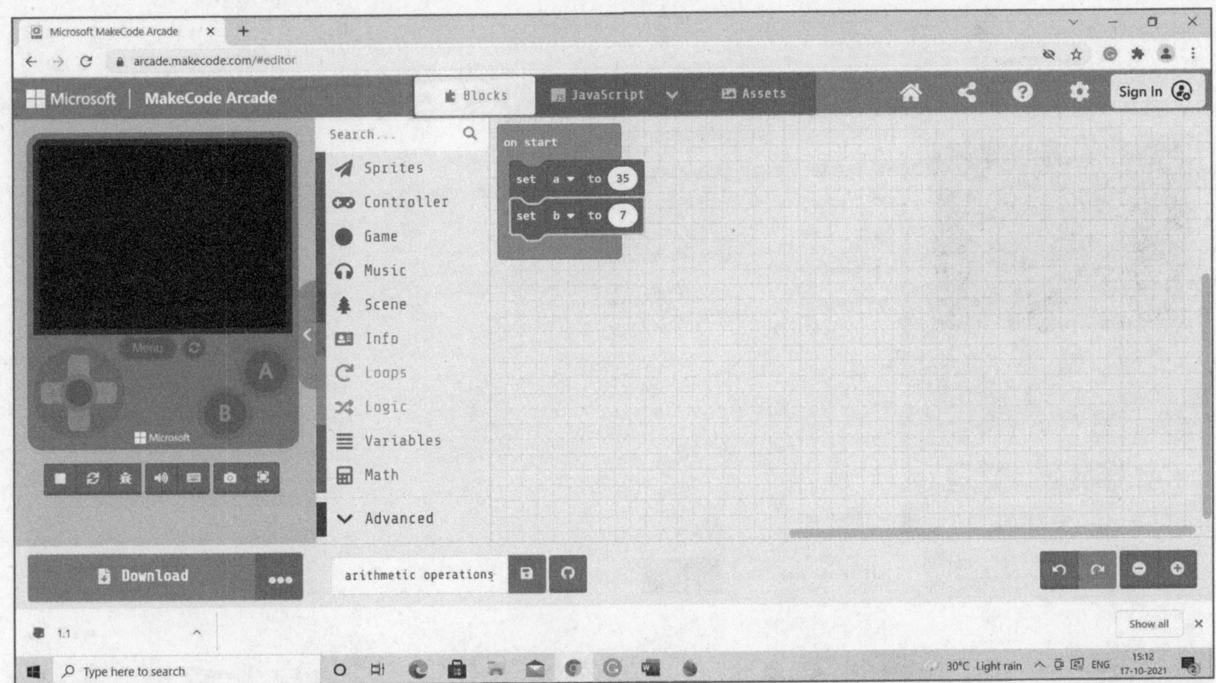

Figure 1.24

Step 8: Now, click on the "Math" link from the centre of the page and click on division operation.

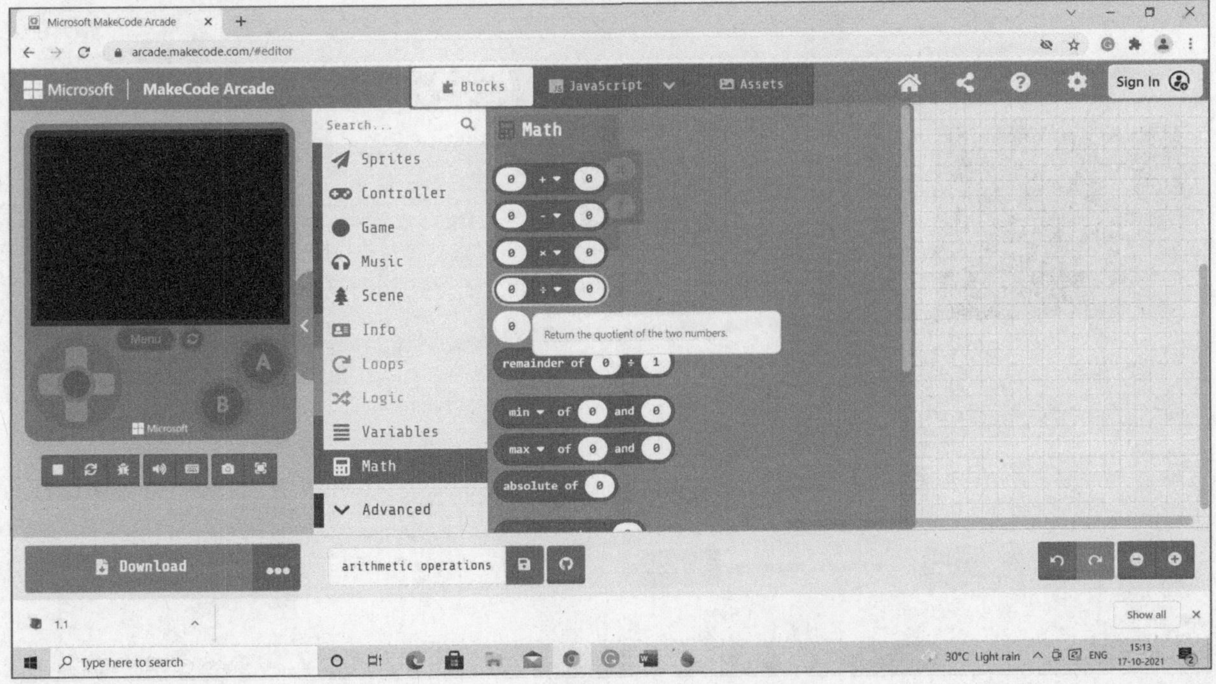

Figure 1.25

Step 9: Now, click on the "Variables" link from the centre of the page and drag and drop variables "a" and "b" in the division box as seen in the screenshot.

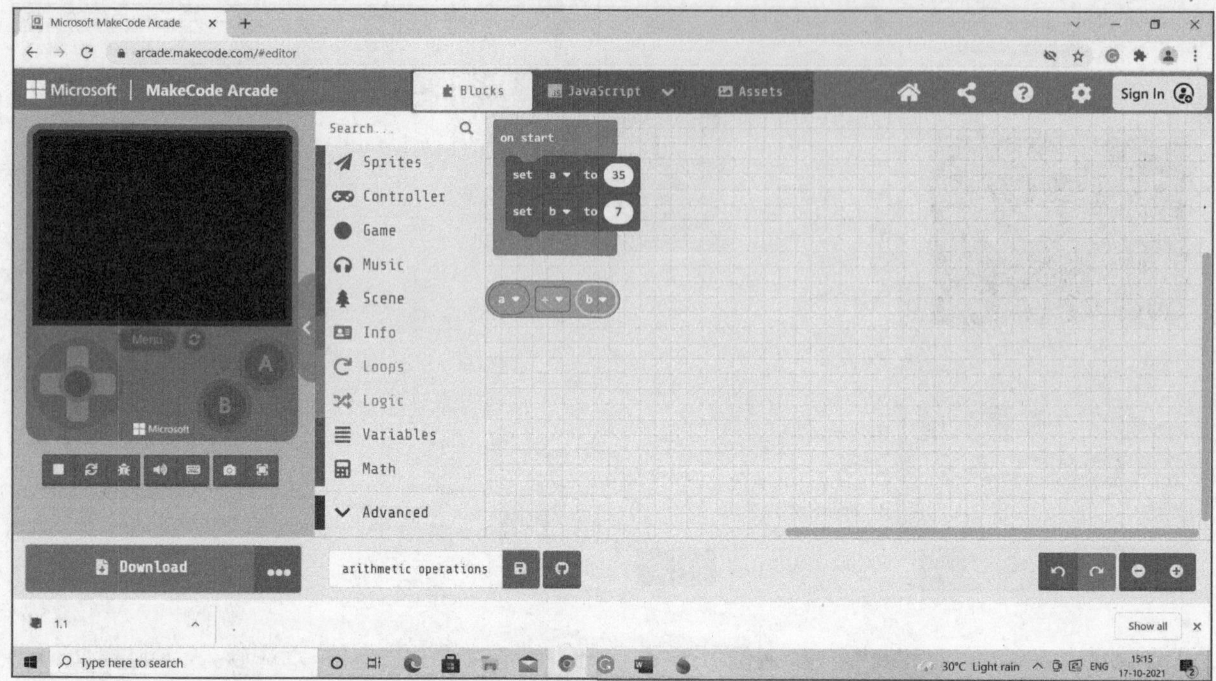

Figure 1.26

Step 10: Like the way we had created variables a and b, now create variable c. Drag and drop a block of variable c to in the play area.

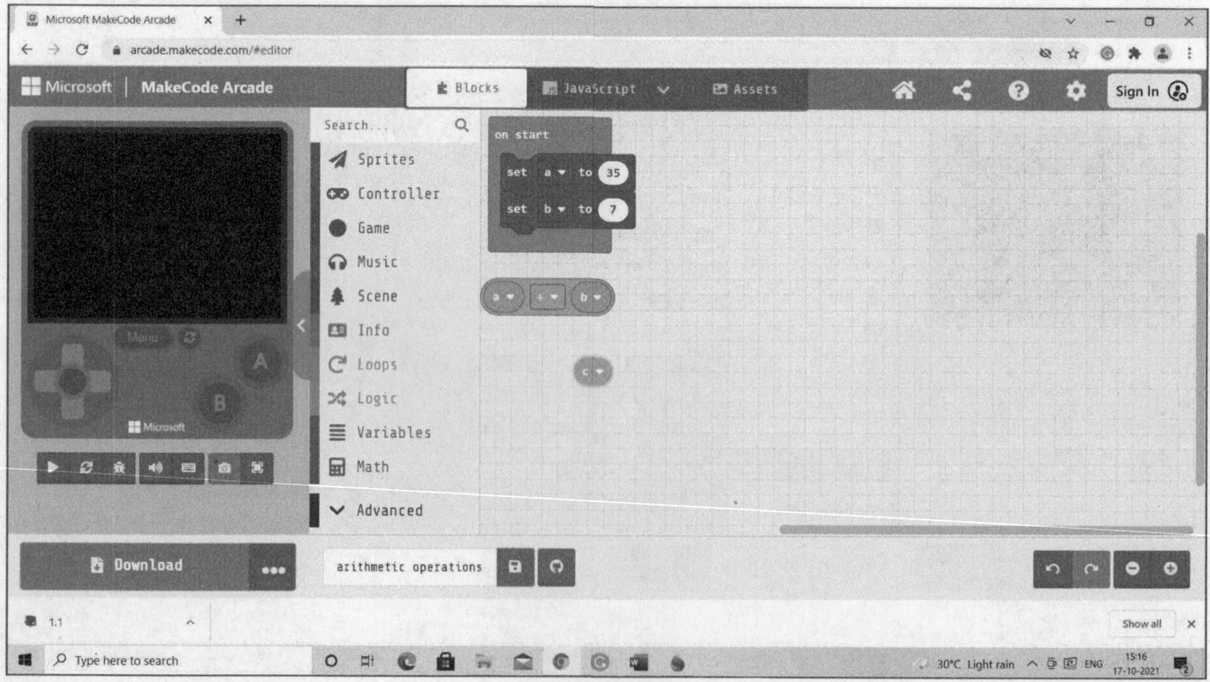

Figure 1.27

Step 11: Now, drag and drop the division block in the "set c to" block, as seen in the screenshot.

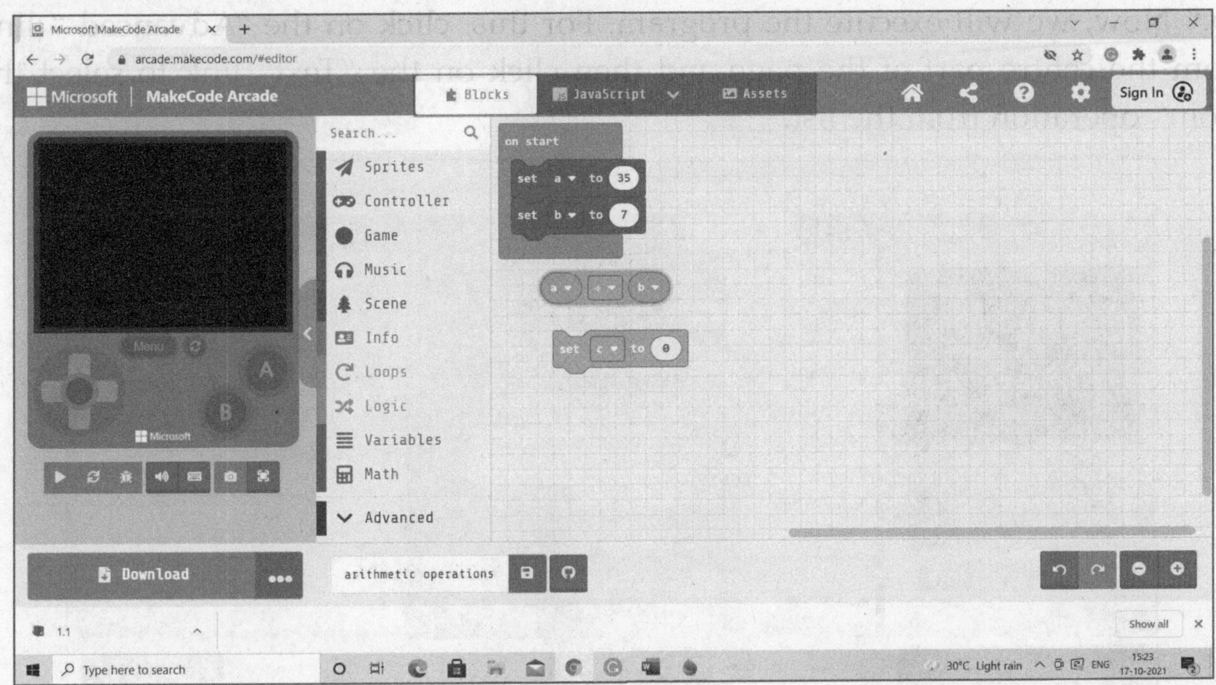

Figure 1.28

Step 12: Now, drag and drop the block of "set c to" to "a" * "b" in the green block.

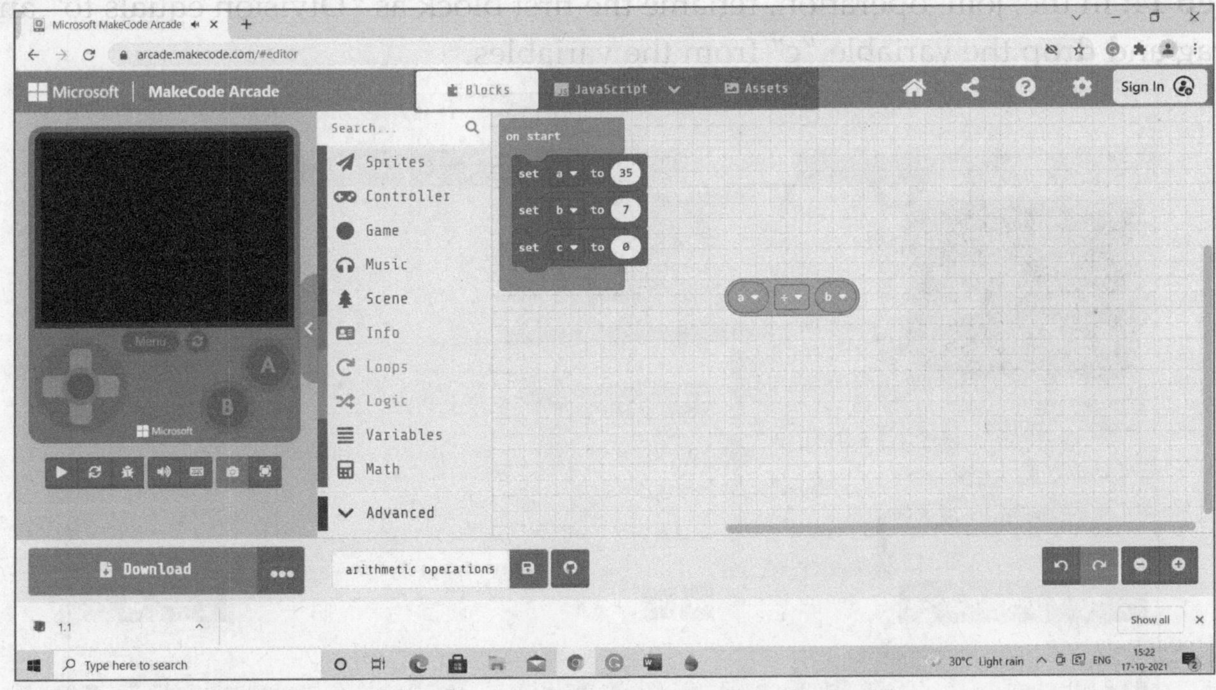

Figure 1.29

Step 13: We have created the variables and assigned them the values, and then created a third variable, "c," which will have the output of division of "a" and "b." Now, we will execute the program. For this, click on the "Advanced " link from the centre part of the page and then click on the "Text" link to select the "Join" operation from the list.

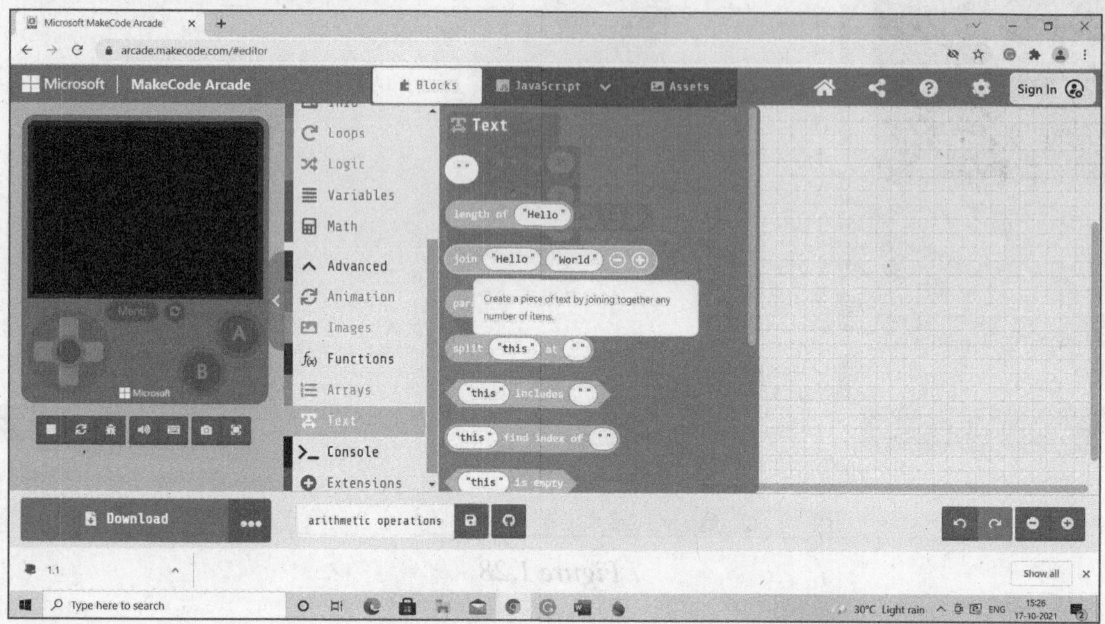

Figure 1.30

Step 14: In the 'join' operation, rename the first block as "Division equals to" and drag and drop the variable "c" from the variables.

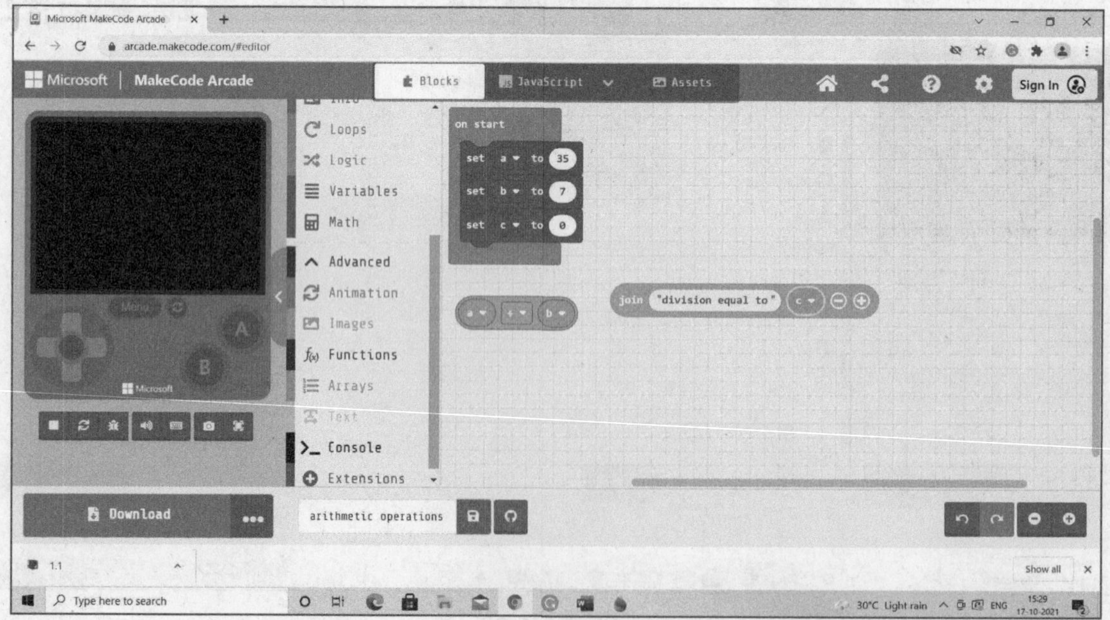

Figure 1.31

Step 15: Click on the "Games" link from the centre part of the page and click on the "Splash" block. On becoming visible, drag and drop the "join" block into it.

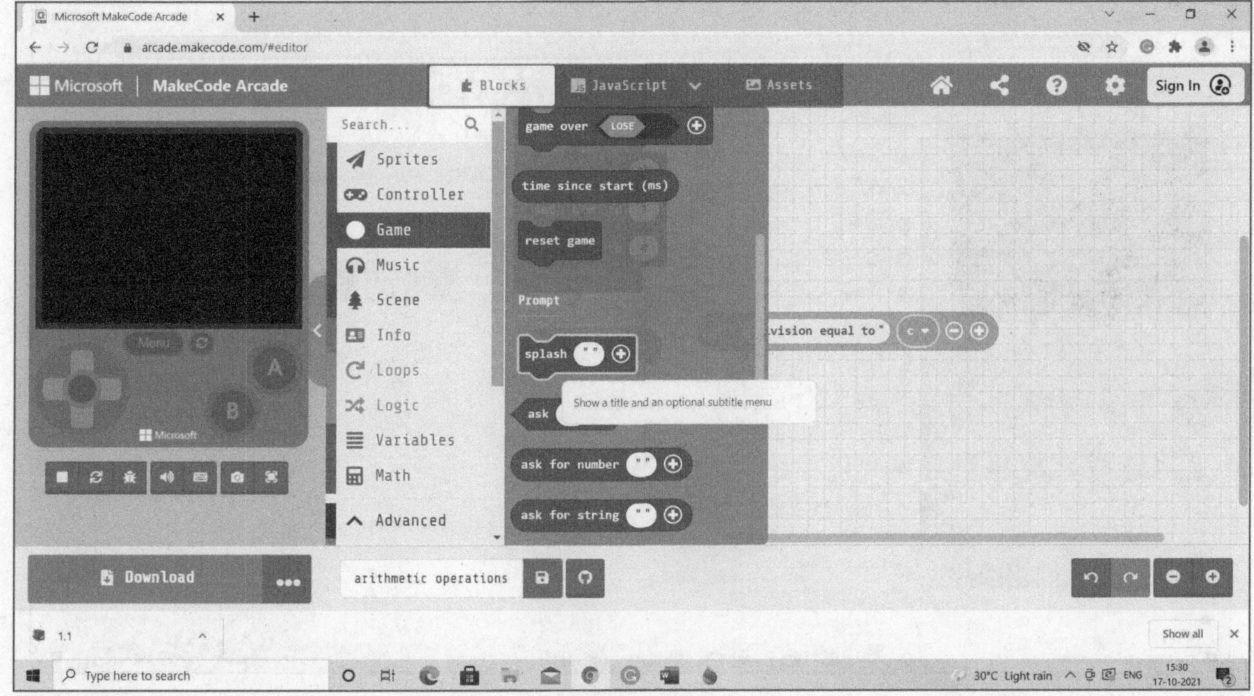

Figure 1.32

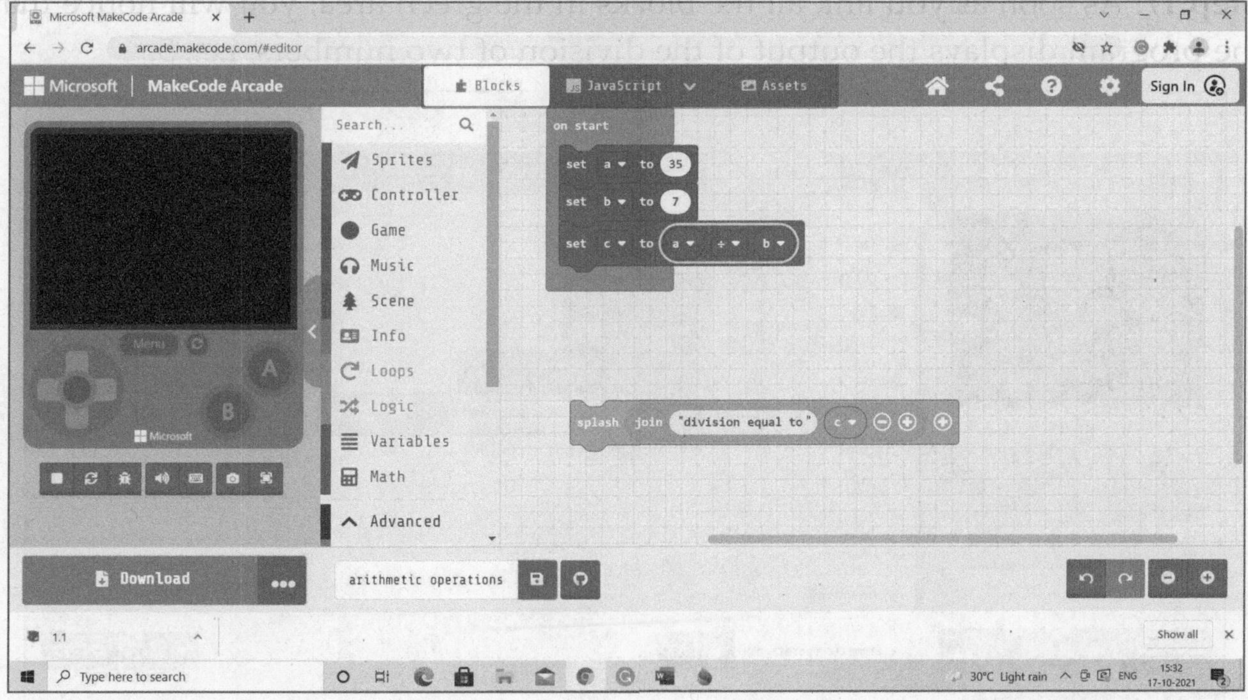

Figure 1.33

Step 16: Drag and drop the splash block into the green block below the set "c" block.

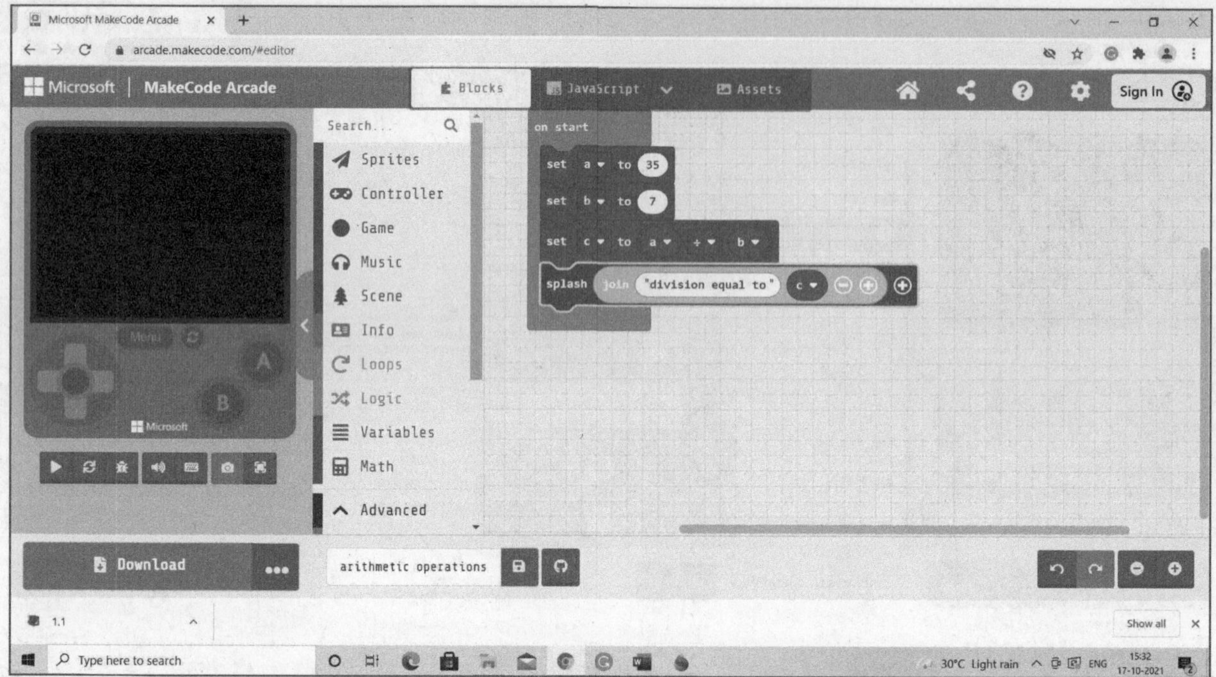

Figure 1.34

Step 17: As soon as you link all the blocks in the green area, you will notice that the program displays the output of the division of two numbers, i.e., 5.

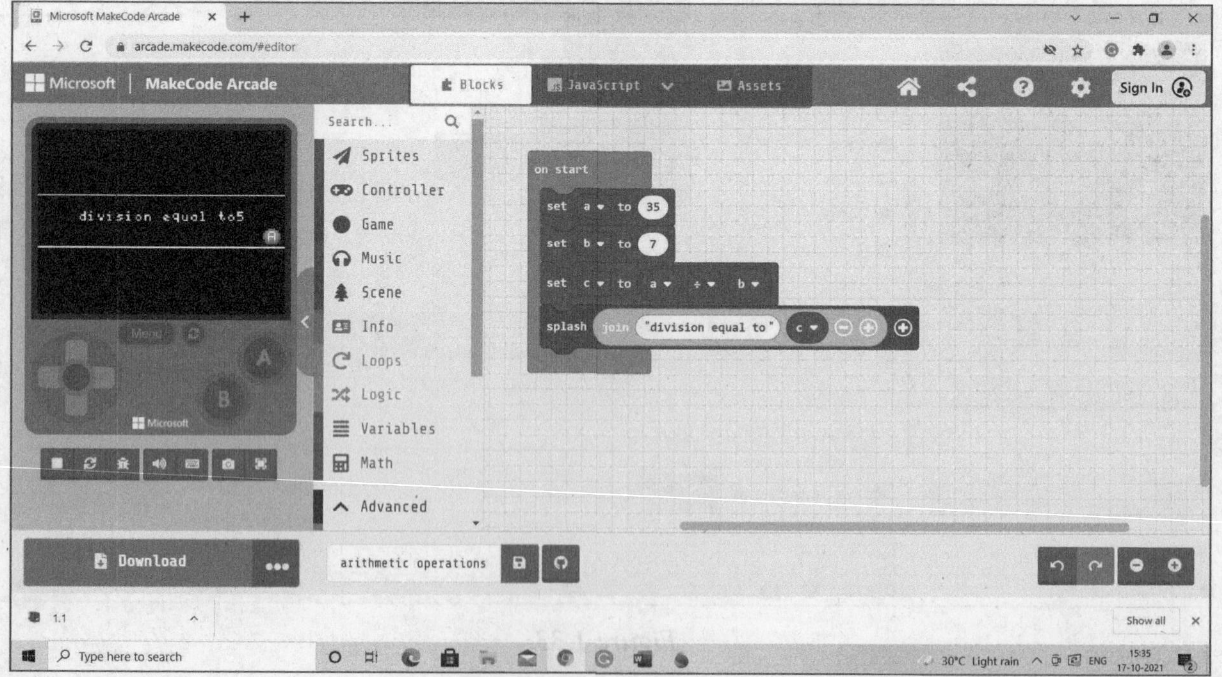

Figure 1.35

Step 18: When we reset the values of an as 750 and b as 5, we get the outcome 150.

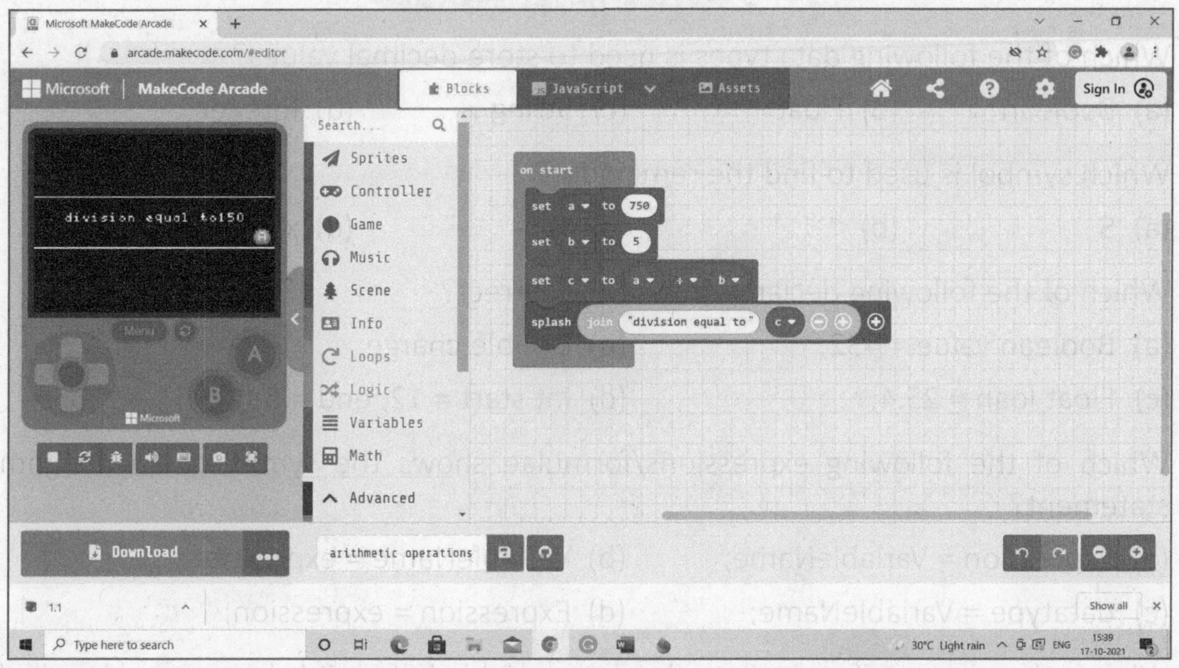

Figure 1.36

Step 19: When we reset the values of an as 22340 and b as 32, we get the outcome 698.125.

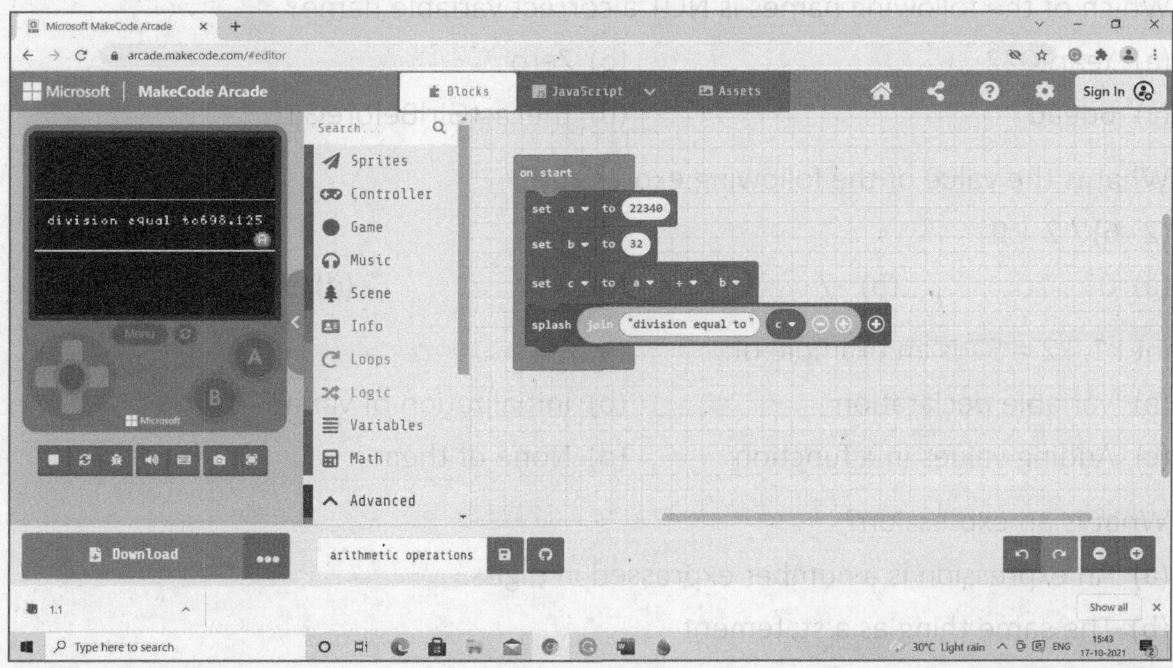

Figure 1.37

Change the values of a and b and find out the outcomes for different pairs.

Coding Quiz

1. Which of the following data types is used to store decimal values?
   (a) Boolean (b) Float (c) String (d) Integer

2. Which symbol is used to find the remainder?
   (a) $ (b) * (c) % (d) x

3. Which of the following declarations is NOT correct?
   (a) Boolean value = 432; (b) Double charge;
   (c) Float loan = 25.4; (d) Int start = 12, end = 53;

4. Which of the following expressions/formulae shows the syntax of an assignment statement?
   (a) Expression = VariableName; (b) VariableName = expression;
   (c) datatype = VariableName; (d) Expression = expression;

5. What is the process of assigning value to a variable before it is being used is called?
   (a) Realisation (b) Operation
   (c) Initialization (d) None of the above

6. Which of the following names is NOT a correct variable name?
   (a) Year2022 (b) Zero
   (c) 6dead (d) theLastGirlBeforeGiri

7. What is the value of the following expression?
   (2- 6) / 2 + 9
   (a) 0 (b) -7 (c) 7 (d) 9

8. int k1, k2 = 57 is an example of:
   (a) Variable declaration (b) Initialization of variable
   (c) Adding values in a function (d) None of them

9. What is an expression?
   (a) An expression is a number expressed in digits.
   (b) The same thing as a statement
   (c) An expression is defined as a list of statements that make up a program

(d) An expression is also a combination of literals, operators, variables, and parentheses used to calculate a value

ANSWERS								
1. (b)	2. (c)	3. (a)	4. (b)	5. (c)	6. (c)	7. (c)	8. (a)	9. (d)

SUMMARY

- Coding is used in many devices used by humans to make life comfortable.
- A variable is defined as a named location that is used to store data in the memory of the computer.
- A variable is like a container (like an envelope or bucket) holding data that can be changed later throughout programming.
- Scope of a variable normally refers to the part of the code where the variable can be used.
- In programming, a user is not allowed to use the same name of a variable more than once.
- The name of a variable also suggests what information the variable contains.
- Data type identifies the type of data that the declared variable can hold.
- The declaration of a variable in a program contains two components: the name of the variable and its type.
- Integer data type variables store integer values only. They store whole numbers which have zero, positive and negative values but not decimal values.
- Variables of the integer data type are only capable of holding single values.
- Floating-point numbers data types are used to store decimal values.
- There is another type of floating-point number known as a "double" data type, which is used to store even bigger values.
- Character type variables are used to store character values only.
- Syntax of declaring a character variable is specific to the programming language that you are using.
- Any character value can be declared as a character variable.
- The String data type stores value in a sequence of characters, i.e., in String format.
- Boolean Data Type stores values in Boolean type only, i.e., "true" or "false."
- Boolean is a subtype of integer data type that stores two values: true and false, where true means non-zero and false means zero.

- Operators are special symbols that represent computation. They are applied to operand(s), which can be values or variables.
- Operators, when applied to operands, form an expression.
- An arithmetic operation combines two or more numeric expressions using the Arithmetic Operators to form a resulting numeric expression.

PRACTICE TIME

(A) True/False Type Questions

1. A variable is defined as a named location that is used to store data in the memory of the computer.
2. The name assigned to a variable acts as an identifier for that variable.
3. Scope of a variable normally refers to the part of the code where the variable can be used.
4. In programming, a user is not allowed to use the same name of a variable more than twice.
5. Integer data type variables store decimal values only.
6. An assignment operator is used to assign a value to a variable.
7. The declaration of a variable in a program contains two components: the name of the variable and its type.
8. Naming variables make it easier to call them while performing operations.
9. If a user tries to create an integer variable and assign it a non-integer value, the program returns an output.
10. The Boolean, known as the "double" data type, is used to store bigger values.

ANSWERS					
1. T	2. T	3. T	4. F (once, not twice)	5. F (integer values)	6. T
7. T	8. T	9. F (error, not output)	10. F (floating-point number, not Boolean)		

(B) Fill in the blanks

1. A variable acts like a container (like an envelope or bucket) holding ____________ that can be changed later throughout programming.
2. Floating-point numbers are used to store ____________ values.
3. Variables of the ____________ data type are only capable of holding single values.
4. Character type variables are used to store ____________ values.

5. ____________ identifies the type of data that the declared variable can hold.

6. ____________ Type stores two values only, i.e., "true" or "false."

7. ____________ data type stores value in a sequence of characters, i.e., in String format.

8. The ____________ of a variable also suggests what information the variable contains.

9. Integer data type stores ____________ numbers which have zero, positive and negative values but not decimal values.

10. ____________ are special symbols that represent computation. They are applied to operand(s), which can be values or variables.

ANSWERS				
1. data	2. decimal	3. integer	4. character	5. Data type
6. Boolean Data	7. String	8. name	9. whole	10. Operators

(C) Very Short Answers Questions

1. What is block coding?
2. What do you mean by variable in programming?
3. What do you mean by variable initialization?
4. Can we declare two variables in a program with the same name?
5. Which data type can store exponential values?
6. What is Boolean data type?

(D) Short Answer Questions

1. What is the syntax to initialize a variable in programming?
2. Why do you think validating user input is important in programming?
3. What are your opinions on the naming convention of variables declared in programming?
4. Write down three best practices that you think one should follow while declaring variables.
5. What do you mean by floating-point data type? Give two examples.
6. Name the common Data Types in programming.
7. Write the pseudocode to perform an addition operation on two variables in a program.
8. Define and illustrate Boolean data types.

(E) High Order Thinking Skill Questions (HOTS)

1. Write a program to count the occurrence of the letter "e" in the string "We are a group."

   (The teacher will explain to the students the logic to count the number of occurrences of the letter "e" in the given string. This will help the students to understand how to apply this logic in a program. The teacher will encourage the students to do the problem on their own.)

2. Write a program to check if a given String is palindrome or not.

   (The teacher will explain to the students the logic to figure out if the string is palindrome or not. This will help the students to understand how to apply this logic in a program. The teacher will encourage the students to do the problem on their own.)

(F) Projects

1. Problem statement: To create a program in Arcade to display a square of numbers from 1 to 10.
2. Problem Statement: To perform a 'Modulus/Remainder' operation by using Block Coding.

(The teacher will explain the students the project so that they can understand it and create the corresponding program in Arcade. The teacher will encourage the students to do the problem on their own. The block code will be different for all the students.)

Sequencing with Block Coding

Structure

In this chapter, you will learn:

- Definition of sequencing
- Importance to follow a sequence in programming
- Methods to reduce steps in a sequence with loops and conditional operators

INTRODUCTION

In the previous class, we have studied that a loop is defined as a series, structure, or process, the end of which is related/connected to the beginning. We see various loops in our daily lives. For example, the water cycle is one type of Loop. When we are running along the borders of the ground of our school, it makes a loop provided we return to the beginning point. Loop is regarded as one of the basic logical structures of computer programming. Computers perform particular tasks repeatedly when loops are used with the proper definition.

Figure 2.1

An algorithm consists of many steps which are to be done in a step-by-step process. Moreover, this is to be done in the correct order to complete a task or to solve a problem. The process of deciding the position/sequence of the steps of a program is called sequencing.

In this chapter, we shall study the sequencing in programming/coding, loops and types of loops, what conditional operators are, and how to reduce steps in a sequence with loops and conditional operators.

Learning Objectives:

At the end of this chapter, you will be able to:

- have an understanding of the basics of algorithms.
- have an understanding of sequencing and its importance.
- know how to apply loops and conditions to simplify sequencing.

2.1 RECAP OF LOOPS

Let's understand what a loop is. Suppose Anita is coming to school, attending school and returning home. What are the different steps for going to school and coming back home? Think and write.

Perhaps the following steps might be followed by her:

- Walk out of the home to the bus stop
- Wait for the school bus
- Get on the school bus
- Arrive at school
- Walk to the school and then to the classroom.
- Attending the school assembly/ classes/participating in all activities
- Walk to the school gate
- Get on the school bus.
- Get down at the bus stop near the home.
- Walk to the home from the bus stop.

Figure 2.2

Thus, the walk to school and returning home is a loop every student performs every day. Similarly, there are many more tasks in our day-to-day life that we repeat at specific intervals, like eating meals, taking a bath, going to the weekly market, etc. These are a few examples of loops.

Activity 2.1

- Participate in the 'Larger Group Discussion' on **"Examples of Loops in Our Lives."**
- All the students will participate in the discussion on the topic that will be initiated by the teacher in the class.

Figure 2.3

- One volunteer student will record all the examples shared by the participants and will share the complete list with the whole class.

A very similar concept to this is used in programming, where we need to repeat certain lines of code at a specific interval or till a specified condition is met. In programming, repetition of a line or a block of code is also known as iteration. A loop is an algorithm that executes a block of code multiple times till the time a specified condition is met. Therefore, we can conclude that a loop iterates a block of code multiple times till the time mentioned condition is satisfied.

Loops in programming help in:

- ❖ Reducing the number of steps in algorithms.
- ❖ Reusing specific parts of the code.

In Short

- ❖ In programming, the repetition of a line or a block of code is called iteration.
- ❖ A loop is an algorithm that executes a block of code multiple times till the time a specified condition is met.

- The break statement modifies the normal flow of execution while it terminates the existing Loop and continues execution of the statement following that Loop.
- Whenever a program encounters a continuous statement, the control skips the execution of remaining statements inside the Loop for the present iteration and jumps to the beginning of the Loop for the next iteration.
- When a loop is present inside another loop, it is known as a nested loop.

In coding, loops allow us to repeat something again and again. Loops will repeat until the coder/programmer gives instructions for the computer to stop. In some cases, a programmer might tell the computer to stop after it has repeated the Loop a certain number of times. In other cases, the programmer may tell the computer to stop once a certain condition is met.

For example, consider that you want to print alphabets A to C on the screen. We can do so by printing the values a, b and c by writing three lines of code.

Let us now look at the following pseudocode:

```
Start
This program demonstrates printing alphabets A to C
Print A
Print B
Print C
End
Output:
A
B
C
```

This was easy. Now, consider a requirement where we need to print numbers in incremental order from 1 to 200. Although it is possible to print it following the above pseudocode, it will get a very tedious and lengthy process. This is the situation where loops come into the picture to make this task easier. We can use the concept of loops and get the desired output by writing just a few lines of code.

Table 2.1 Some Examples of Loops

- When the software of the ATM machine is programmed to process transaction after transaction until you acknowledge that you have no more to do, then it is a loop.
- Suppose someone puts his/her favourite song on a repeat mode. It is also a loop.
- A software program in a mobile device allows users to unlock the mobile with 5 password attempts. After that, it resets the mobile device.
- If someone wants to run a particular analysis on each column of the data set, then it is a loop.
- Salary preparation software is used by some organisations.
- A bhajan (devotional song) that is intentionally put on a repeat mode just to deep dive into the feeling.
- Software used to get the printout of salary slips of all employees of an organisation.
- Water Cycle

2.2 WHAT IS SEQUENCING?

An algorithm is defined as a detailed step-by-step process that is required to be followed in order to complete a task and/ to solve a problem. There are three basic building blocks that can be used when designing algorithms:

- Sequencing
- Selection
- Iteration

These building blocks help us to convert any complex problem into a well-defined solution that can be understood and implemented by others using programming.

For example, how would you design an algorithm for your morning routine? It may be like as follows:

- Wake up
- Brush your teeth
- Take a bath
- Have breakfast
- Go to school

Thus, a sequence is a list of activities that are done one after another. Sequencing refers to the specific order in which we require to act or to carry the activities to get the desired output.

Every day, we do many activities in a sequence. For example, think of how you would make a sandwich. If we wish to write down the steps for making a sandwich, it may be like the steps given below.

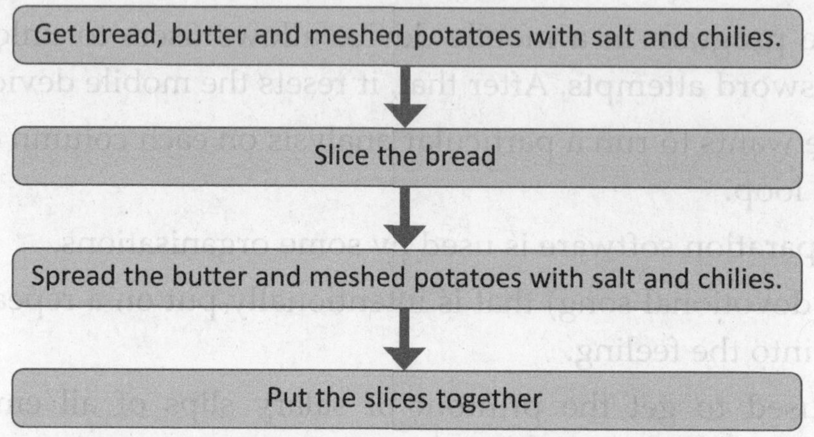

Figure 2.4: An algorithm for 'Making a Sandwich.'

If we do these steps in any other order, would the result still be a sandwich? Definitely No!

Similarly, in programming, tasks need to be done in the correct sequence to get the desired output.

In both daily tasks and coding, if we don't put every step in the right sequence, the result will not be what we wanted. Sequencing is a foundational concept in programming, and everything we learn in the future will build on this concept.

Activity 2.2

- Participate in the larger group activity on **"Examples of Sequencing in Real Life"**.
- The teacher will initiate the discussion on the topic in the class and all students will provide their inputs in the form of examples of sequencing.
- A volunteer student will make a list of all such examples and will put them before the full class.

In Short

- A sequence is a list of activities to be done one after another.
- Sequencing refers to the specific order of activities/actions in which the computer need to perform the activities to get the desired output.
- When creating algorithms or programs, then the instructions are presented in a particular correct order.
- A sequence can contain any number of instructions, but each instruction must be run in the order they are presented.
- No instruction can be skipped.

2.3 EXAMPLES OF SEQUENCE, SELECTION, AND ITERATION

To understand the concept of sequencing in programming, take a look at the below algorithm to swap two numbers:

Here, we need to follow the algorithm step by step to get the final output.

First, Read the two numbers that need to be swapped. Then, assign the value of num1 to a temporary variable called "temp." Next, assign value of num2 to num1. Later, assign a value of "temp" to num2. Finally, Print the values of num1 and num2, which are now swapped.

It is interesting to note that the steps that followed to achieve this output are in a sequence. Skipping any step from this sequence or altering the sequence will lead to errors in the program, and that may generate the wrong output.

```
Step 1: Start
Step 2: READ num1, num2
Step 3: temp = num1
Step 4: num1 = num2
Step 5: num2 = temp
Step 6: PRINT num1, num2
Step 7: Stop
```

This is how sequencing in programming works.

Now, let us understand the concept of selection using an example.

Take a look at below pseudocode to check if the age entered by the user is of a pensioner or not. Consider that person is named as a pensioner if his/her age is above 60 years.

```
int age = 61;
if (age>=60)
print("Person is a pensioner");
else
print("Person is not a pensioner");
```

Here, the pseudocode is trying to check if the age defined in the program is of a pensioner or not.

When we follow the sequence of pseudocode, then we will see that the program makes a "selection" of which flow to enter depending on the age defined in the program.

When the age is more than or equal to 60 years, then the program enters the 'if' block. When the age is less than 60 years, then the program enters the 'else' block. This is how concept of selection is applied in programming.

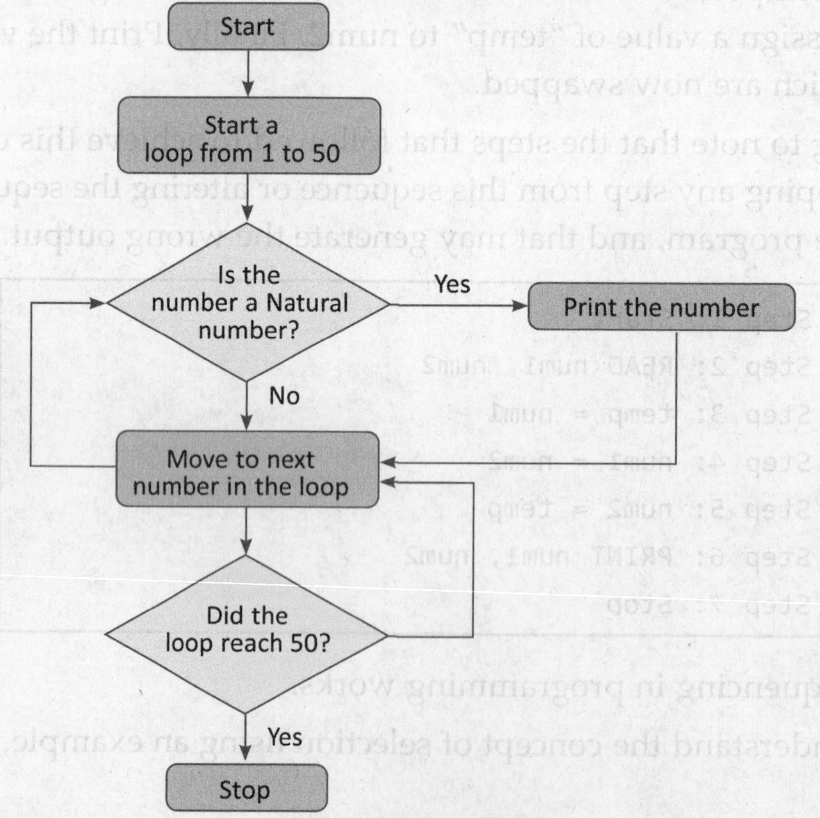

Figure 2.5: Flowchart

Now, look at this example of iteration. Iteration simply means repetition. In programming, loops follow the iteration depending on the condition. Every Loop iterates at least once, if not more.

Consider a program to print all the natural numbers from 1 to 50. It will follow the flow as shown in the Fig 2.5 flowchart.

As we can see in the flowchart, the flow of the program will repeat or iterate for each number from 1 to 50. For every single iteration it will check for the condition and take the appropriate workflow. This is how iteration works in programming. It will repeat the block of code multiple times till the specified condition is achieved.

2.4 WHAT IS A BUG?

Any unexpected problem in a program is called a bug. We need to follow a sequence of activities to complete a program to get a specific output. Any deviation in the actual and expected and actual output of the program is called a bug.

Figure 2.6

Example: suppose we want to create a boat that can sail in the ocean. Now, when the boat is ready and we try to sail it in the water, we realise that there is a very small hole in the bottom of the boat from where water is seeping in. This water seeping into the boat at a very slow speed may create a big problem for the boat in the long run. Thus, this hole in the bottom of the boat can be termed as a "bug" in programming.

Factz Funda

The process of removing bugs from a code/program is called debugging.

2.5 TYPES OF LOOPS

As we have studied that the applications of loops make the code manageable and organisd. There are three different types of loops:

- While Loop
- For Loop
- Nested Loop

2.5.1 While Loop

The 'While' Loop can execute a set of commands till the condition is true. 'While' Loops are also called conditional loops. The 'While' loop can execute a set of commands till the condition is true. Once the condition is met, then the Loop is finished.

Thus, 'while' loops are those loops that will continue to go until a condition is no longer true. They are called 'while' loops because of the fact that the code will repeat while a condition is still true. We can think of while loops as telling our app "while this happens, repeat this" or "while this hasn't changed, repeat this."

Factz Funda

A user uses the 'while' loop until a condition is true.

2.5.2 For Loop

'For' Loop is needed for iterating over a sequence. A 'For' Loop executes a specific number of times. Thus, 'For' loops will repeat a block of code a set number of times as directed. These loops are called 'for' loops because we can tell our app how many times we want it to repeat the code. We can think about for loops as telling our app, "Repeat this, for 12 times" or "Repeat this, for 5 times."

'For' loops use a variable to count how many times the program/code has been repeated, and it is called a 'counter.' We control how many times the Loop repeats by setting where the counter starts and ends. We also set how much the counter goes up by each time the code repeats. In most cases, the counter increases by one each time the loop repeats.

Factz Funda

A 'For' Loop is to be used when the user is sure that exactly how many iterations are needed to be carried out.

2.5.3 Nested Loops

Any loop in the program may contain another loop inside it. When there is a loop inside another loop, it is called a nested loop. This combination of loops inside Loop is helpful while working with requirements where the user wants to work on multiple conditions simultaneously. There is no restriction on how many loops can be nested inside a loop.

To understand the concept of Nested loops in a better way, consider the example of an Analogue clock. An analogue clock has one hand as the nested Loop, and every full rotation knocks the minute hand on by one and so on. We can take this even further to say that clocks are just a form of the counting system. This is how nested loops work in real life.

Activity 2.3

- Participate in the individual activity on "**Building a music player.**"
- During this activity, the participants will implement the concept of incrementing loops with the help of the Arcade platform (https://arcade.makecode.com/).

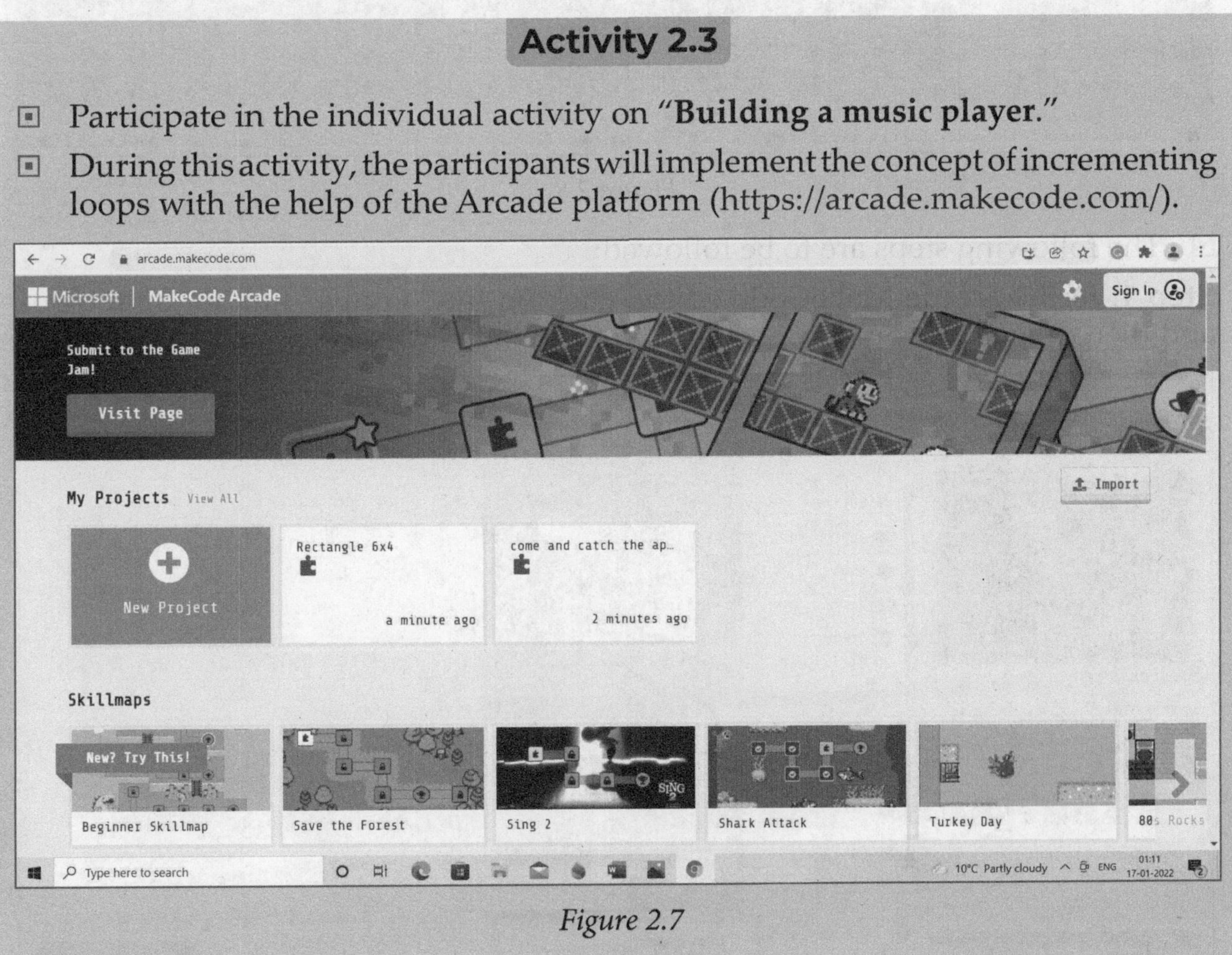

Figure 2.7

▣ Create the project "Building a Music Player."

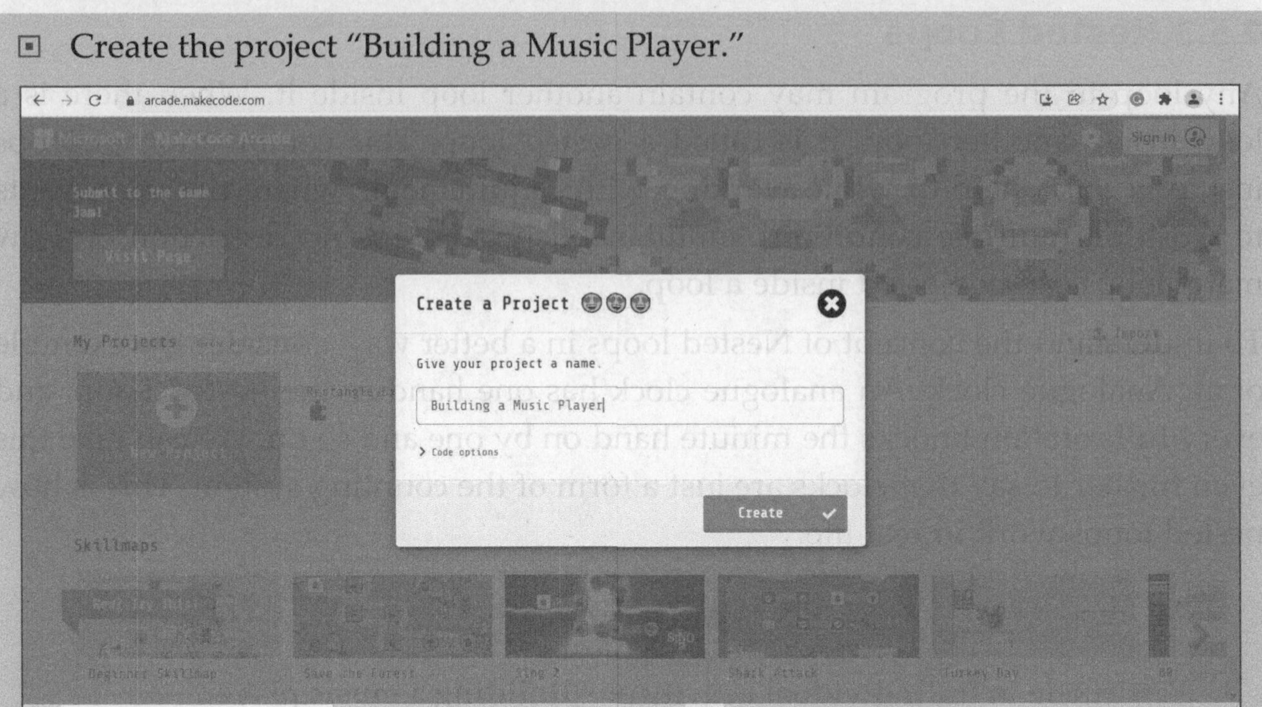

Figure 2.8

▣ The following steps are to be followed:

Step 1: In the arcade MakeCode editor, click on the "Loops" link in the toolbox and then drag and drop the "on start" block to the play area.

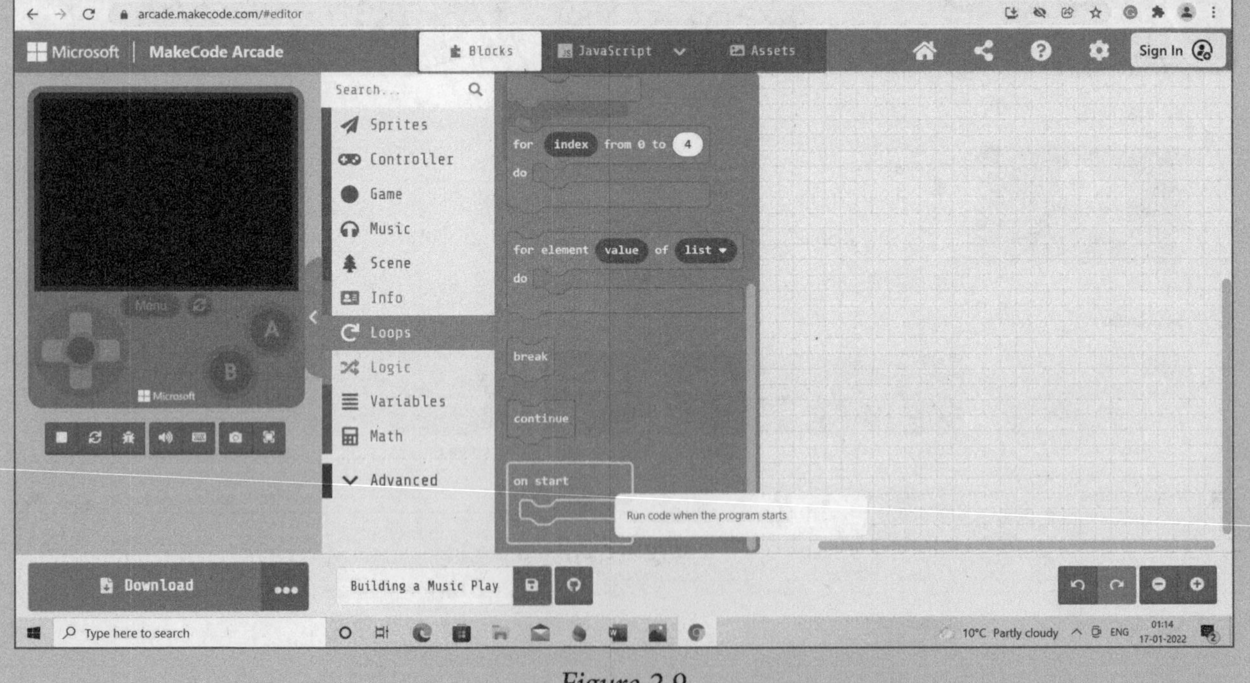

Figure 2.9

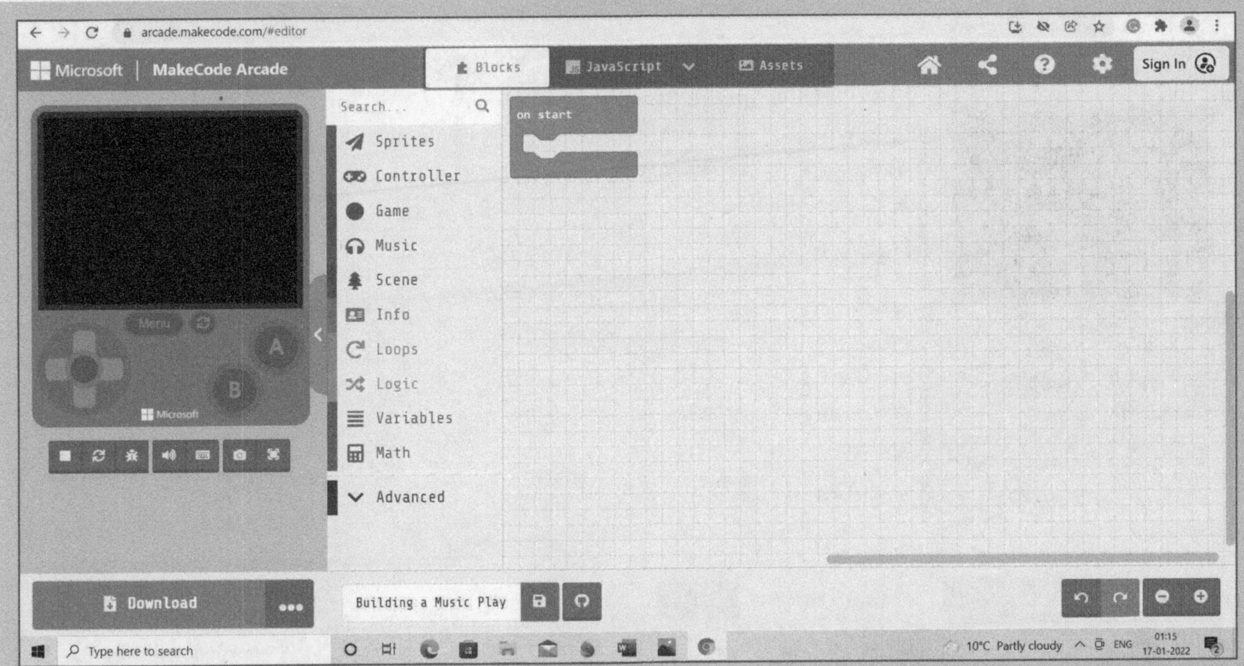

Figure 2.10

Step 2: Again, click on the "Loops" link in the toolbox in the centre of the page. Drag and drop the "repeat 4 times do" block to the play area.

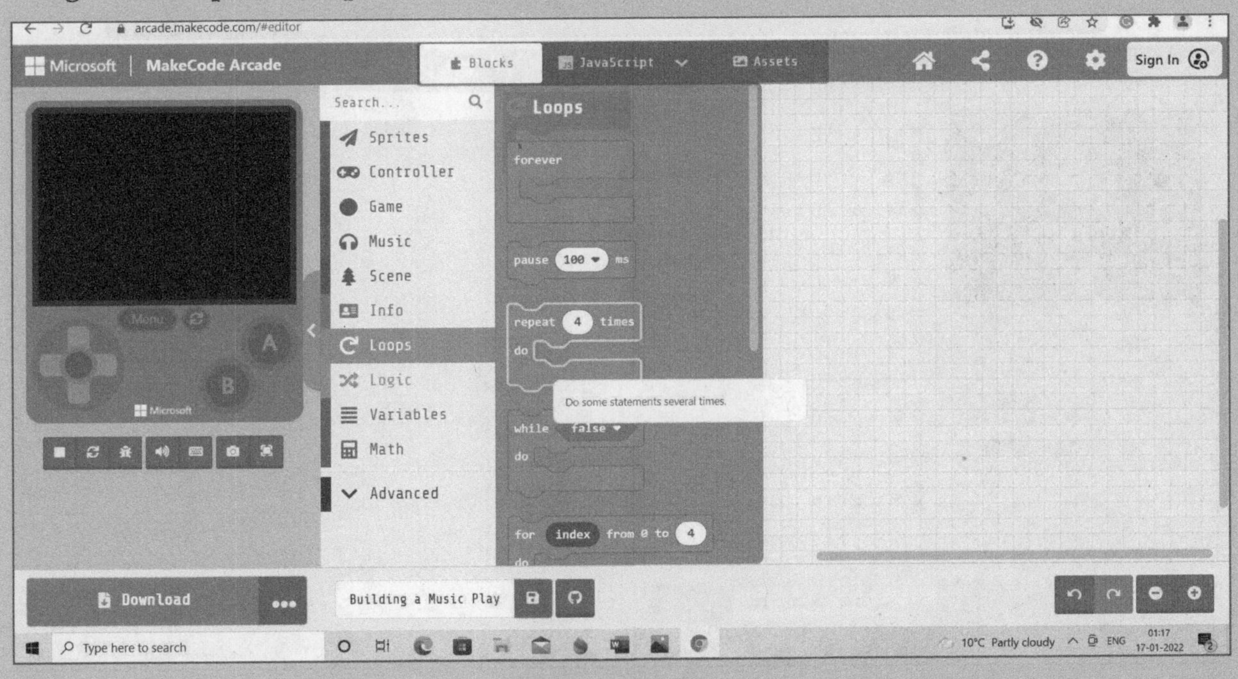

Figure 2.11

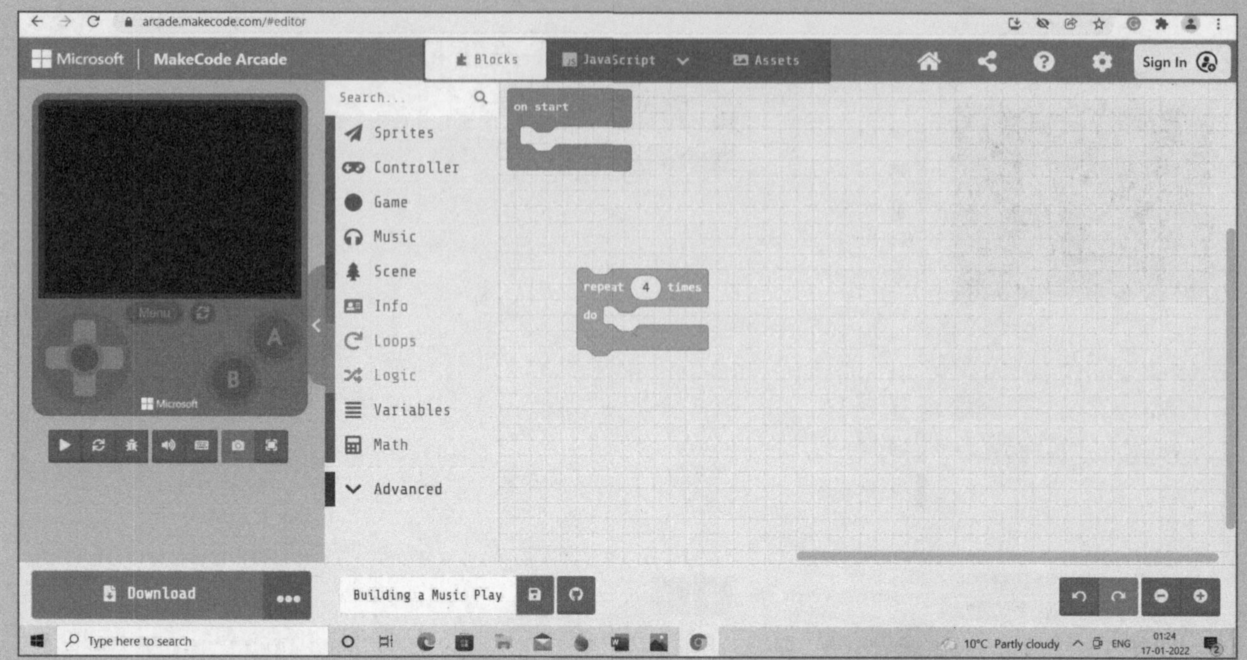

Figure 2.12

Step 3: Now, move the other "repeat "block and place it inside the "start" block. Also, reset the value in the "repeat" block to "8".

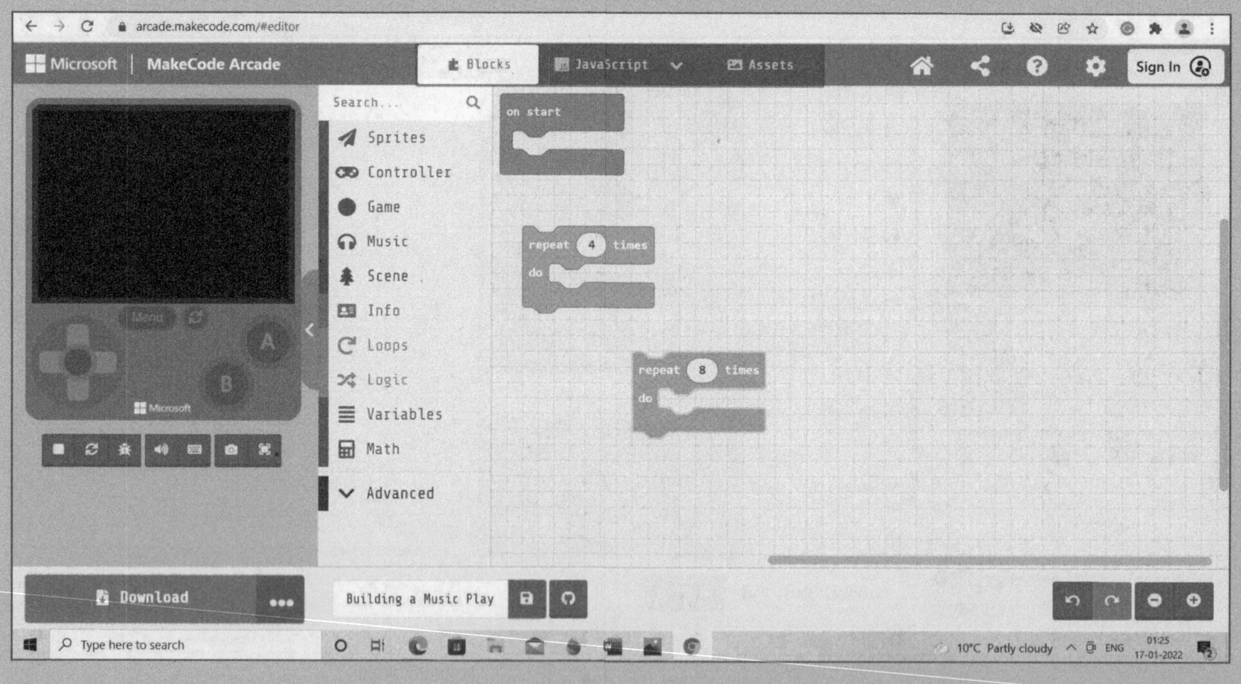

Figure 2.13

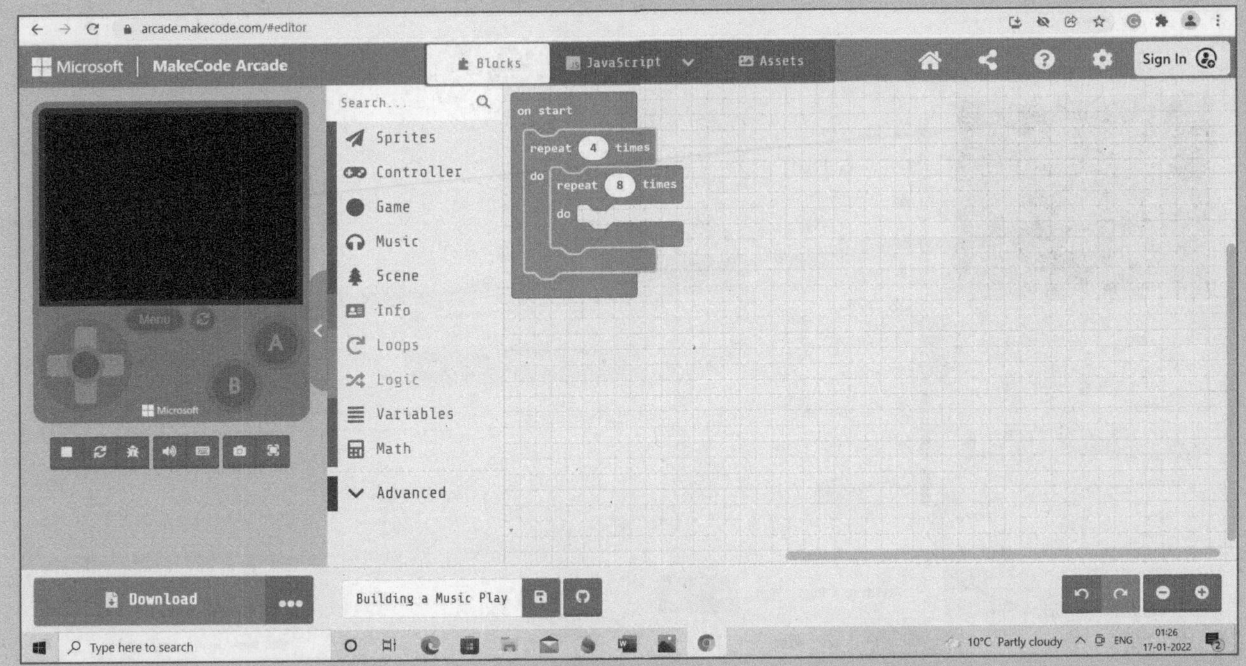

Figure 2.14

Step 4: Click on the "Music" link from the toolbox and drag and drop the "play sound until done" block in the play area.

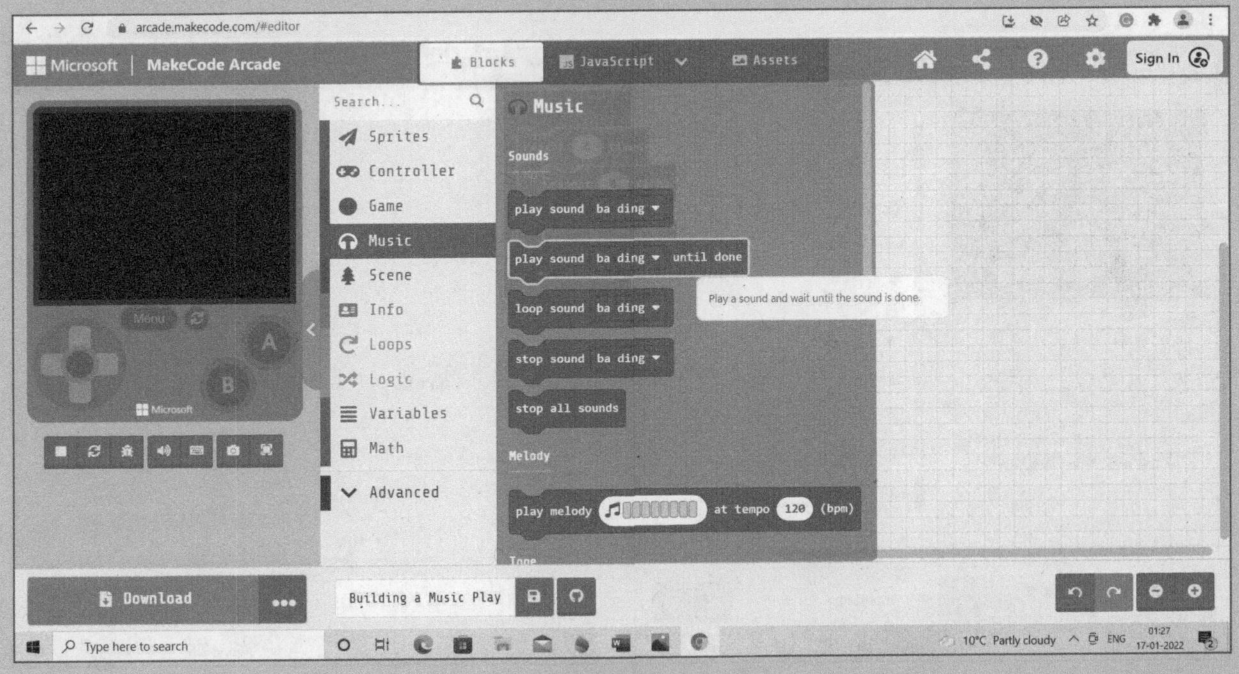

Figure 2.15

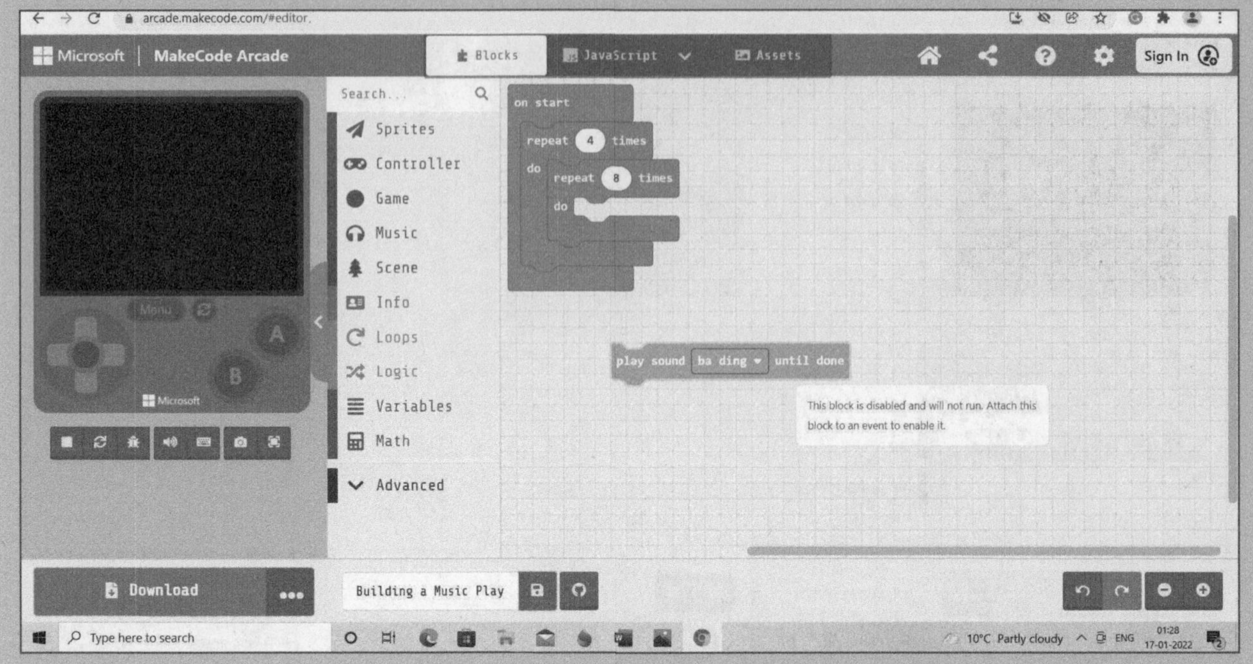

Figure 2.16

Step 5: Click the 'ba ding' soundbox and change it to the 'pew pew' sound in the "play sound until done" block.

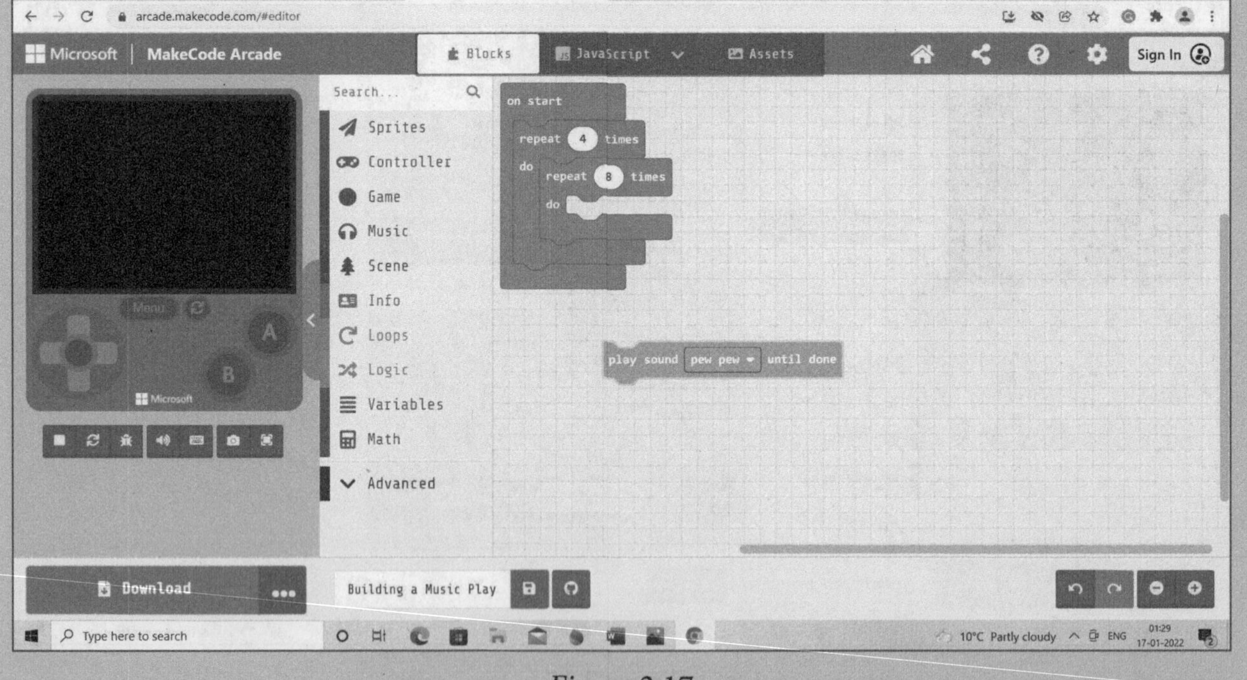

Figure 2.17

Step 6: Fix the "play sound until done" block in the "repeat" block.

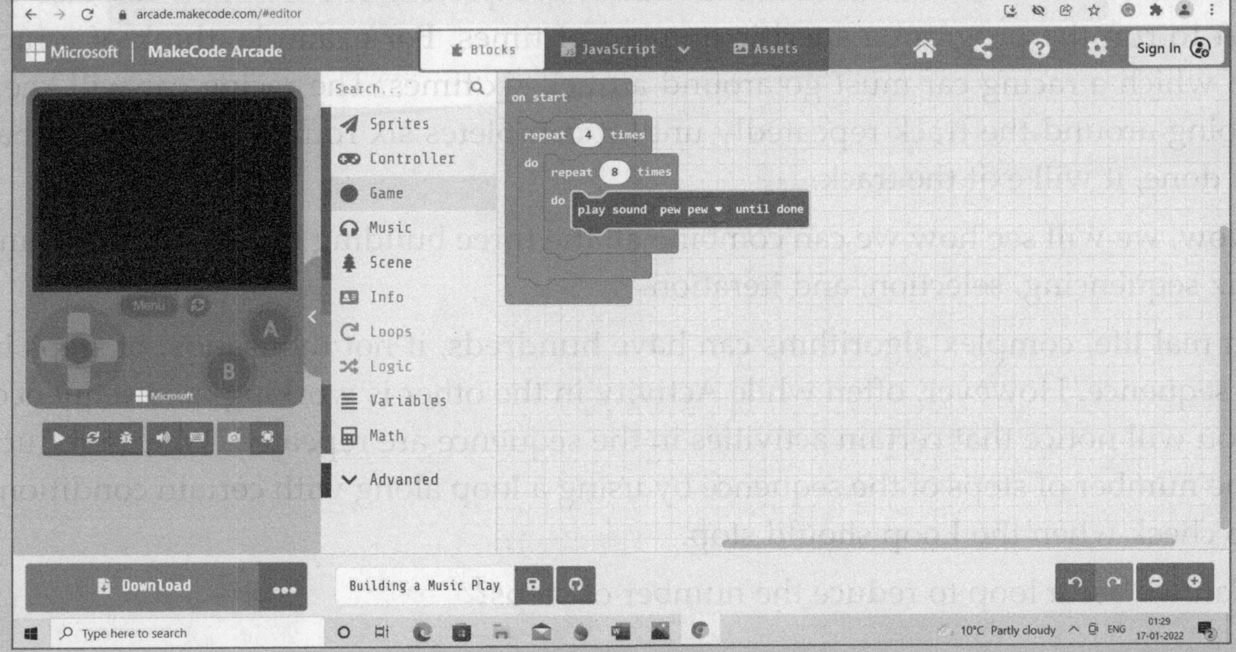

Figure 2.18

When we click on the play for the above exercise that we have created, we will hear the music 8 times. The Loop repeats itself 8 times (counter that we had set). The flow starts with 1, and in each iteration, it increments once. Each time loop completes once iteration, and we will hear music once.

Factz Funda

The process of doing something repeatedly is called iteration. In computing, iteration is the technique of marking out a block of statements within a computer program for a defined number of repetitions.

2.6 APPLY LOOPS AND CONDITIONALS WITH SEQUENCING

There are two important aspects of an algorithm for discussion: selection and iteration. Selection refers to the situation in which the algorithm needs to make a choice between two or more alternatives. It is just like asking questions like "Is it raining?". If the answer to the question is true, the algorithm follows one path. When the answer is false, the algorithm follows a different path.

Iteration refers to the process of doing the same task over and repeatedly until a certain condition is met or a certain task is completed. The iteration can also be set to run the program a specific number of times. For example, think of a race in which a racing car must go around a track six times. The racing car will keep going around the track repeatedly until it completes six rounds/ laps. Once that is done, it will exit the track.

Now, we will see how we can combine all the three building blocks of algorithms viz sequencing, selection, and iteration.

In real life, complex algorithms can have hundreds, if not thousands, of steps in a sequence. However, often while Activity in the other is working on a sequence, you will notice that certain activities in the sequence are repeated. We can reduce the number of steps of the sequence by using a loop along with certain conditions to check when the Loop should stop.

Can we use a loop to reduce the number of steps?

2.7 IS THERE A BETTER WAY TO APPLY TO SEQUENCE?

By combining sequencing with loops and conditionals, we can have successfully come up with an algorithm.

Project Time

Project 2.1

Aim: To understand iteration by the activity **'Distributing Chocolates on Birthday'**.

Learning Outcomes: After this project, the learners will be able to understand the iteration process.

Problem Statement: It is Shalu's birthday on a particular day. The entire class wishes birthday to Shalu. Later, Shalu takes out the chocolate from his bag and starts distributing it to her classmates in the class. Prepare a flowchart.

Solution: The class will be distributed into four groups randomly without any bias. Each group will discuss the problem and will prepare a flowchart. All flowcharts prepared will be shared by the group representative, followed by a class discussion.

Look at the flowchart given in Figure 2.19 to understand how Shalu uses the concept of iteration while distributing chocolates in the class.

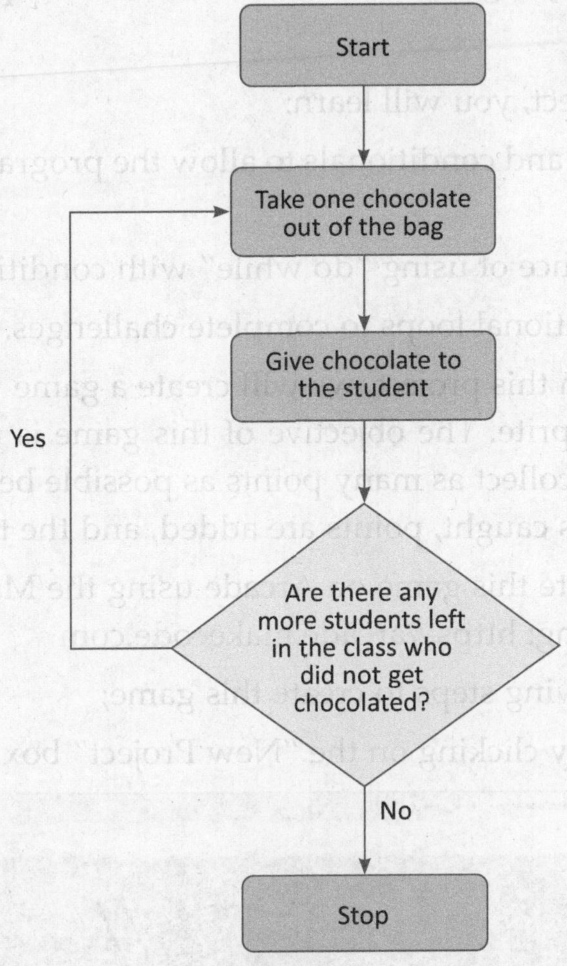

Figure 2.19

You will notice that there is a pattern that Shalu follows while distributing chocolates. She takes the chocolates out from his bag, gives one chocolate to a student, moves to the next student and repeats the same steps again till the sweets are distributed to all the students.

This is an example of an iterative process. Repetition of a set of steps with a defined end – in this case the repetition ended when all the students in the class were given chocolates.

Project 2.2

Aim: To create and play a game, **"Come and Catch the Apple."**

Learning Outcomes:

At the end of this project, you will learn:

- Learn to use loops and conditionals to allow the program to perform repeated tasks.
- Learn the importance of using "do while" with conditional loops.
- Learn to use conditional loops to complete challenges.

Problem Statement: In this project, we will create a game with 2 sprites, a Player sprite and an Apple sprite. The objective of this game is to chase and catch the wandering apple and collect as many points as possible before the time runs out. Every time the apple is caught, points are added, and the timer is restored.

Solution: We will create this game on Arcade using the MakeCode editor, which can be found by clicking: https://arcade.makecode.com

Now, follow the following steps to create this game;

Create a new project by clicking on the "New Project" box.

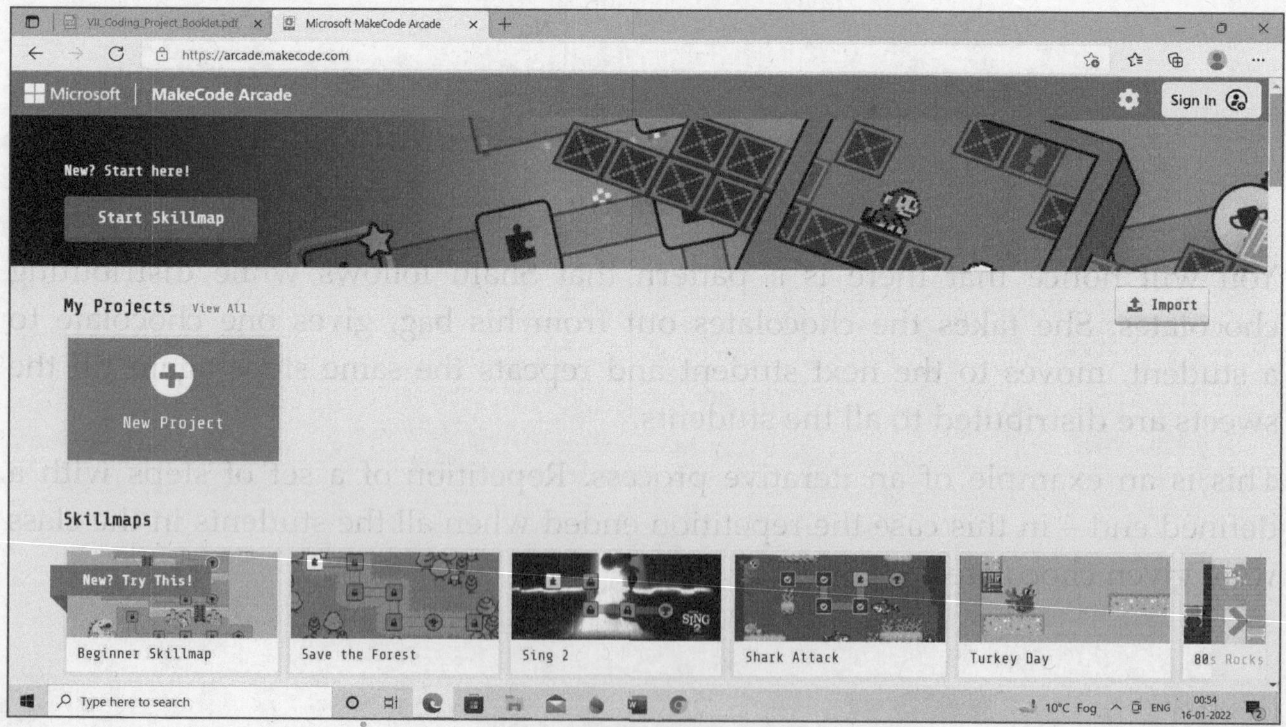

Figure 2.20

In the appeared dialog box, give a name to your project, "Come and Catch the Apple," and click the "Create" button and you will get the following:

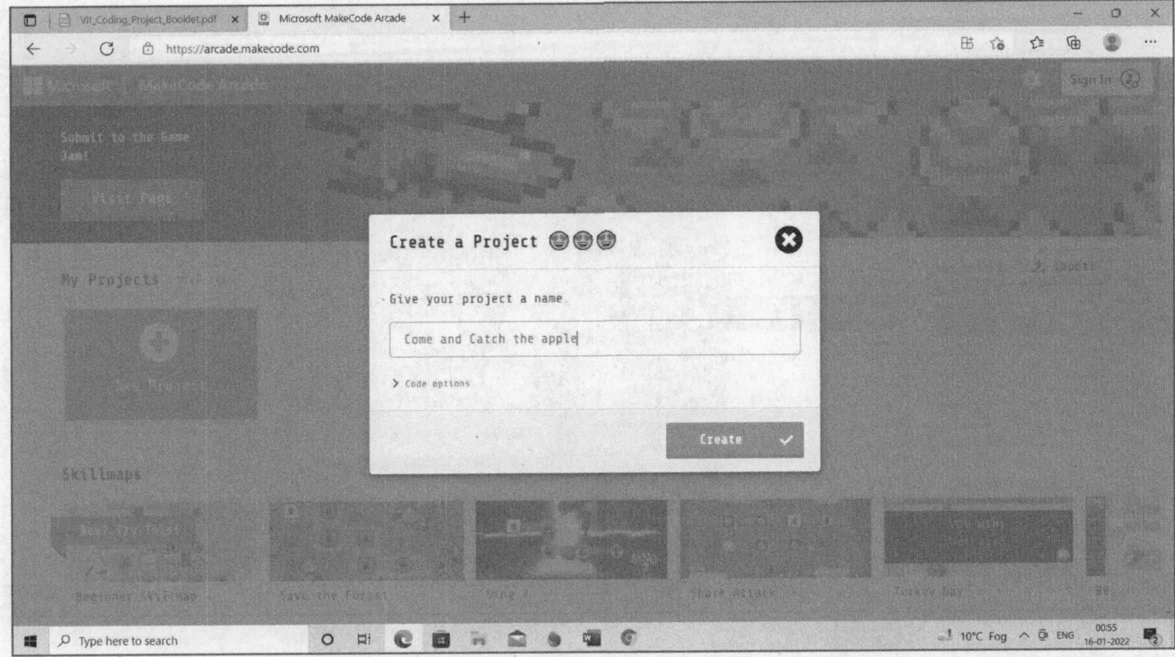

Figure 2.21

Follow the following steps:

Step 1: Open the scene toolbox drawer and drag the "set background image" block into the "On start" block on the workspace.

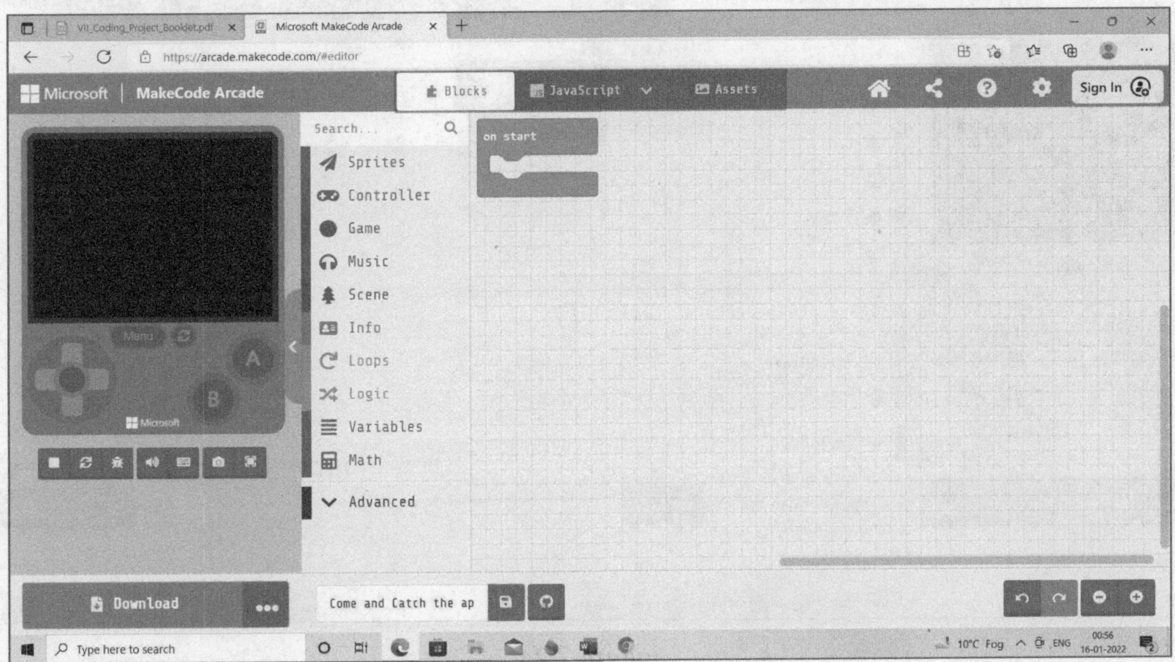

Figure 2.22

Step 2: In the "Set background image" block, click on the gray square to open the image editor, select a colour (yellow) to fill in the background colour.

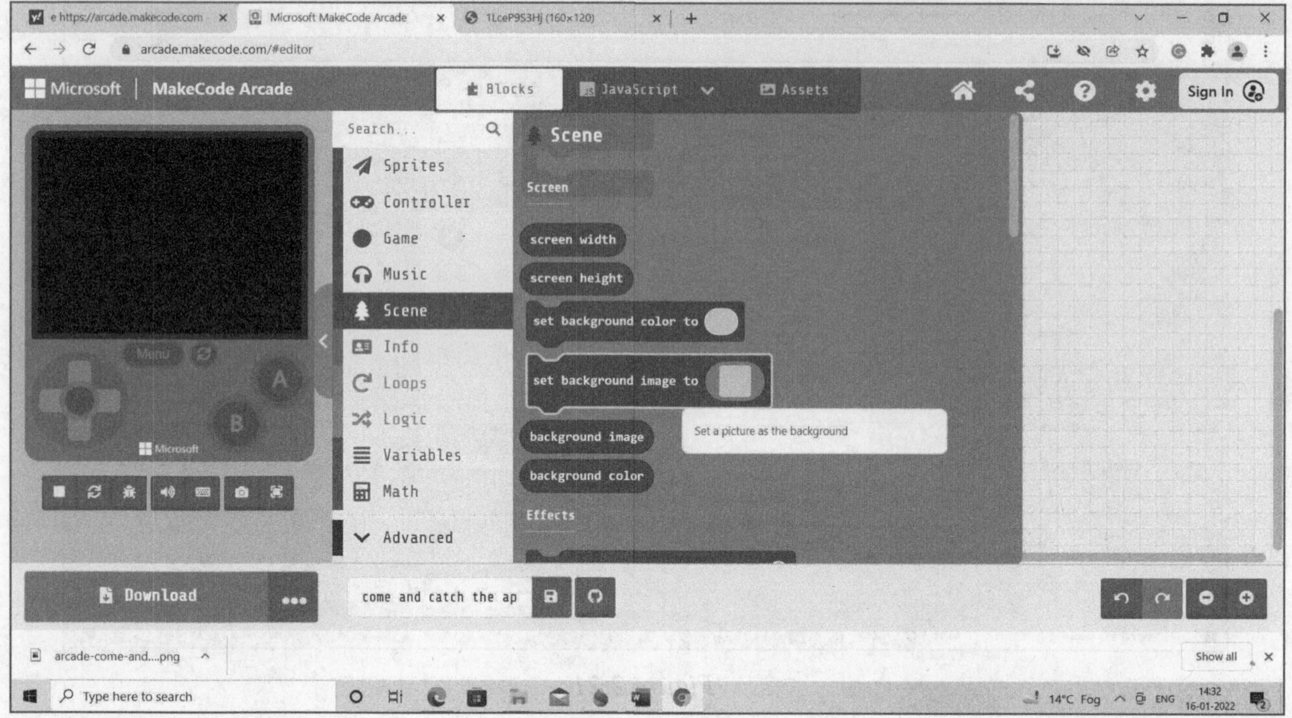

Figure 2.23

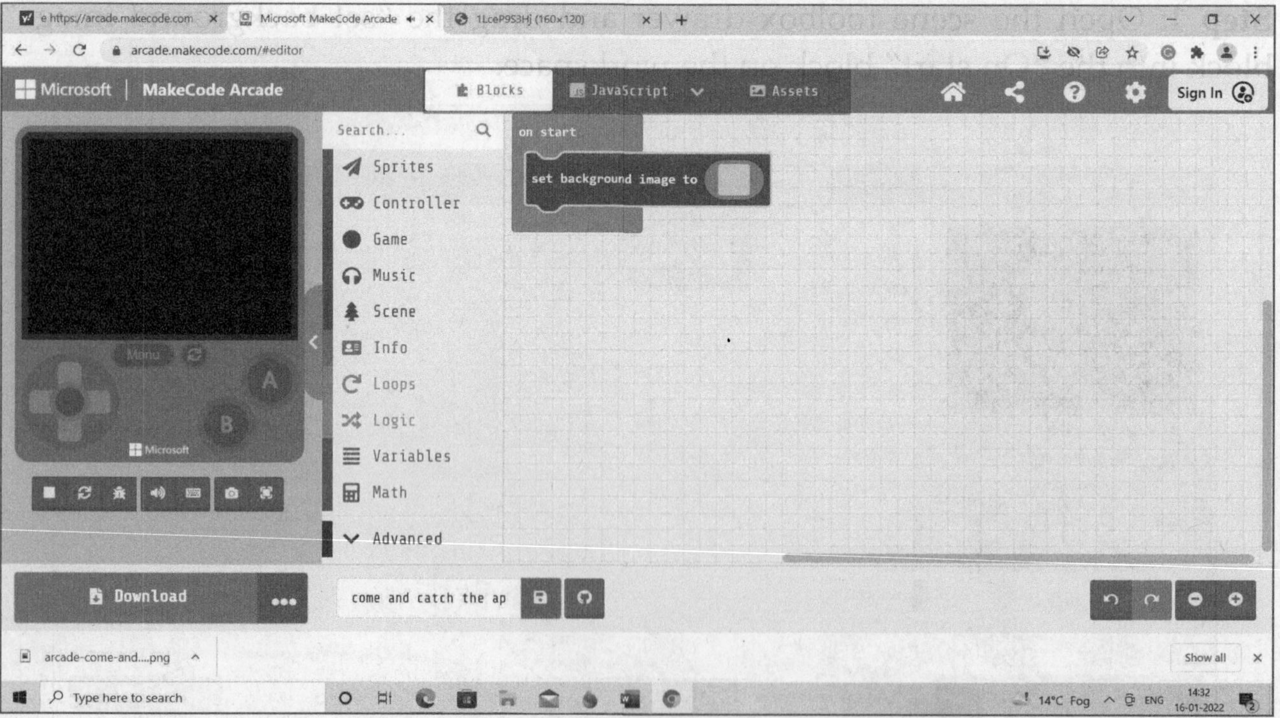

Figure 2.24

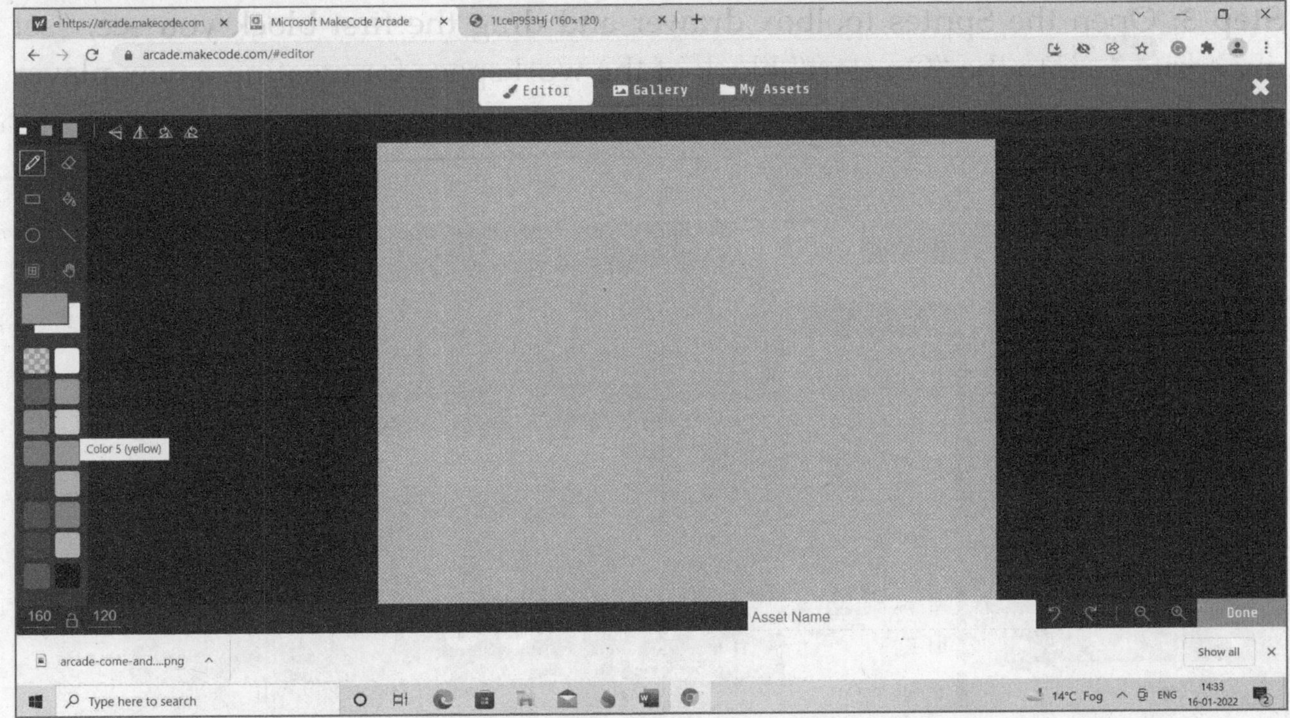

Figure 2.25

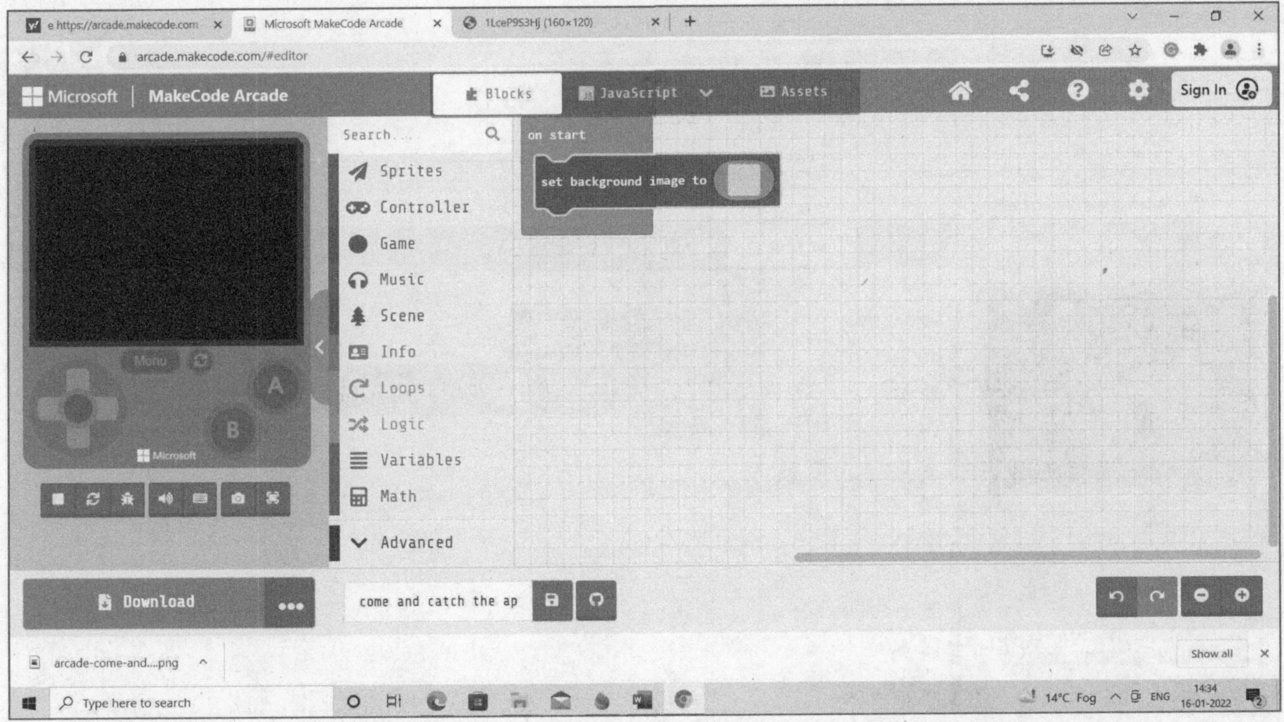

Figure 2.26

Step 3: Open the Sprites toolbox drawer and drag the first block you see, "set my sprite," into the "On start" block of the workspace for creating a new player character for the game.

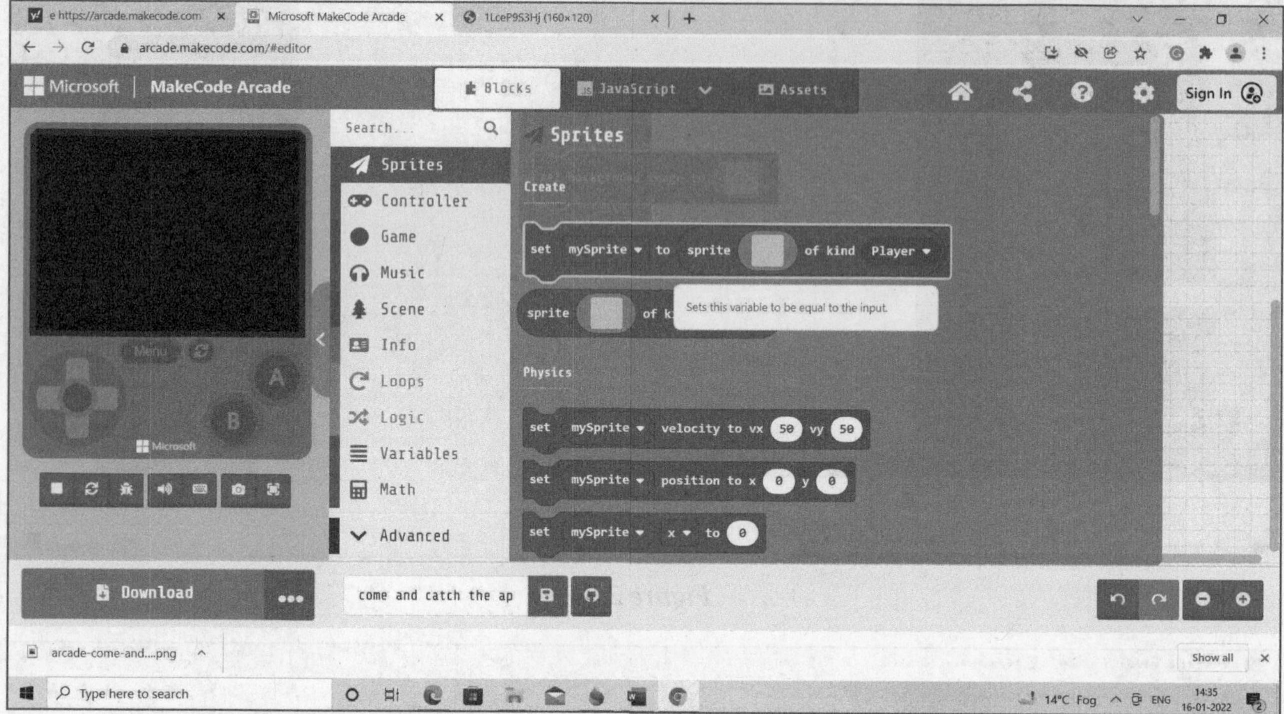

Figure 2.27

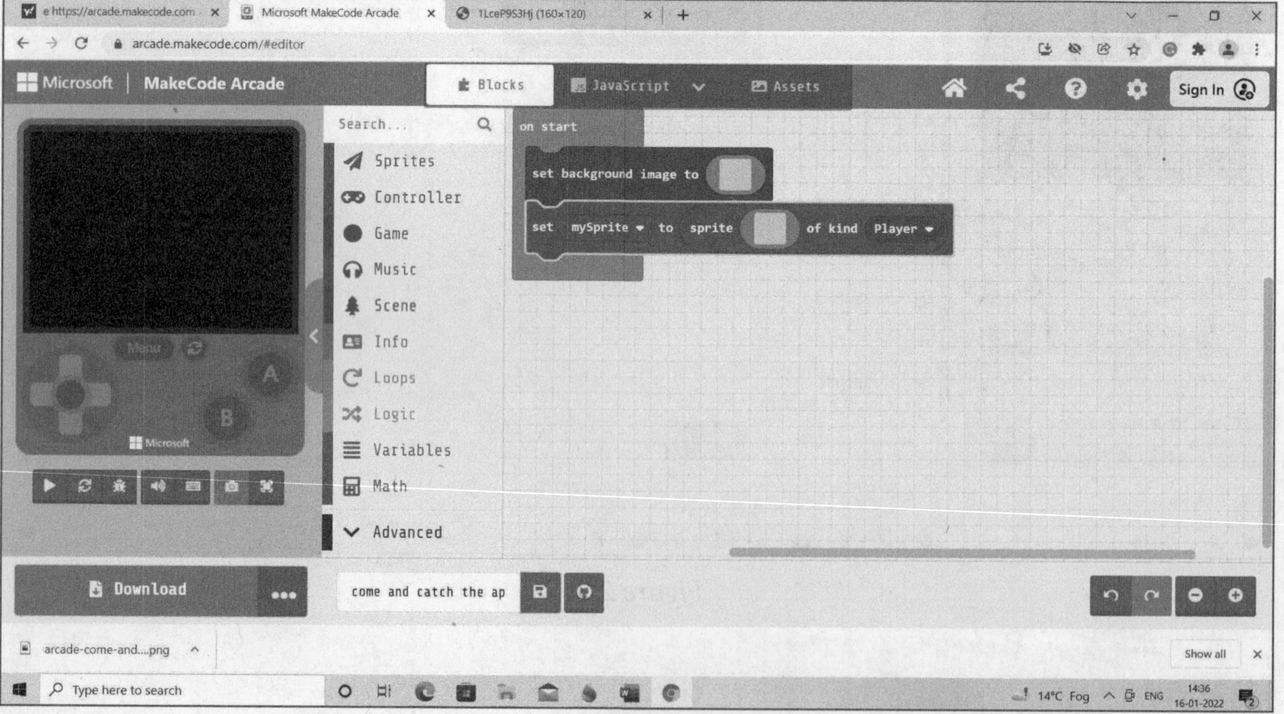

Figure 2.28

Step 4: In the "Player" block, click the gray square to open the image editor and select the gallery view. Find and select a character of your choice. (here we have selected '').

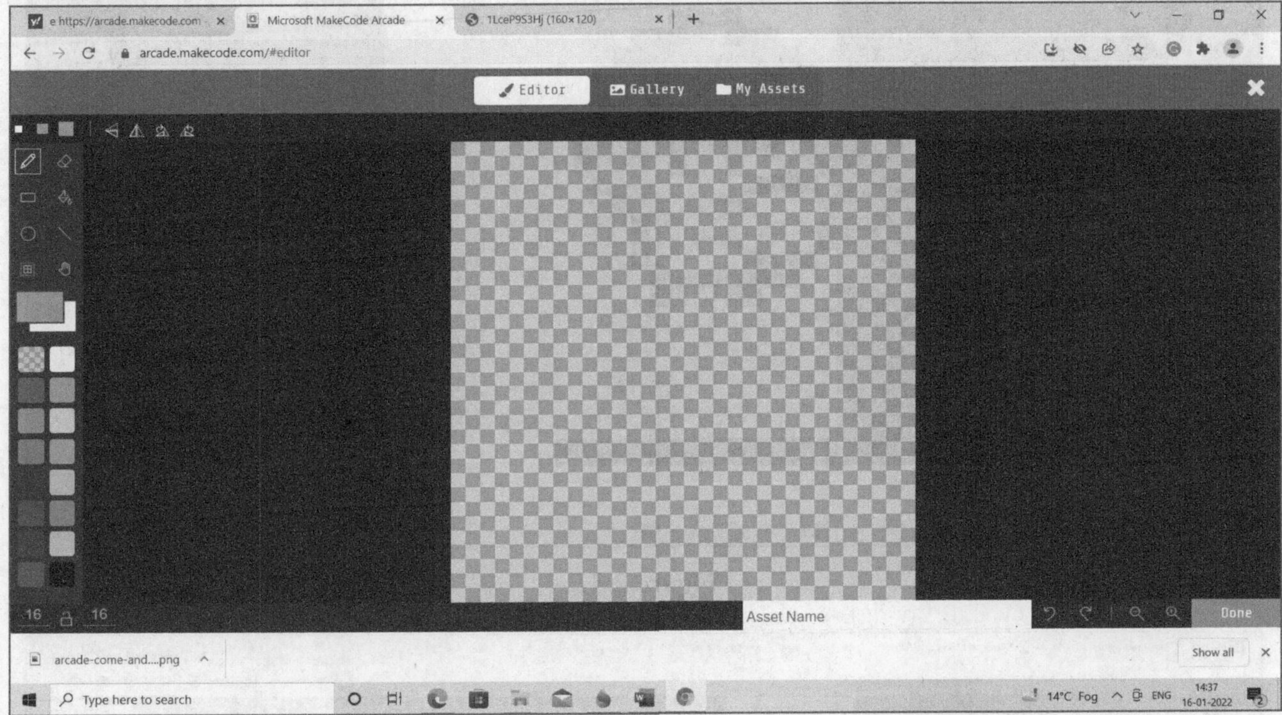

Figure 2.29

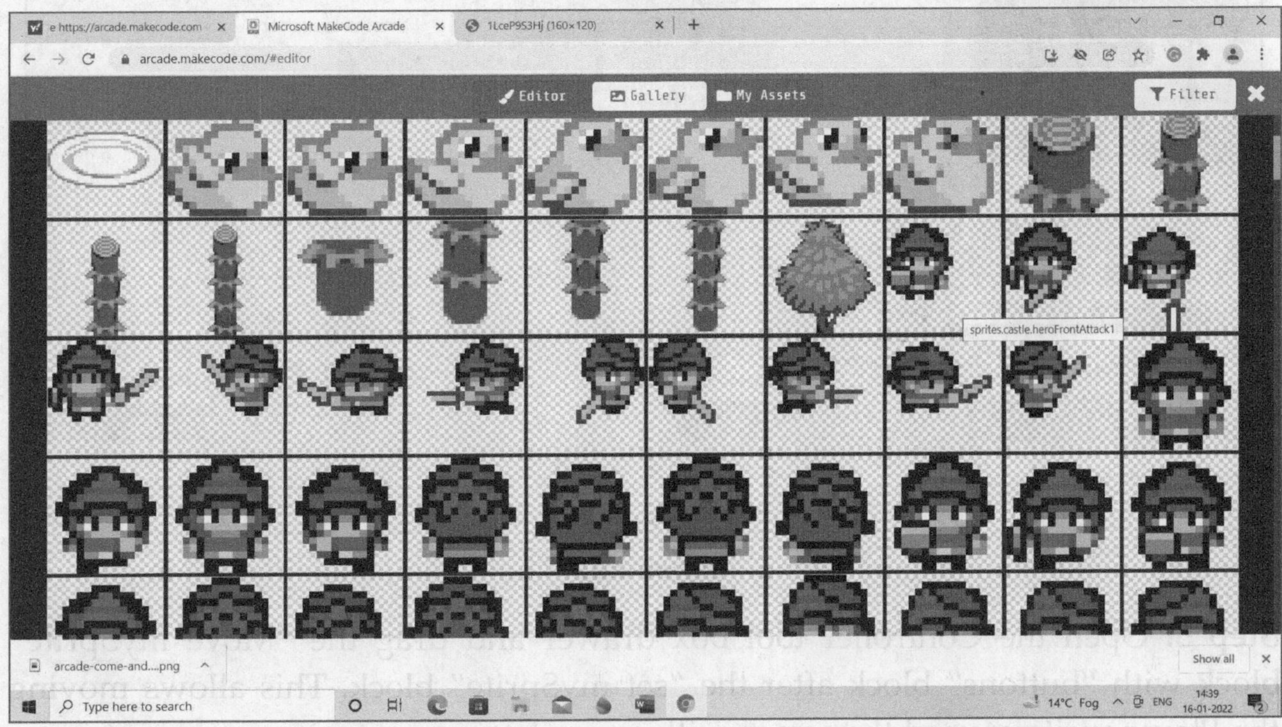

Figure 2.30

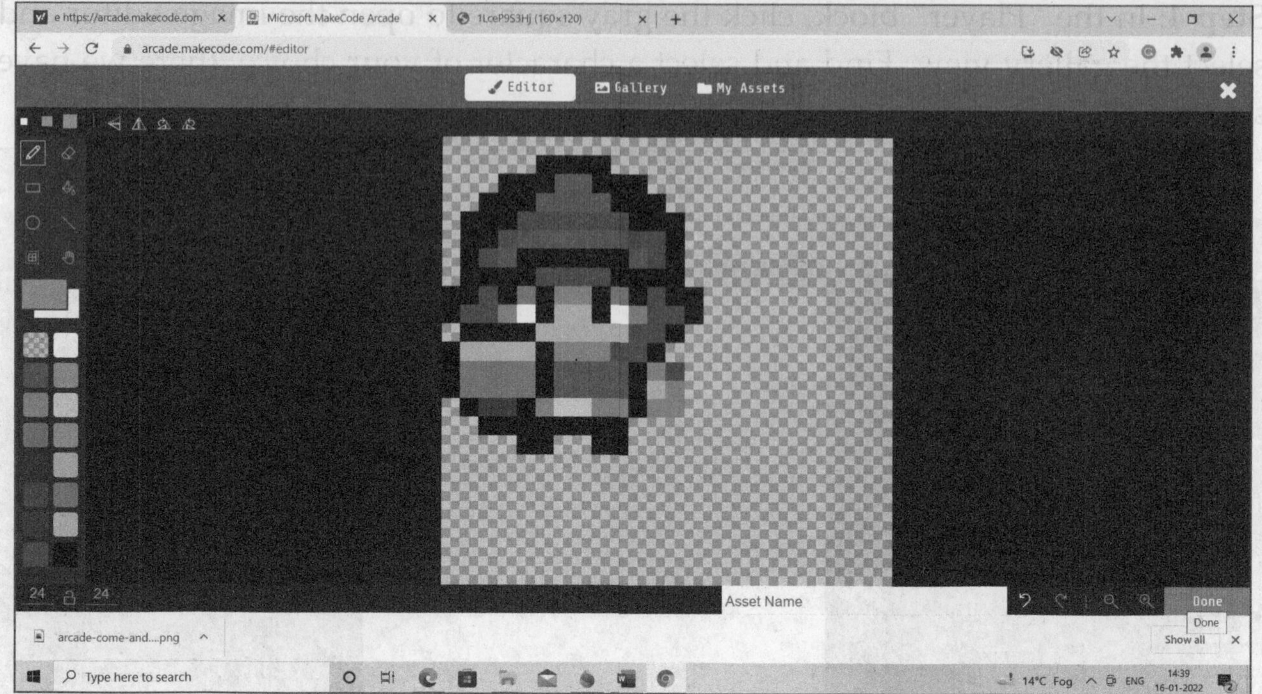

Figure 2.31

Figure 2.32

Step 5: Open the Controller tool box drawer and drag the "Move mySprite" block with "buttons" block after the "set mySprite" block. This allows moving the Player sprite around the screen with arrow keys.

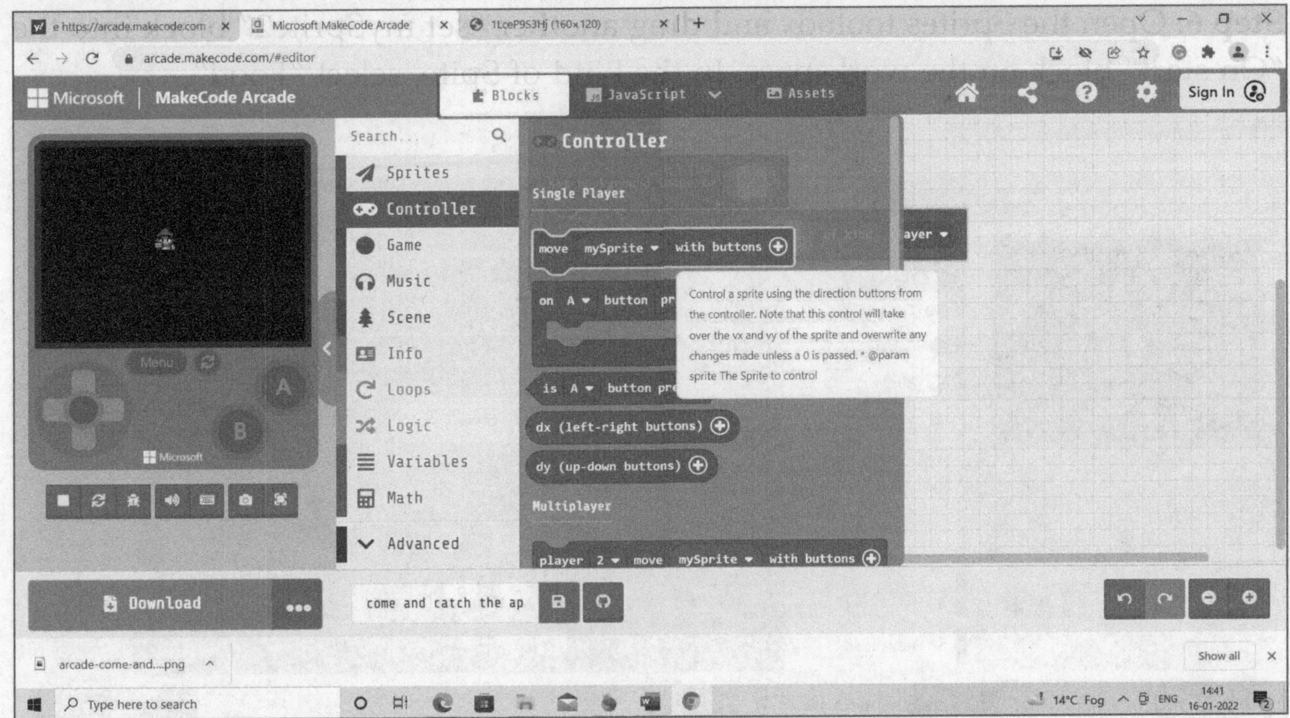

Figure 2.33

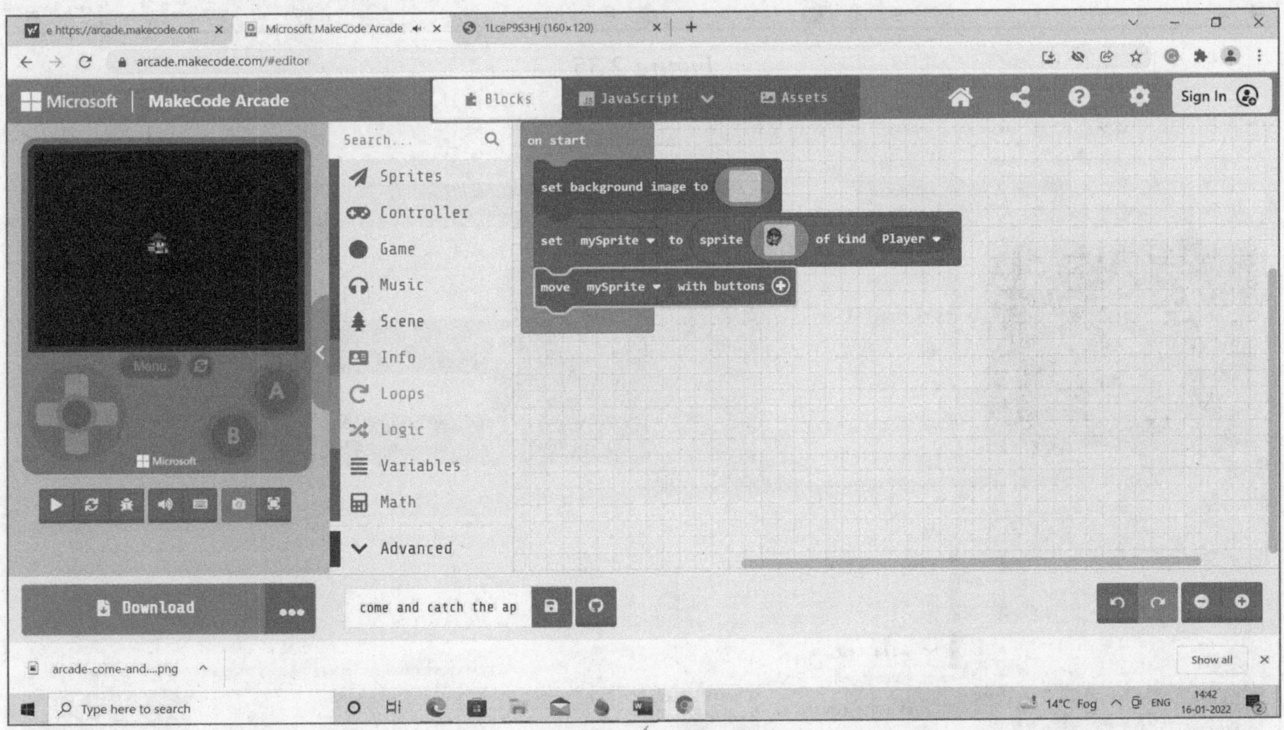

Figure 2.34

Step 6: Open the Sprites toolbox and drag another "set mySprite2" block into the "On start" block on the workspace. In the kind of Spite, select "Food".

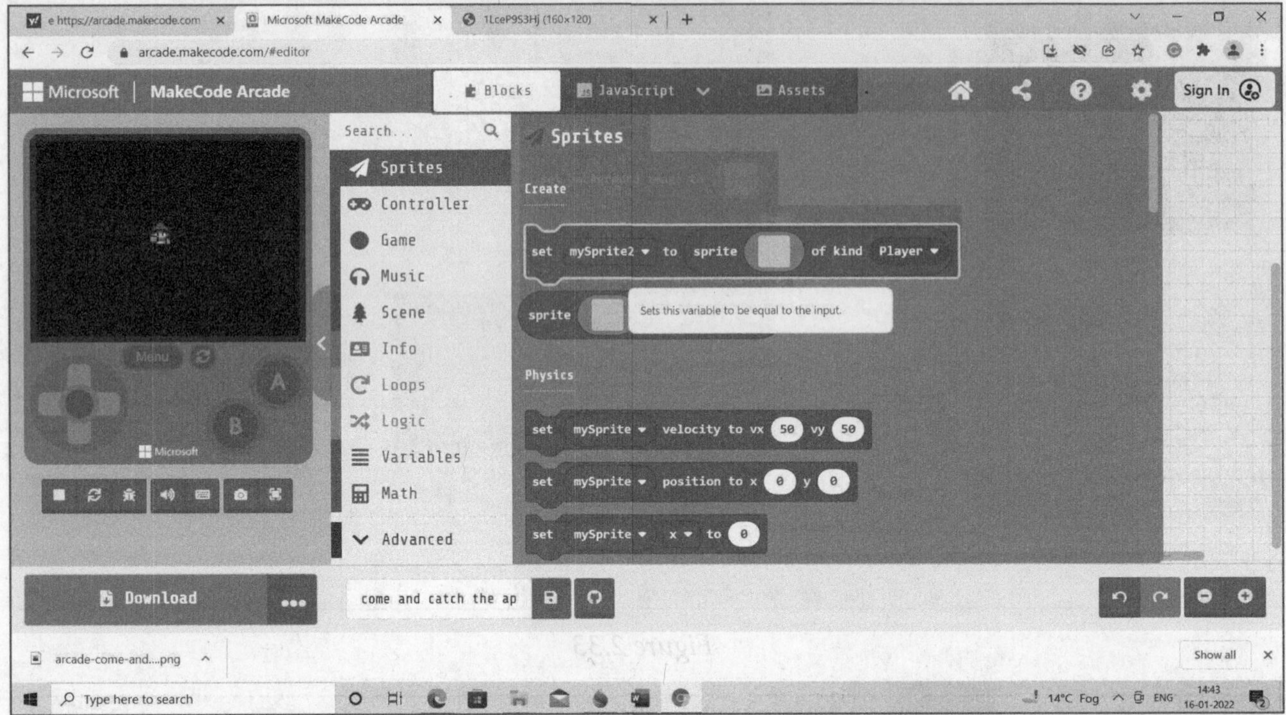

Figure 2.35

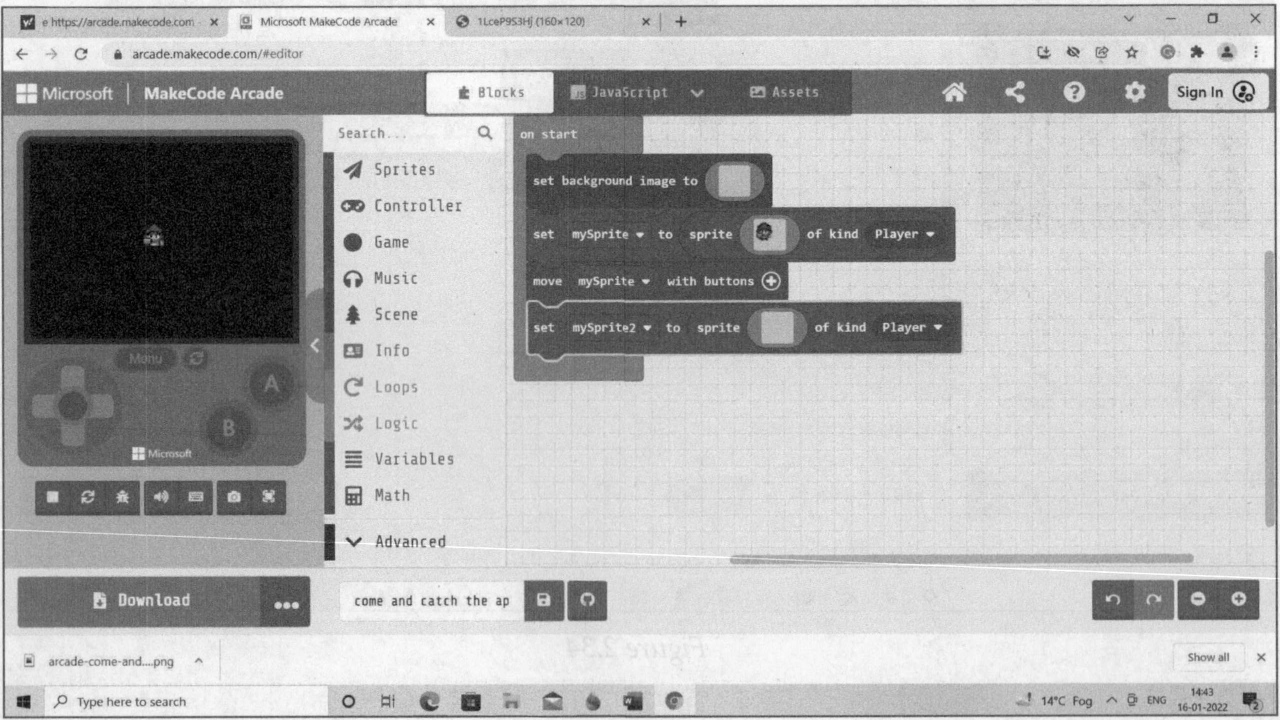

Figure 2.36

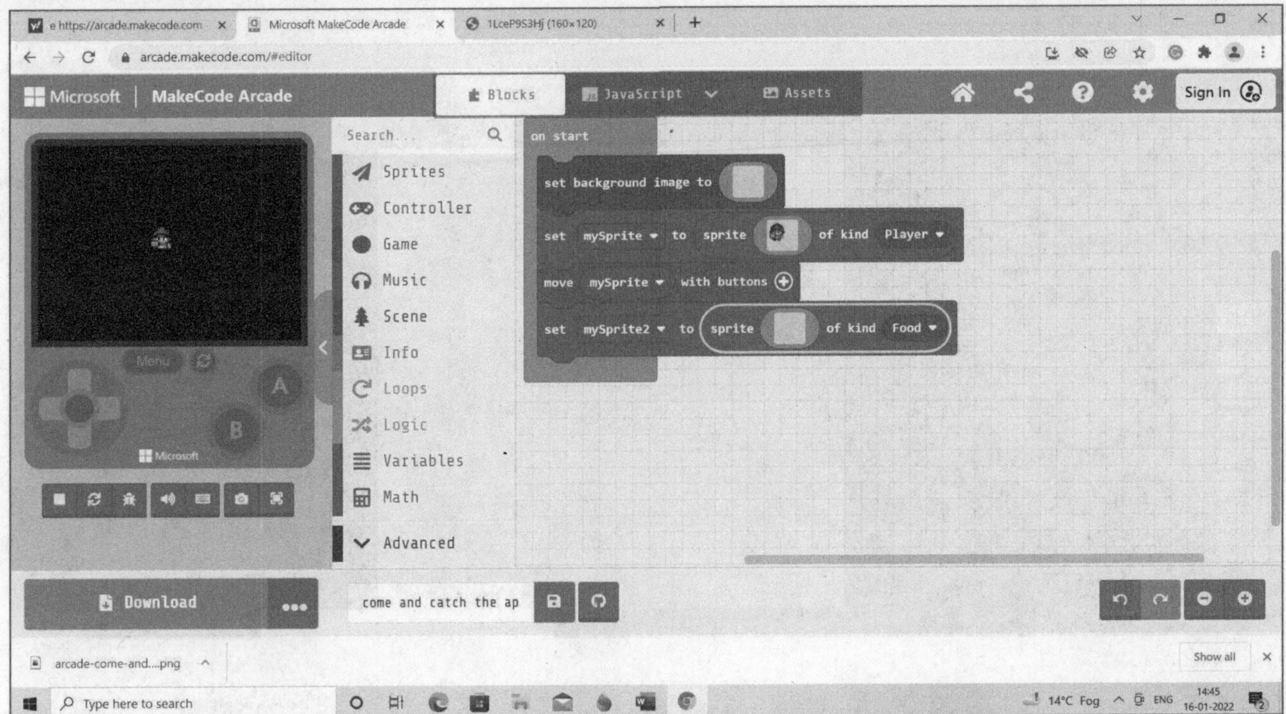

Figure 2.37

Step 7: In the "Food" block, click on the gray square to open the image editor and select the gallery view. Find and select the image of an apple.

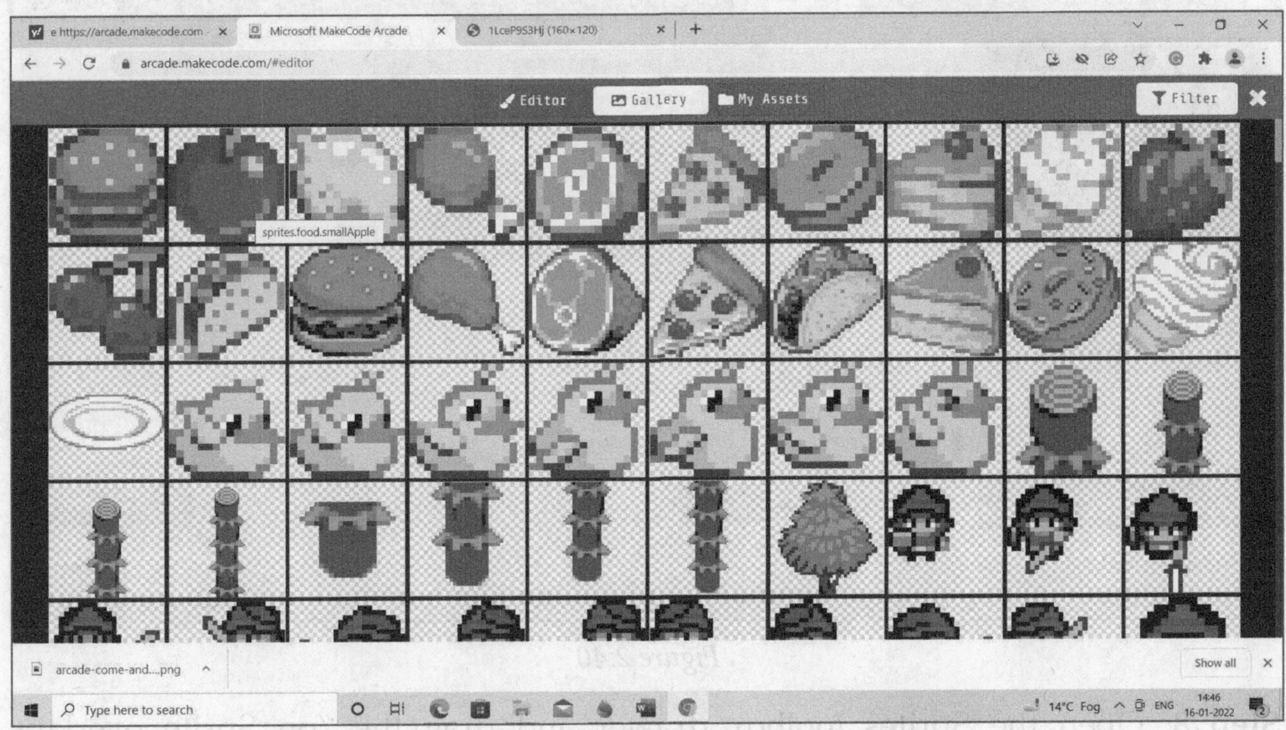

Figure 2.38

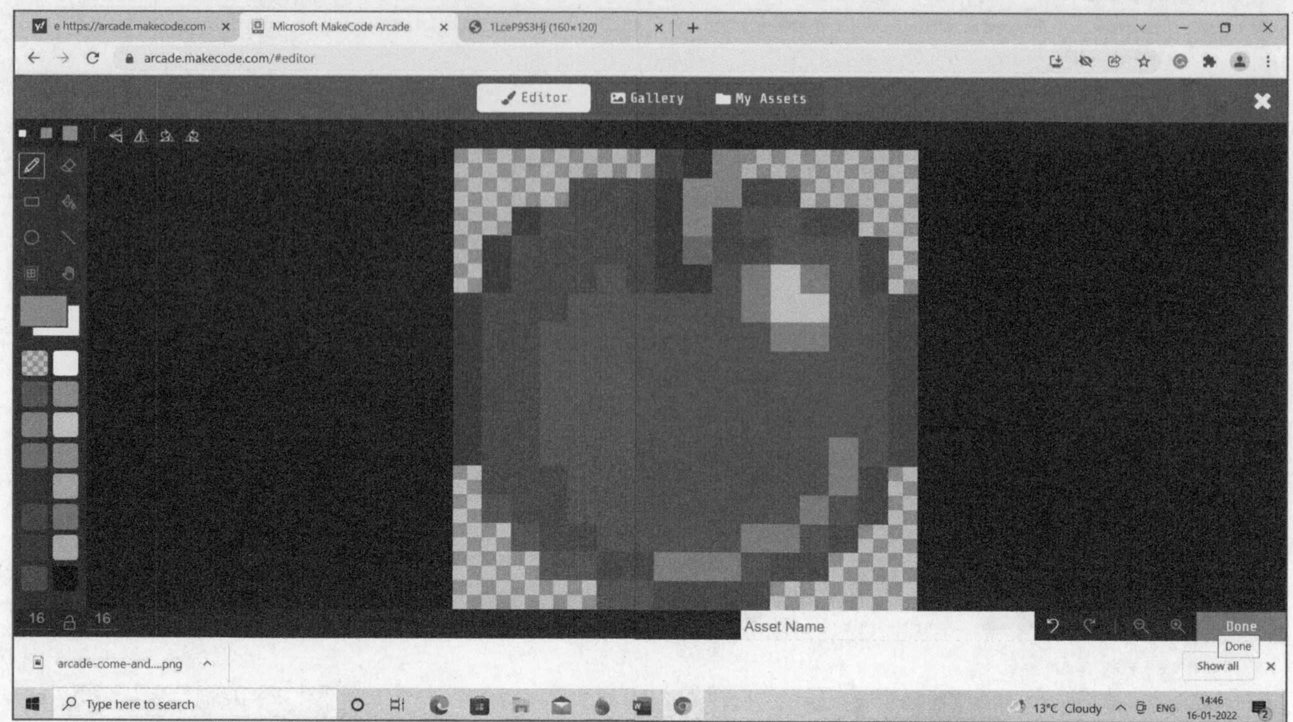

Figure 2.39

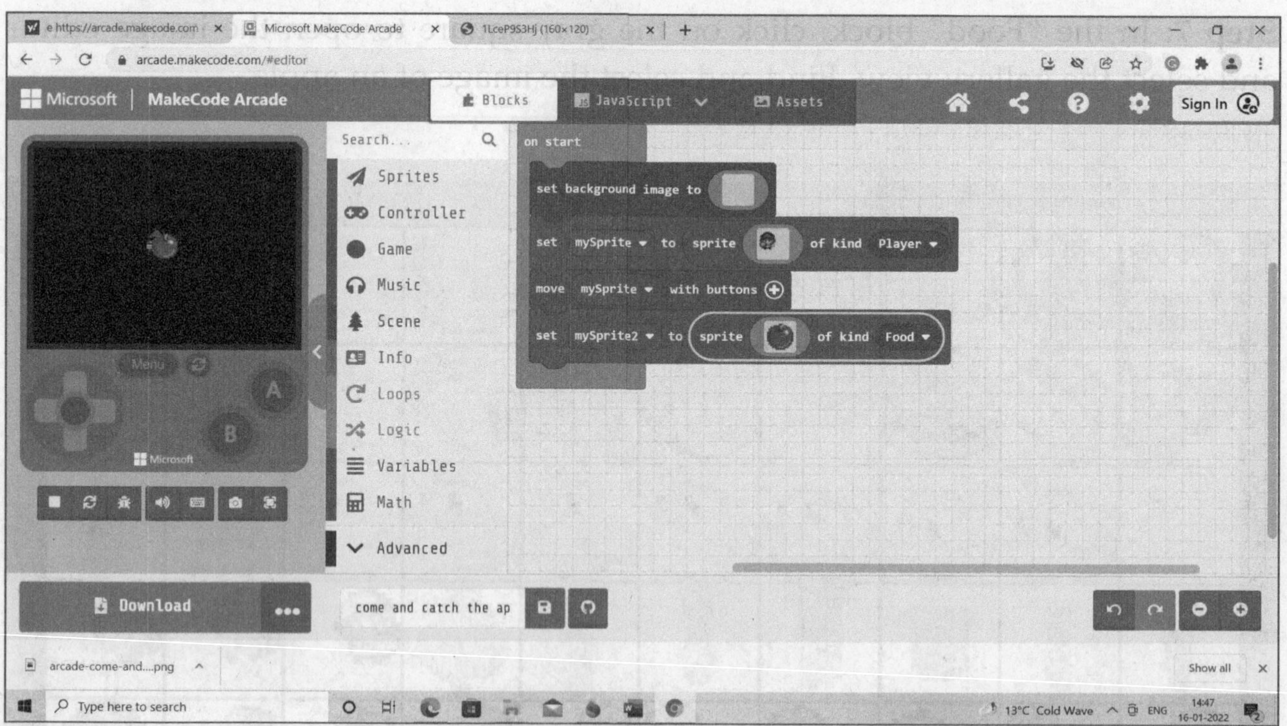

Figure 2.40

Step 8: Open the Sprites toolbox drawer and drag the "on Sprite overlaps otherSprite" block into the workspace to place anywhere.

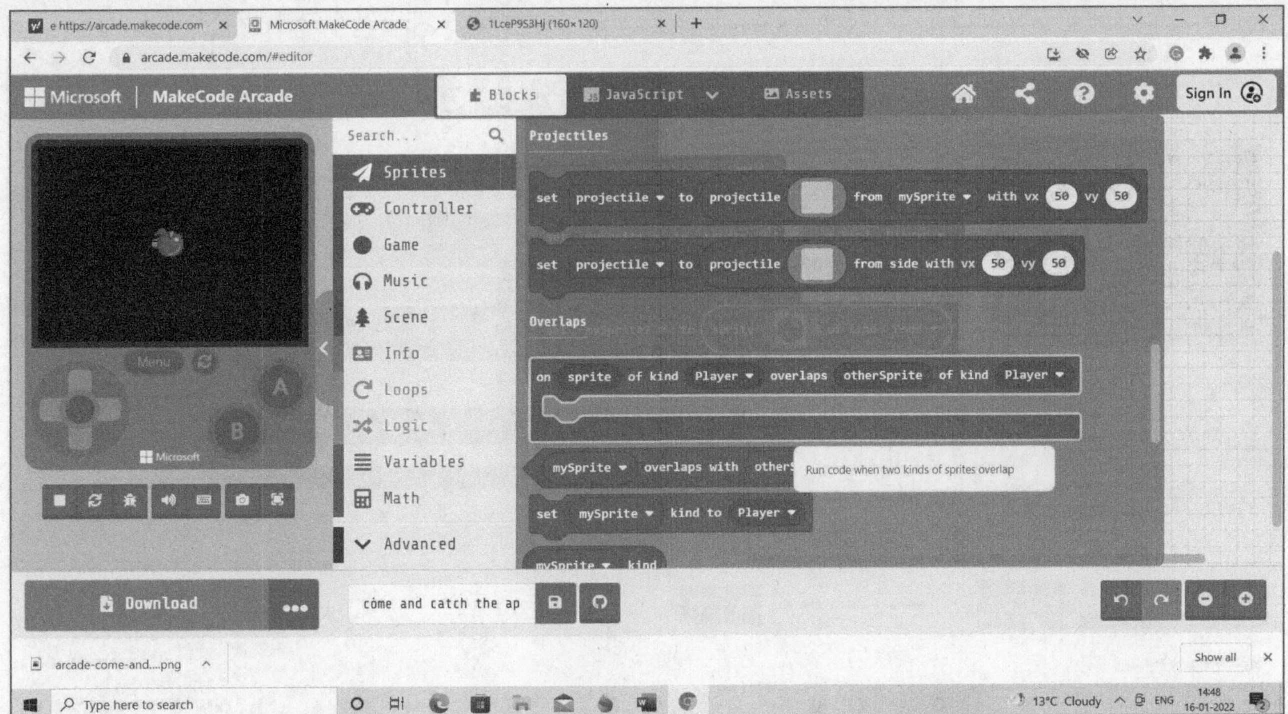

Figure 2.41

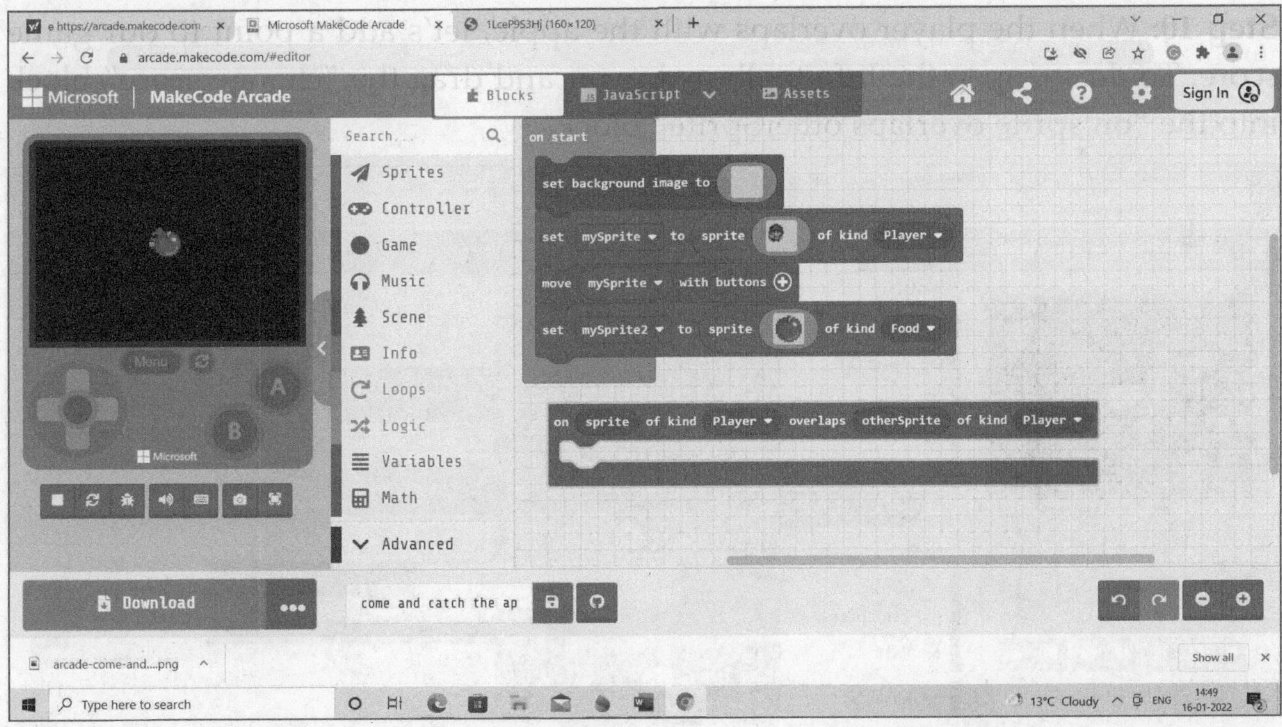

Figure 2.42

Step 9: In the "On sprite overlaps otherSprite" block, click on the second Player kind after otherSprite to open the menu. Select Food as the kind.

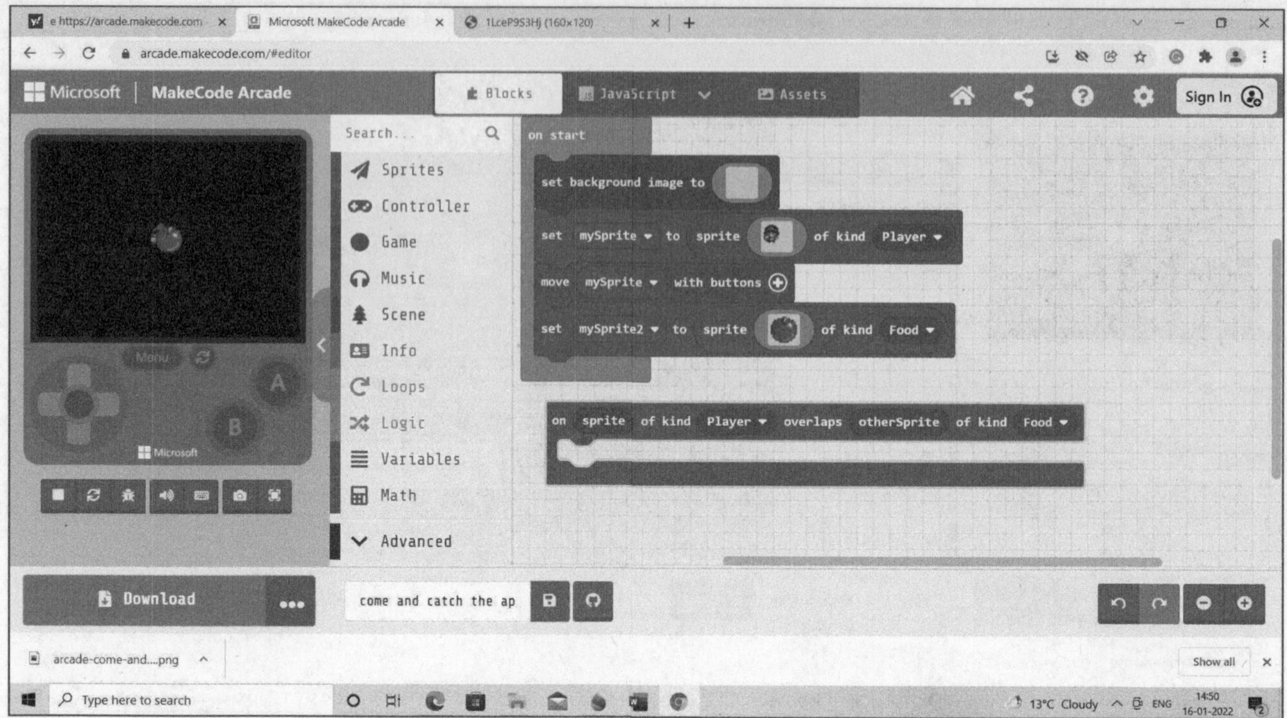

Figure 2.43

Step 10: When the player overlaps with the apple, let's add a point to our game score. To do so, open the Info toolbox drawer and drag the "change score" block into the "on sprite overlaps otherSprite" block.

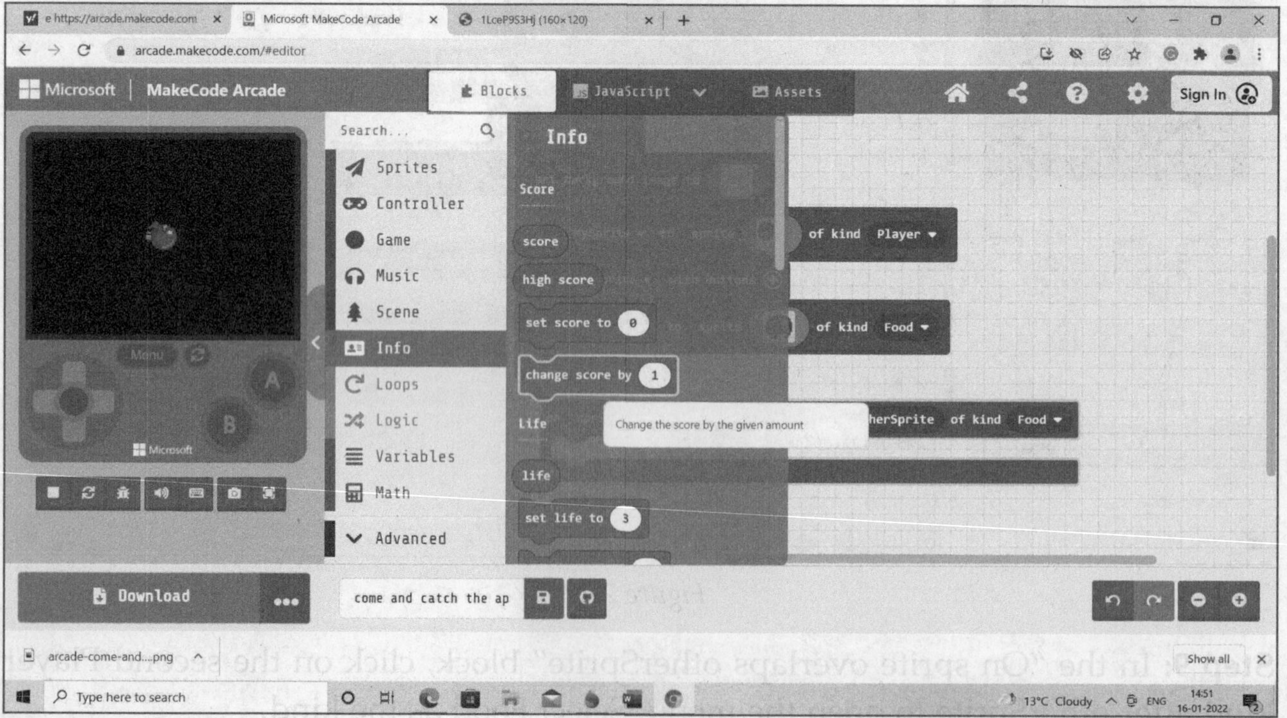

Figure 2.44

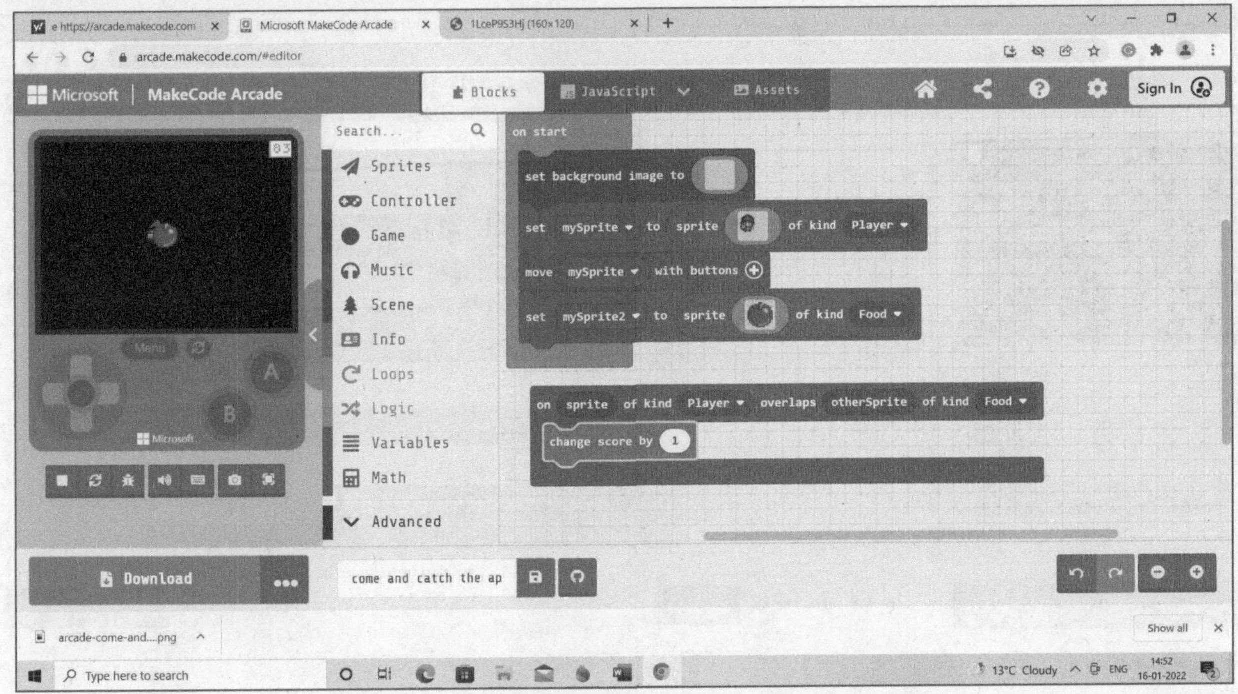

Figure 2.45

Step 11: Once the sprites overlap, let's set the position for the apple to random locations around the screen. To do so, open the "Sprites" toolbox drawer and drag the "set mySprite Position" block into the "On sprite overlaps otherSprite" block.

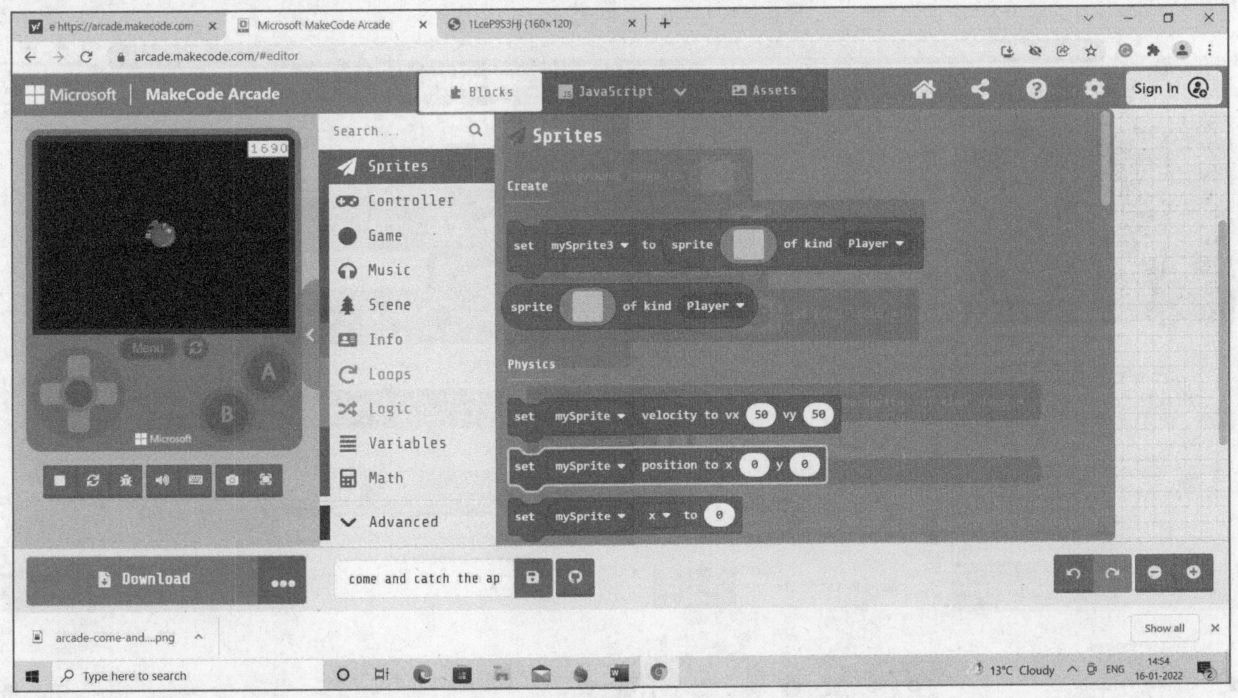

Figure 2.46

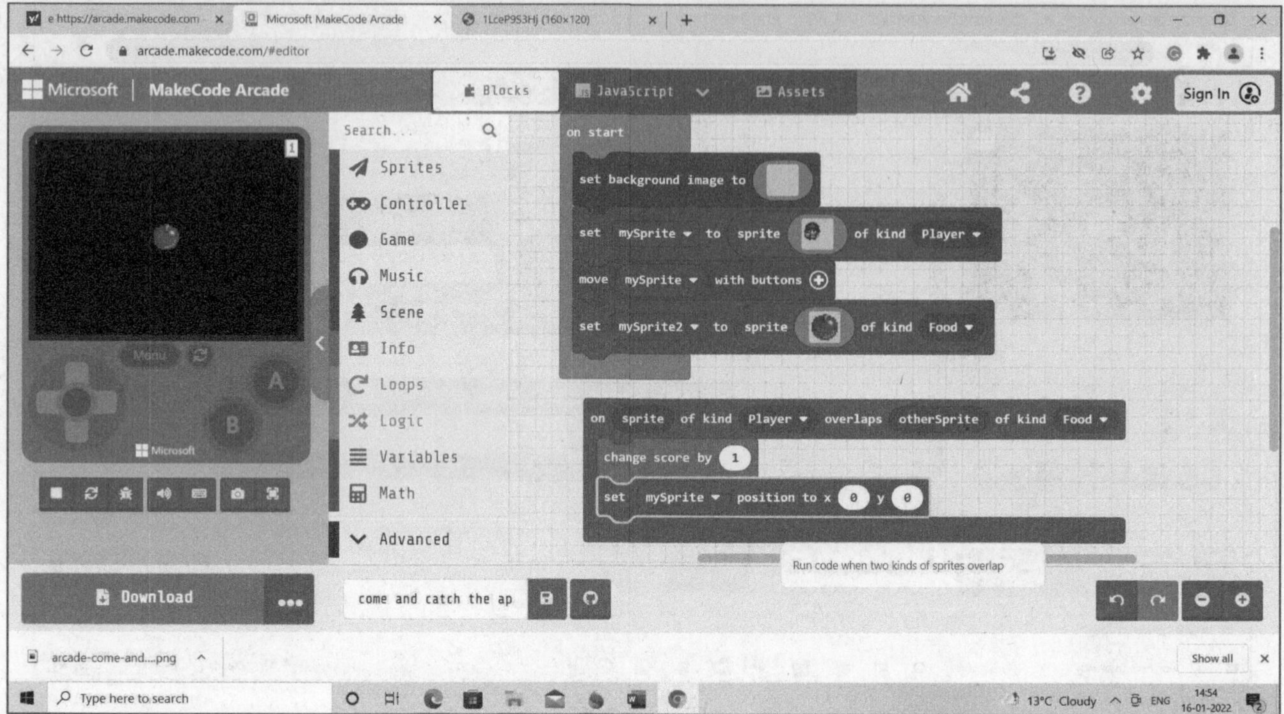

Figure 2.47

Step 12: In the "set mySprite position" block into the "on sprite overlaps otherSprite" block, click on mySprite variable to open the menu, and select the sprite "mySprite2".

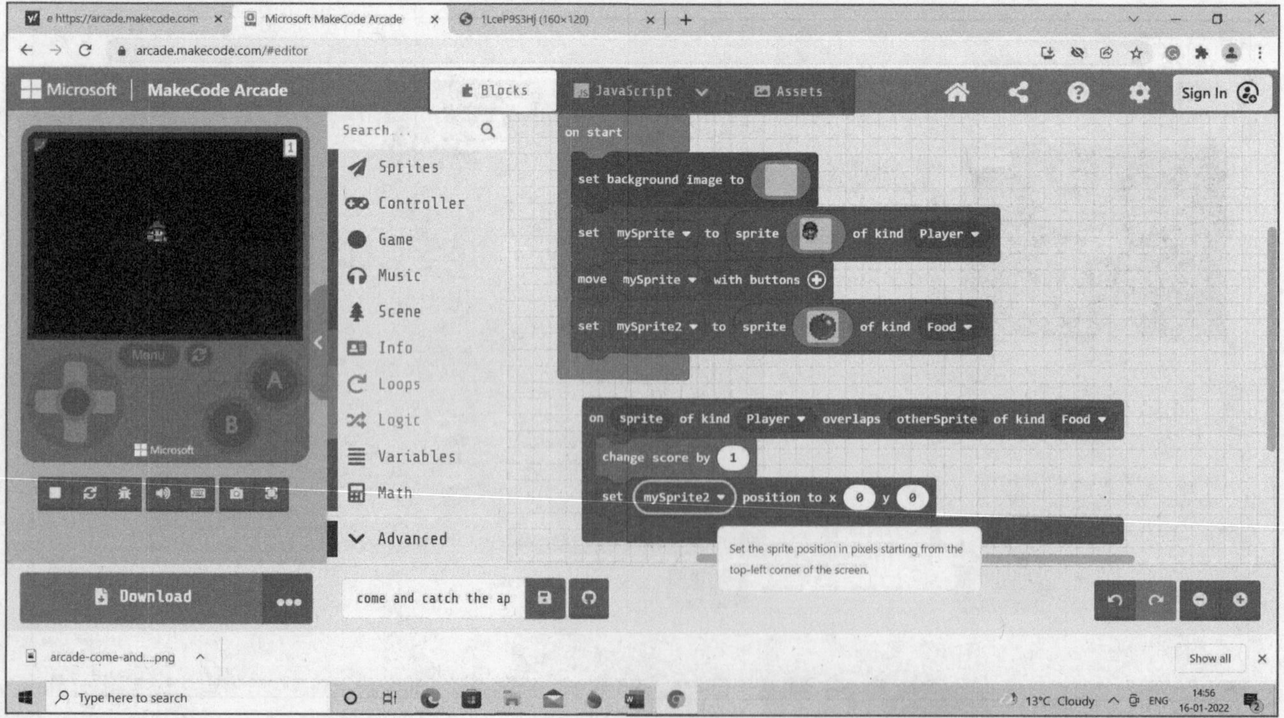

Figure 2.48

Step 13: Open the 'Math' toolbox drawer and drag two 'pick random blocks' onto the workspace. Drop one into the x coordinate of the "set mySprite2 position" block, and the other into the y coordinate, replacing the 0 values.

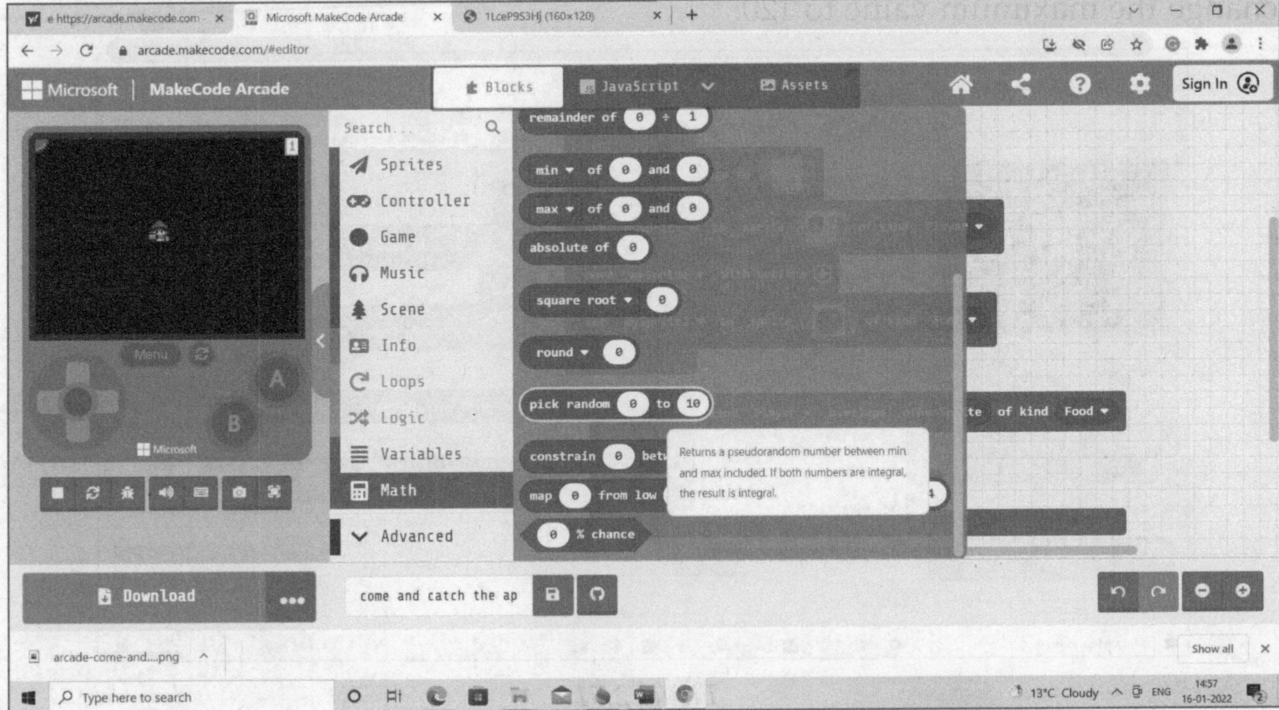

Figure 2.49

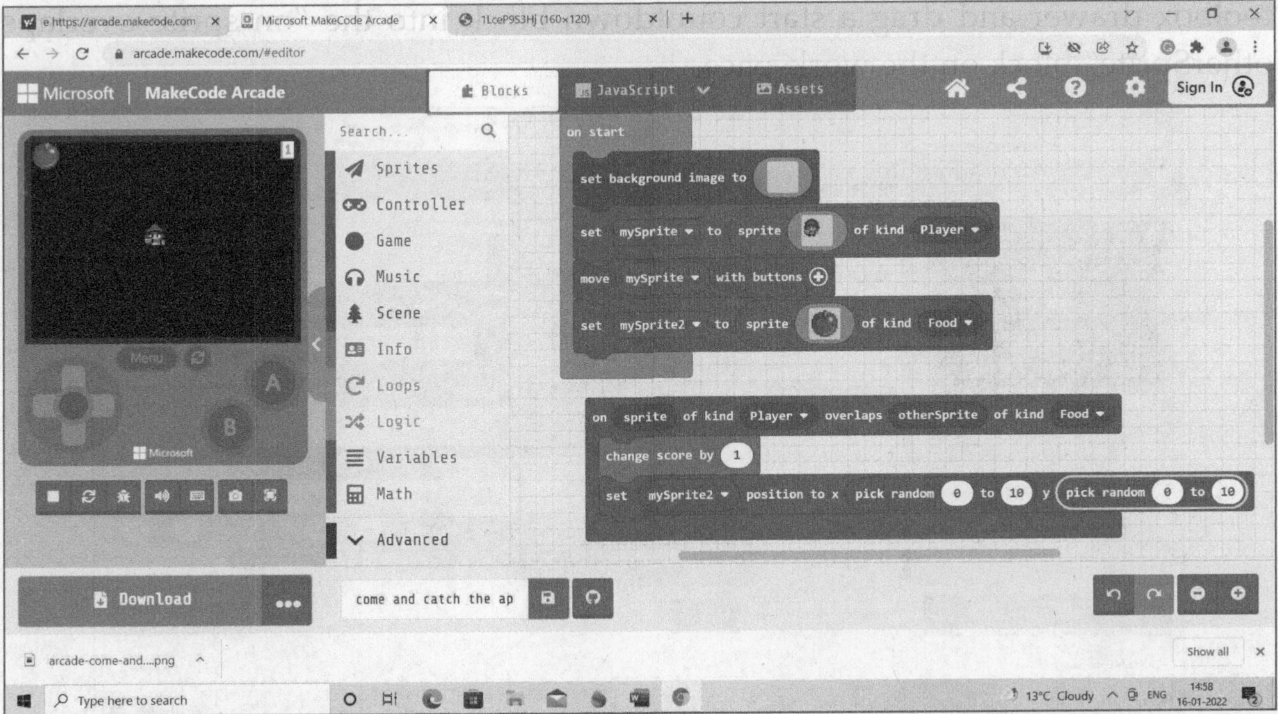

Figure 2.50

Step 14: the arcade game screen is 160 pixels wide and 120 pixels high. In the first pick random block in the x coordinate of the set mySprite2 position block, change the maximum value to 160. In the second pick random block in the y coordinate, change the maximum value to 120.

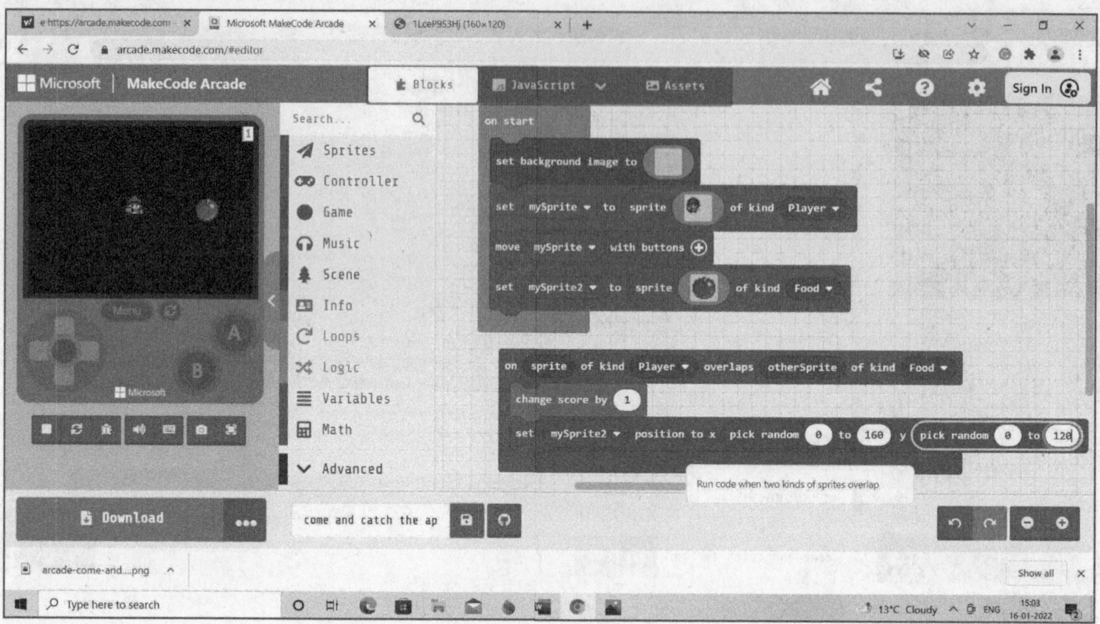

Figure 2.51

Step 15: In order to restart the countdown of the timer each time, open the "Info" toolbox drawer and drag a start countdown block into the "on sprite overlaps otherSprite" block on the workspace.

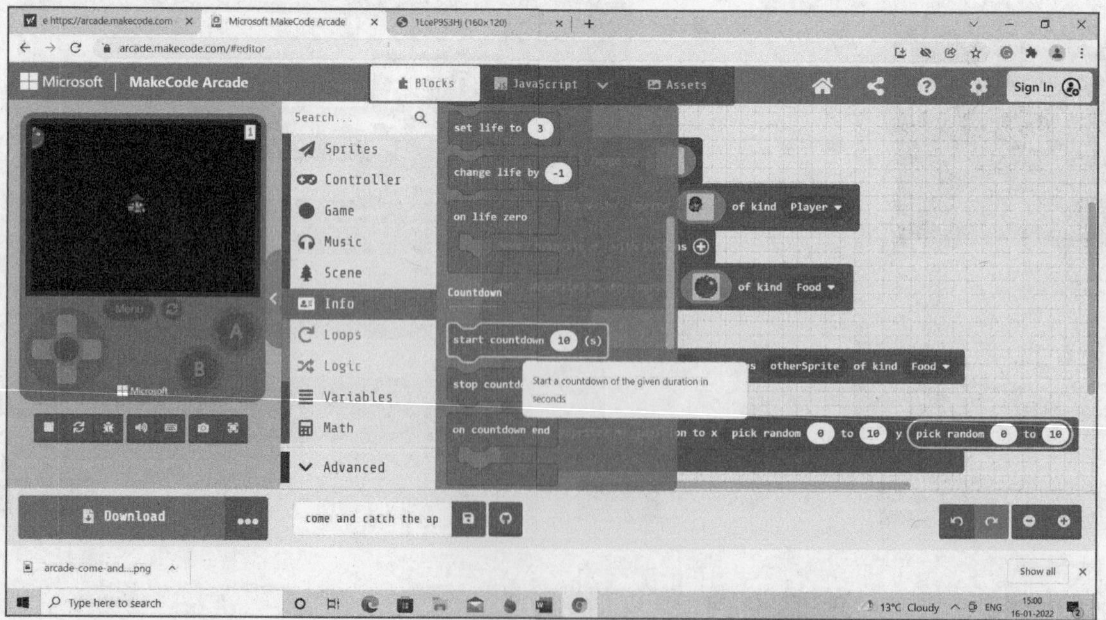

Figure 2.52

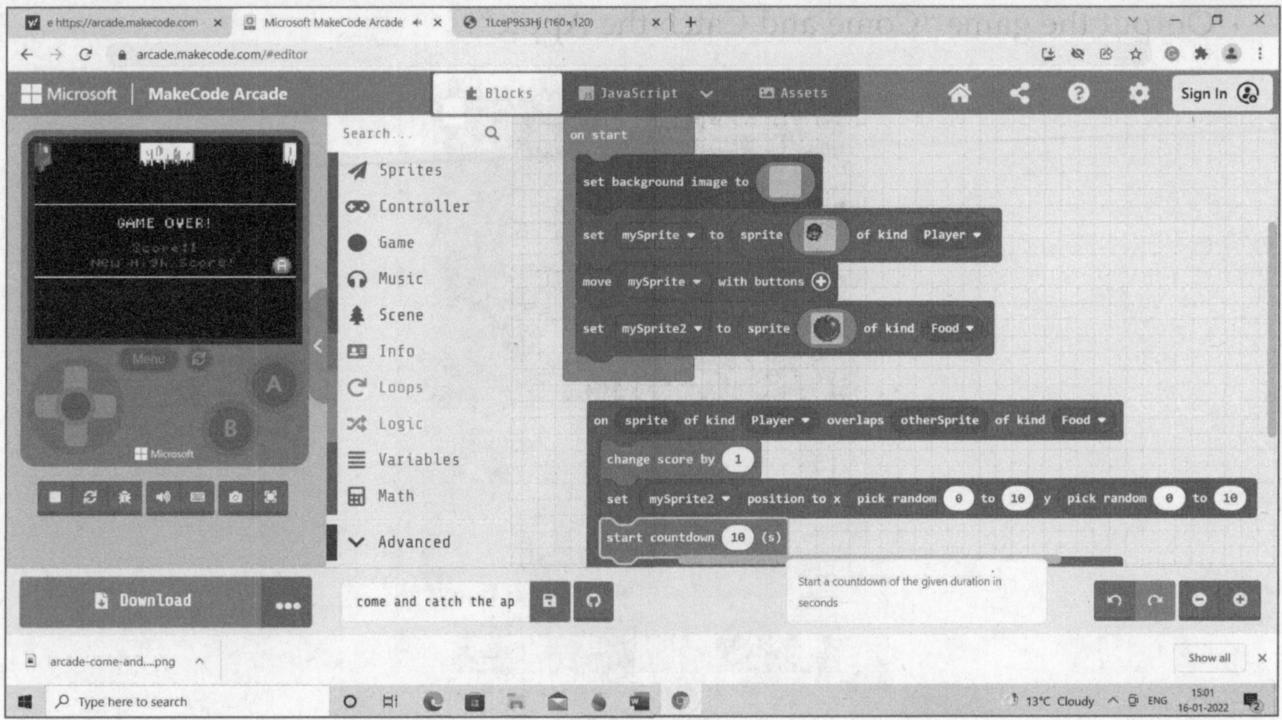

Figure 2.53

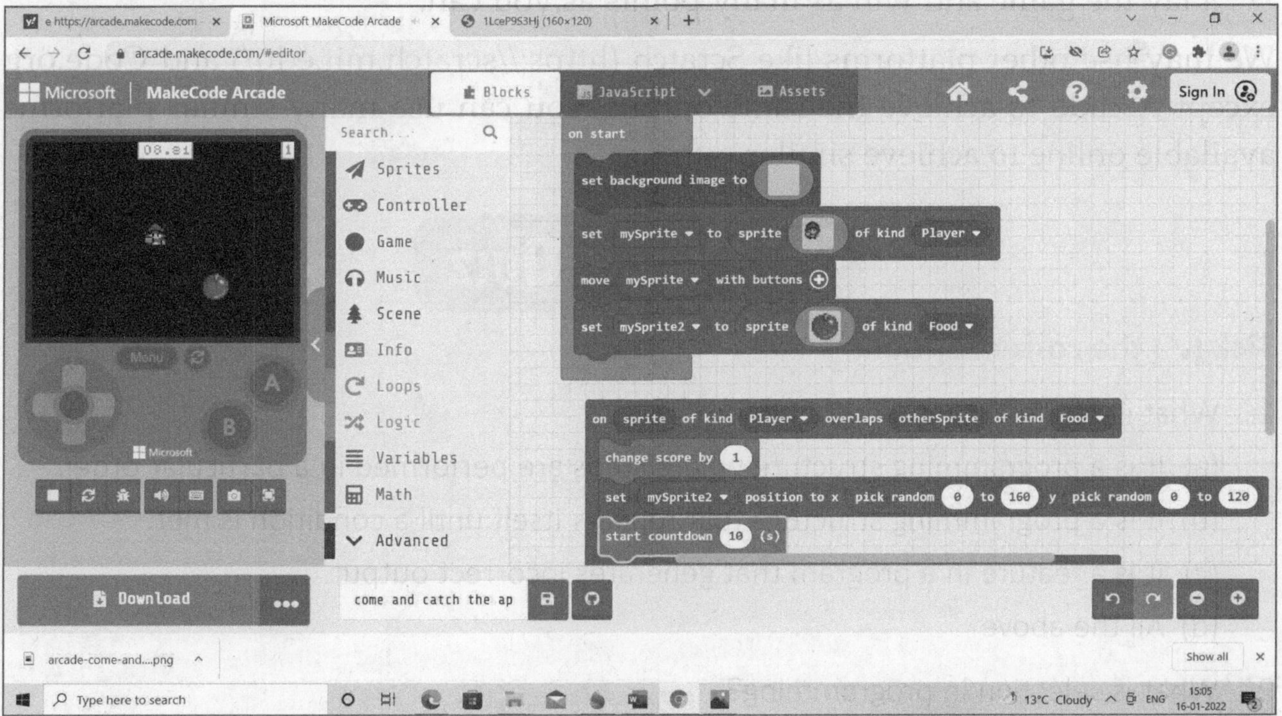

Figure 2.54

❖ Output the game "Come and Catch the Apple".

Figure 2.55

❖ Play the game and win as many points as you can.

We may use other platforms like Scratch (https://scratch.mit.edu/) and Code.org except Arcade to achieve the same output. You can use many similar platforms available online to achieve similar output

Tick (✓) the correct option.

1. What is sequencing in programming?
   (a) It is a programming structure where steps are performed in a particular order.
   (b) It is a programming structure that repeats itself until a condition is met.
   (c) It is a feature in a program that generates incorrect output.
   (d) All the above

2. What is selection in programming?
   (a) A list of instructions that are followed in a set order
   (b) A list of instructions where a choice based on a condition is available
   (c) A list of instructions that will loop based on a condition
   (d) A list of instructions that will loop forever

3. What is looping in programming?

(a) It is a programming structure where steps are performed in an order.

(b) It is a programming structure that repeats itself until a condition is met.

(c) It is a feature in a program that generates incorrect output.

(d) All the above

4. A bug in programming is:

(a) A feature in a code/program that causes it to run correctly

(b) A feature in a code/program that can predict the output

(c) A feature in a code/program that generates incorrect output

(d) None of the above

5. What is an iteration in programming?

(a) It is a list of instructions which are followed in a set order.

(b) It is a list of instructions where there is a choice based on a condition.

(c) It is a list of instructions which will loop based on a condition.

(d) It is a list of instructions that will loop forever.

ANSWERS
1. (a) 2. (c) 3. (b) 4. (c) 5. (b)

SUMMARY

- A loop is an algorithm that executes a block of code multiple times till the time a specified condition is met.
- A sequence may contain any number of instructions, but all instructions must be run in the order they are presented.
- A sequence is a list of activities that are done one after another.
- A loop iterates a block of code multiple times till the time mentioned condition is satisfied. A loop statement allows users to execute a statement or group of statements multiple times.
- 'For' loops will repeat a block of program/code a set number of times as directed.
- 'While' Loops are also called 'conditional' loops. 'While' loops are those loops that will continue to go until a condition is no longer true.
- Each time the condition is true, and the block of code executes once; it is counted to be one iteration.

- Entry criteria is defined as a condition that must be met before starting a specific task.
- Exit criterion is a set of conditions that must exist before you can declare a program to be completed.
- In computing, iteration is the technique marking out of a block of statements within a computer program for a defined number of repetitions.
- In programming, repetition of a line/ a block of code is called iteration.
- Loop is regarded as one of the basic logical structures of computer programming.
- Loops provide the facility to execute a block of code repetitively, based on a condition and till the time a specified condition remains true.
- Most loops have a variable which in programming terms is called counter variable.
- Sequencing refers to the specific order in which we need to perform the activities to get the desired output.
- The 'While' loop can execute a set of commands till the condition is true.
- Counter variable keeps the record of how many times the Loop is executed.
- The Loop will exit when the condition becomes false.
- The need for defining the Loop in a computer program is due to various reasons that are based on the tasks to be performed.
- The reason these loops are called 'for' loops is that we can tell our app how many times we want it to repeat to the code.
- To run a block of code in a loop, one needs to set a condition and set its number of iterations.
- We might tell the computer either to stop after it has repeated the Loop a certain number of times or to stop once a certain condition is met.
- When creating algorithms or programs, then the instructions are presented in a particular correct order.
- When a loop is present inside another loop, then it is called a nested loop.
- While programming, the coder states the condition that should result false at a certain point in time to avoid its entry in an infinite loop.

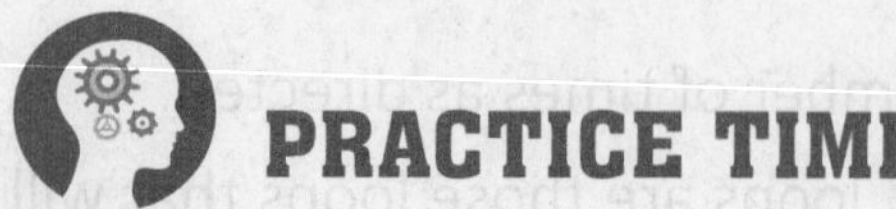

PRACTICE TIME

(A) Fill in the blanks

1. A ____________ is defined as a shape produced by a curve that bends round and crosses itself. Grammatically, Loop means encircling.
2. Execution of loops is based on ____________.

3. The ______________ () function returns a sequence of numbers, starting from 0 by default, and increments by 1 (by default), and ends at a specified number.
4. In programming, repetition of a line/a block of program/code is known as ______________.
5. The Loop will exit when the condition becomes ______________.
6. Each time the condition is true and the block of code executes ______________, it is counted to be one iteration.
7. The ______________ variable keeps track of how many times the Loop executed.
8. ______________ criterion is defined as a condition that must be met before starting a specific task.
9. ______________ criterion is a set of conditions that must exist before we can start a task.
10. When a loop is present inside another loop, it is called a ______________ loop.

ANSWERS				
1. loop	2. iterations.	3. range	4. iteration	5. false
6. once	7. counter	8. Entry	9. Exit	10. nested

(B) True/ False type

1. A loop is defined as a structure, series, or process, the end of which is connected to the beginning.
2. Most loops do not have a counter variable.
3. A loop statement allows users to execute a statement or group of statements multiple times.
4. 'For' Loops are also called 'conditional' loops.
5. The 'While' loop can execute a set of commands till the condition is true.
6. 'Nested' loops will repeat a block of code a set number of times as directed.
7. A loop iterates a block of code multiple times till the time mentioned condition is satisfied.
8. Loops provide the facility to execute a block of code repetitively, based on a condition and till the time a specified condition remains true.
9. An iterator is an object which allows a programmer to traverse through all the elements of a collection, regardless of its specific implementation.
10. Exit criteria are defined as a condition that must be met before completing a specific task.

ANSWERS						
1. (T)	2. (F)	3. (T)	4. (F, while)	5. (T)	6. (F, For loops)	7. (T)
8. (T)	9. (T)	10. (T)				

(C) Very Short Answers Questions

1. Define loops.
2. What do you mean by nested loops in programming?
3. What is an exit criterion?
4. What do you mean by iteration?
5. What is sequencing in programming?

(D) Short Answer Questions

1. Explain 'loop' with the help of an example.
2. Have you encountered a bug in any program/application in real life? If yes, explain in your own words.
3. Whether sequencing, selection, and iteration can be used together or not? Support your answer with a proper explanation.
4. Give three examples where you can apply Loop and conditionals to simplify sequencing.

(E) High Order Thinking Skill Questions (HOTS)

1. Why is while loops called so?
2. Write an algorithm to print cube of numbers from 1 to 5.
3. Draw a flowchart to explain the iterative process that a student followed while distributing birthday sweets in the class.

Fun with Functions

Structure

In this chapter, you will learn:

- The usefulness of using functions in code
- How to define and call a function
- Different Parameters in a function
- Different types of values returned by a function

INTRODUCTION

In our life, we perform many tasks in a particular sequence to get the desired result. In computer programming too, various tasks are undertaken by the computer in a sequence. Functions are groups of code that always run together. They are similar to modules that we stack together to build programs. Programmers/developers create functions to simplify tasks that occur often. A function usually requires data as an input. This data is called an argument. Functions can have many arguments. When we call a function, we actually supply its arguments.

In this chapter, we will learn about functions, parameters in a function, and different types of values returned by a function.

Figure 3.1

Learning Objectives:

At the end of this chapter, you will be able to:

- have an understanding of using functions in code.
- know how to define a function and pass parameters in a function.
- know how different types of values are returned by a function.

3.1 WHAT ARE FUNCTIONS?

What type of picture do we make in our mind on hearing the word pattern? A pattern is formed when something or a series of things are repeated in a particular sequence. We may come across many patterns in day-to-day life like in making rangoli, colour arts, music, or sometimes in mathematics.

Likewise, there may be patterns in code too. As a programmer/coder, there will be times when we want the computer to repeat certain lines of code in sequence. A function is a block of code that is made up of a set of steps for giving results in a single specific action. Then, the programmer will give this action a simple name that increases the chances that the set of steps can easily talk about and reused again and again in the program.

Thus, a function is a group of instructions (sometimes known as a named procedure) that is used by coding/programming languages to return a single result and/ a set of results.

Functions are also defined as "self-contained" modules of code that attain specific task. Functions usually take in data as input, process it, and "return" a result. A written function can be used many times.

Function Parameters are the names that are defined in the function definition, and real values passed to the Function in the function definition are known as arguments.

3.1.1 Function flow

The function "flow of control" is as follows:

- The program comes to a line of code containing a 'function call.'
- The program enters the Function . It means that it starts at the first line in the function code.
- All instructions inside of the Function are executed from top to bottom.

- The program leaves the Function and goes back to where it started from.
- Any data processed/computed and RETURNED by the Function is used in place of the Function in the original line of code.

A function usually requires data as an input, and this data is called an argument. Functions may have many arguments. When we call a function, we actually supply its arguments.

Example: Assume that Sukriti is traveling on a road trip, and someone calls her and asks, "What time will you get there?". To answer that question, Sukriti needs to have some information like the destination, where she is now, what time it is now, and how fast she is traveling. These four pieces of information are like the arguments to a function. Once she has them, she can do some calculations and return the output: her estimated time of arrival.

Factz Funda

A data value is redundant if we can delete it without information being lost. Simply, redundancy is unnecessary duplication.

3.1.2 Purposes of Writing Functions

Functions are written and used for the following purposes:

a) Functions allow the users to conceive of their programs as a bunch of sub-steps. (Remember that each sub-step may have its own Function. A too-hard program may be broken into sub-steps.)

b) Functions allow users to reuse code instead of rewriting it.

c) Functions allow users to keep the variable namespace clean.

d) Functions allow users to test small parts of the program in isolation from the rest.

3.1.3 Steps to Writing a Function

a) Understand clearly the purpose of the Function to be created.

b) Define the data that enters into the Function from the caller (in the form of parameters).

c) Define the data variables that are needed inside the Function to attain its goal.

d) Define and decide the set of steps that the program will use to attain the goal (Algorithm).

3.2 Examples of simple functions in Arcade MakeCode

Example 1: Calling a function that has no parameters.

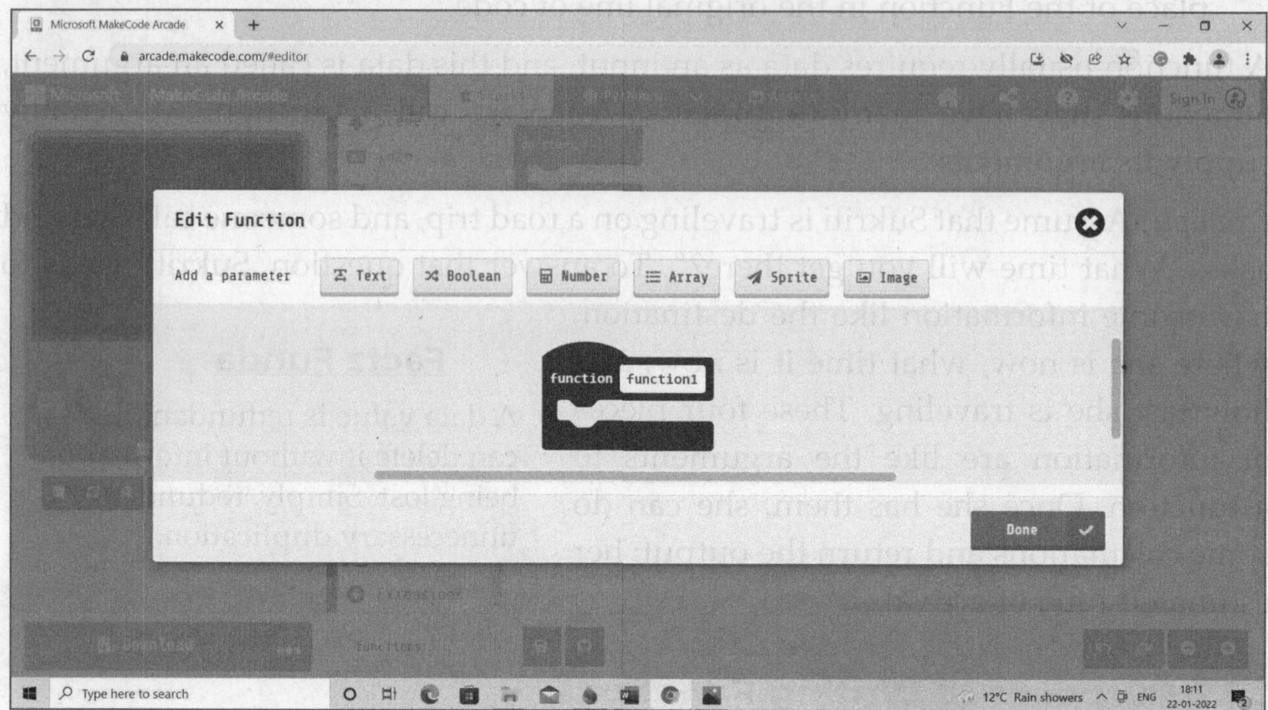

Figure 3.2

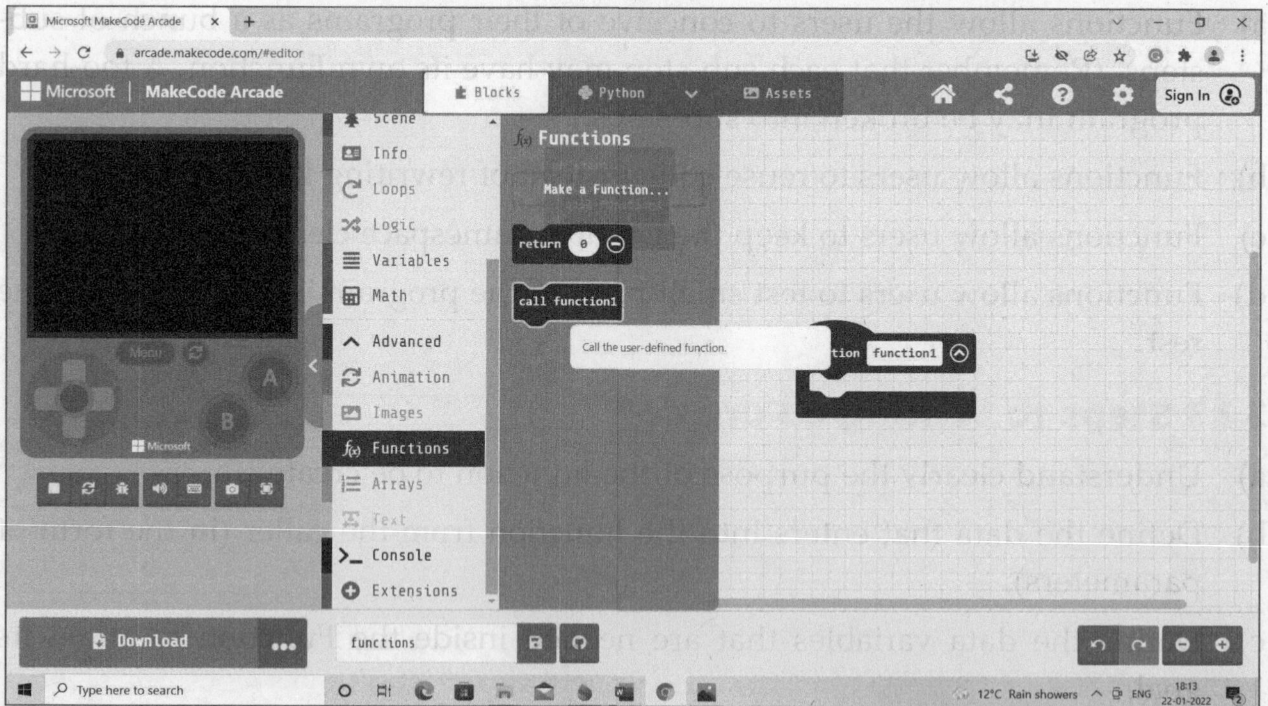

Figure 3.3

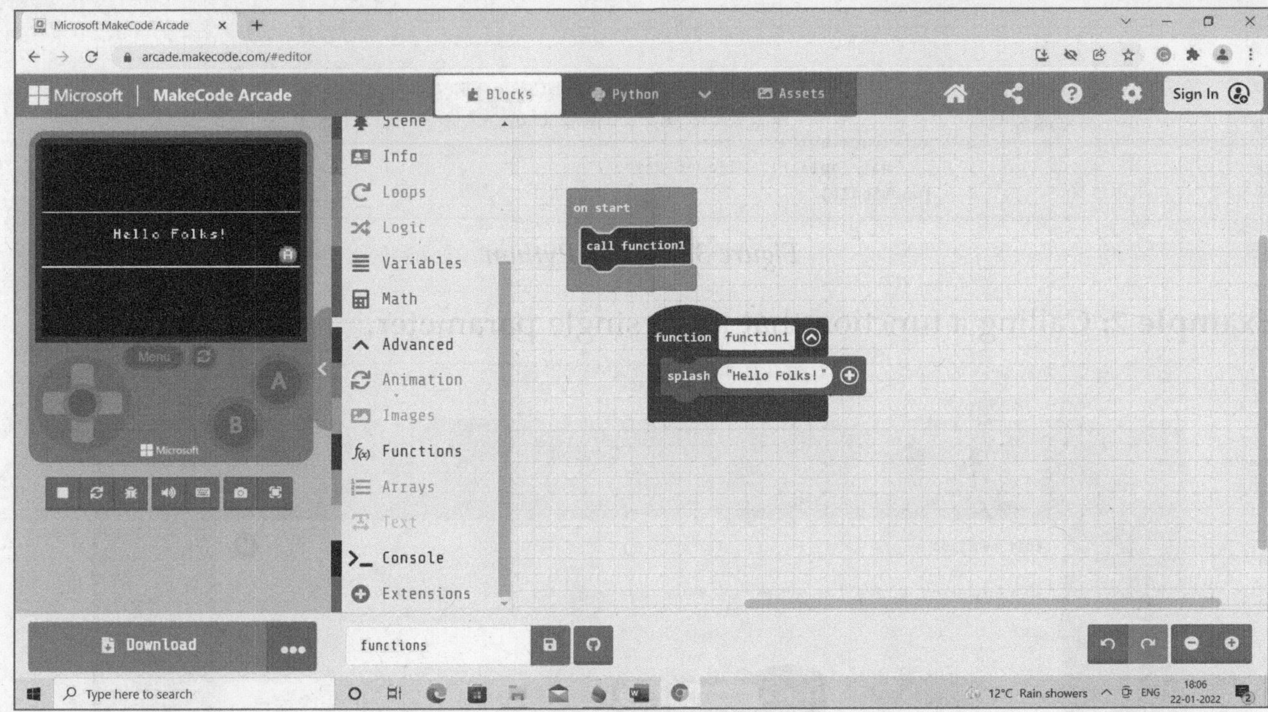

Figure 3.4

Output for calling a function without any parameter

Figure 3.5

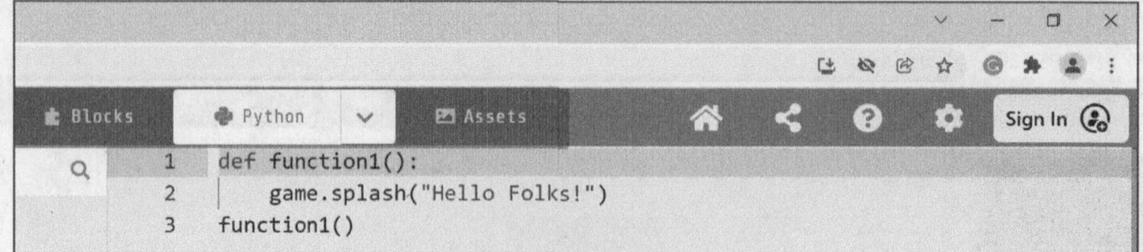

Figure 3.6: Using Python

Example 2: Calling a function that has a single parameter.

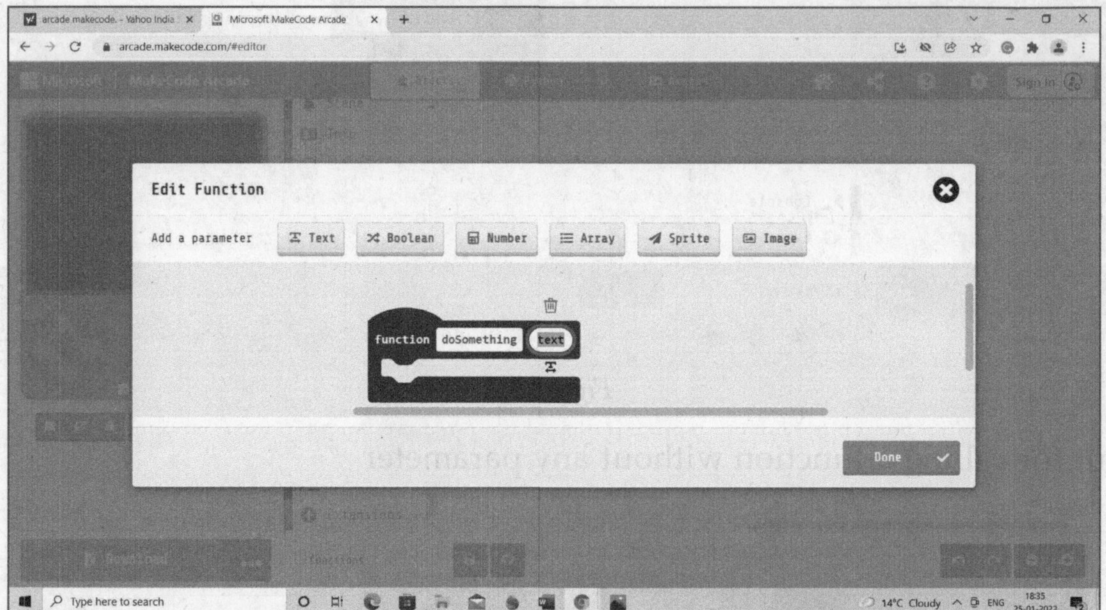

Figure 3.7

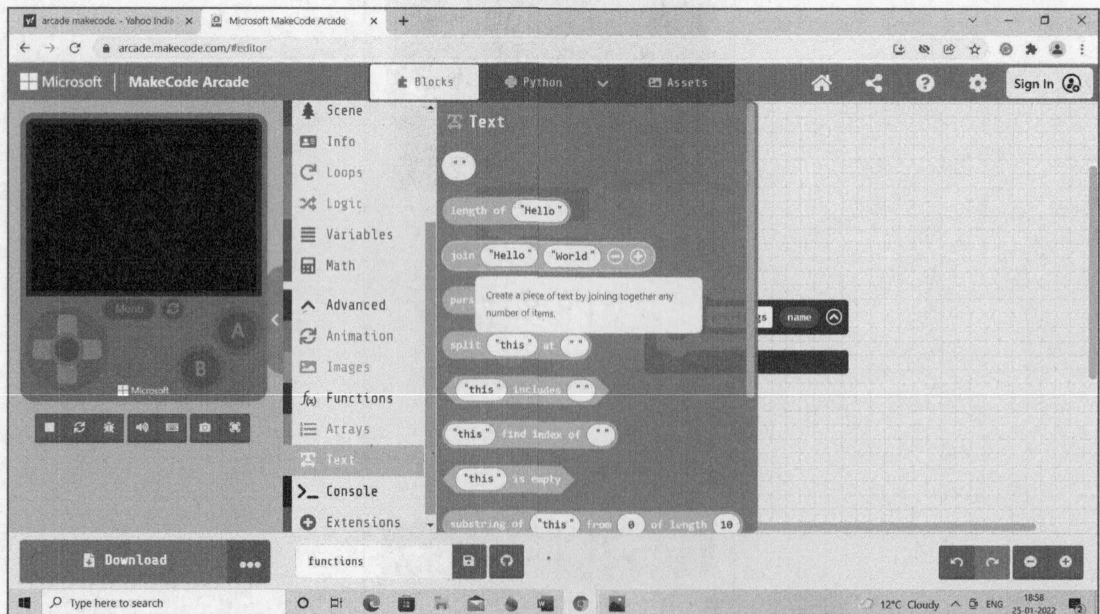

Figure 3.8

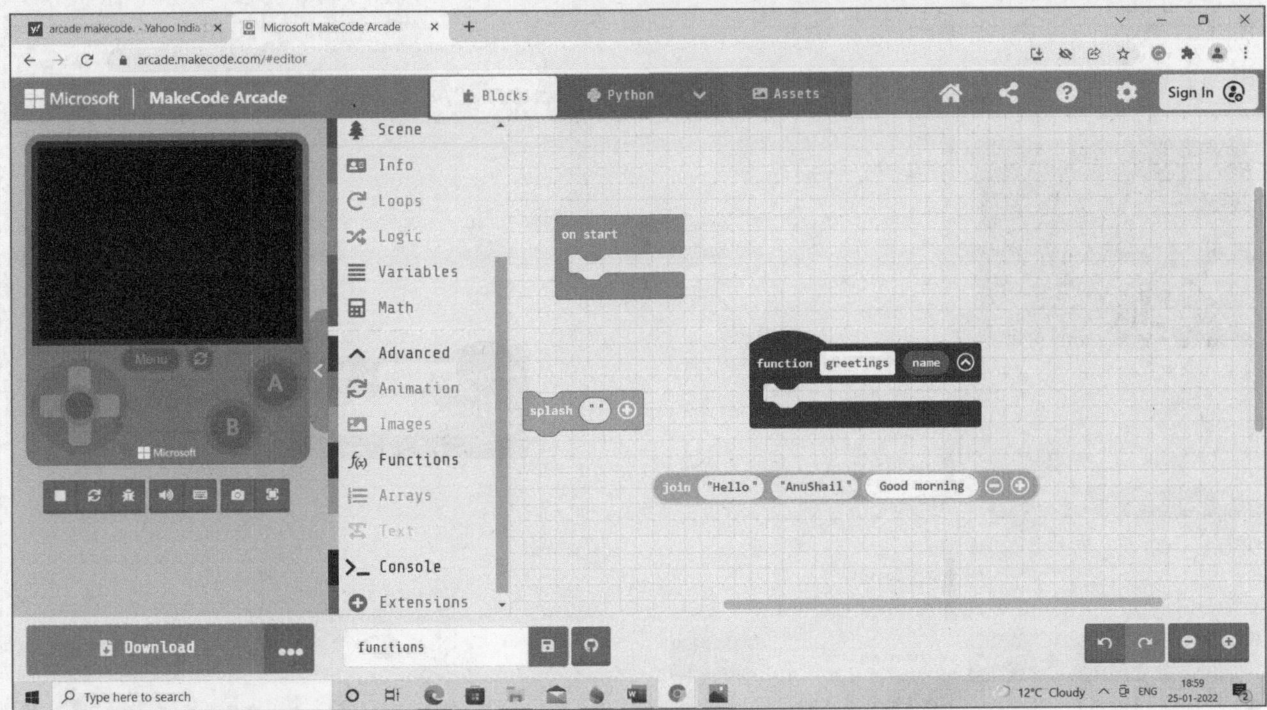

Figure 3.9

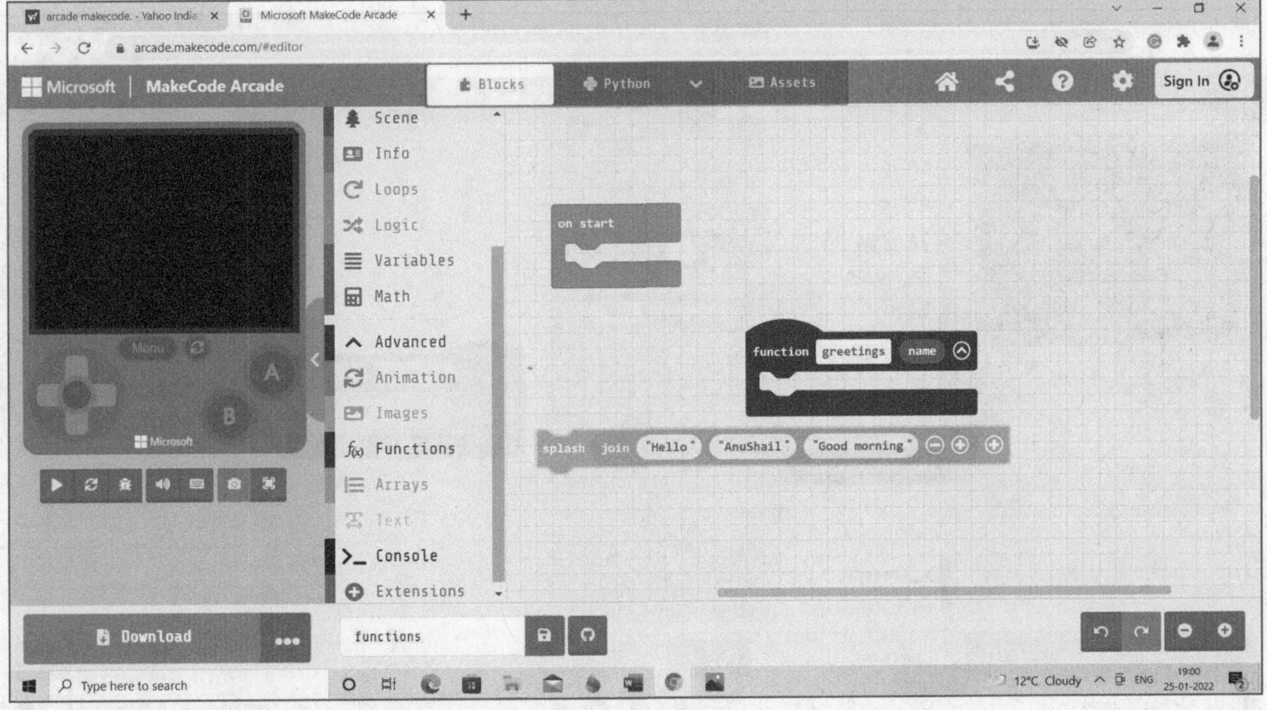

Figure 3.10

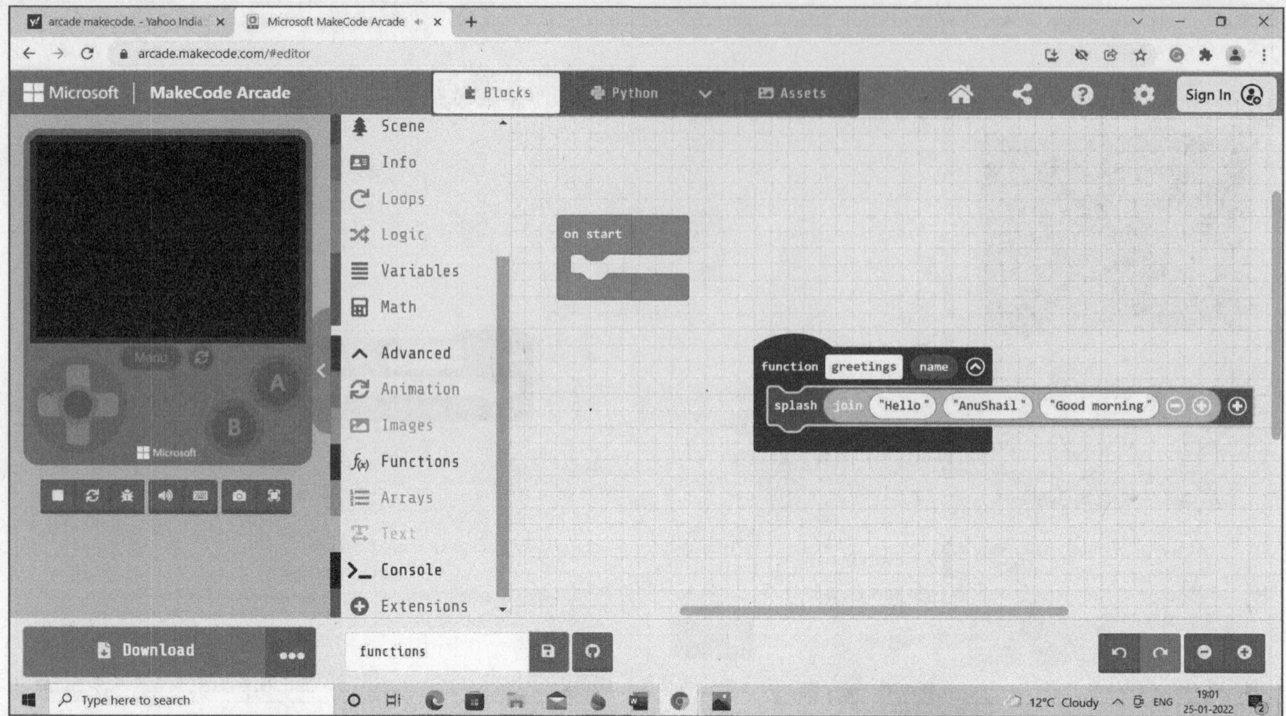

Figure 3.11

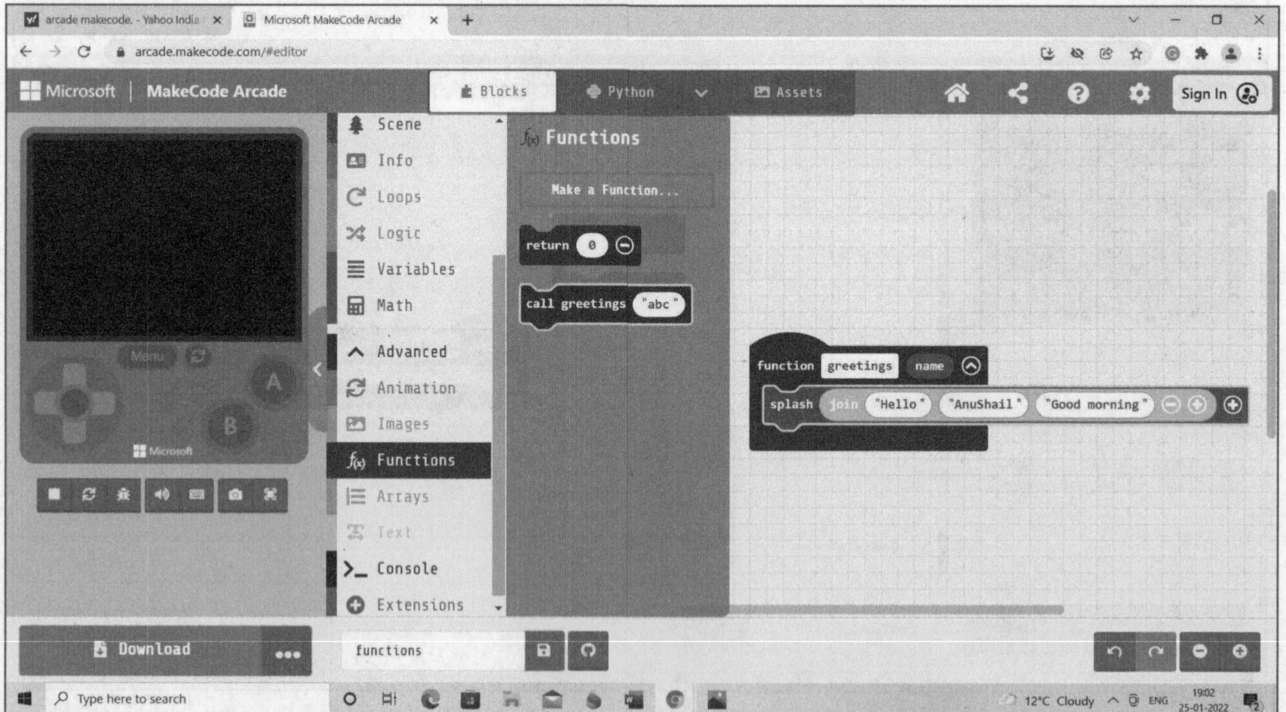

Figure 3.12

Output for calling a function without a single parameter

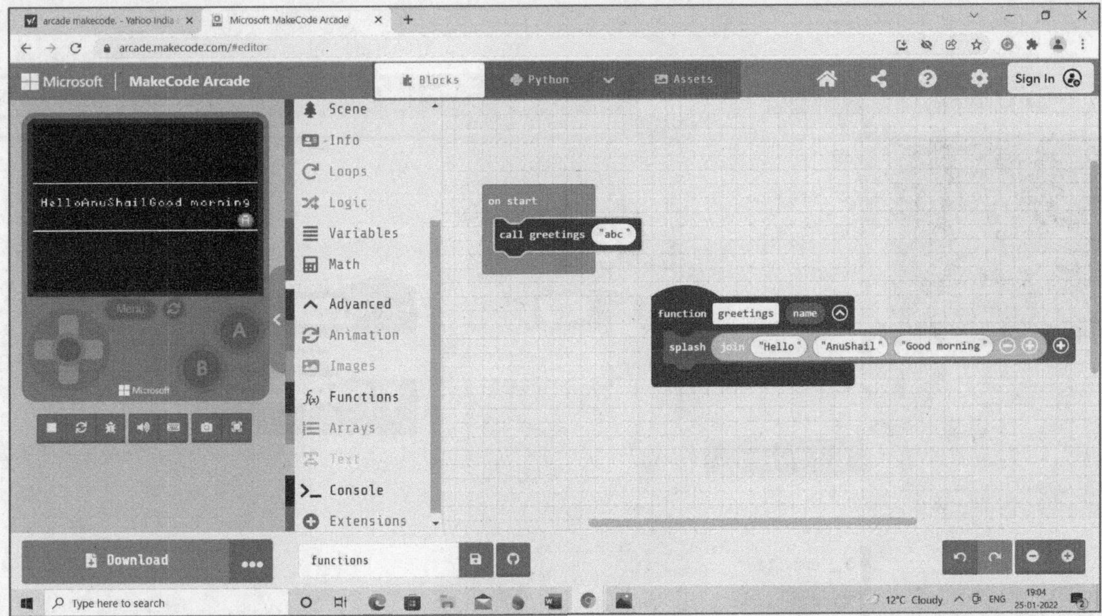

Figure 3.13

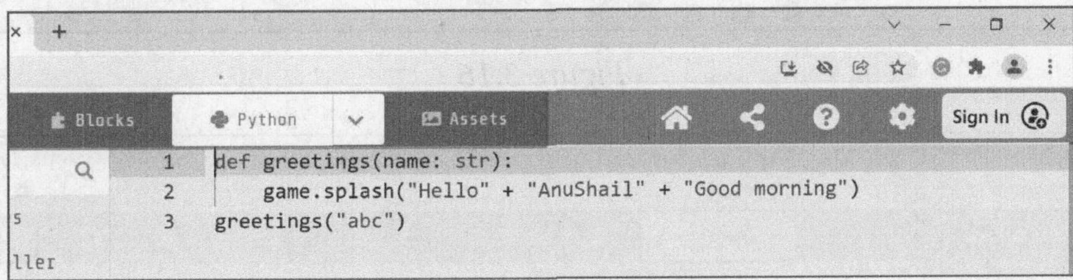

Figure 3.14: using Python

Example 3: Calling a function to print statements.

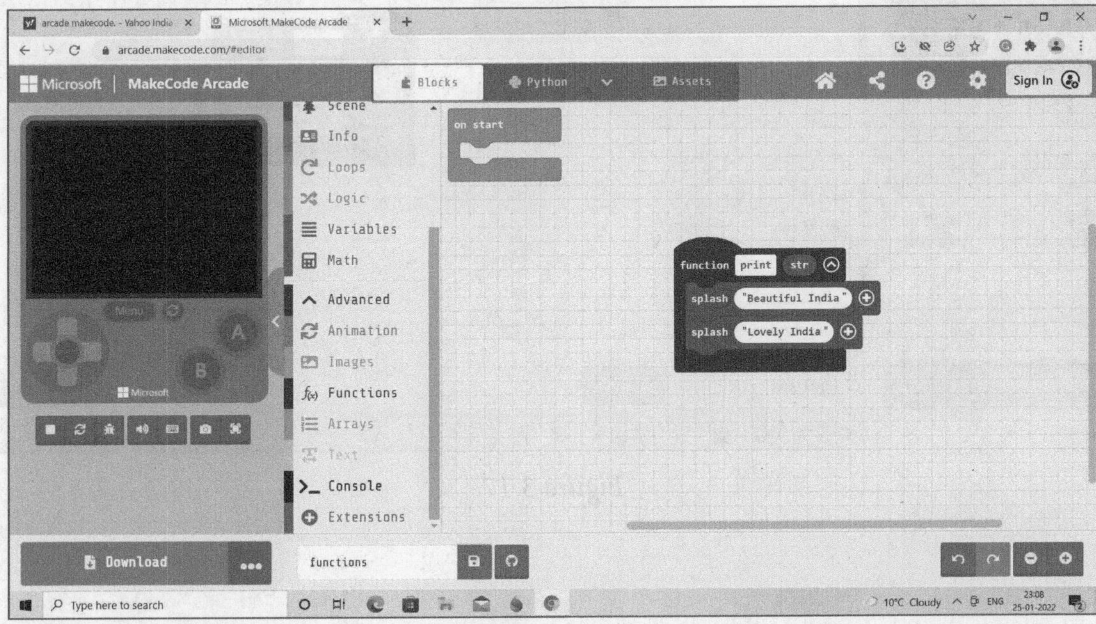

Figure 3.15

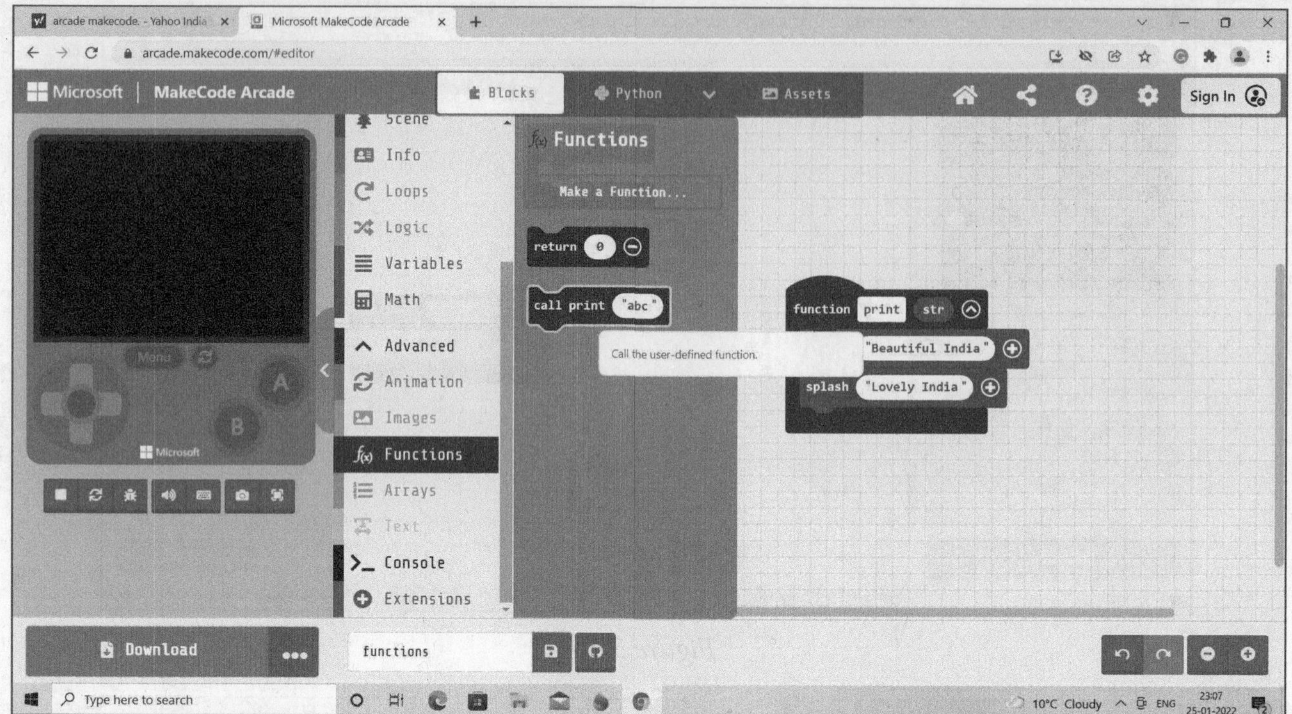

Figure 3.16

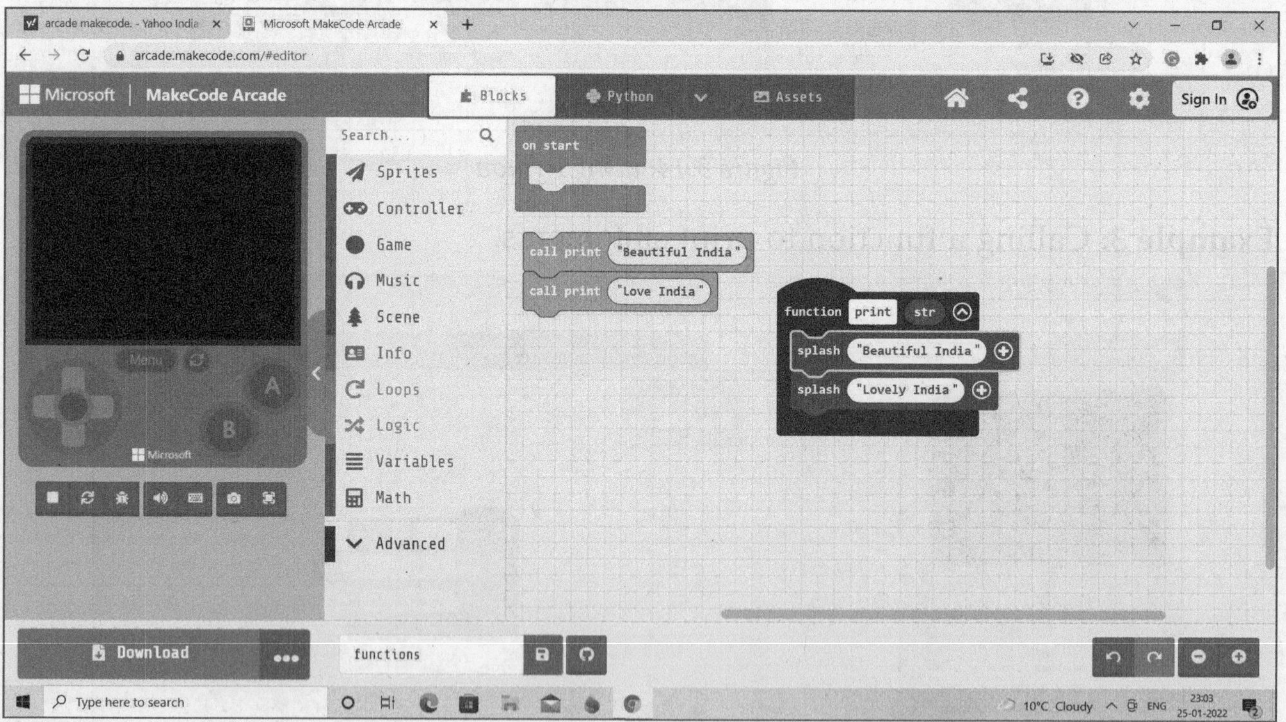

Figure 3.17

Output for calling a function to print statements.

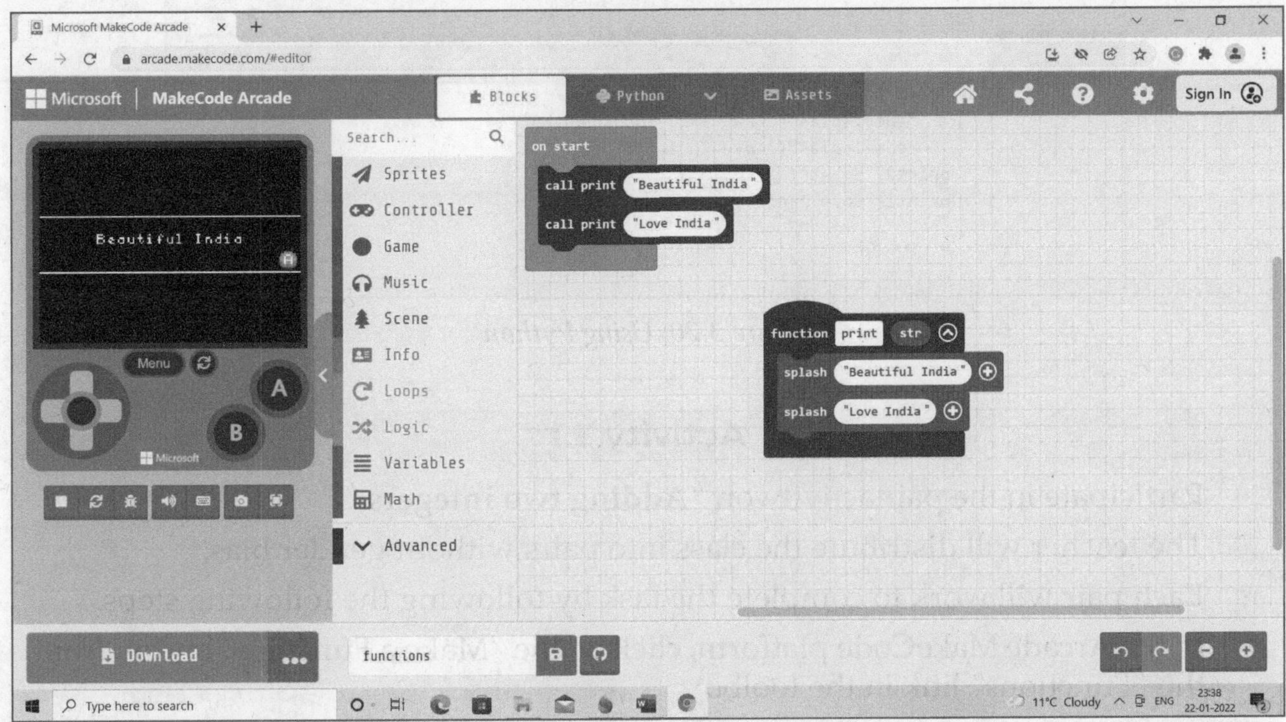

Figure 3.18

On clicking the 'A' button, we get the next string printed/displayed as follows:

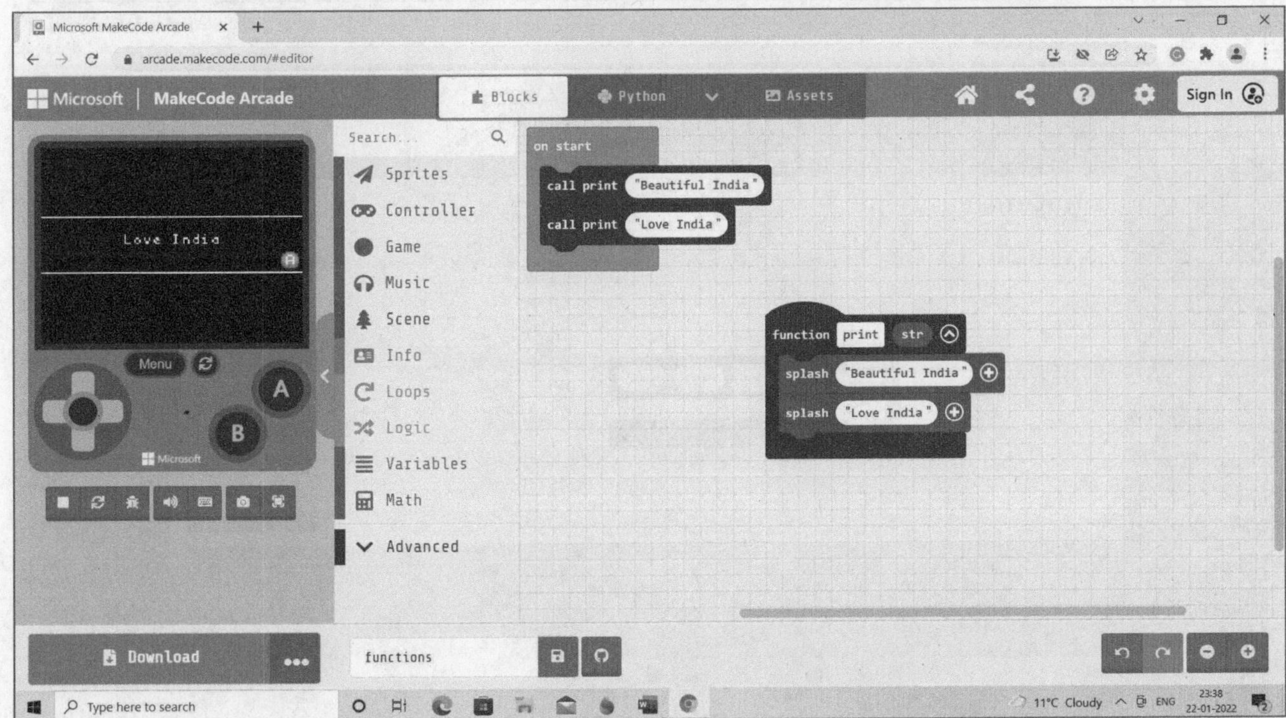

Figure 3.19

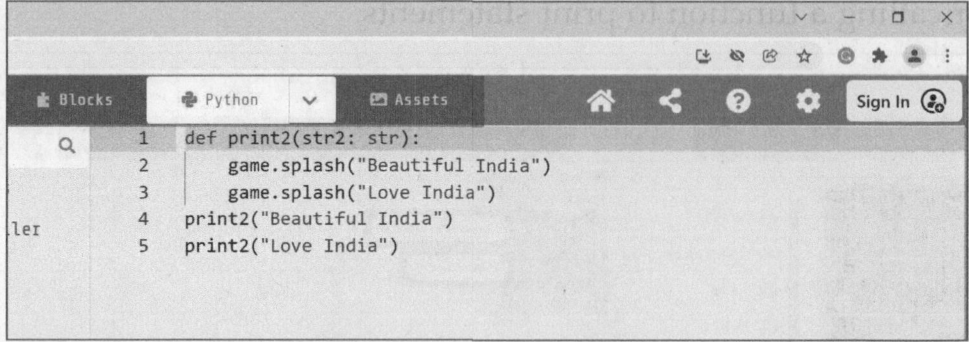

Figure 3.20: Using Python

Activity 3.1

- Participate in the pair activity on "**Adding two integers.**"
- The teacher will distribute the class into pairs without gender bias.
- Each pair will work to complete the task by following the following steps.
- In the Arcade MakeCode platform, click on the "Make a Function" button from the "Functions" link in the toolbox.

Step 1: Click on the "Make a function" button from the "Functions" link in the toolbox. Name the functions as "doAddition". Click on the "number" button, add "num1" and "num2" as input parameters and click the "Done" button.

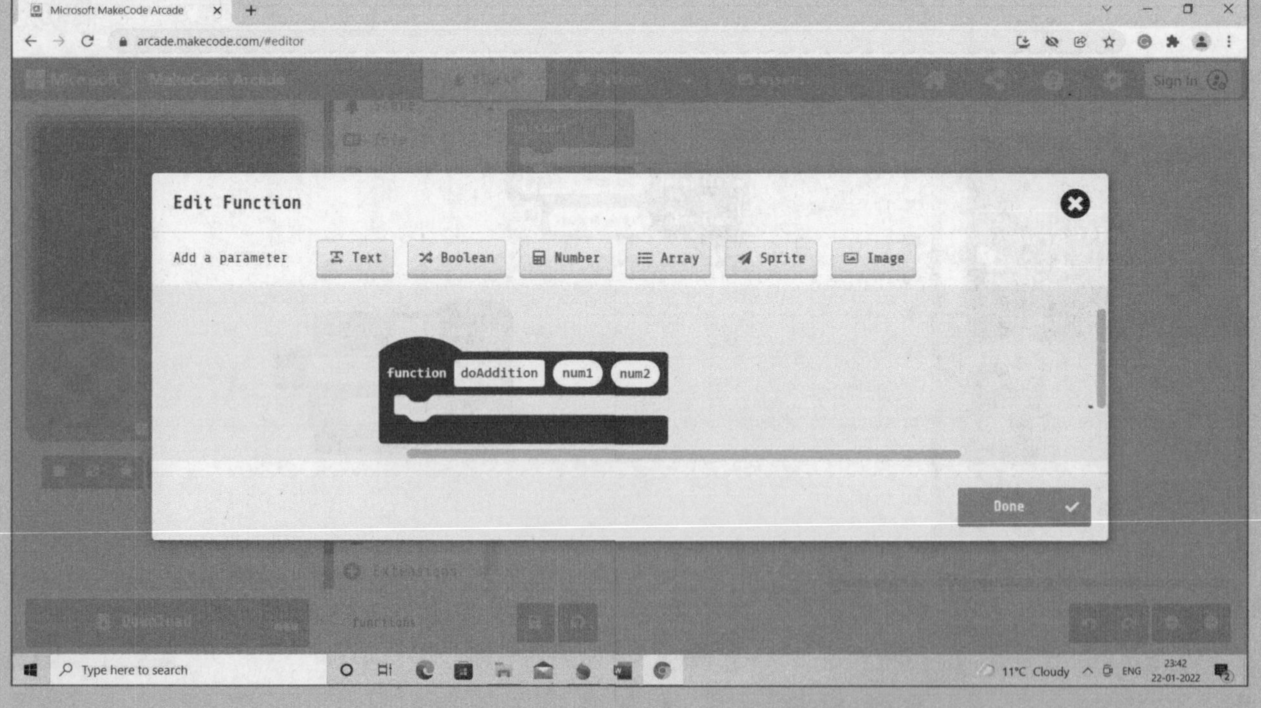

Figure 3.21

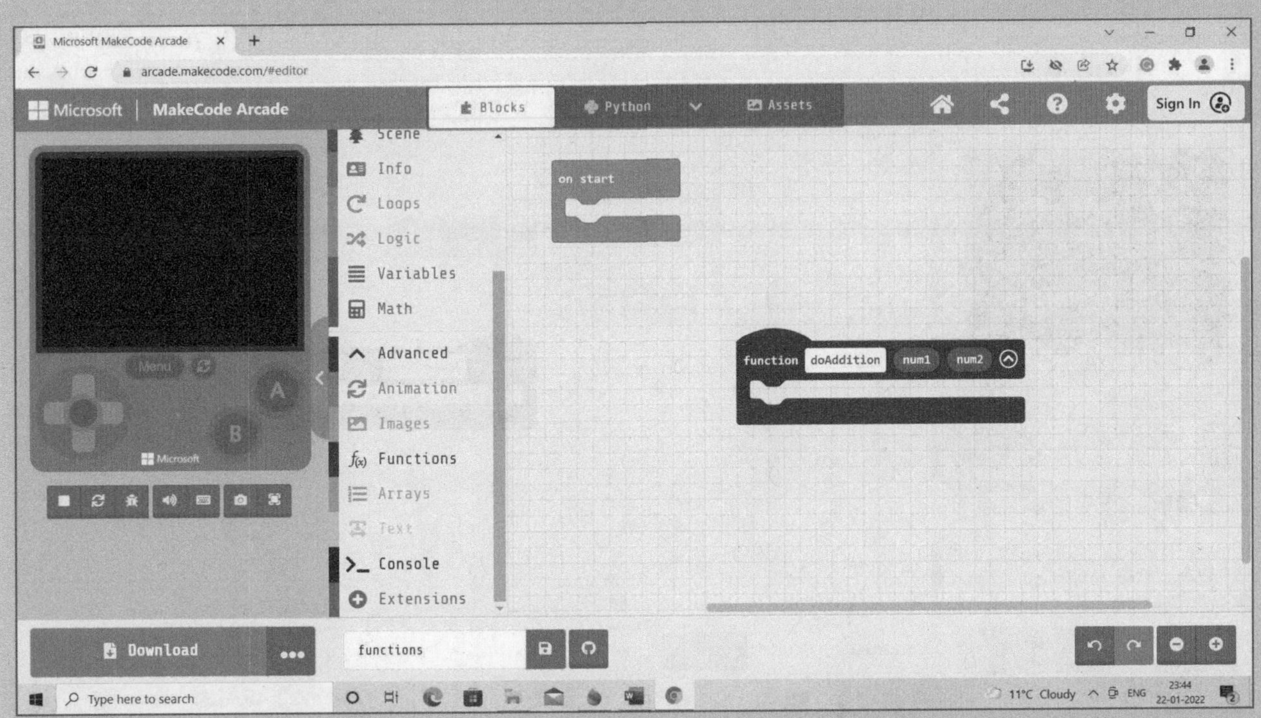

Figure 3.22

Step 2: Create two variables, "num1" and "num2," and assign their values to "15" and "35," respectively. Attach these blocks to the "On start" block.

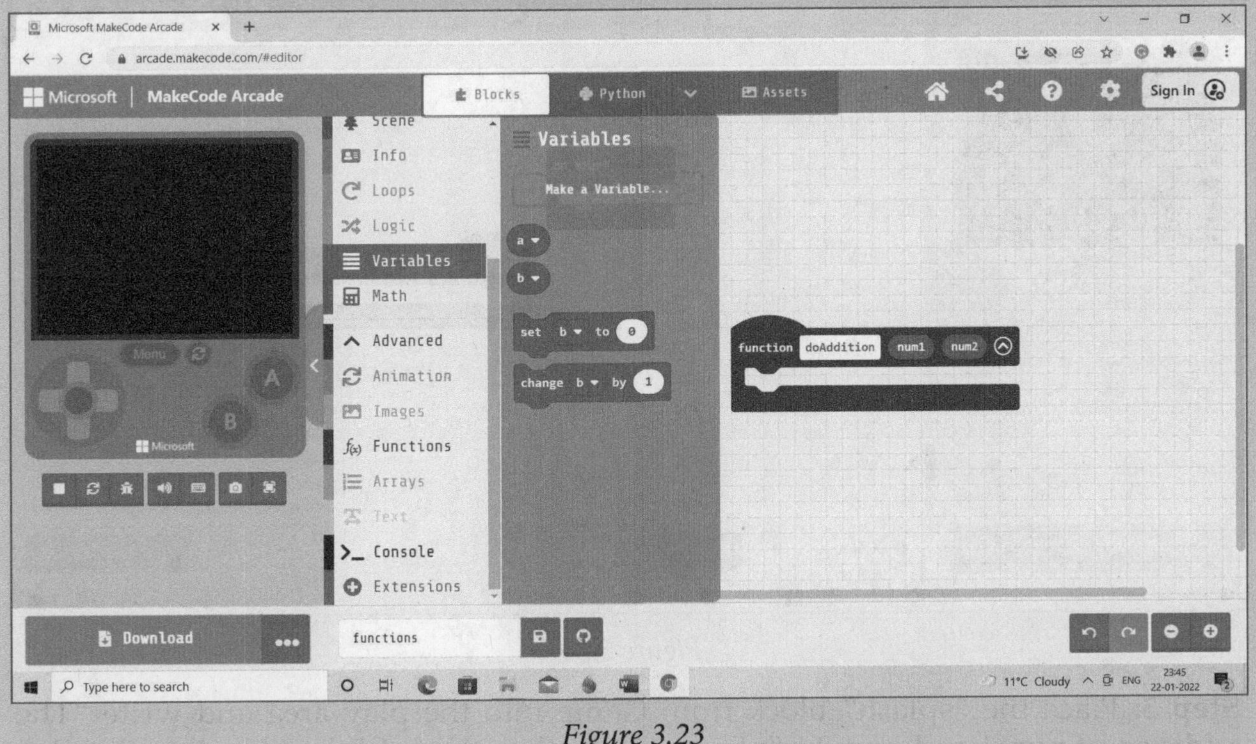

Figure 3.23

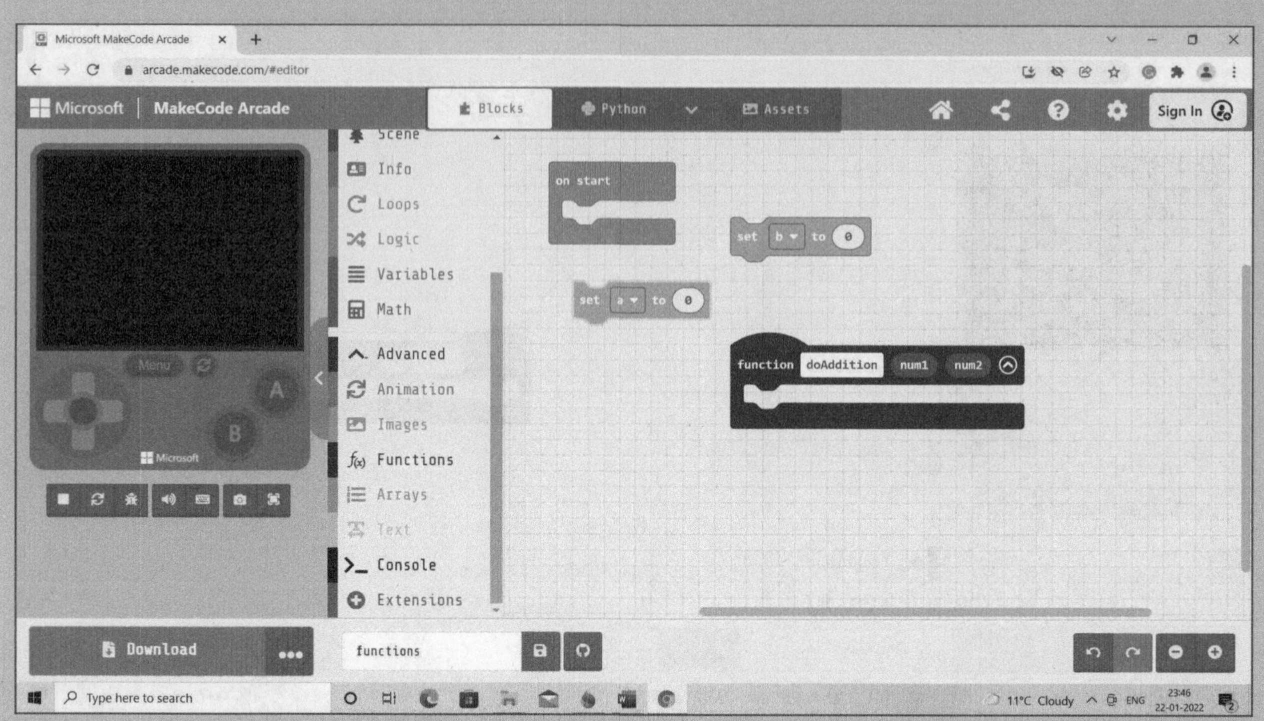

Figure 3.24

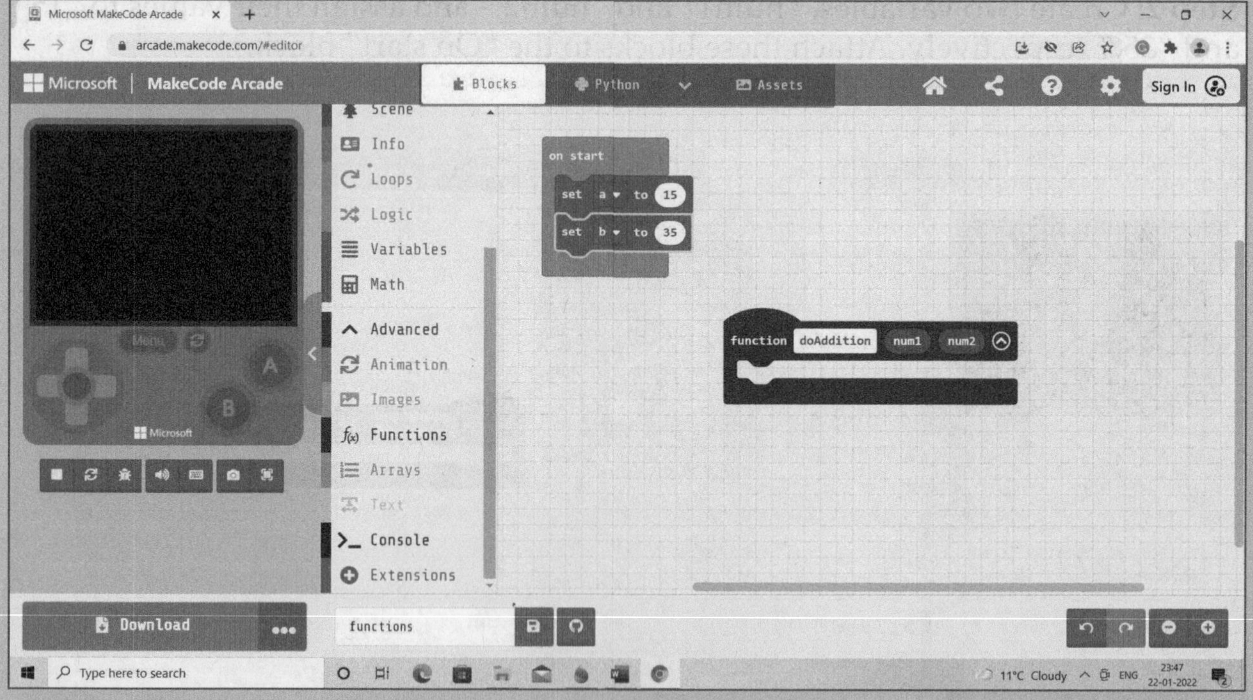

Figure 3.25

Step 3: Place the "splash" block from Game into the play area and write "The addition of num1 and num2 is". From math, click the 'addition' block to the play area, pick up num1 and num2 variables from the "Variable" toolbox as shown, and add in the 'splash .'Now, put it inside the "doAddition" function that is created in step1.

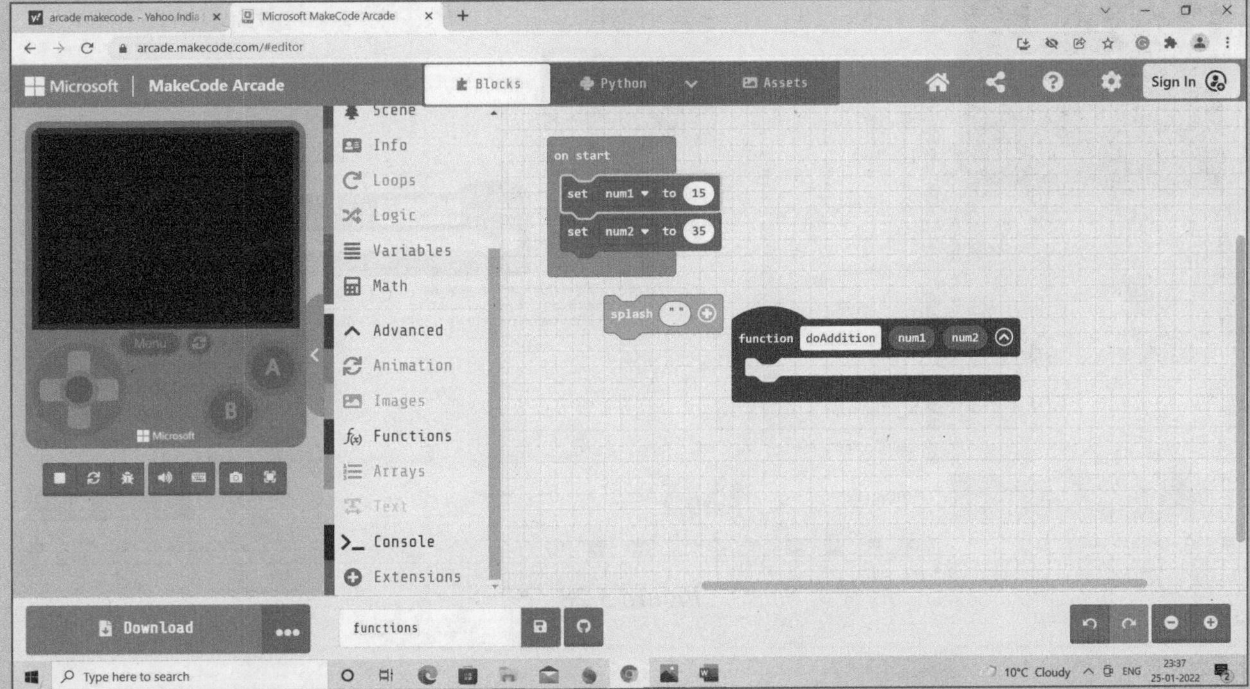

Figure 3.26

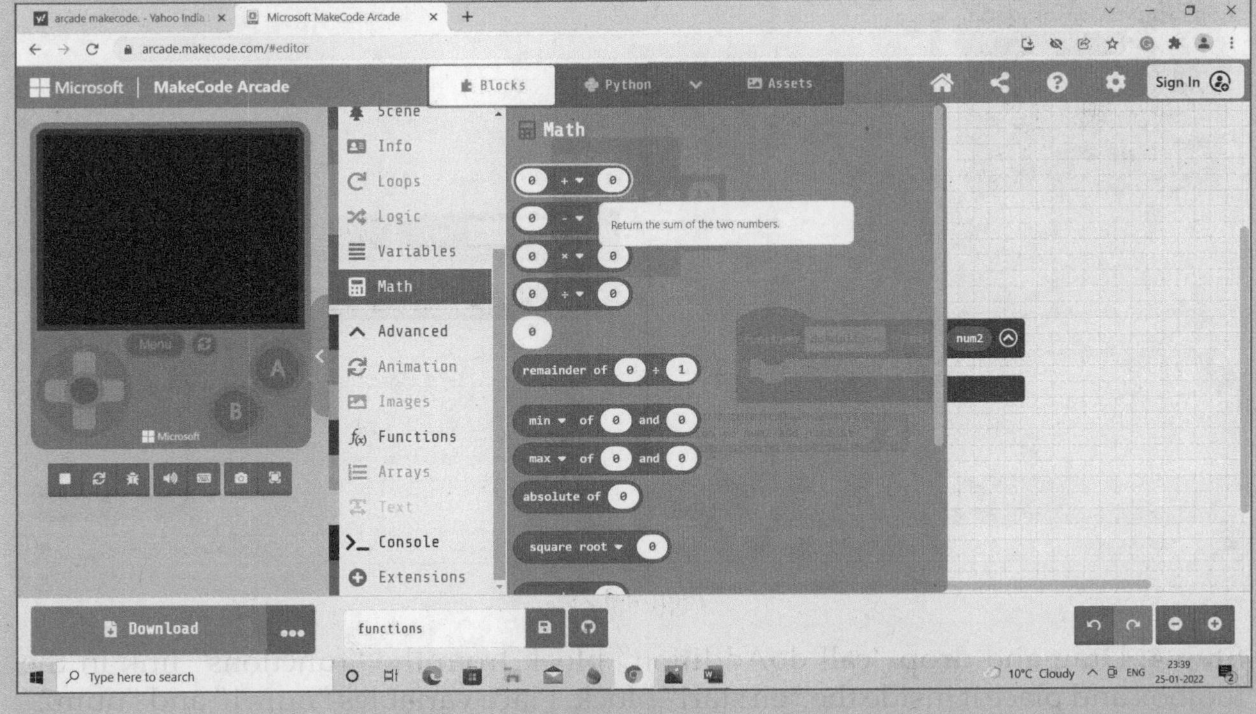

Figure 3.27

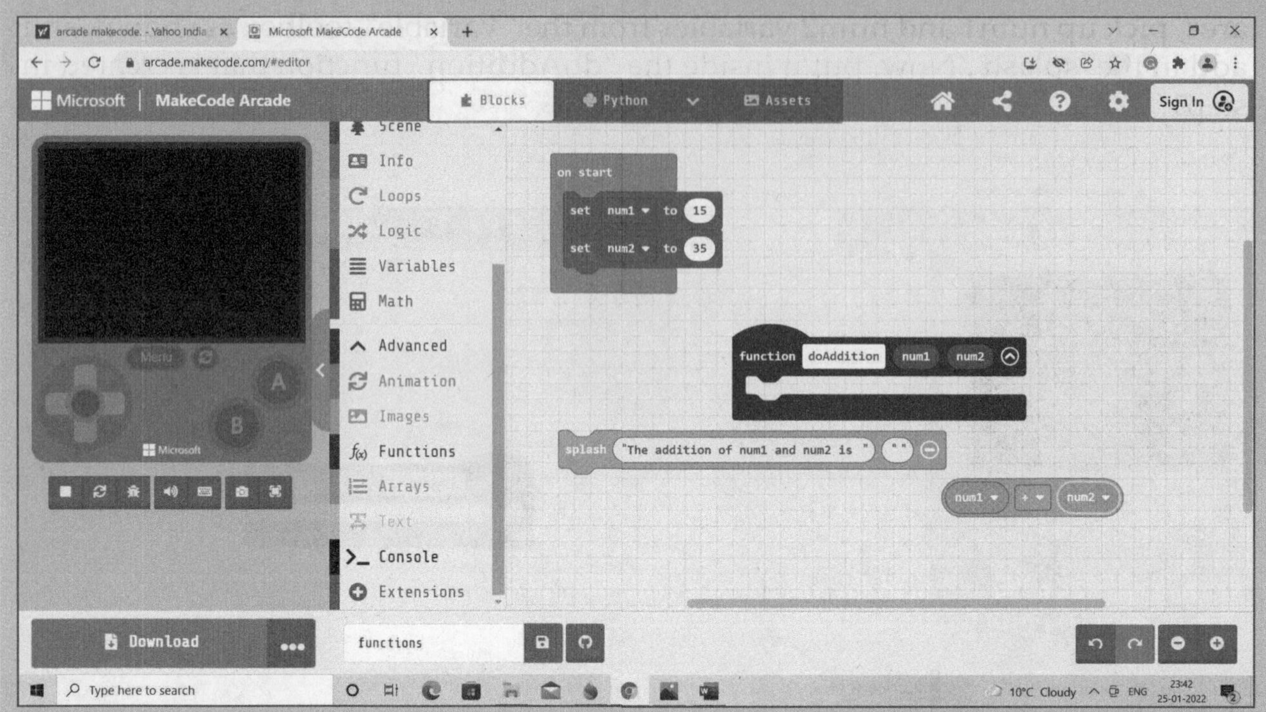

Figure 3.28

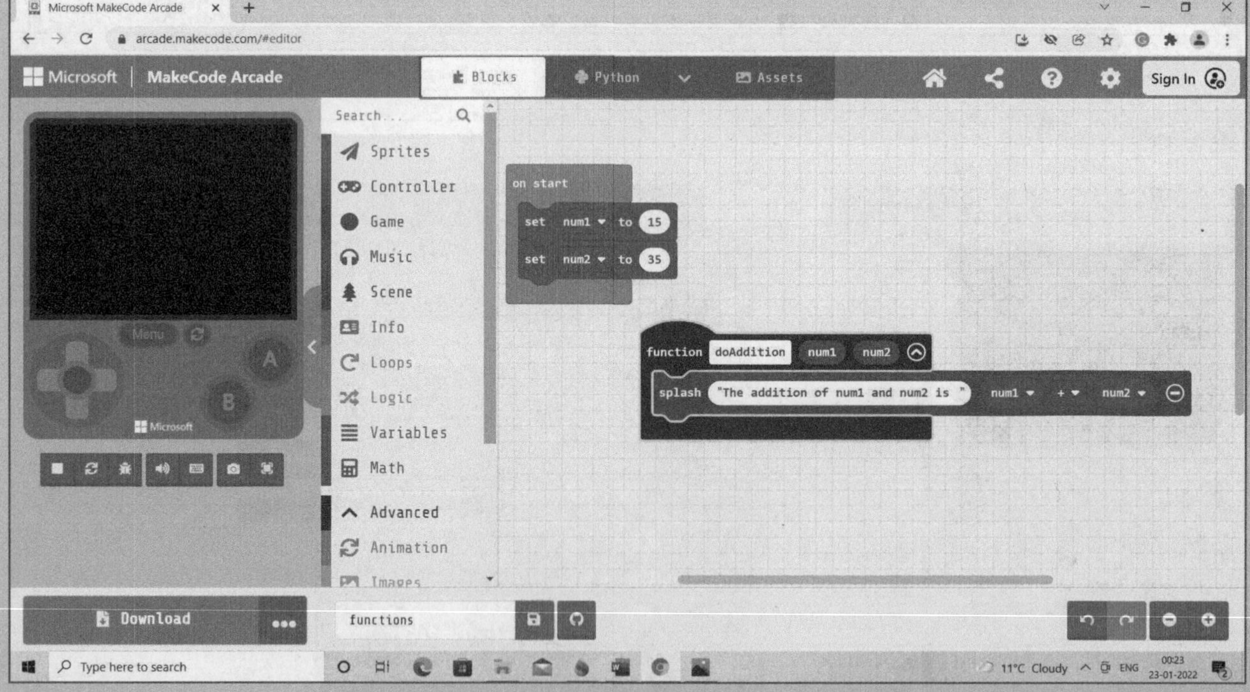

Figure 3.29

Step 4: Drag and drop "call doAddition" block from the "functions" link in the toolbox and place it inside the "on start" block. Place variables "num1" and "num2" inside "call doAddtion" block.

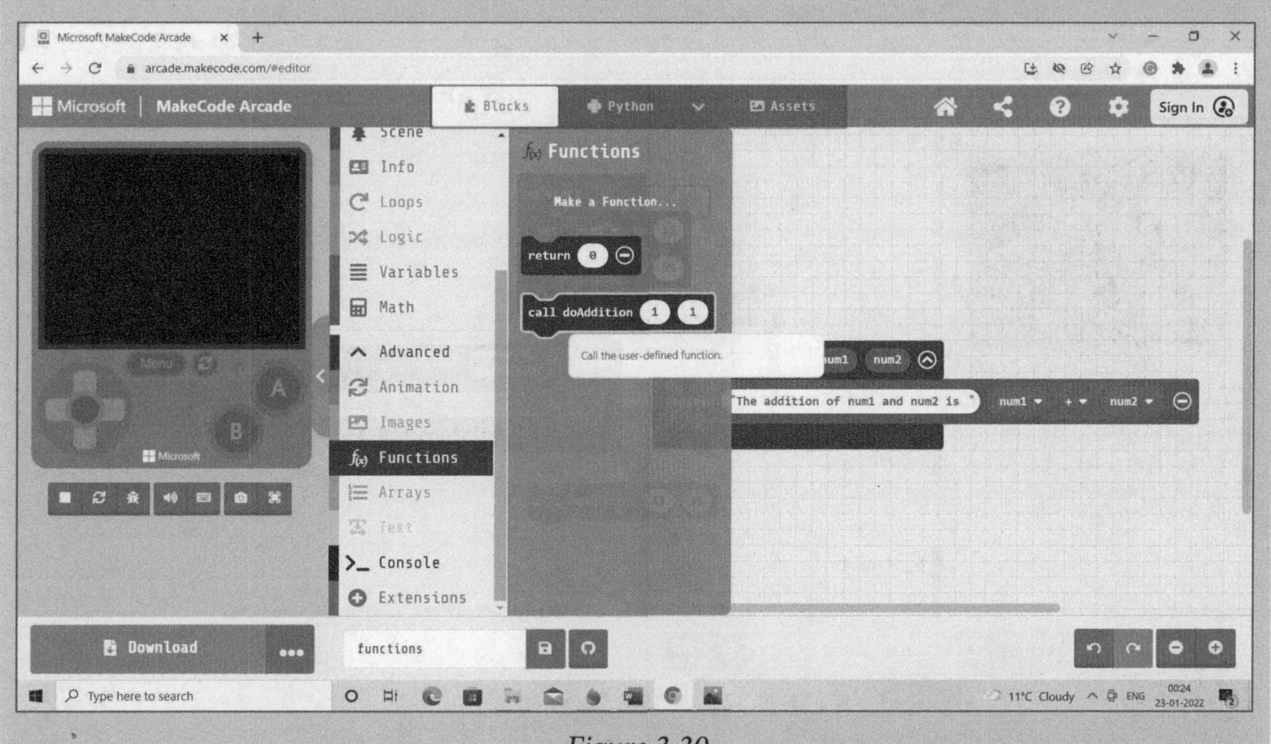

Figure 3.30

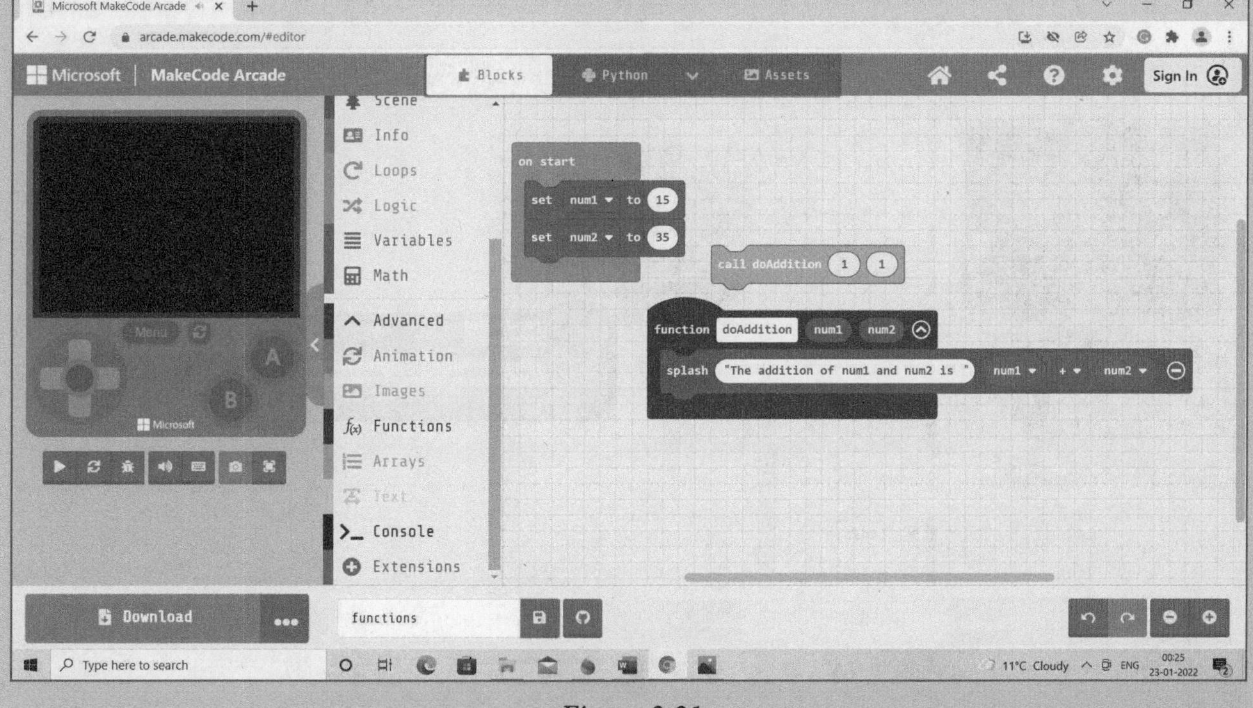

Figure 3.31

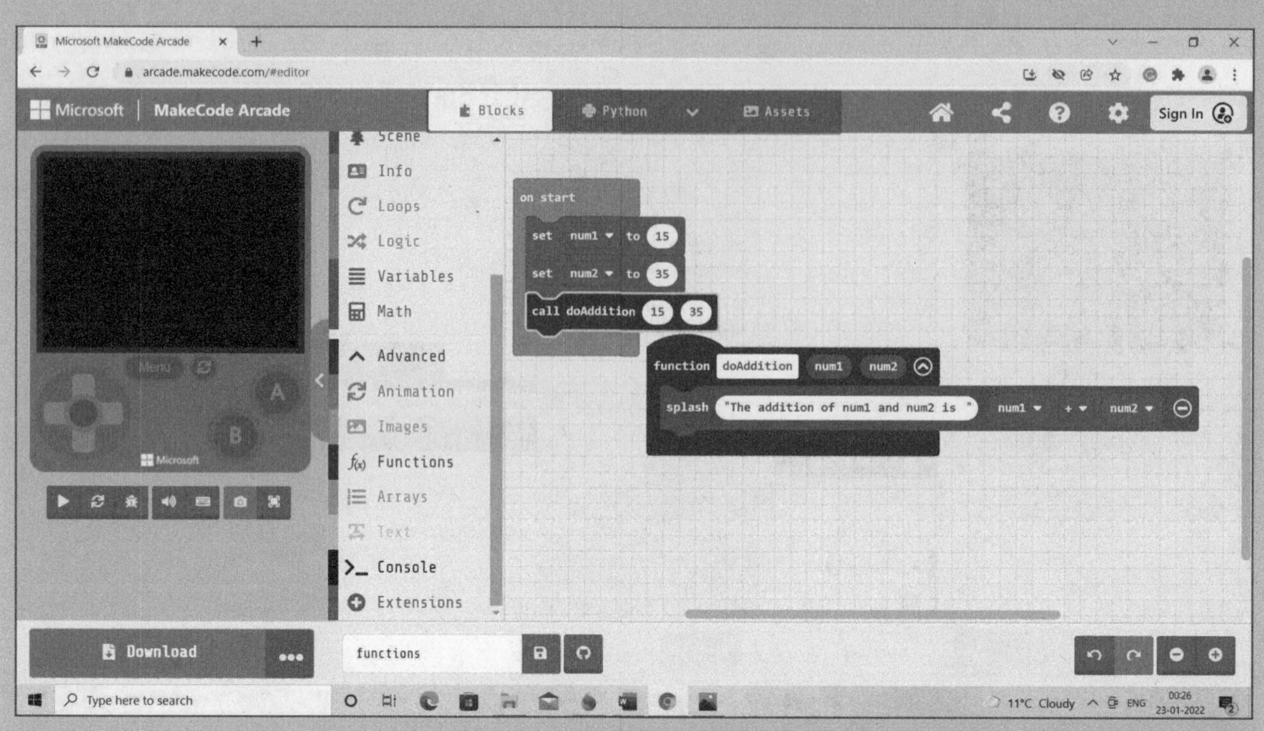

Figure 3.32

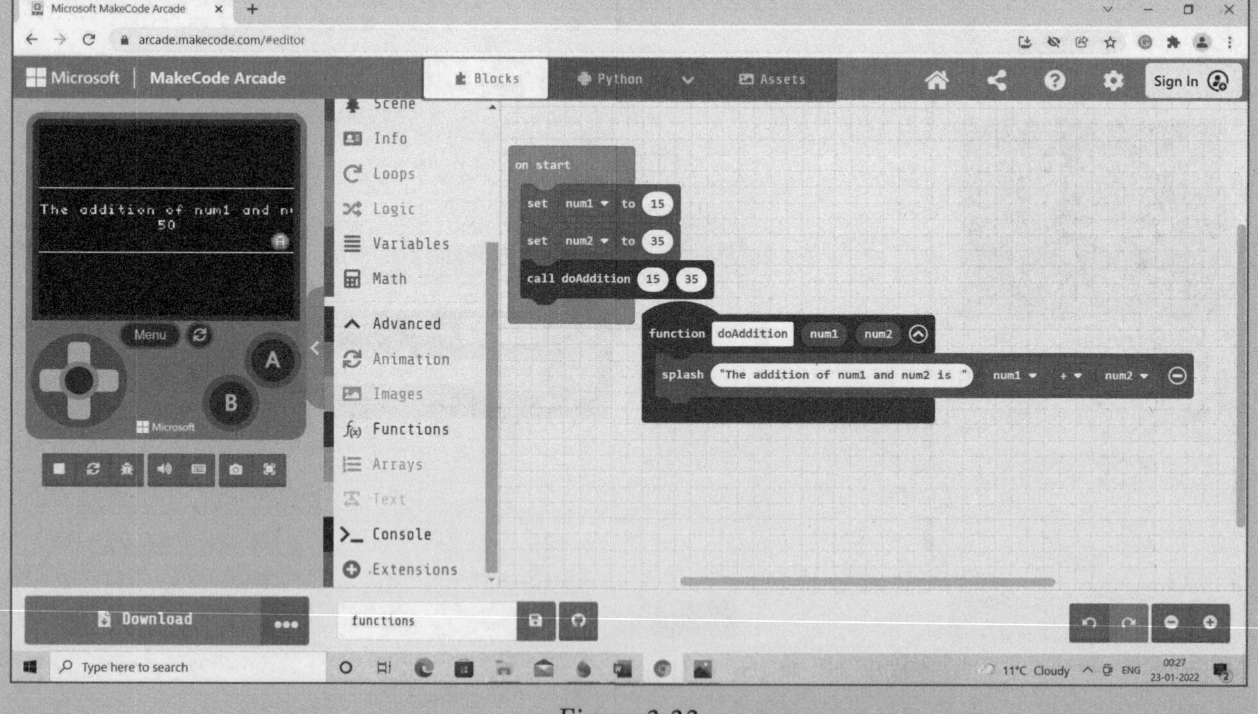

Figure 3.33

Step 5: Click on the play button at the bottom of the screen to see the final output.

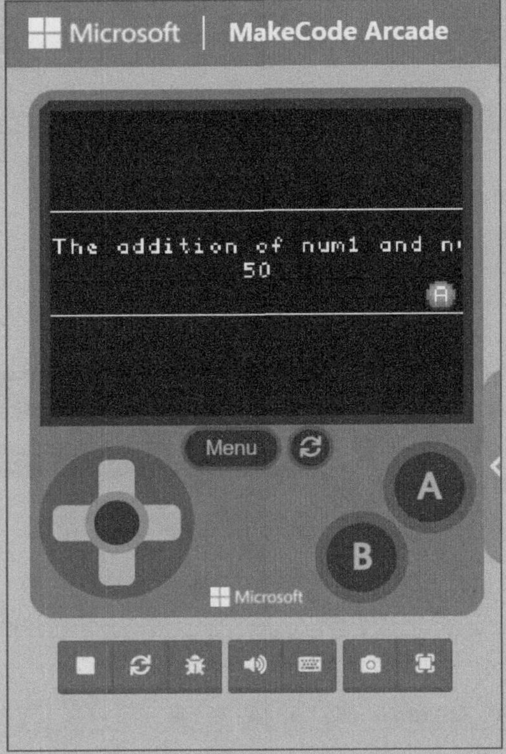

Figure 3.34

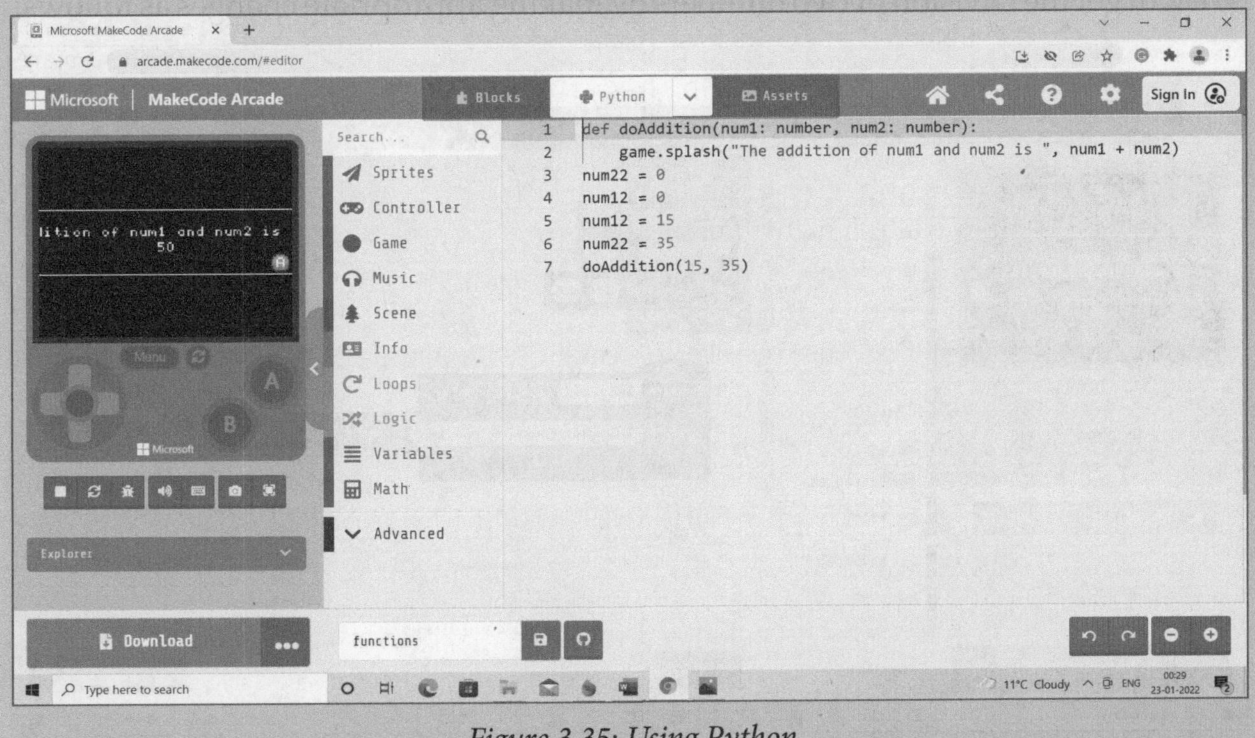

Figure 3.35: Using Python

We will get the multiplication of two numbers by making appropriate changes as follows:

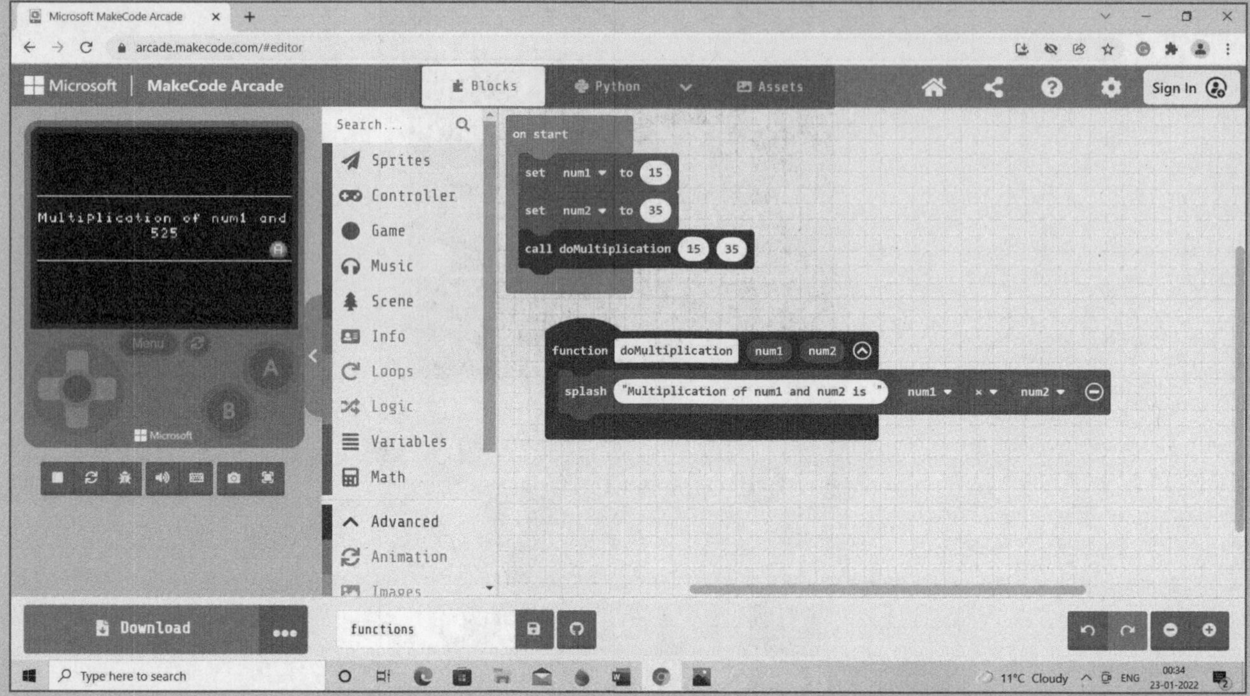

Figure 3.36

We will get the Division of two numbers by making appropriate changes as follows:

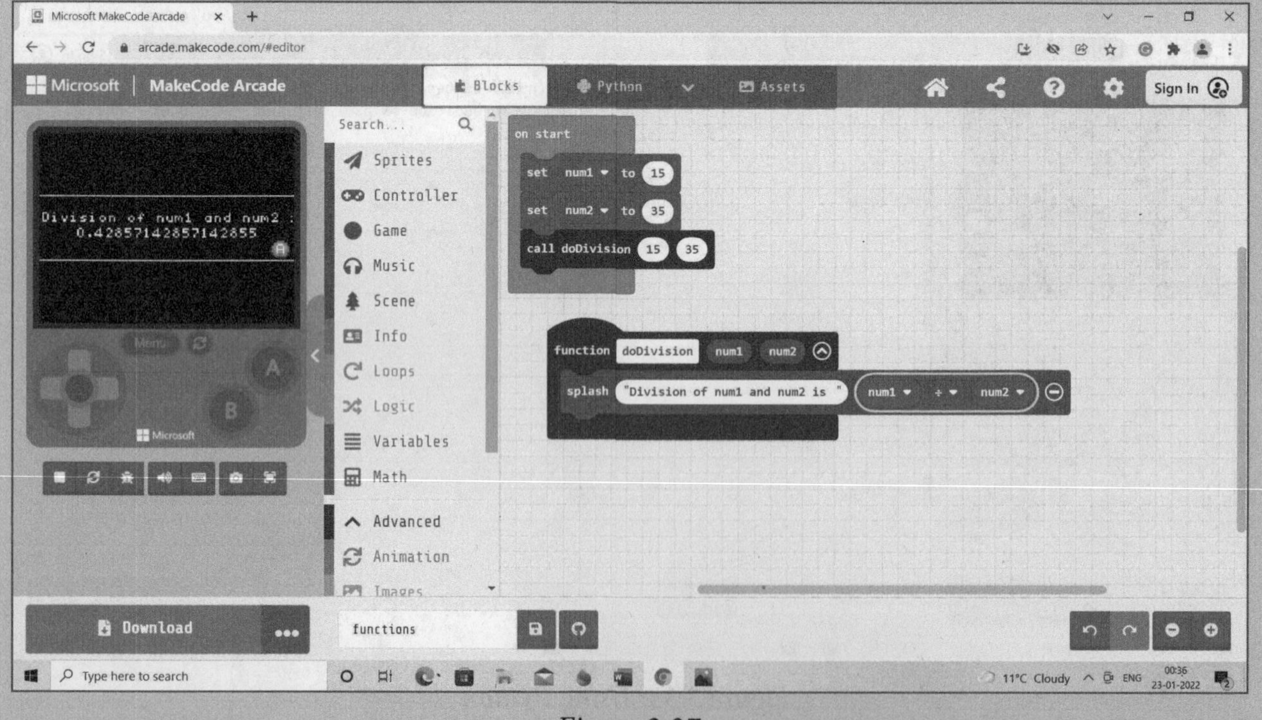

Figure 3.37

We will get the subtraction of two numbers by making appropriate changes as follows:

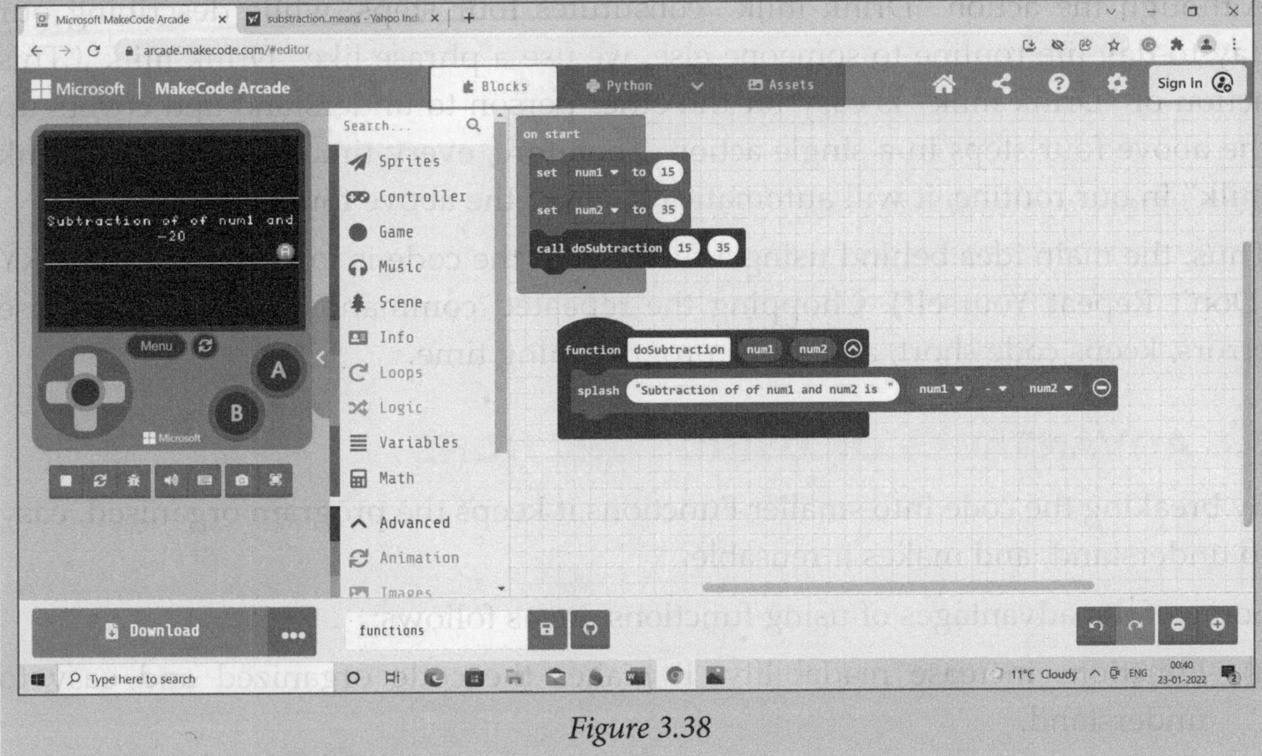

Figure 3.38

3.2.1 Types of Functions

There may be four different types of user-defined functions as follows:

a) Functions with no arguments and no return value.

b) Functions having no arguments and a return value.

c) Functions having arguments and no return value.

d) Function with arguments and a return value.

3.3 HOW TO REDUCE REDUNDANCY USING FUNCTIONS?

A data value is redundant if we can delete it without information being lost. In simple words, redundancy is unnecessary duplication.

Let us take an example -a very basic child's habit of drinking milk. If we look at the action of drinking milk, it involves four main steps only:

- Take a glass of milk/bottle of milk.
- Sip the milk from the container (glass/bottle).

- Gulp the milk down the throat.
- Put down the glass/bottle after finishing it.

Although the action "Drink milk" constitutes four steps, while describing our day-to-day life routine to someone else, we use a phrase like "Drink milk ."This action of "Drink milk" is easy for the other person to understand and covers up the above four steps in a single action. Therefore, every time we include "Drink milk" in our routine, it will automatically cover the above four steps.

Thus, the main idea behind using a function in the code is to keep the code DRY (Don't Repeat Yourself). Chopping the repeated commands helps to minimise errors, keeps code short, and saves programming time.

3.4 ADVANTAGES OF USING FUNCTIONS

By breaking the code into smaller Functions,it keeps the program organised, easy to understand, and makes it reusable.

Some of the advantages of using functions are as follows:

a) Functions increase readability. It makes the code organized and easy to understand.

b) Functions reduce code length. Redundant code is removed and replaced by functions.

c) Code reusability increases by the use of functions.

d) Functions help users in reducing code redundancy.

e) Functions make code modular.

f) Functions provide abstraction.

Factz Funda

Modular programming allows many programmers to collaborate on the same application.

3.5 FUNCTION PARAMETERS

Function Parameters are the names that are defined in the function definition, and real values passed to the Function in the function definition are known as arguments. Thus, a parameter refers to an unknown data value capable of being set through a command by the user.

Example 1: Suppose we have a problem statement wherein we are required to calculate the area of a circle. For doing so, we need to know the 'Radius' of the circle whose area we are required to calculate. Here, 'Radius' will be a function parameter.

However, the formula for calculating the area of a circle always remains the same.

```
Function to calculate and print area of a circle
Area of a circle (Radius)
{
    Area = 3.14*radius*radius
    Print Area
}
Here, Radius is the function parameter for the function 'Area of Circle.'
```

Example 2: Suppose that we want to calculate the area of a rectangle, we need to know the length and breadth of the rectangle. Here too, the formula for calculating the area of the rectangle always remains the same. Length and breadth are function parameters here.

Thus, in the above-mentioned two scenarios, if we consider the task of calculating the area of circle and rectangle as functions, respectively, then the formulae used to calculate the area can be considered as the body of the Function. However, to get a concrete value from the functions, we need to provide the value of Radius in case of calculating the area of a circle and the value of length and breadth in case of calculating the area of the rectangle.

Hence, the variables accepted by a function to perform the set of tasks defined in its body are called function parameters.

Activity 3.2

- Participate in the group activity on "**Finding the square of a number.**"
- The teacher will divide the class into groups of 3-4 students without gender bias.
- Each group will participate in the activity using the Arcade MakeCode platform by following the steps given below:

Step 1: Open the link www.arcademakecode.com and create a new project "functions"

Step 2: Click on the "Make a variable" button from the "Variables" link in the toolbox.

Step 3: Create a variable and give its name as "num1".

Step 4: Drag and drop "set num1 to" block from "Variables" link into the play area and set its value to'9'.

Step 5: Place the created variable inside the "on start" block.

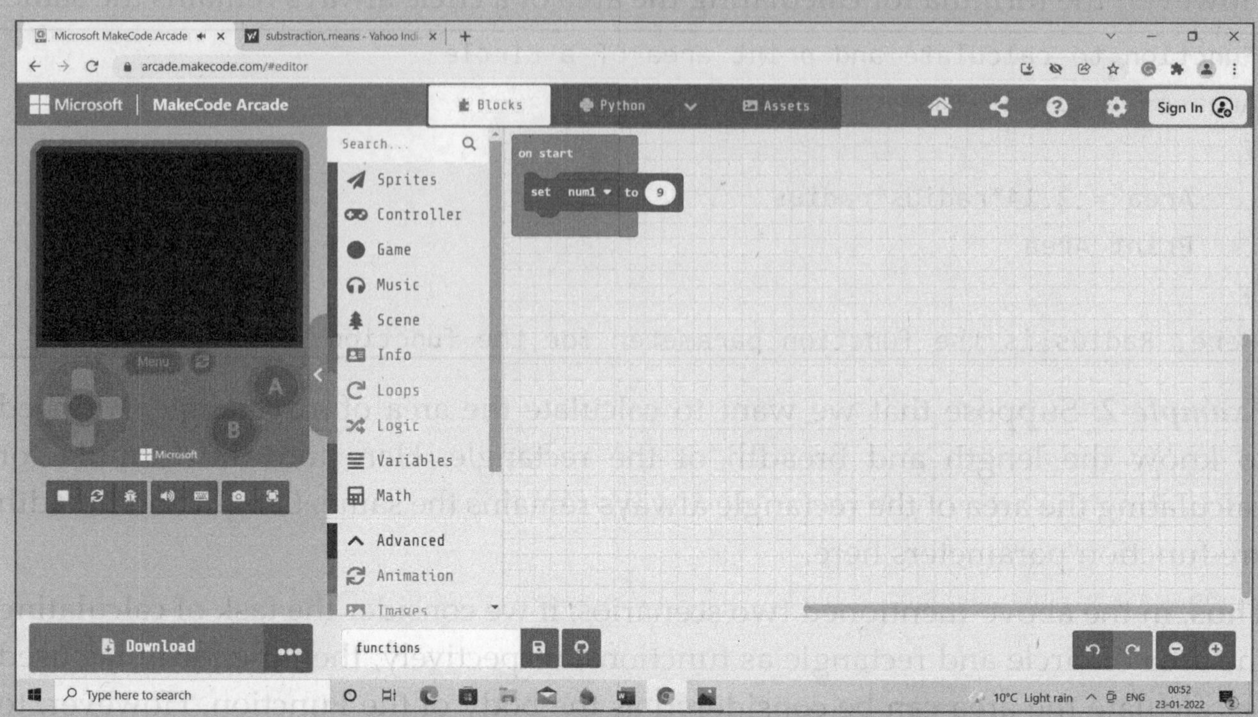

Figure 3.39

Step 6: Place the "splash" block from the Game toolbox and add a "multiplication" block in it, having both numbers as num1. Now, place it inside the "on start" block as shown here.

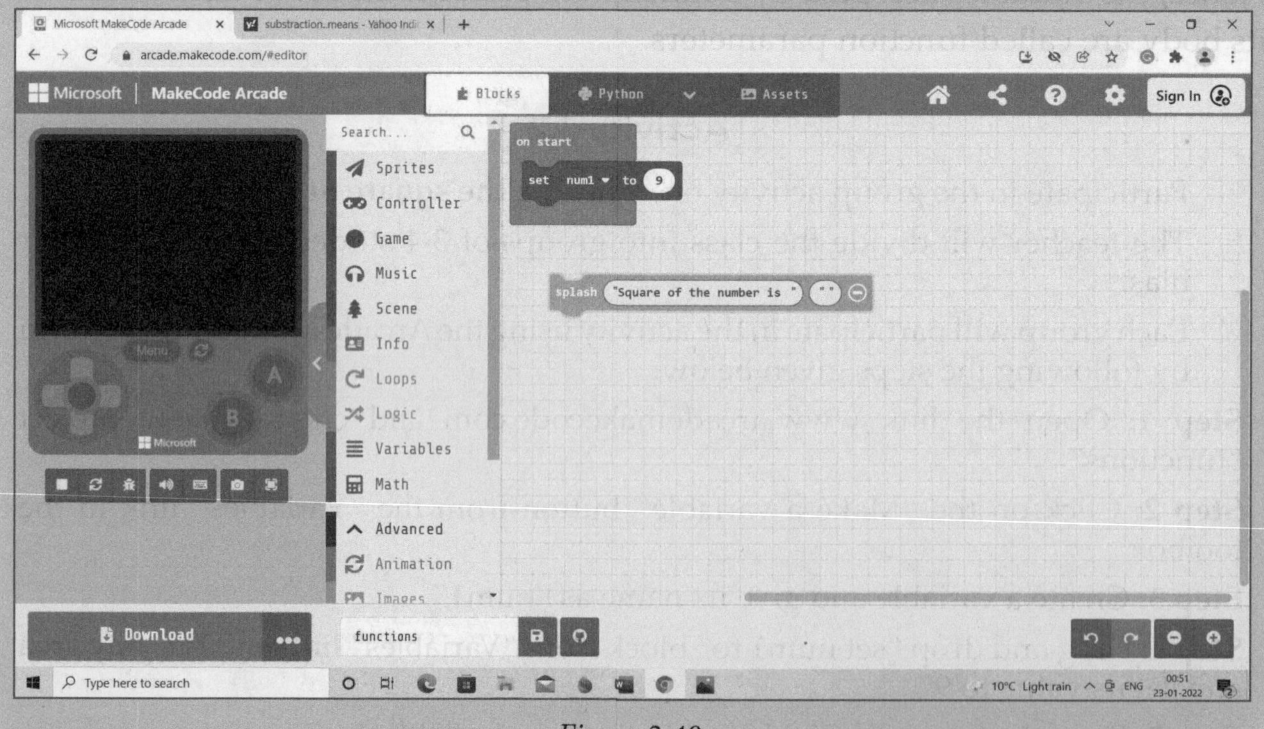

Figure 3.40

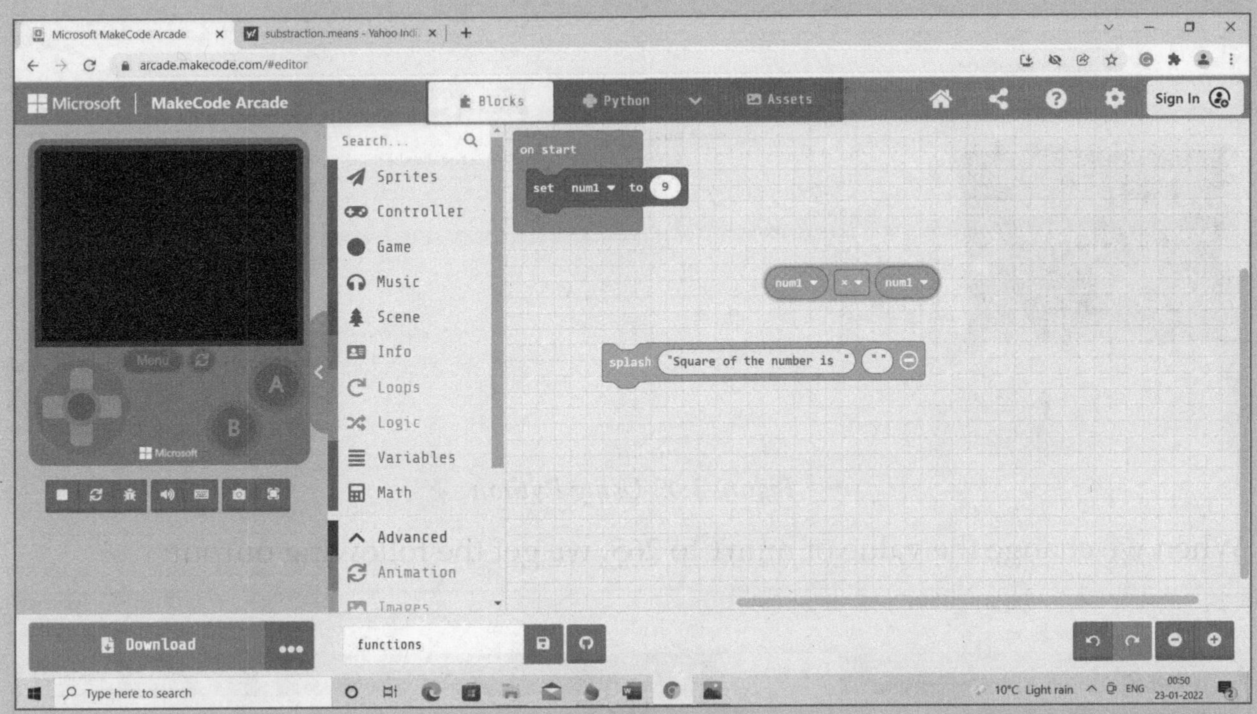

Figure 3.41

Step 7: on clicking the play button, the final output is obtained, as shown here.

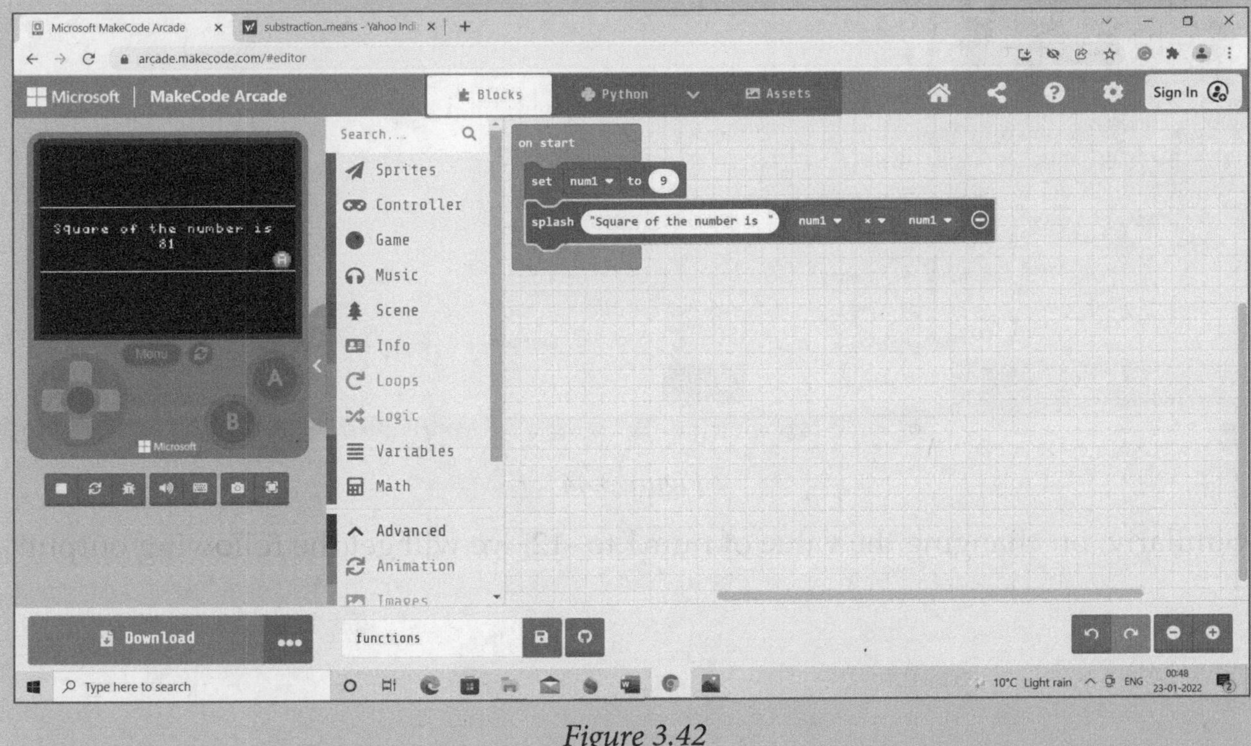

Figure 3.42

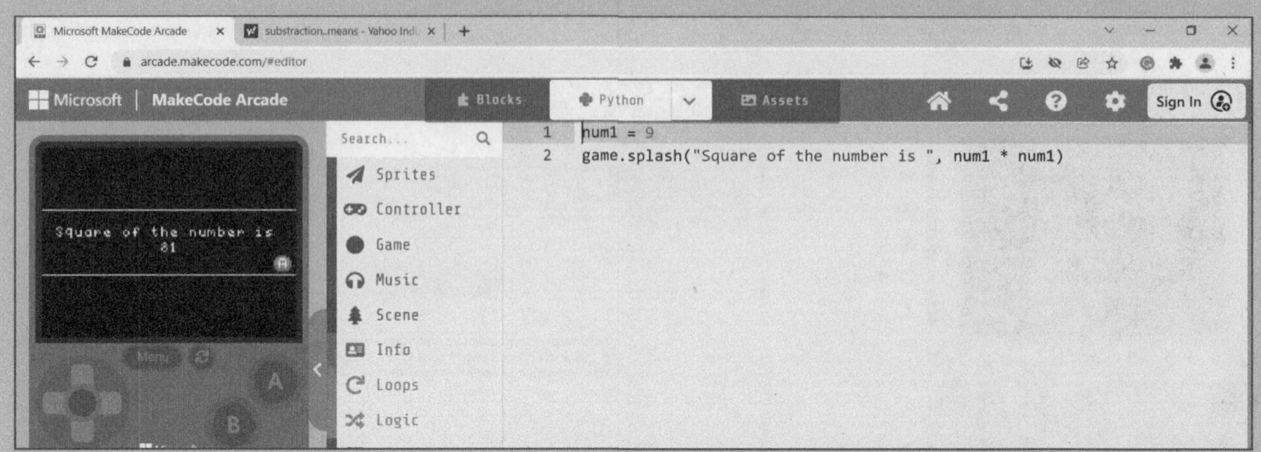

Figure 3.43 Using Python

When we change the value of num1 to 265, we get the following output:

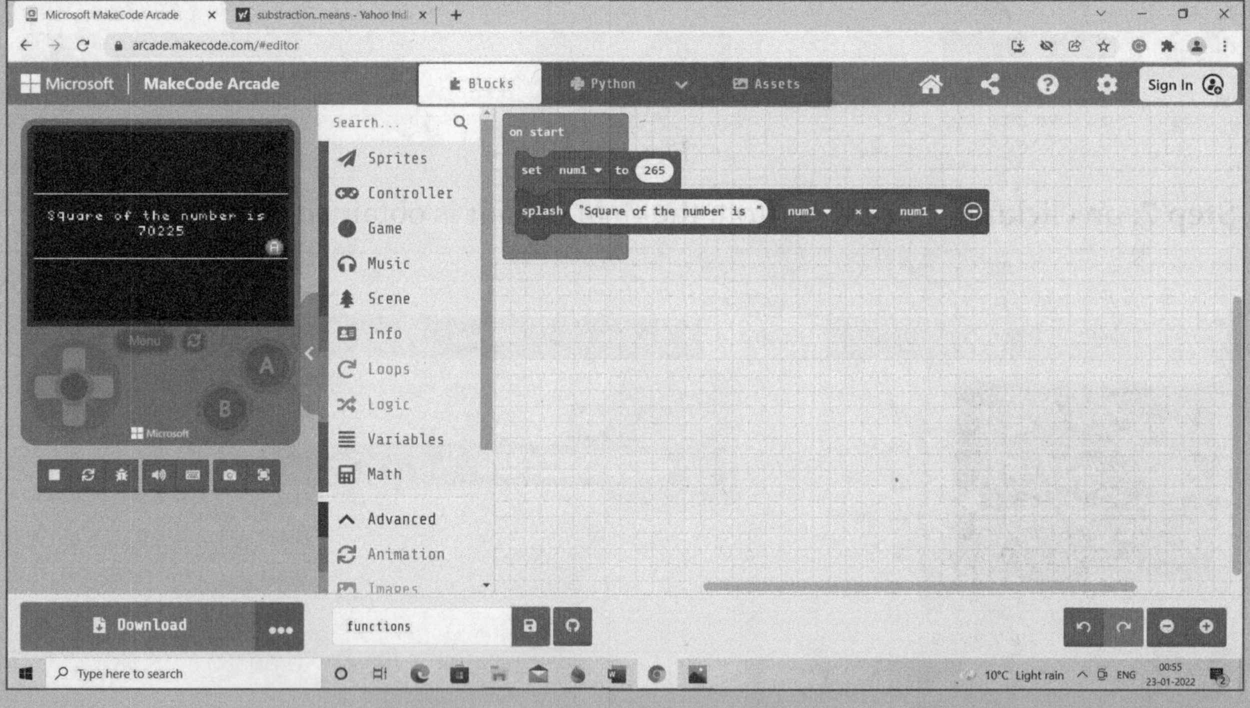

Figure 3.44

Similarly, on changing the value of num1 to -12, we will get the following output:

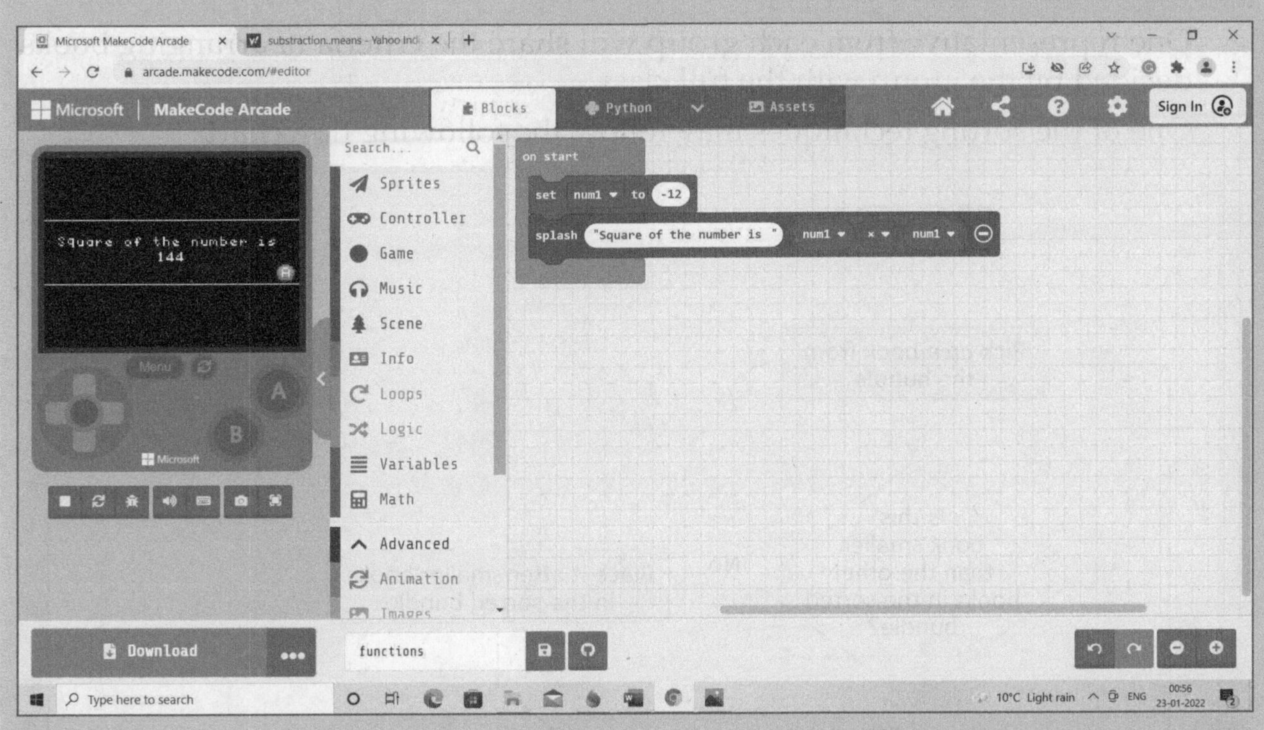

Figure 3.45

Activity 3.3

- Participate in the group activity on "**Arranging the Books.**"
- Divide the class into small groups (4-6 students in a group) without gender bias.
- In this activity, each group of students will learn about the concept of "Sorting" in programming.
- Each group will be given a mixture of various books (10-20) to arrange them properly.
- The arrangement of books can be made in many ways, like:
  - Arranging the books according to their heights (from smallest to tallest).
  - Arranging the books alphabetically (titles of books).
  - Arranging the books categorical (Hindi (Novels/poems/Drama/Travel…) /English (Novels/poems/Drama/Travel…) / Science (Physics/Chemisrty/ Biology/Astronomy…)/ Maths/ History/GK/..etc)
  - Arranging the books as the frequency of their uses. And so on…
- The group will discuss and arrange the books as per the criteria selected after the group discussion.

- One representative from each group will share the criteria of arranging books decided by the group with the full class.

One of the sorting techniques may follow the following flowchart:

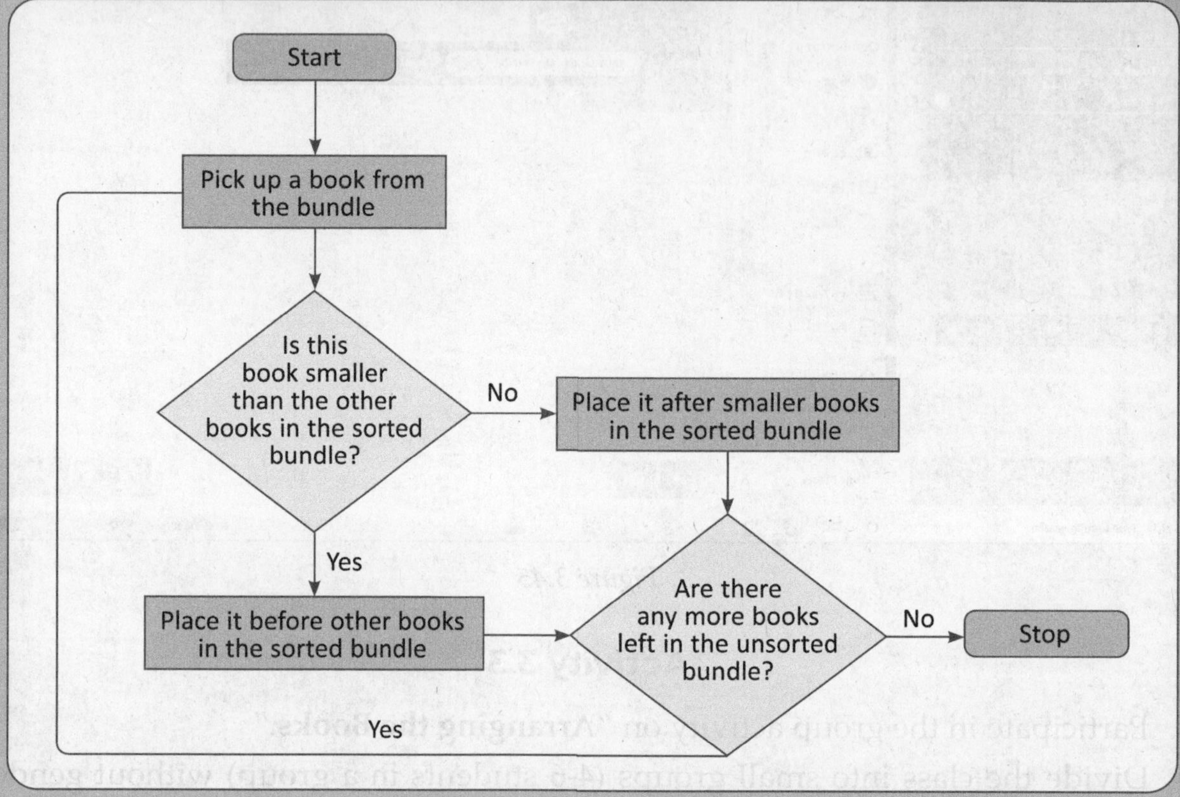

Figure 3.46

3.6 SORTING IN PROGRAMMING

We understand that arranging the data in ascending or descending order is known as Sorting. Sorting is very important in our practical life. The best example of Sorting can be phone numbers in the phone directory/our phones. If the directory is not maintained in alphabetical order, it will be difficult to search any number effectively. Sorting is a classic problem of reordering items (that can be compared, e.g., integers, strings, floating-point numbers, etc.) of an array (or a list) in a certain order (increasing, non-decreasing).

The different ways and methods used for arranging items are called "Sorting" in programming. In Sorting, we take a jumbled set of objects and arrange them in some kind of order. Thus, Sorting is a term used to describe the process of organising data in a particular order to allow for information to be found easier.

For Sorting, we need to know how to compare two items. Hence, we will ask questions like Which book is taller/shorter?

3.7 ADVANTAGES OF SORTING

There are many clever sorting algorithms that computers use. They help you sort different kinds of items very quickly. Sorting is helpful because:

Sorting a collection helps you answer questions like "which is the tallest/ smallest/ fastest item in this collection?"

Arranging things in order can make other algorithms work better.

3.8 TYPES OF SORTING

A large number of sorting techniques/methods based on data structures are used. However, these can be divided into basic sorting techniques, which may be thereafter combined and enhanced to make more complex sorting techniques.

The basic sorting techniques are as follows:

- Bubble sort,
- Insertion sort,
- Selection sort,
- Bucket sort,
- Heapsort,
- Quicksort,
- Radix sort, etc.

Factz Funda

Quicksort is considered as one of the fastest sorting algorithms and the best sorting algorithm.

The best sorting technique can be decided by a variety of factors like the size of data to be sorted, machine capabilities, memory requirements, etc.

Activity 3.4

- Participate in the individual activity on "**Calculating the area of a circle**".
- You have to calculate the area of a circle in MakeCode using the above steps. You should try this exercise using the Arcade MakeCode editor, which can be found by clicking the website: https://arcade.makecode.com/.
- Create new project by clicking on the green box labelled as "New project." In the prompted dialog box, write the name of the project.
- Click on 'Create' button for creating the project.

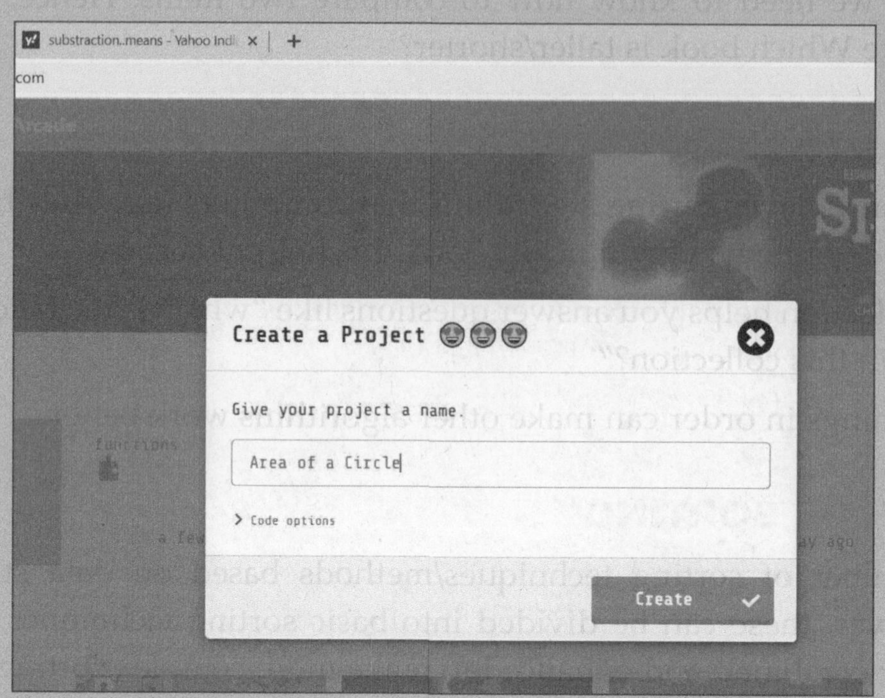

Figure 3.47

- On clicking create button, we will get the following screen:

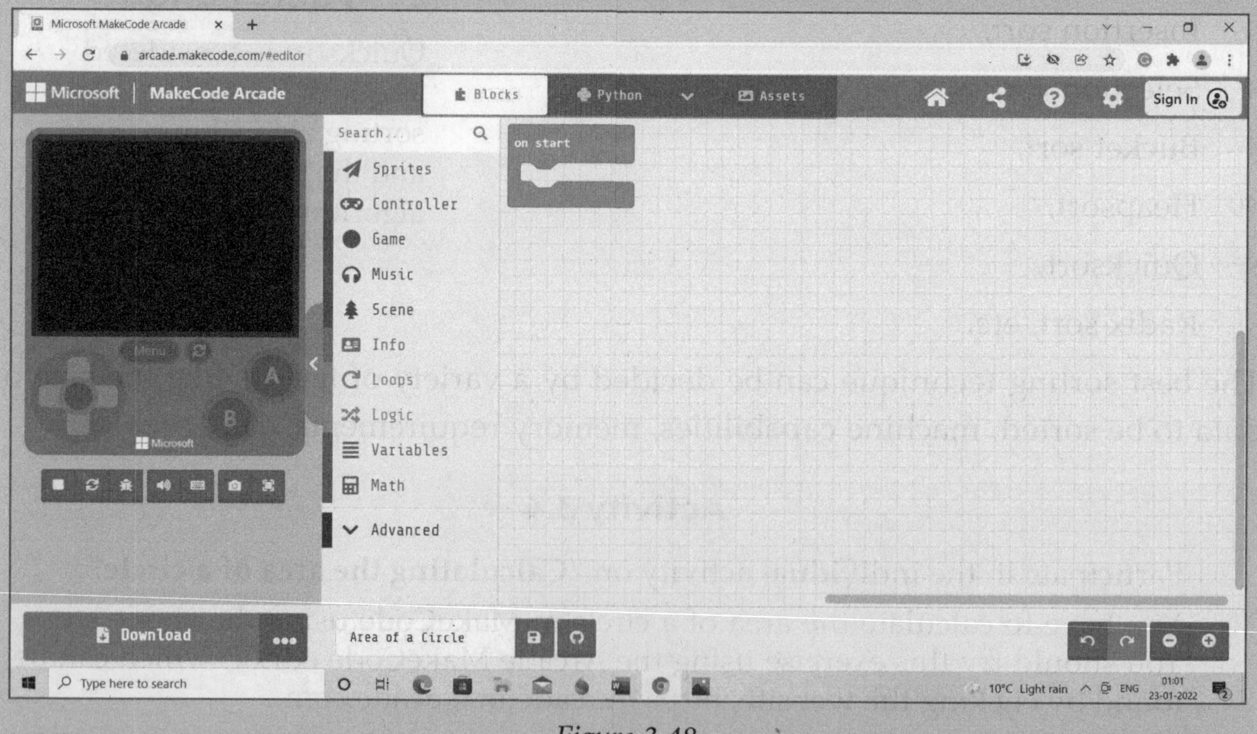

Figure 3.48

Step 1: Click variable block from the toolbox and select "Make a variable."

Step 2: Create a new variable and name it "Radius."

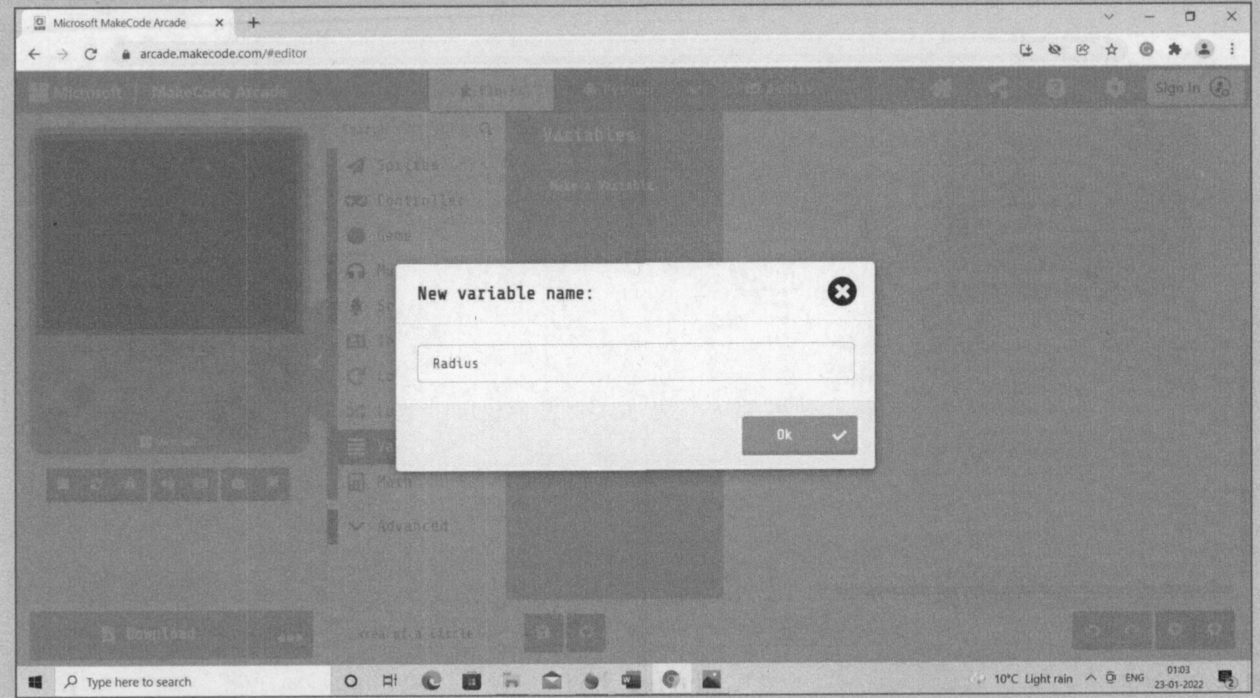

Figure 3.49

Step 3: From the 'variables' menu, select the "Set Radius to" block.

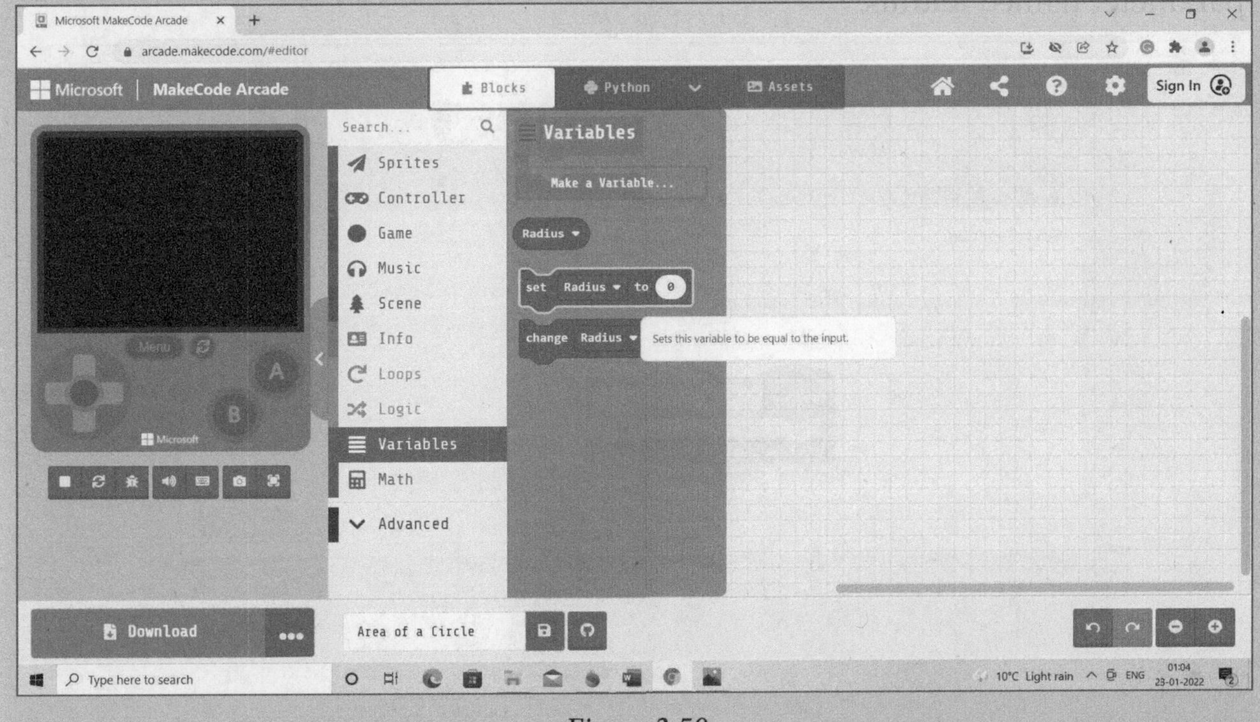

Figure 3.50

Step 4: Place the "set Radius to" block inside the "On start" block and change the value to '14'.

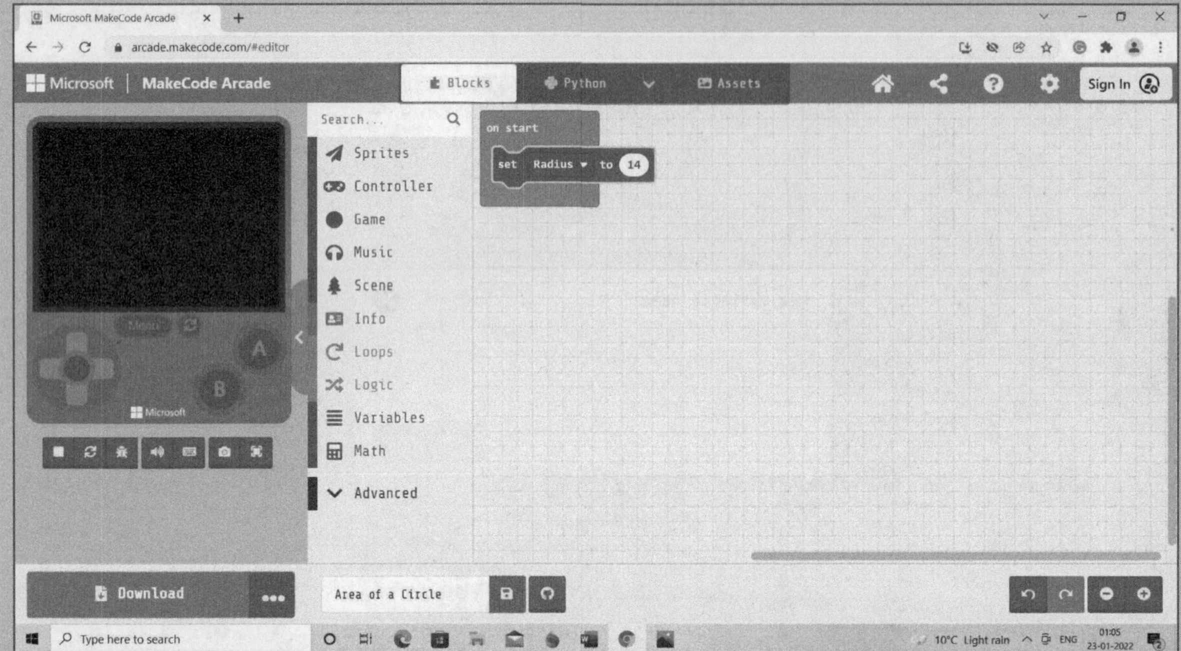

Figure 3.51

Step 5: Go to block type 'Functions' and click on "make a function."

Step 6: Create a function with the name "AreaOfCircle" having one numerical parameter named Radius.

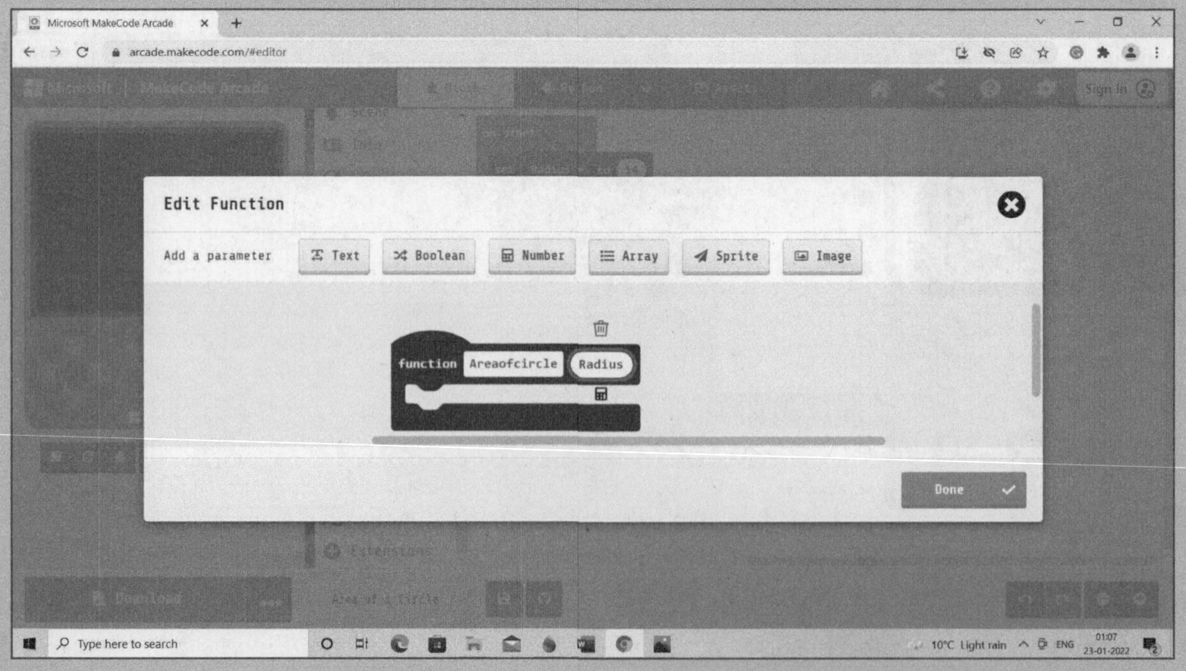

Figure 3.52

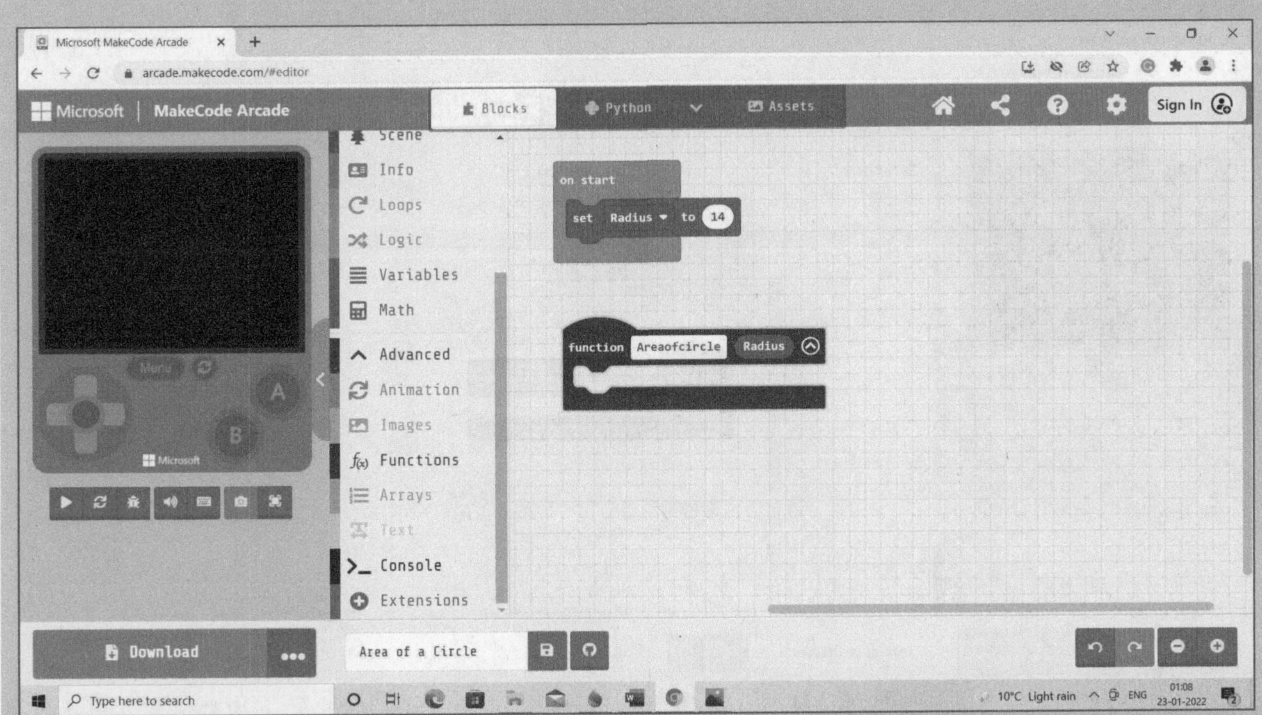

Figure 3.53

Step 7: Click "splash" from the 'Game' toolbox to the play area. Write "Area is" and add one more area by clicking + sign.

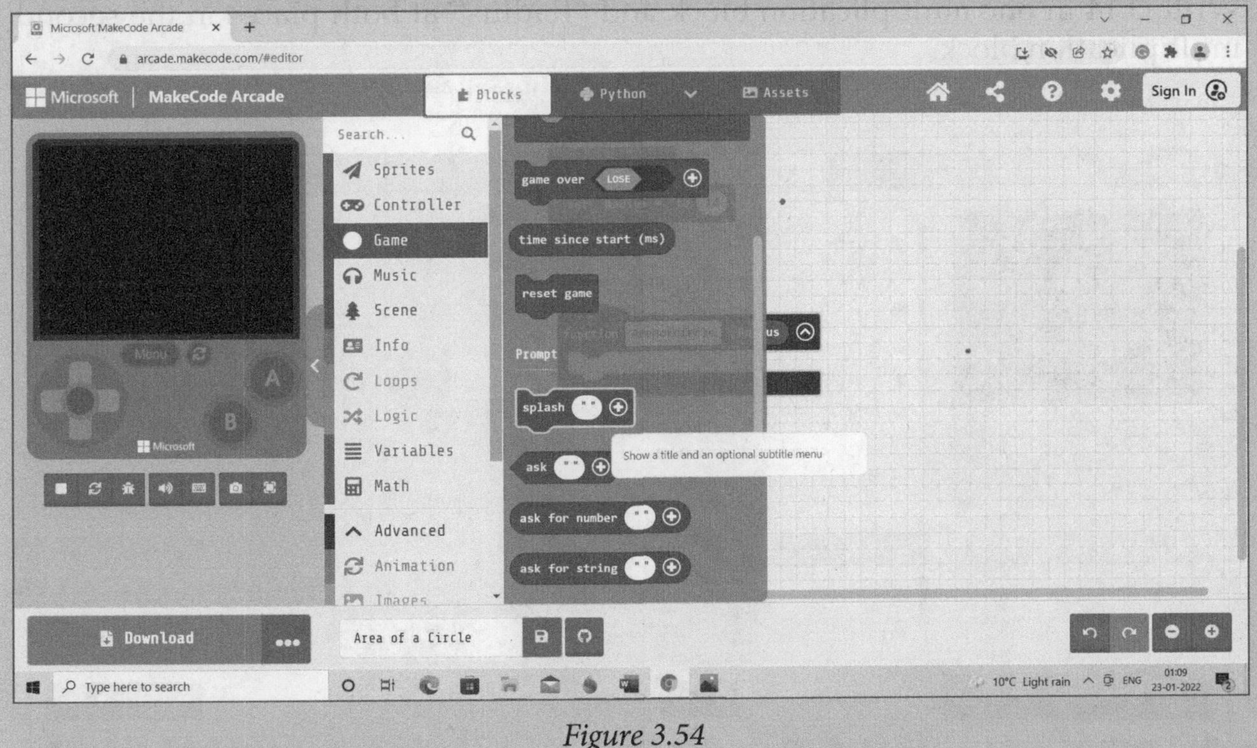

Figure 3.54

Figure 3.55

Step 8: Click on the Math block type and select the instance of the highlighted ("multiplication"). We need to do this twice to create two multiplication blocks. Write 3.14 in one multiplication block and "Radius" at both places in the second multiplication block.

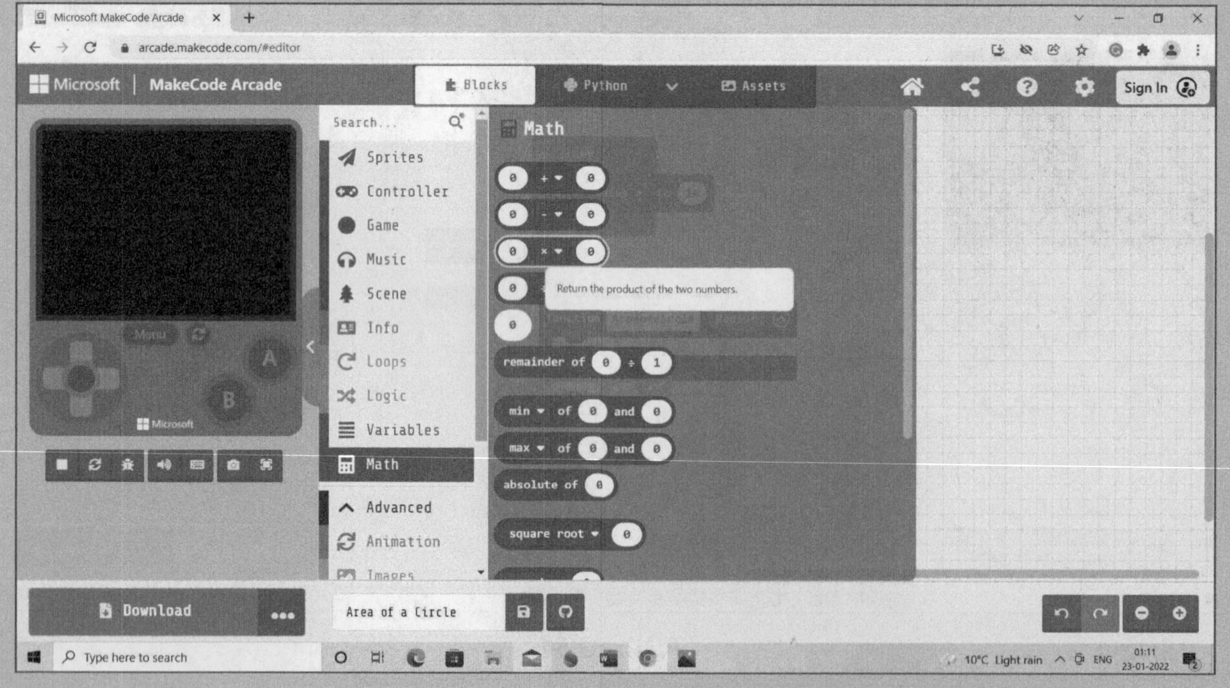

Figure 3.56

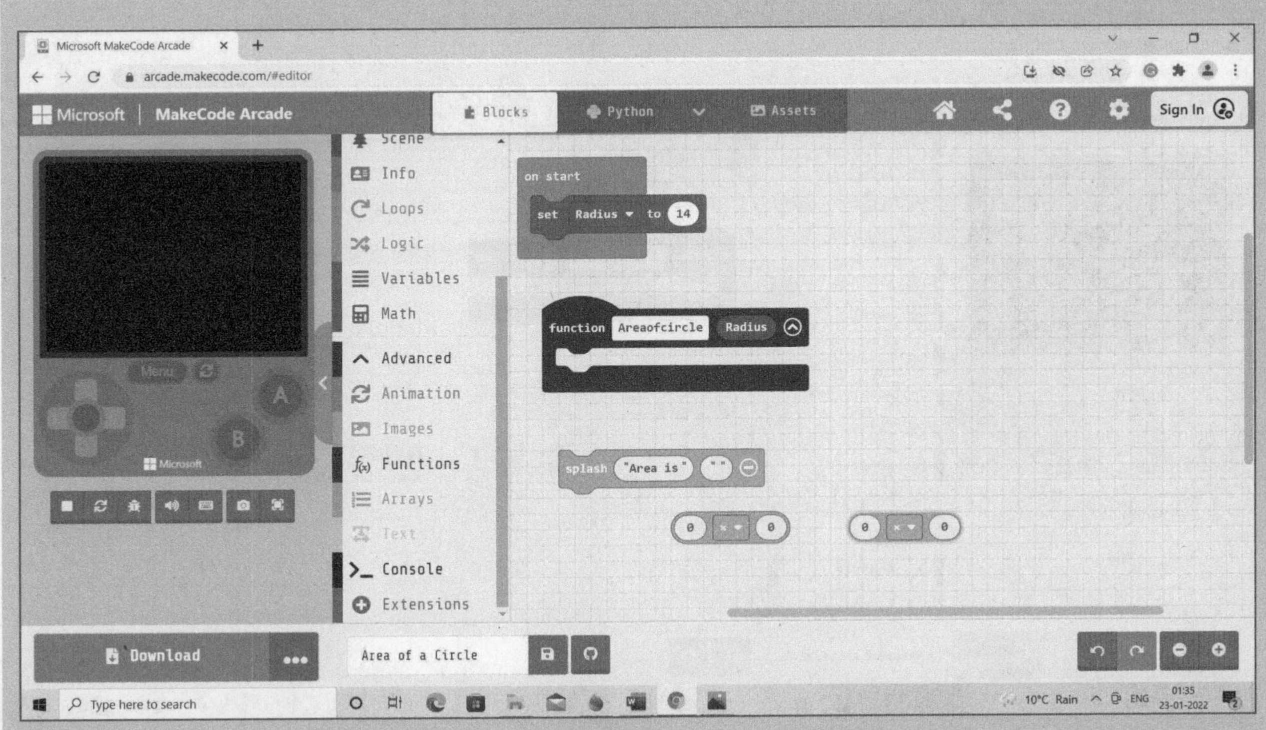

Figure 3.57

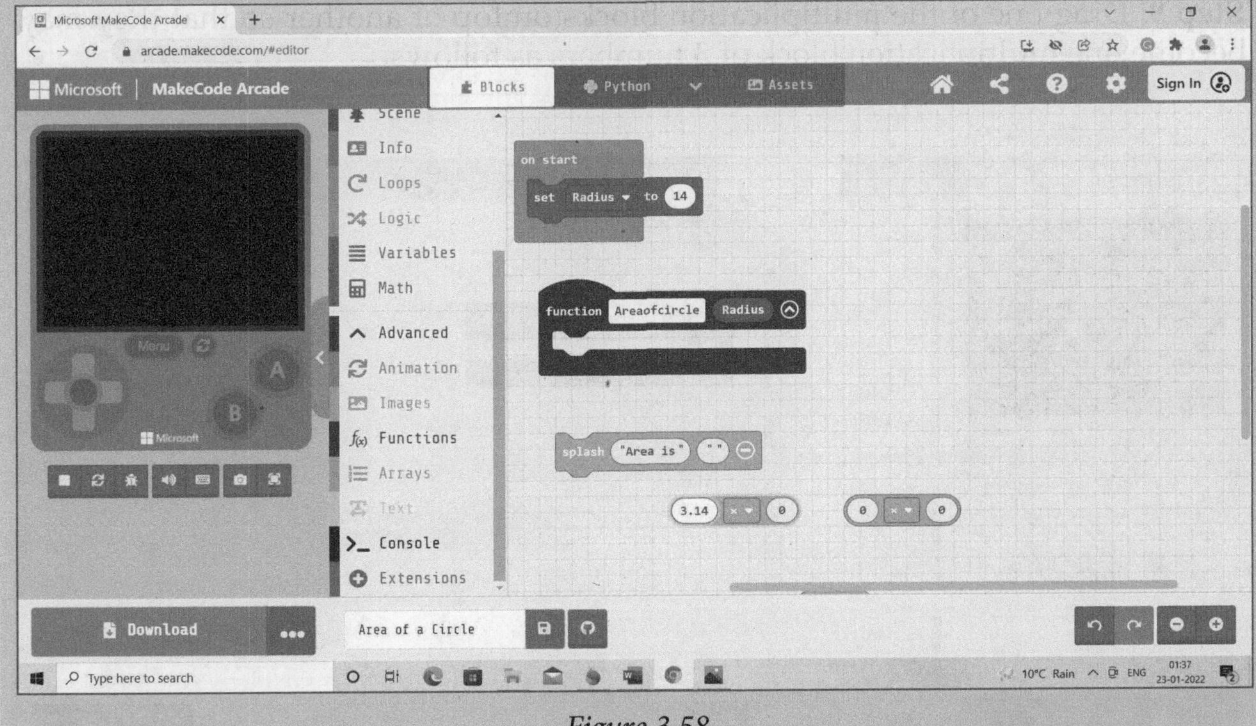

Figure 3.58

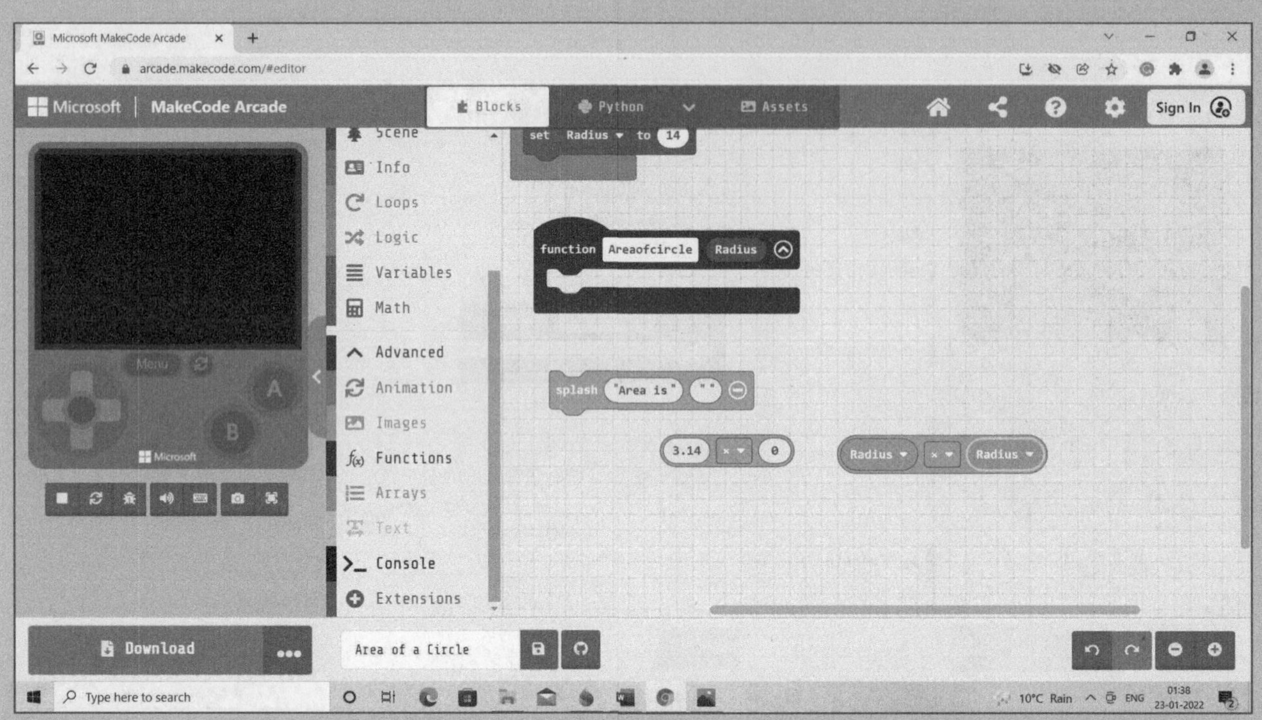

Figure 3.59

Step 9: Drag one of the multiplication blocks on top of another so that they may become one multiplication block of 3 numbers as follows.

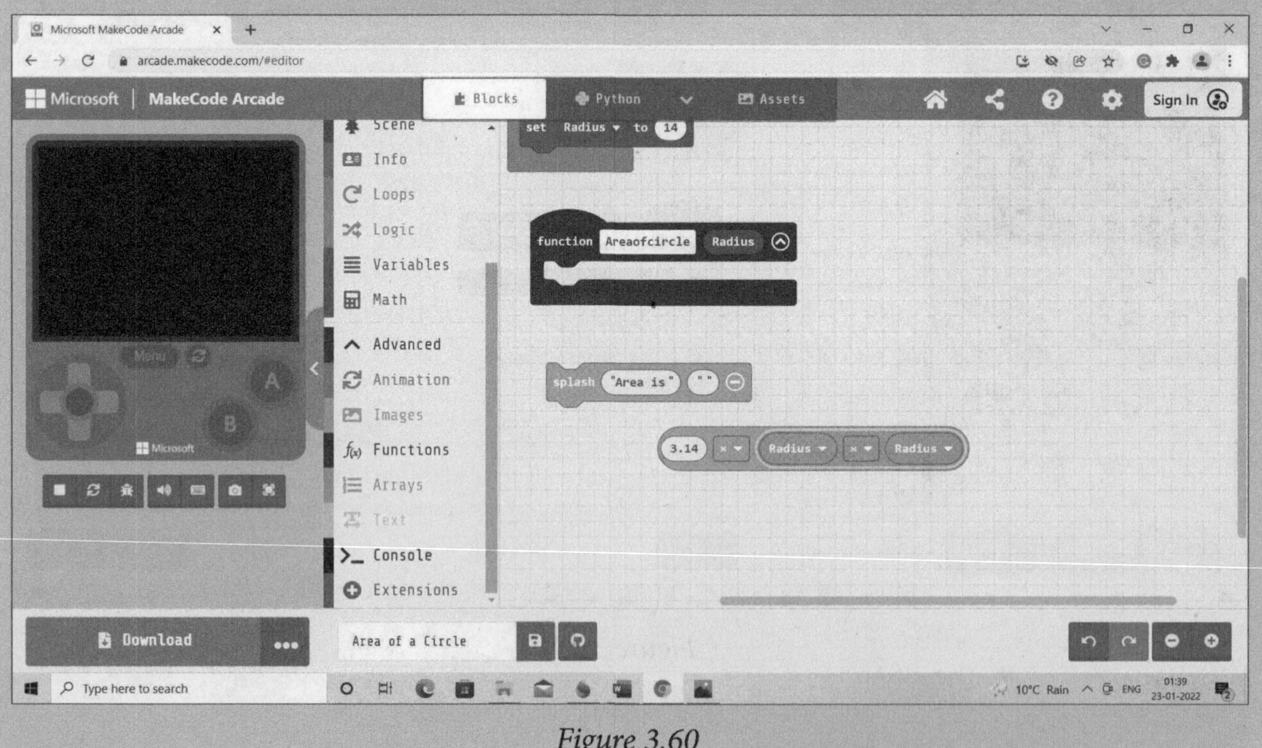

Figure 3.60

Step 10: Drag the multiplication block of 3 numbers to the "splash" block and put it inside the function block "AreaOfCircle."

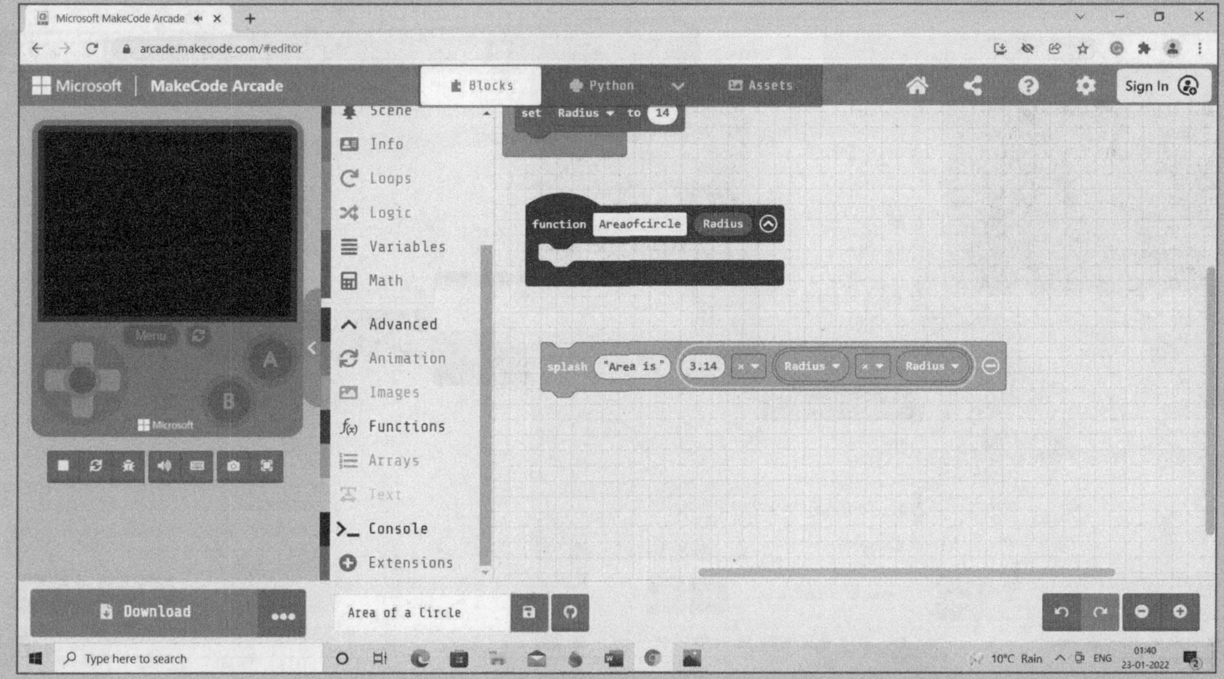

Figure 3.61

Step 11: Inside the function "AreaOfCircle," inside the "set Area to" block, set the first number as 3.14 and the second and the third number to the parameter radius.

Figure 3.62

Step 12: Open the function block type and select the "call AreaOfCircle" block.

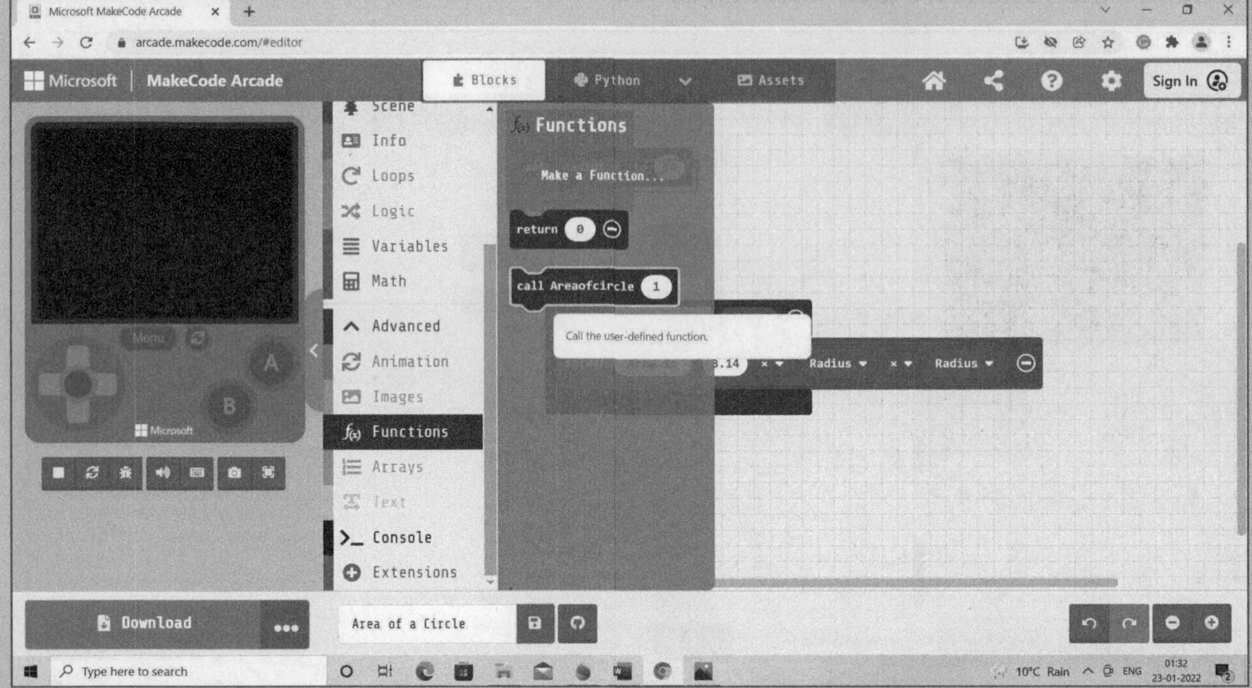

Figure 3.63

Step 13: drag the "call AreaOfCircle" block into the "on start" block below the "set Radius to" block.

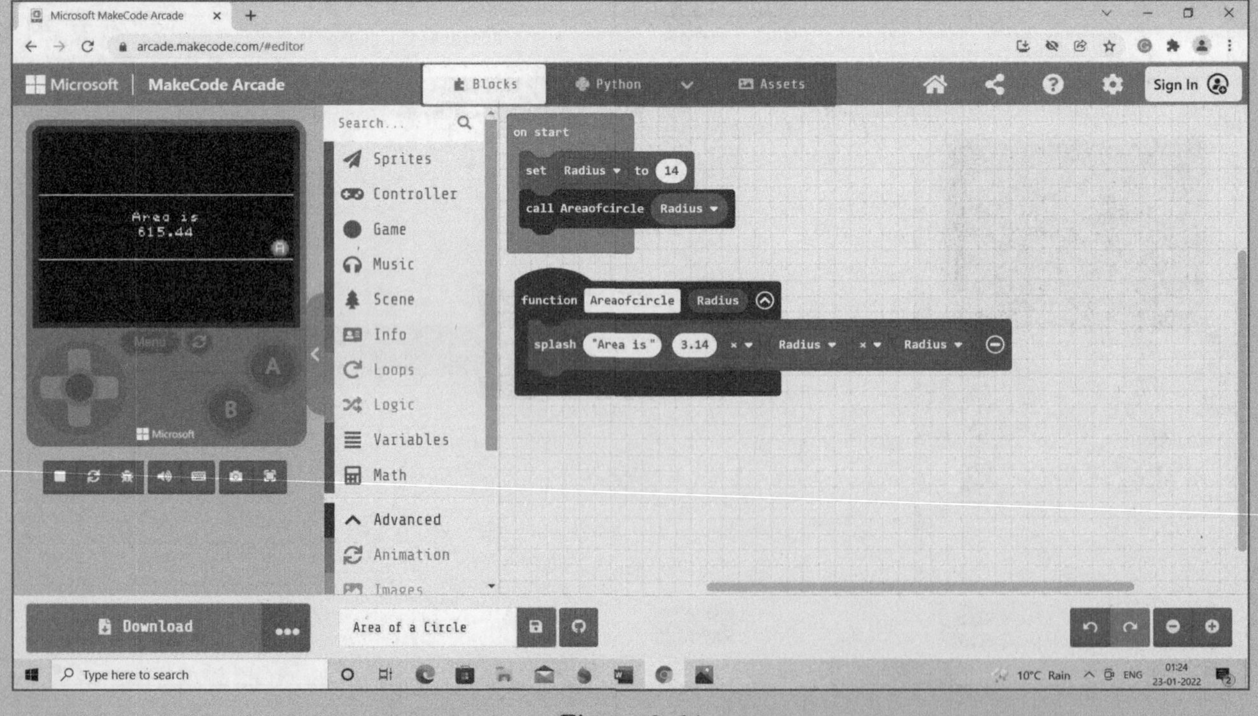

Figure 3.64

Step 14: We get the final output as below:

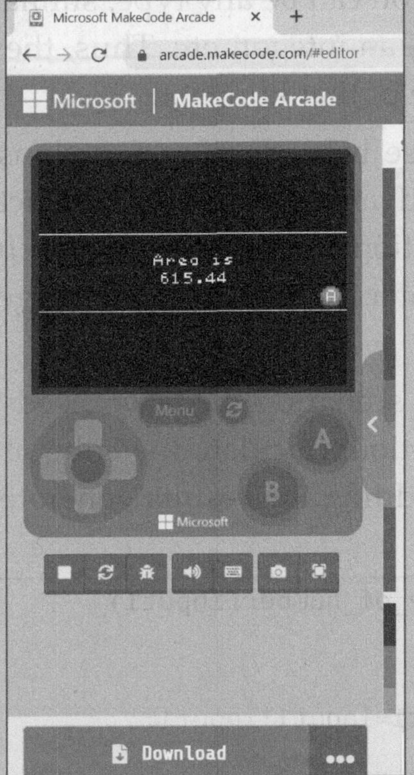

Figure 3.65

Factz Funda

The name of the value is called a parameter, while the actual value itself is called an argument. Functions always return a value.

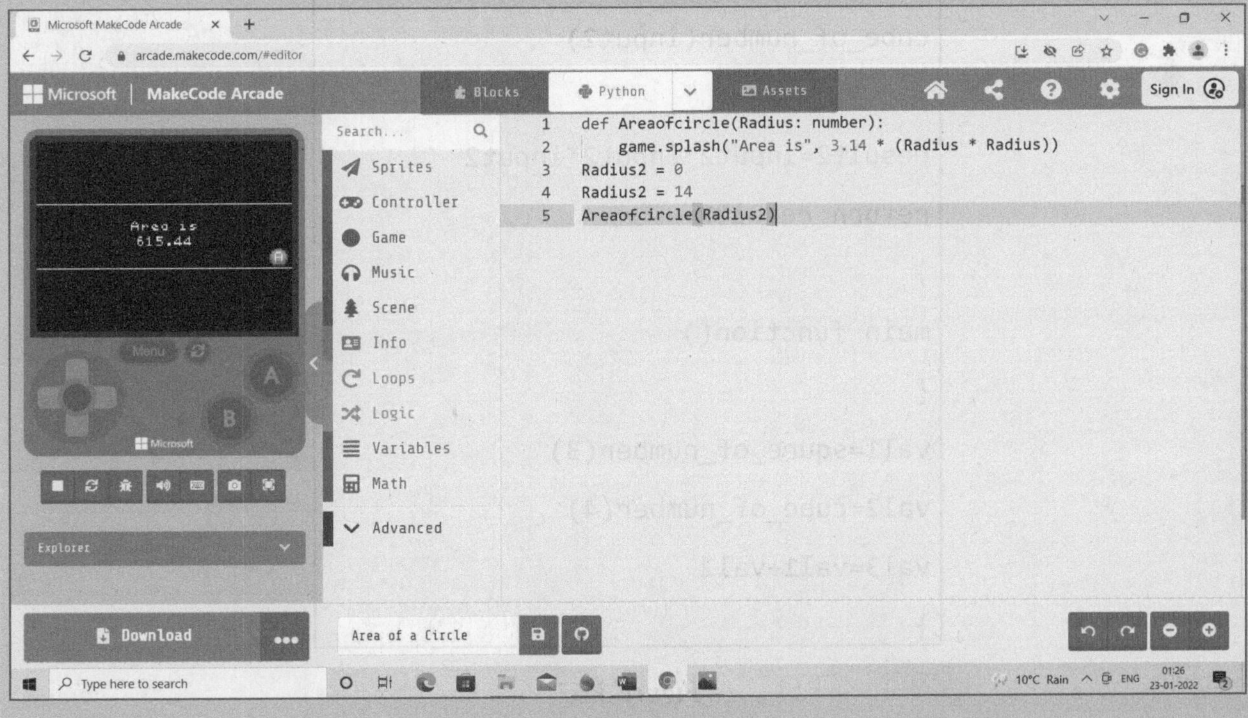

Figure 3.66 Using Python

3.9 CAN FUNCTION RETURN A VALUE?

The return value of a function can be any type, similar to the type of a variable. It can be a character, a string, an integer, etc. Thus, the return type of a function is the type of the return value of that Function.

However, the main purpose behind using functions is not to allow repetitive tasks of code. Thus, the advantage of using a function in a program becomes important when an operation performed inside a function gives back a value. This value can be used later in the program to generate meaningful output/results.

As an example, consider a scenario where we need to calculate the square of a given number using a function; calculate the cube of other given number using other function; and then, adding the results generated from these two functions and display/print them.

```
square_of_number(input1)
{
result1=input1*input1
return result1
}
cube_of_number(input2)
{
result2=input2*input2*input2
return result2
}
main function()
{
val1=squre_of_number(3)
val2=cube_of_number(4)
val3=val1+val2
}
```

Figure 3.67

Now, we will understand how we can implement the above example via Arcade MakeCode editor.

Step 1: Create a new project, 'Arithmetic with Functions.'

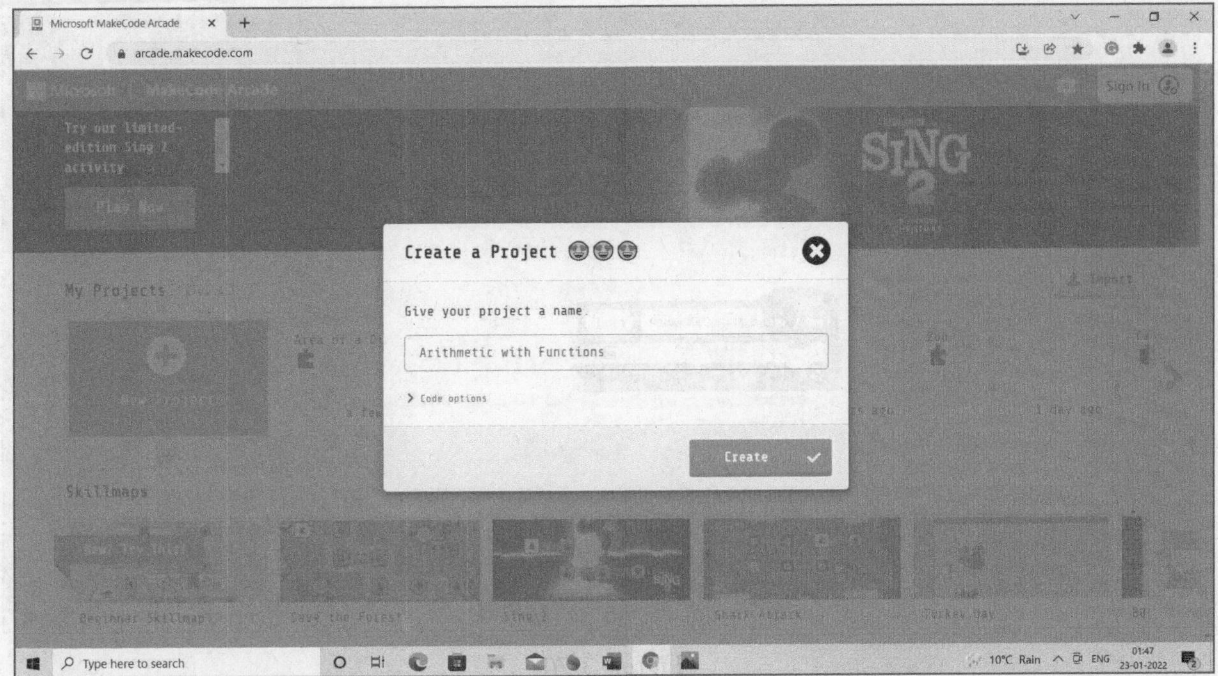

Figure 3.68

Step 2: Create three variables val1,val2 and val3.

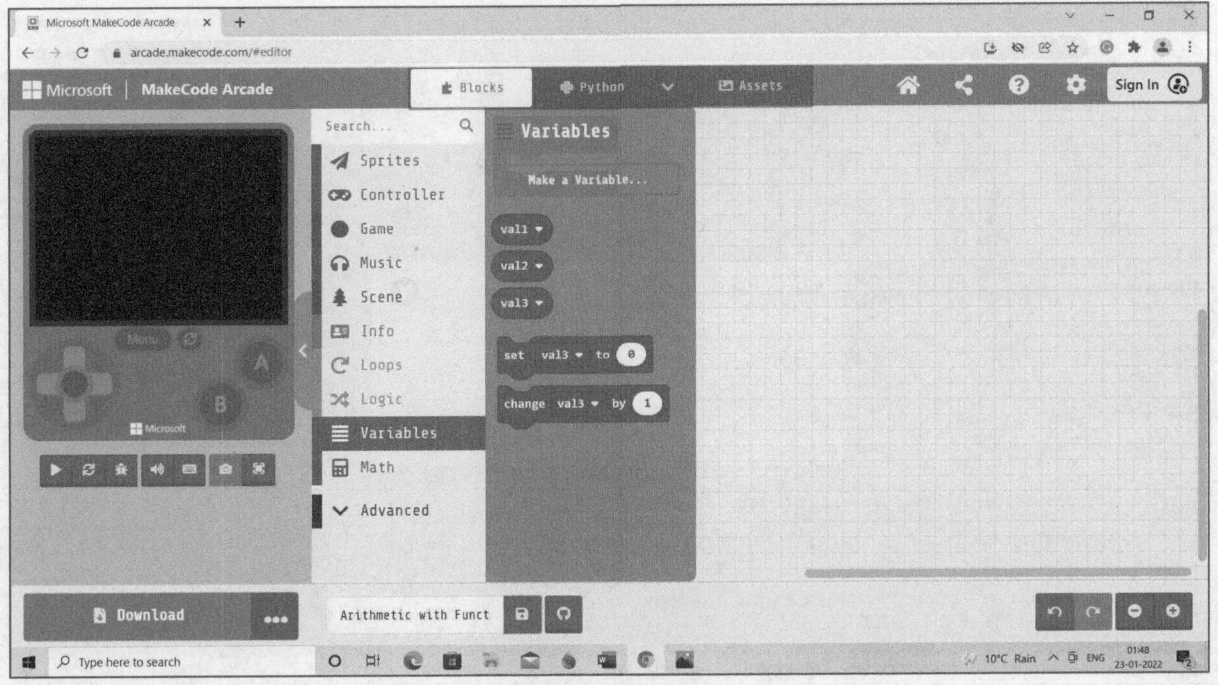

Figure 3.69

Step 3: Create a function named squareOfNumber having a numeric type parameter.

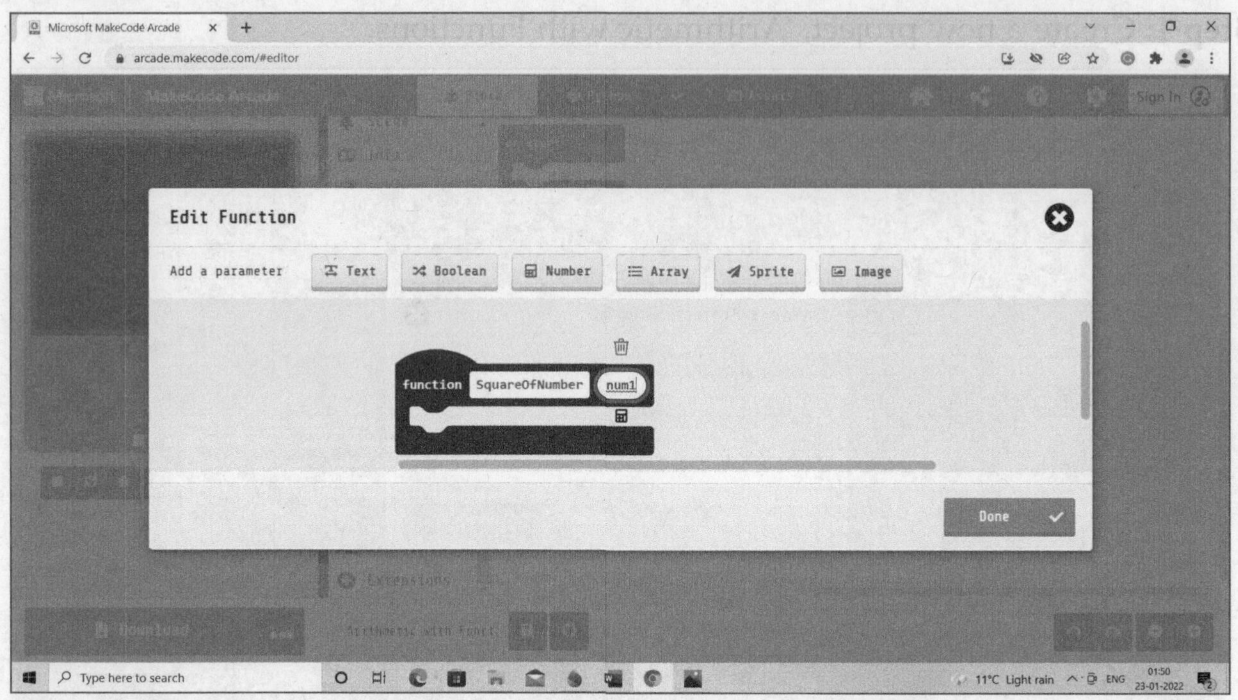

Figure 3.70

Step 4: Create a variable named square and create a block "set square to" and place them inside function squareOfNumber.

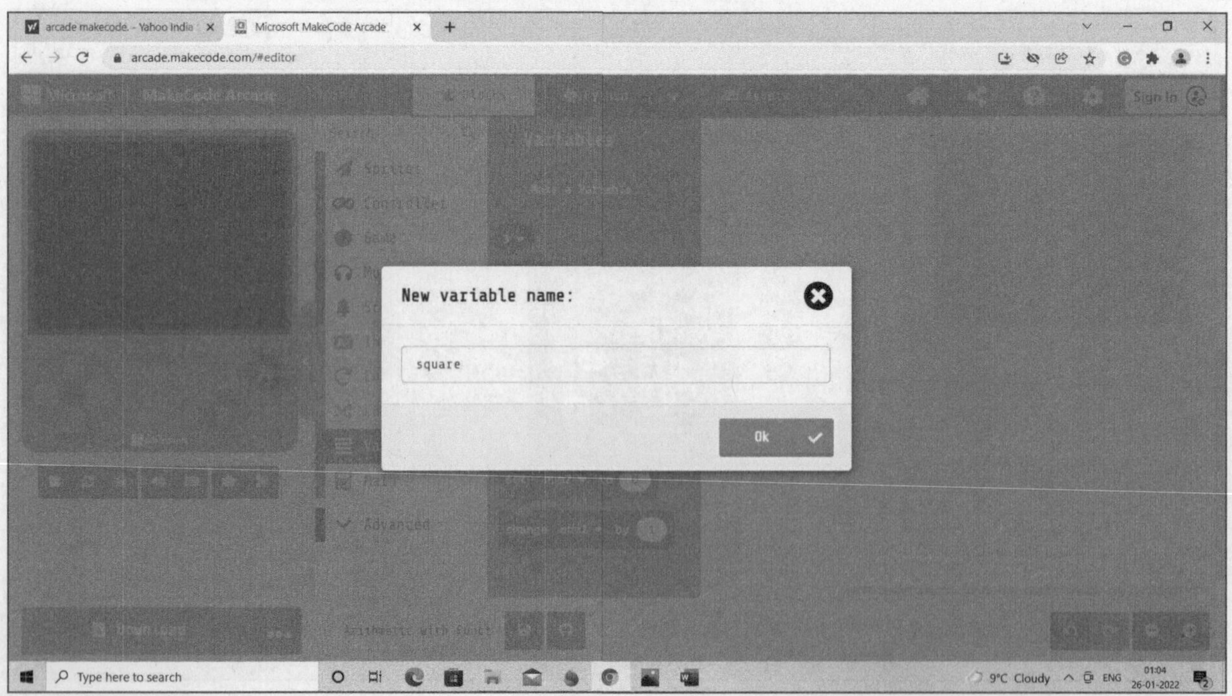

Figure 3.71

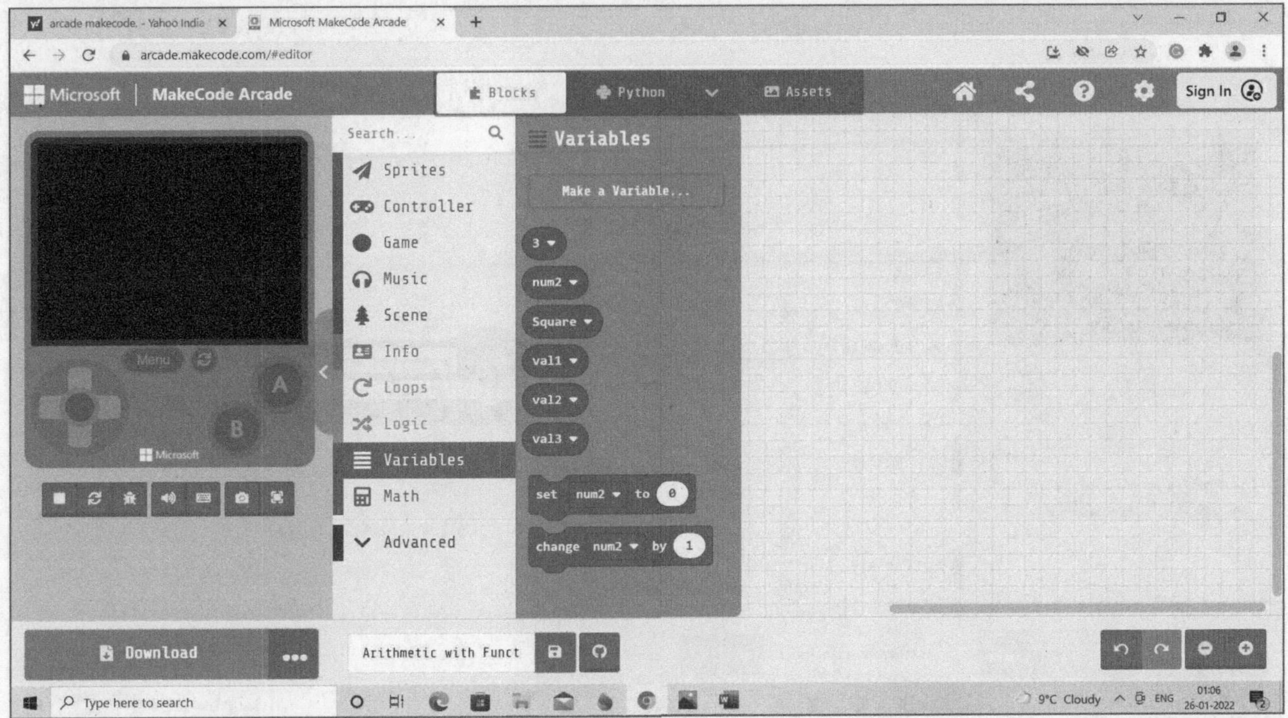

Figure 3.72

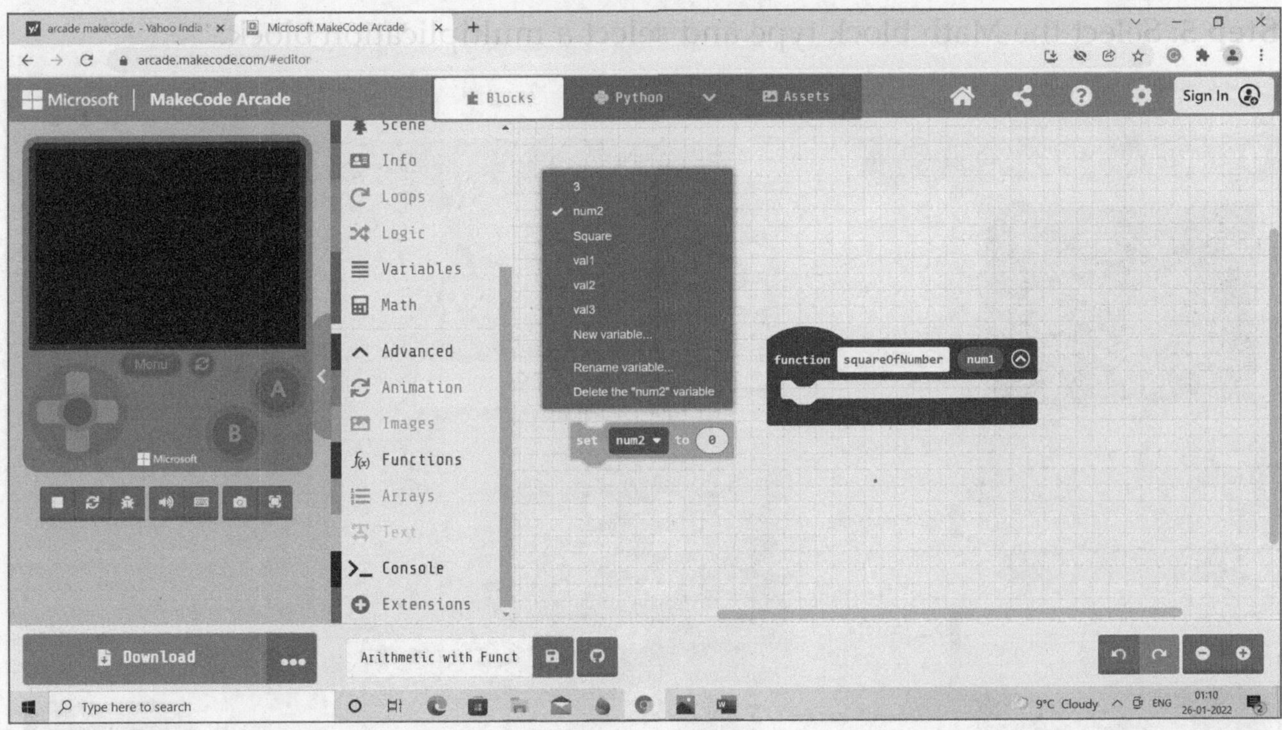

Figure 3.73

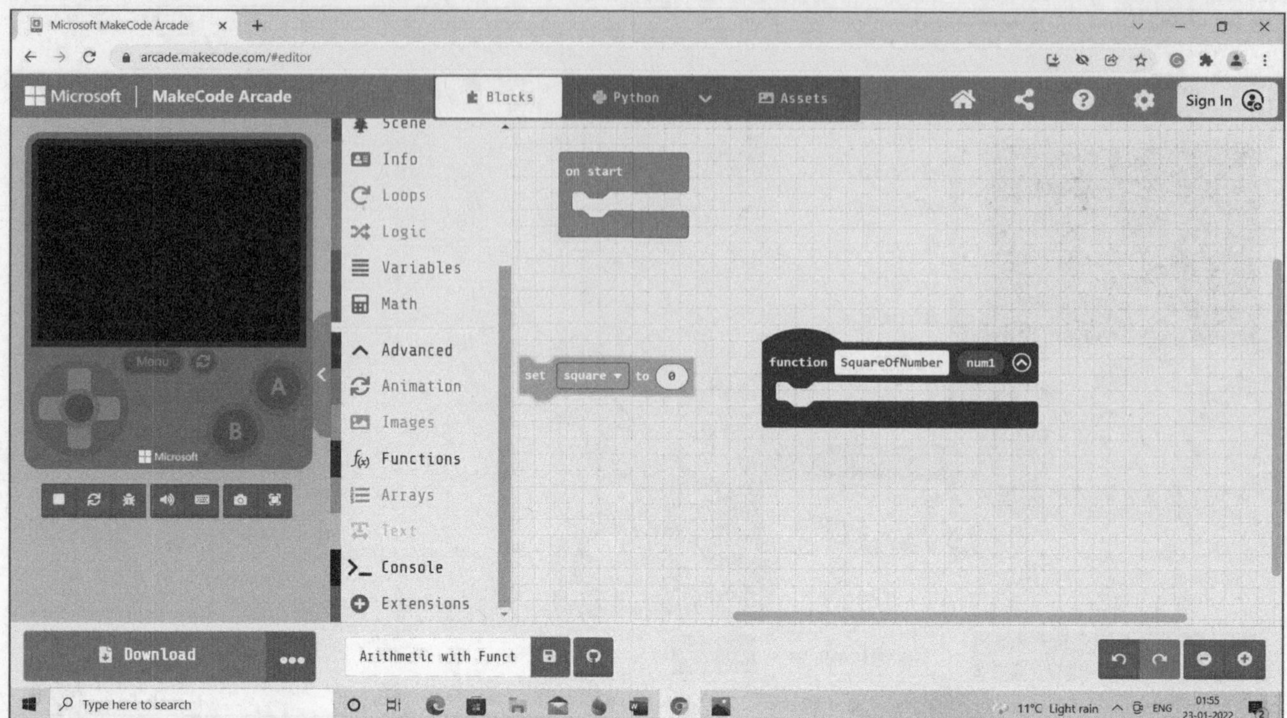

Figure 3.74

Step 5: Select the Math block type and select a multiplication block.

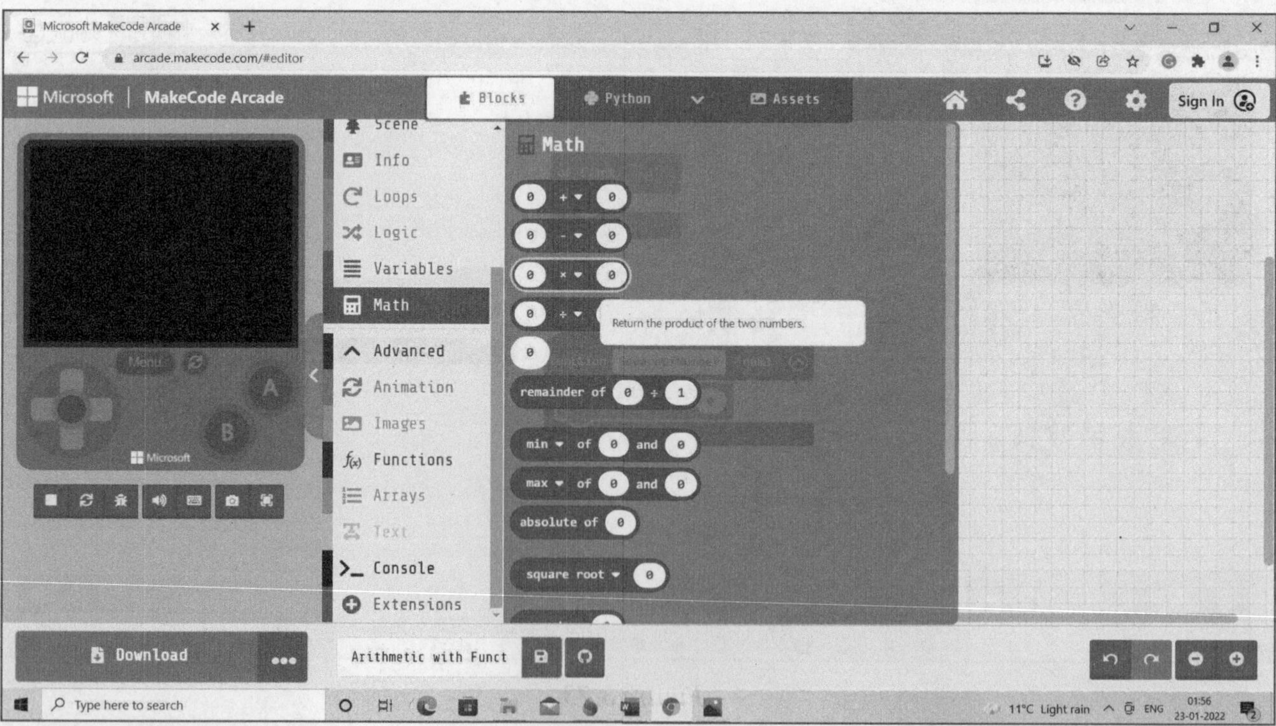

Figure 3.75

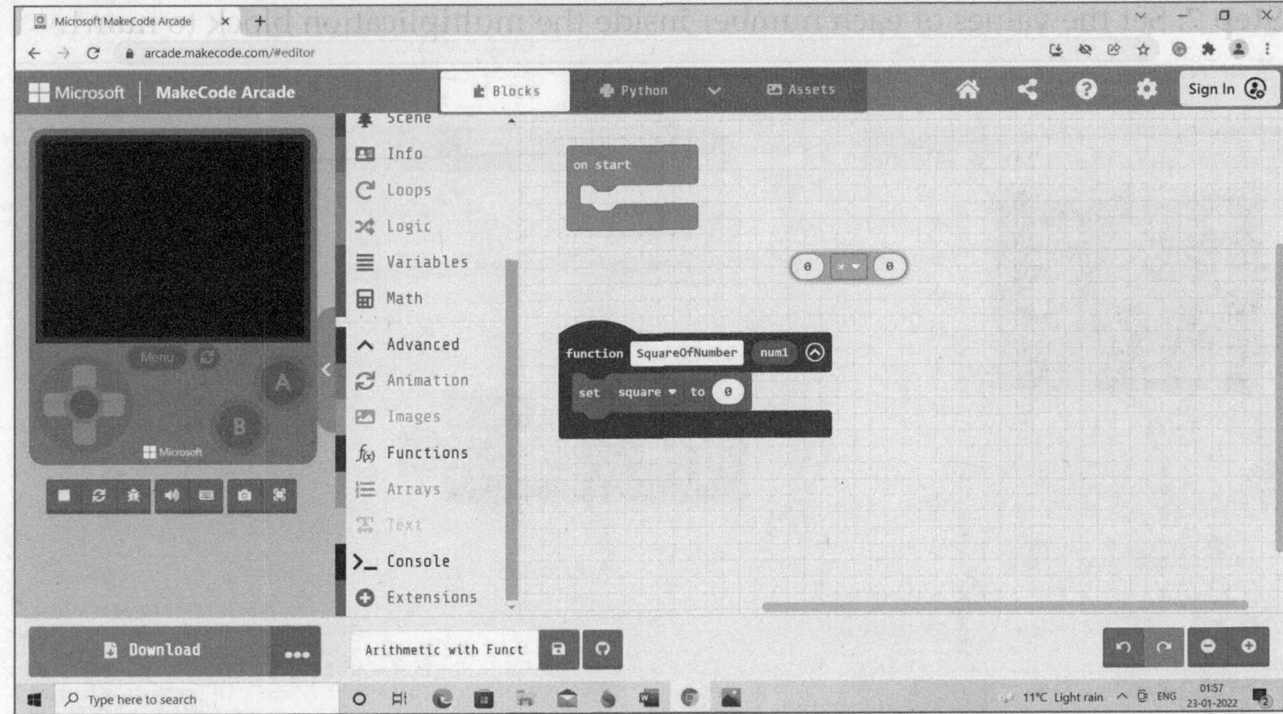

Figure 3.76

Step 6: Attach the multiplication block to the "set square to" block inside the function 'squareOfNumber.'

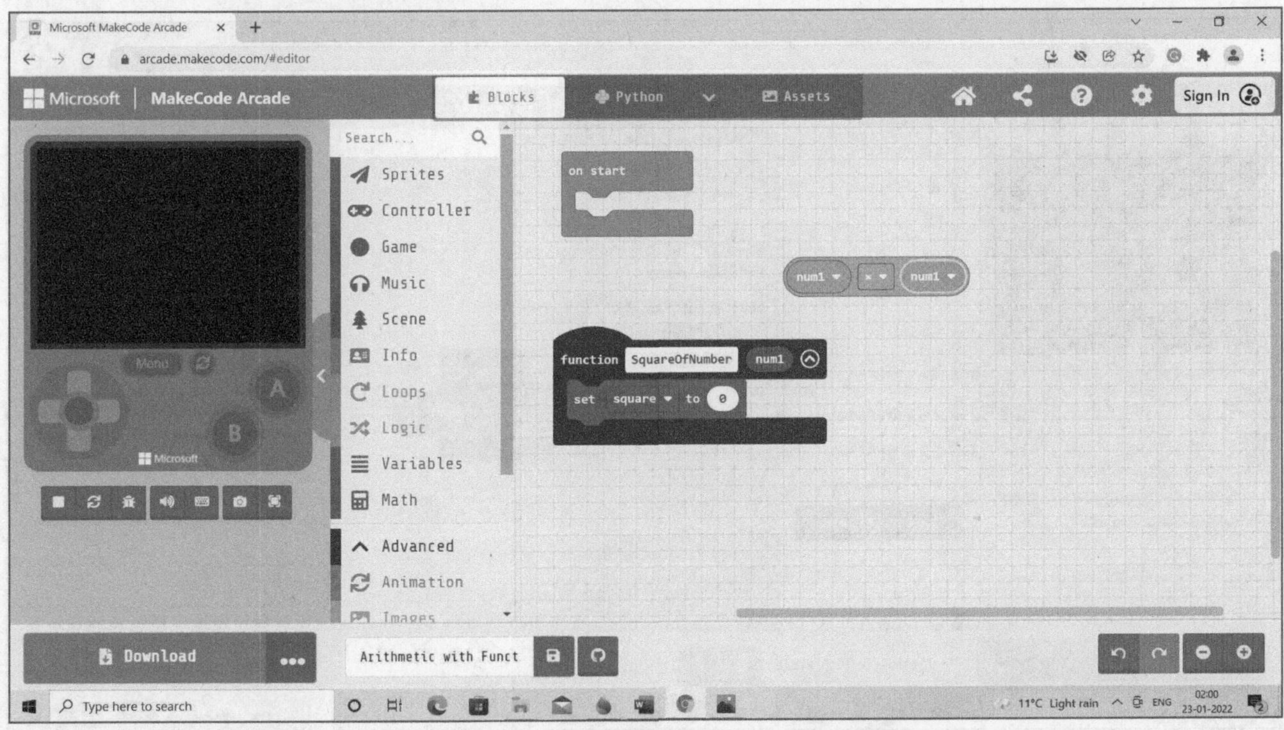

Figure 3.77

Step 7: Set the values of each number inside the multiplication block to num1.

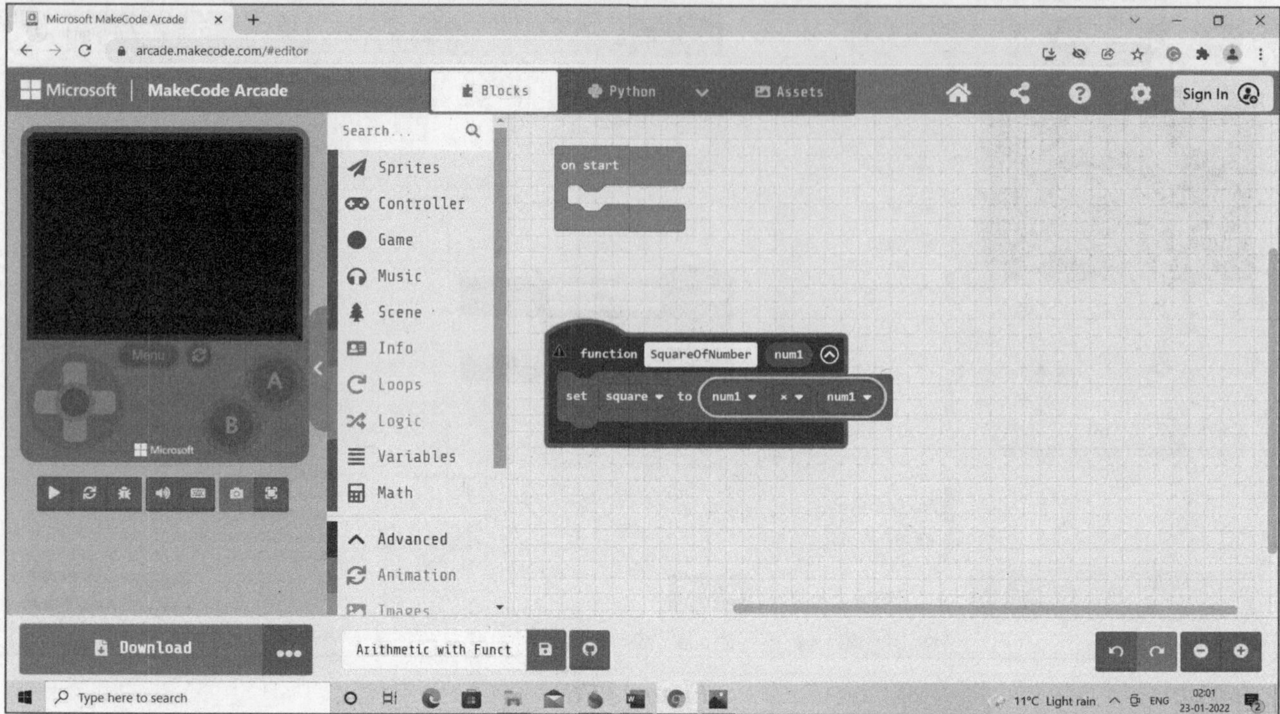

Figure 3.78

Step 8: Select block type functions and select "return" block.

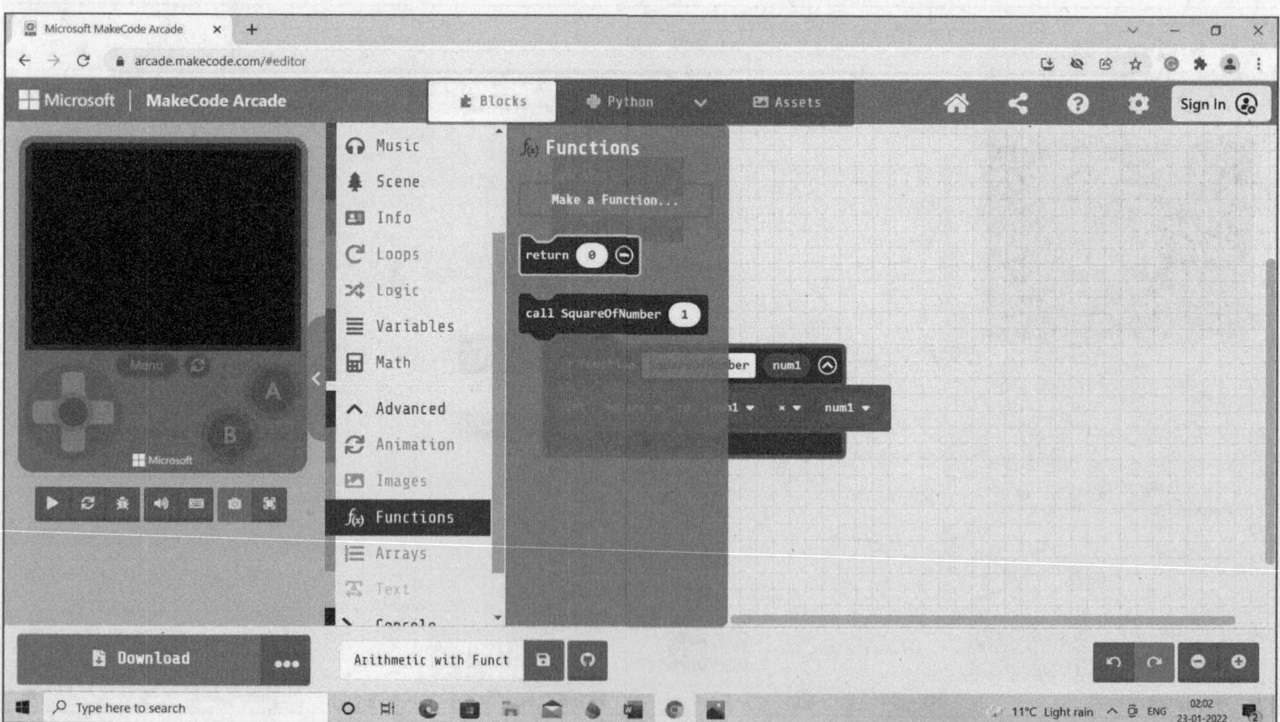

Figure 3.79

Step 9: Place the return block inside the squareOfNumber Function after the "set square to" block.

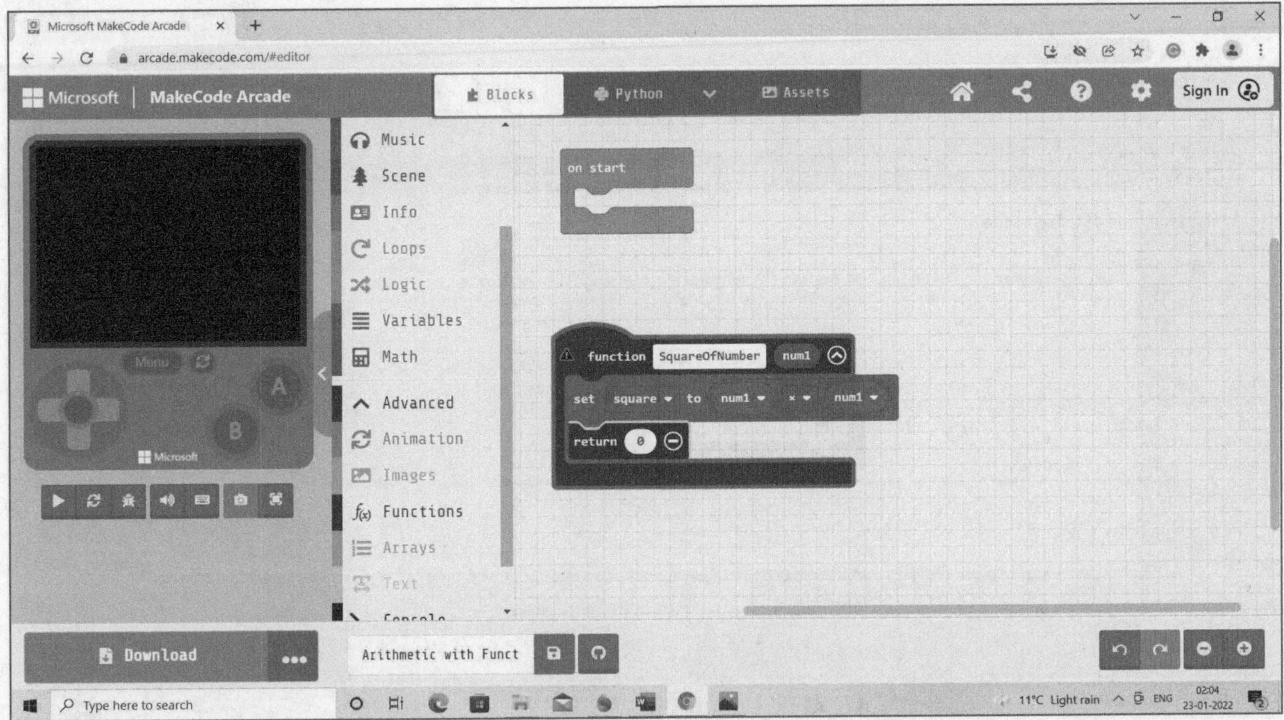

Figure 3.80

Step 10: Set value inside return block to 'square' variable.

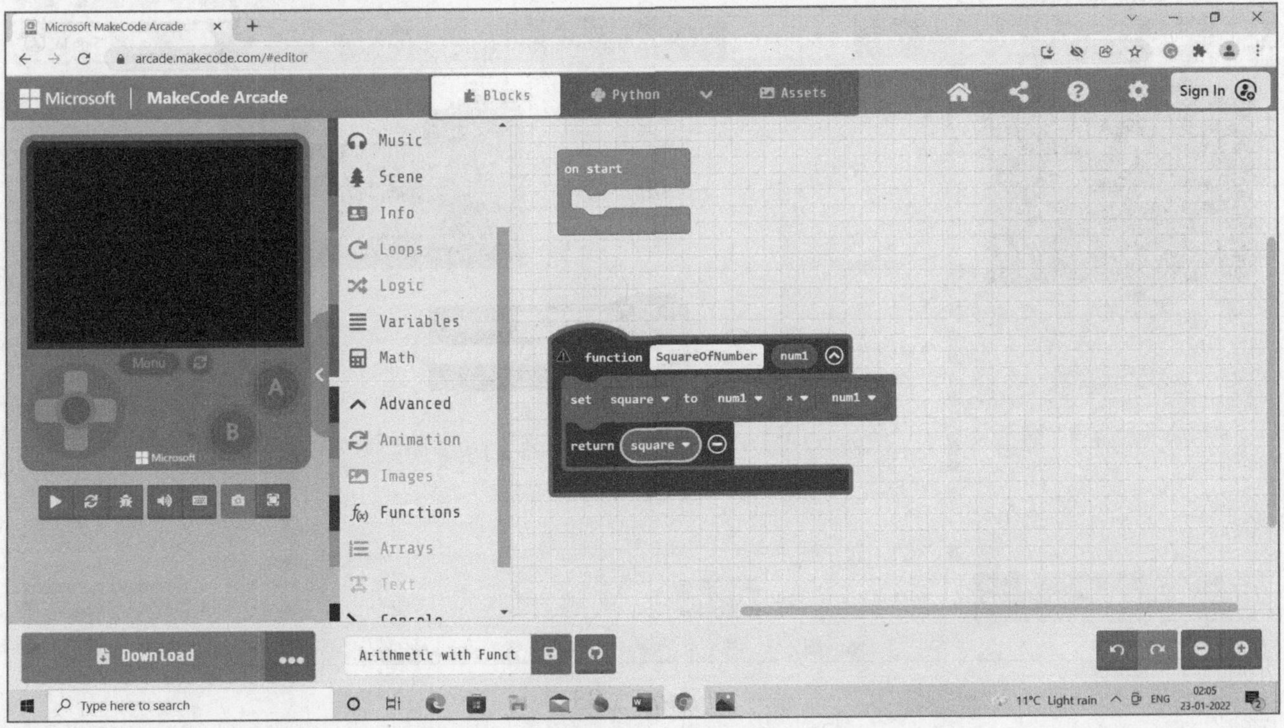

Figure 3.81

Step 11: Similarly, create a function cubeOfNumber having a numeric parameter num2.

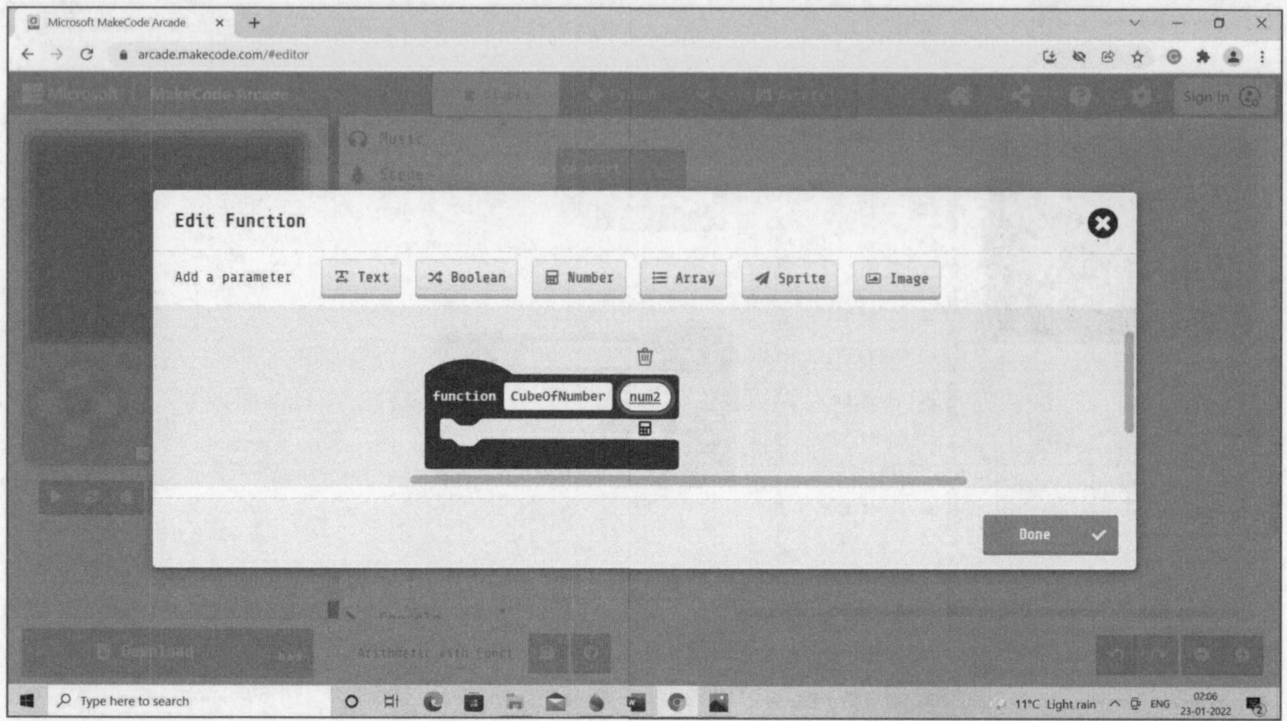

Figure 3.82

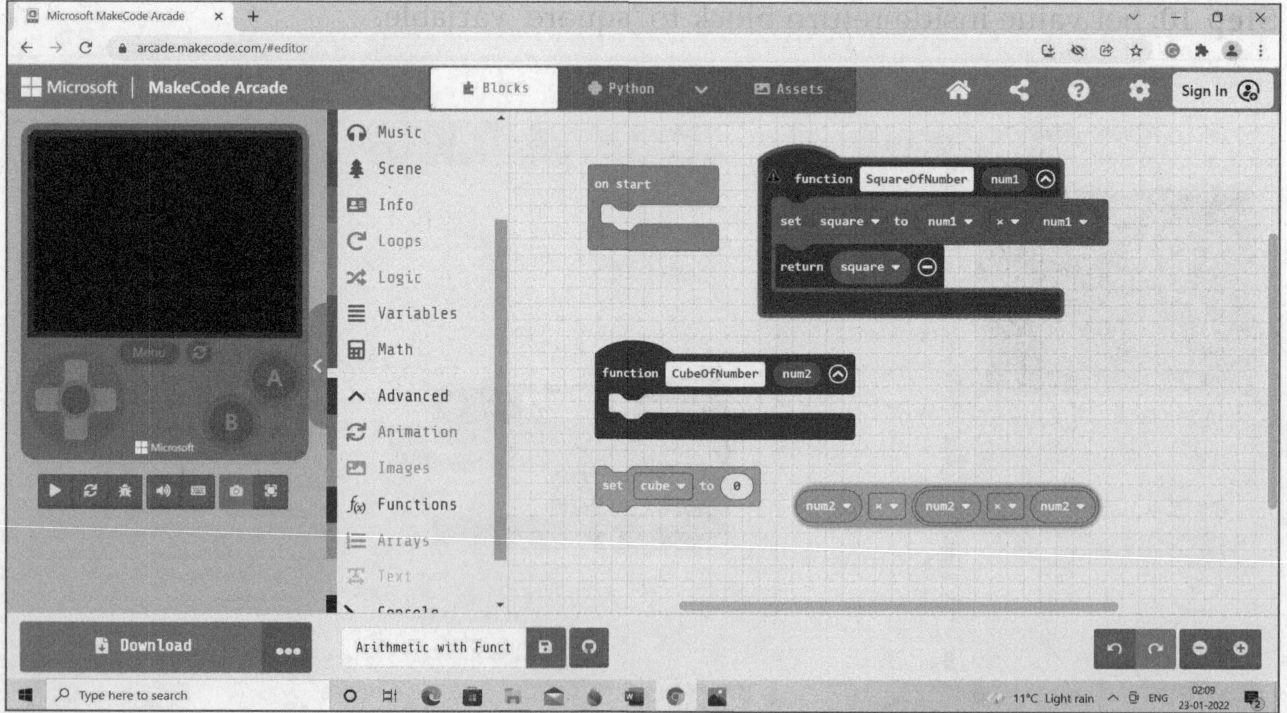

Figure 3.83

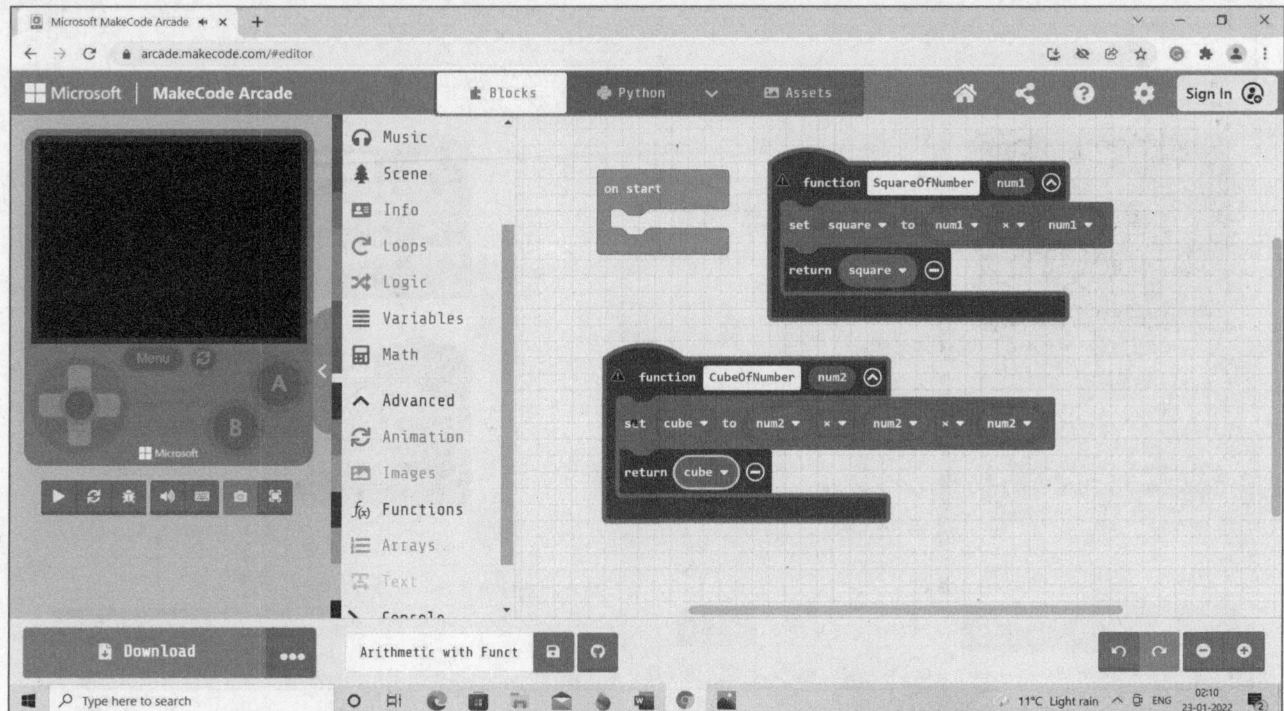

Figure 3.84

Step 12: Open Variable block type Functions. Create three blocks "set val1", "set val2" and "set val3" .

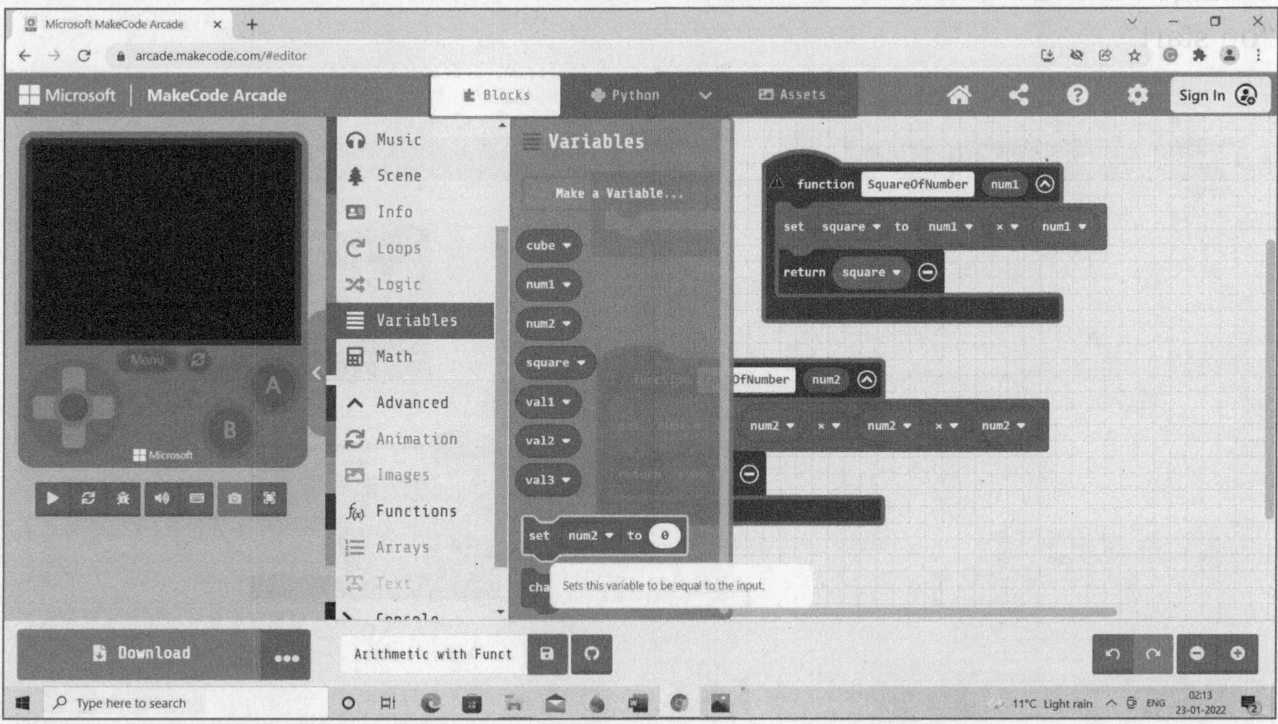

Figure 3.85

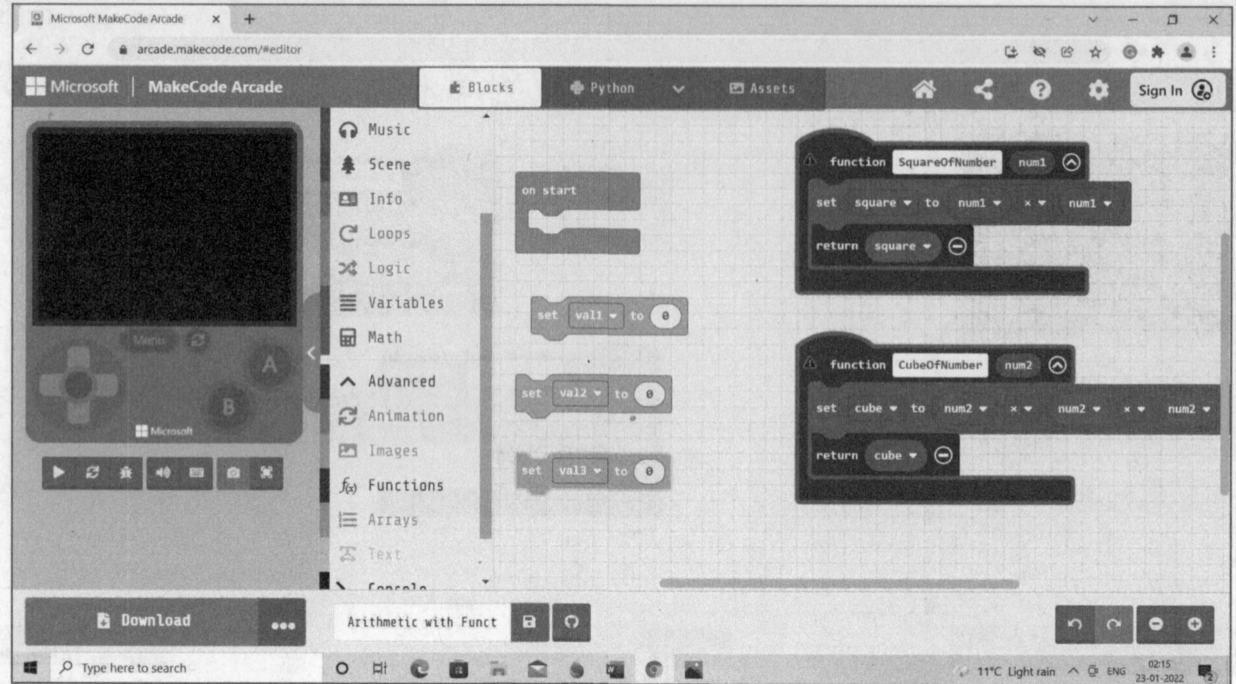

Figure 3.86

Step 13: Attach "call squareOfNumber" block to "set val1 to". Change value in "call squareOfNumber" to 3. Attach "call cubeOfNumber" block to "set val2 to". Change value in "call cubeOfNumber" to 4. Now, attach all these three blocks to "on start".

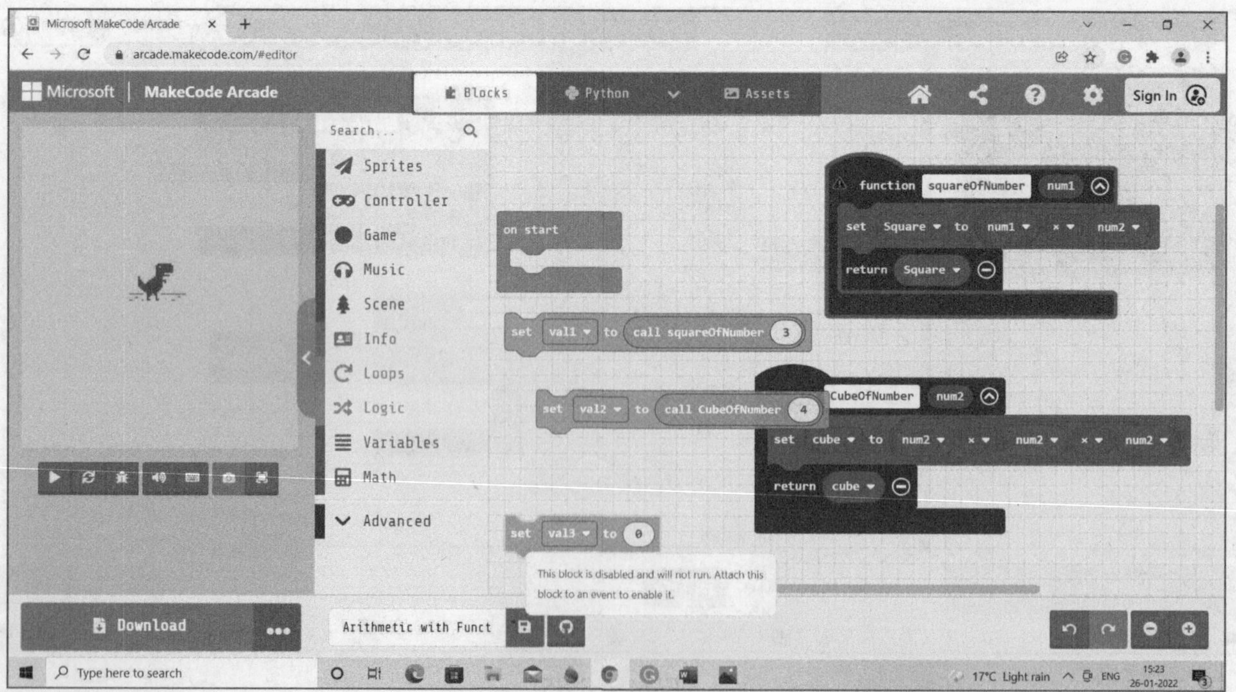

Figure 3.87

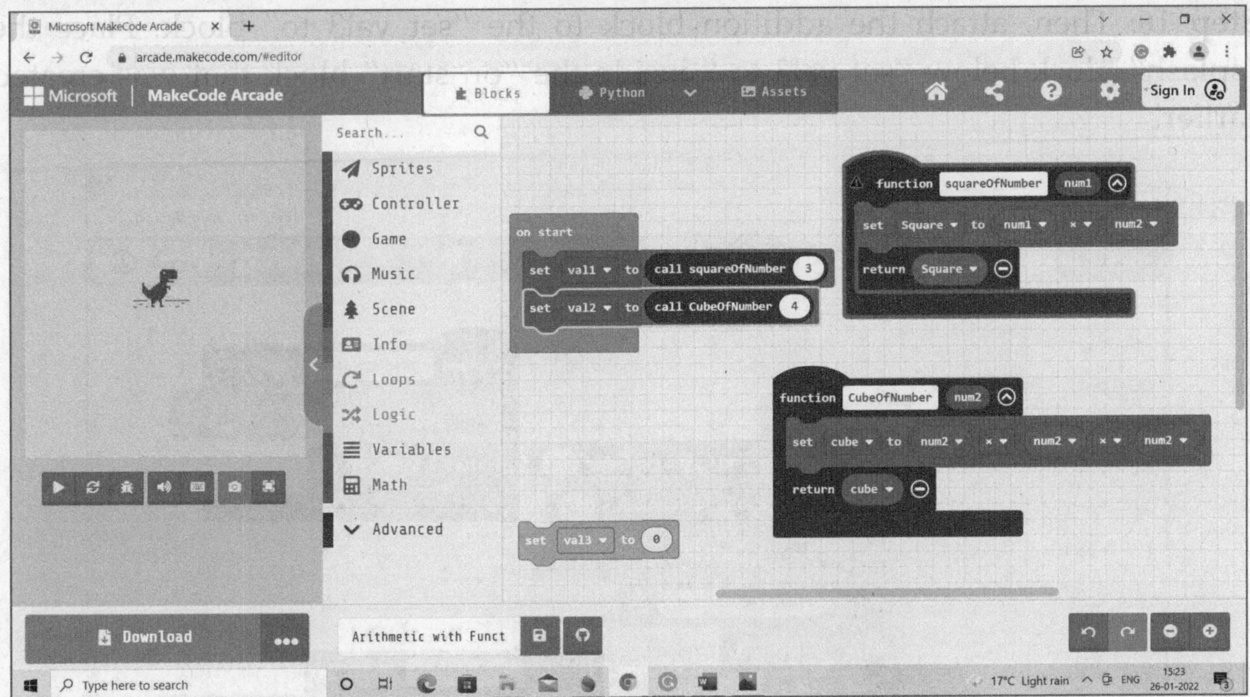

Figure 3.88

Step 14: Select Math block type and select an 'addition' block.

Step 15: In the addition block, set the value on the left-hand side as val1 and on the right-hand side as val2.

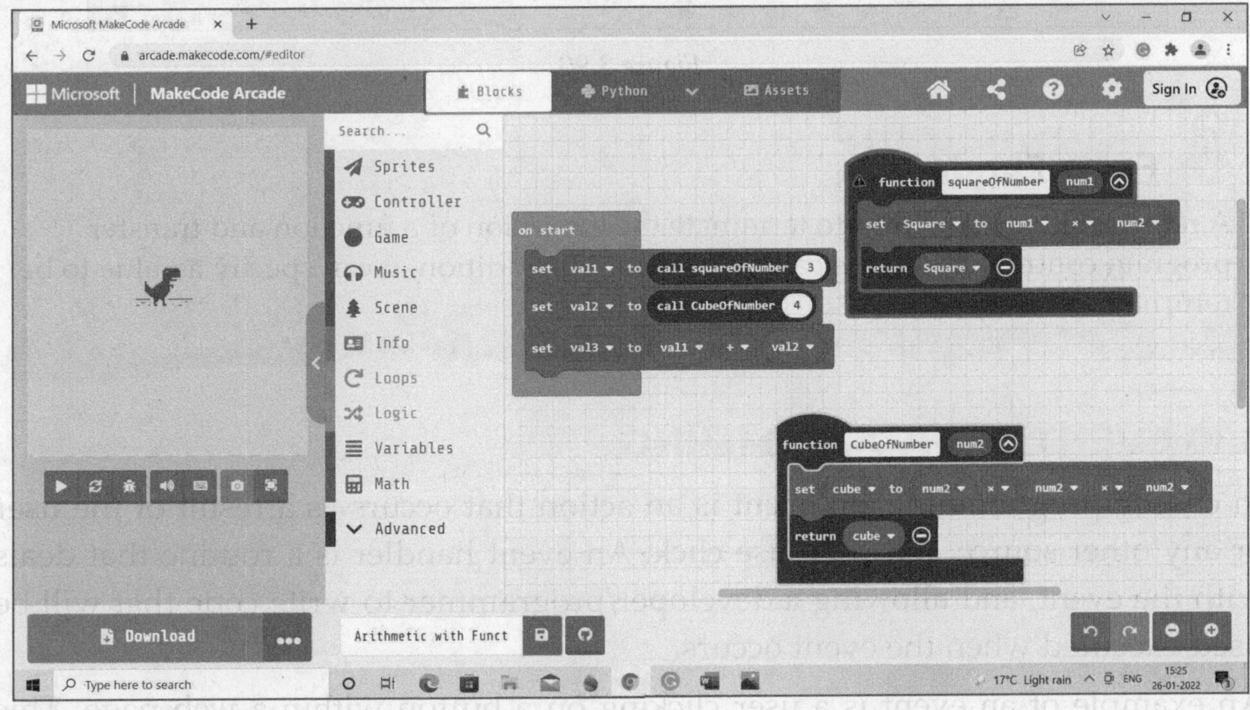

Figure 3.89

Step 16: Then, attach the addition block to the "set val3 to" block. Place the "splash" block below "set val3 to " inside the "on start" block that was created earlier.

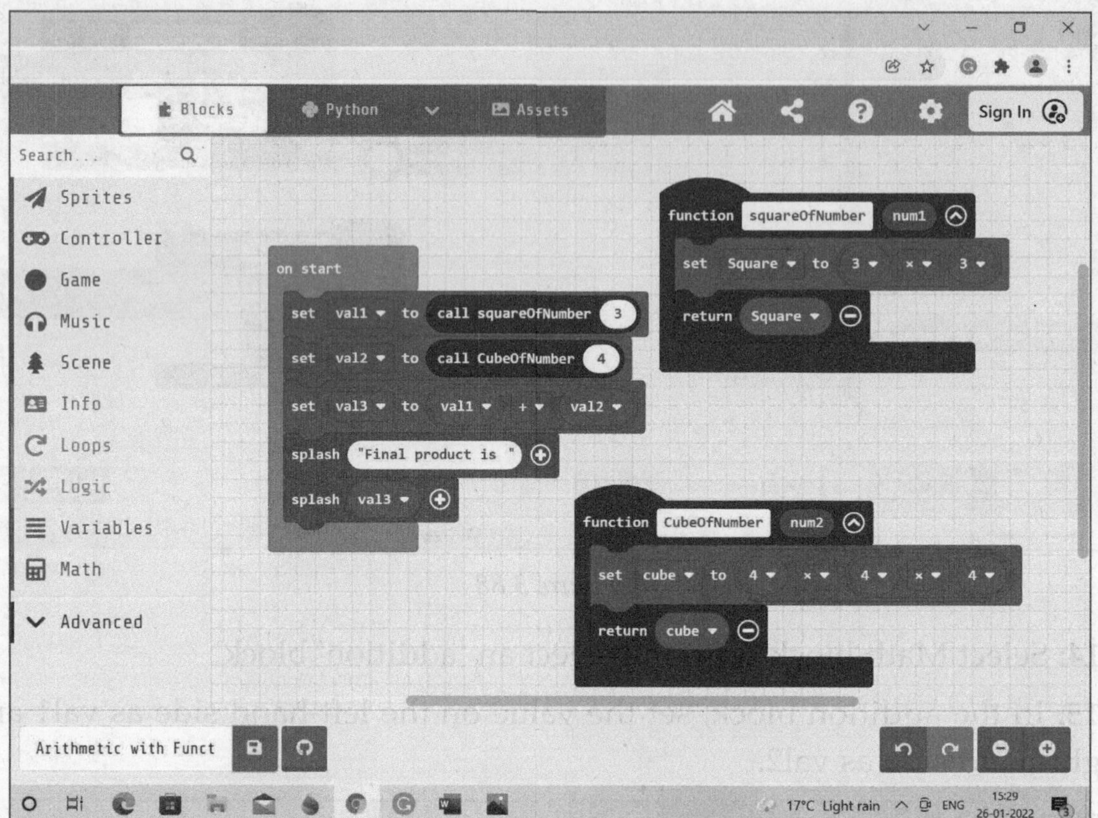

Figure 3.90

Factz Funda

A return statement is used to terminate the execution of a function and transfer program control back to the calling function. In addition, it can specify a value to be returned by the Function.

3.10 EVENT IN PROGRAMMING

In coding/programming, an event is an action that occurs as a result of the user or any other source, like a mouse click. An event handler is a routine that deals with the event, and allowing a developer/programmer to write code that will be used/executed when the event occurs.

An example of an event is a user clicking on a button within a web page. This type of action creates what is known as a "click" event.

Therefore, a return in programming is a value that a function returns to the calling script or Function when it completes its task. A return value may be any one of the four variable types: handle, integer, object, or string.

An event is something that happens due to the action of user or by the presence of any other thing. With refernce to coding, events are a generalisation of all the things that the program can respond to.

Table 3.1 Some common examples of events in programming

- Clicking on a button of a web page
- A web browser while loading a web page
- Keypress inside a desktop application
- A file is created or modified on a file system
- A hardware sensor like a webcam or microphone receives sensory input
- The arrival of incoming network traffic
- The occurrence of an error at the program or system level

3.11 EVENT HANDLER

An event handler is a piece of code associated with an event in the code. An event handler gets executed when that event occurs. For example, in the Arcade MakeCode platform, if we want a player to move forward when the user clicks on the forward icon, we would create a code block like below:

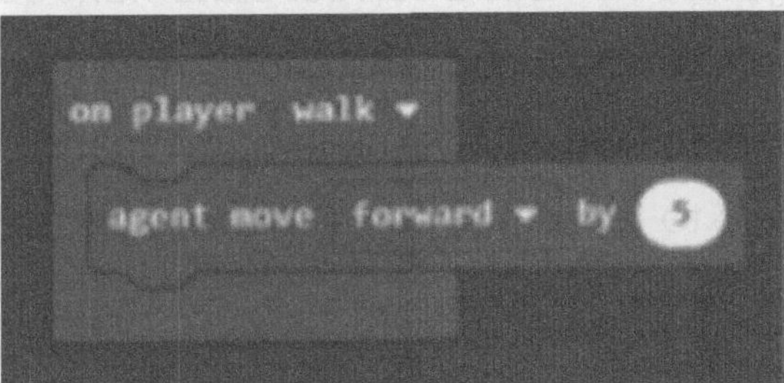

Figure 3.91

Here, this "on player walk" block is acting as an event handler. Agent mode forward is the action that occurs with this event.

1. What is the term given to the variables found in the definition of the Function on which further operations may be performed?
   (a) Return value (b) Parameter(s) (c) Data types (d) Data function
2. Function in a program increases readability.
   (a) True (b) False
3. Function in a program decreases code reusability.
   (a) True (b) False
4. Which of the following is a basic sorting technique?
   (a) Bubble sort, Insertion sort, (b) Selection sort, Bucket sort,
   (c) Heapsort, Quicksort, (d) All the above
5. A Function in programming helps in reducing code redundancy.
   (a) True (b) False
6. Which of the following algorithms is considered as the quickest sorting algorithm?
   (a) Rapid sort (b) Quicksort (c) Heapsort (d) Selection sort
7. A function can return a value.
   (a) True (b) False (c) It cannot be predicted
8. Which of the following statements is a correct statement about functions?
   (a) Functions allow users to reuse code instead of rewriting it.
   (b) Functions allow users to keep the variable namespace clean.
   (c) Functions allow users to test small parts of the program in isolation from the rest.
   (d) All the above
9. Which of the following is not an advantage of functions?
   (a) Functions increase readability.
   (b) Functions reduce code length.
   (c) Redundant code is added in functions.
   (d) Code reusability increases by the use of functions.

ANSWERS								
1. (b)	2. (a)	3. (b)	4. (d)	5. (a)	6. (b)	7. (a)	8. (d)	9. (c)

SUMMARY

- Sorting is a classic problem of reordering items (that can be compared, e.g., integers, strings, floating-point numbers, etc) of an array (or a list) in a certain order (increasing, non-decreasing).
- Functions are groups of code that always run together in a program.
- A function usually requires data as an input. This data is called an argument.
- Functions can have many arguments. When we call a function, we actually supply its arguments.
- A pattern is formed when something or a series of things are repeated in a particular sequence.
- A function is a block of code made up of a set of steps that results in a single specific action.
- A function is a group of instructions (sometimes known as a named procedure) that is used by a programming language to return a single result and/ a set of results.
- Functions may have many arguments. When we call a function, we actually supply its arguments.
- Redundancy is unnecessary duplication in a program. A data value is redundant if we can delete it without information being lost.
- Functions increase readability. It makes the code organized and easy to understand.
- Functions reduce code length. Redundant code is removed and replaced by functions.
- Modular programming allows many programmers to collaborate on the same application.
- A parameter refers to an unknown data value capable of being set through a command by the user.
- The variables accepted by a function to perform the set of tasks defined in its body are called function parameters.
- Sorting a collection helps the user to answer questions like "which is the tallest/ smallest/ fastest item in this collection?"
- Arranging things in order can make other algorithms work better.
- The best sorting technique can be decided by a variety of factors like the size of data to be sorted, machine capabilities, memory requirements, etc.
- Quicksort is considered as one of the fastest sorting algorithms and the best sorting algorithm.
- The name of the value is called a parameter, while the actual value itself is called an argument. Functions always return a value.

- Return value of a function can be a character, a string, an integer, etc. Thus, the return type of a function is the type of the return value of that Function.
- The main purpose behind using functions is not to allow repetitive chunks of code.
- The return statement is used to terminate the execution of a function and transfer program control back to the calling function.
- An event handler is a piece of code that is associated with an event in the code.
- An event handler gets executed on the occurrence of the event.

PRACTICE TIME

(A) True/False Type Questions

1. Functions are groups of code that always run together in a program.
2. A data value is redundant if we can delete it without information being lost.
3. Code reusability decreases by the use of functions.
4. A pattern is formed when something or a series of things are repeated in a particular sequence.
5. A function is a block of code made up of a set of steps that results in a single specific action.
6. Generally, arranging the data in ascending or descending order is known as Sorting.
7. Modular programming does not allow many programmers to collaborate on the same application.
8. A function usually requires data as an output, and this data is called an argument.
9. Functions may have many arguments. When we call a function, we actually supply its arguments.
10. Redundancy is necessary duplication in a program.

ANSWERS							
1. T	2. T	3. F (increases)	4. T	5. T	6. T	7. F	8. T
9. F (data as input)		10. F (unnecessary)					

(B) Fill in the Blanks

1. A ____________ is a group of instructions (sometimes known as a named procedure) that is used by programming languages to return a single result and/ a set of results.

2. A function usually requires data as an input. This data is called an ____________.

3. Functions make ____________ organised and easy to understand.

4. ____________ is a classic problem of reordering items (that can be compared, e.g., integers, strings, floating-point numbers, etc) of an array (or a list) in a certain order (increasing, non-decreasing).

5. Functions ____________ code length. Redundant code is removed and replaced by functions.

6. A ____________ refers to an unknown data value capable of being set through a command by the user.

7. ____________ is considered as one of the fastest sorting algorithms and the best sorting algorithm.

8. ____________ value of a function can be a character, a string, an integer, etc. Function Parameters are the names that are defined in the function definition, and real values passed to the Function in the function definition are known as arguments.

9. An ____________ is a routine that deals with the event, allowing a programmer to write code that will be executed when the event occurs.

10. In programming, an ____________ is an action that occurs as a result of the user or another source, like a mouse click.

ANSWERS				
1. function	2. argument.	3. code /program	4. Sorting	5. reduce
6. parameter	7. Quicksort	8. Return	9. event handler	10. event

(C) Very Short Answers Questions

1. Define Function.
2. What are function parameters?
3. What is the main purpose of using functions?
4. What is an event in programming?
5. Define sorting.

(D) Short Answer Questions

1. Explain the advantages of using functions.
2. Functions help in increasing the readability of code. Explain.
3. Can function return a value? Support your answer with a proper explanation.

4. How does the use of functions in a program help in reducing the redundancy of code?

(E) HOTS Questions

1. Explain what the output of the below program will be:

```
def test(x, y):

    if x > y:
        return y

def testl(x, y, z):
        return text(x, test(y, z))

print(testl(2, 7, –1))
```

Figure 3.92

(Hint Answer: 1)

2. Write a function to print odd numbers from 11 to 50
3. Write a function for sorting the elements [14,12,75,85,99,105] from biggest to smallest.
4. Find an error in the below program:

```
def sum(numbers):
    total =
    for x in number:
        total += x
    return total
print ( sum ((1, 2, 3, 4, 5)))
```

Figure 3.93

(Hint Answer: Variable "number" is not defined anywhere in the program.)

(F) Projects

The practice challenges may be done on the Arcade MakeCode platform or on similar platforms.

1. Create a block code that takes the Radius and height of a cylinder as input to a function and computes its volume. The volume computed should be returned by the Function.

2. Create a block code that computes the product of (sum of two random numbers) with the (difference of two random numbers) using functions.

Understanding Arrays and Collections

Structure

In this chapter, you will learn:

- About collections.
- About Arrays and their practical implementation in computers
- How to work with a large set of data in programming
- To work on some fun exercises to get a better understanding of the concepts.

INTRODUCTION

In our daily life, we all have some groups of similar objects like a Collection of our favourite foods, a Collection of books of our choice, a list of cities visited in our life. These all are sets, i.e., groups of similar objects/things, and are called collections. In the field of computer science, collections and arrays are used for specific functions.

In this chapter, we will learn more about collections, arrays, and their practical implementations in computers.

Figure 4.1

Source: https://www.xtechalpha.com/2019/08/29/new-ai-programming-language-goes-beyond-deep-learning/

Learning Objectives:

At the end of this chapter, you will be able to:

- know about collections.
- Know about arrays and their practical implementations.

4.1 WHAT ARE COLLECTIONS?

A collection is nothing but a container that store together multiple items into a single object—for example, a jar of toffees, a list of names, etc. Collections are normally used in every programming language, and when Java programming language was introduced, it also came with a few Collection classes like Vector, Stack, Hashtable, Array.

In computers, collections are used to store data. We can also retrieve and manipulate data that is stored in the Collections. In the real world, you can consider a collection of cards, a telephone directory, or a mailbox to be an example of Collections.

In programming, a collection is a class that is used to represent a group/set of similar data type items as a single unit, which are then used for grouping and managing related objects.

Activity 4.1

- Participate in the group activity on "**Preparing List of Real-Life Example of Collections.**"
- The class will be divided into four/five groups randomly without any bias.
- Each group will discuss and prepare a list of examples of collections from real life.
- One representative from each group will present the List prepared by his/her group before the full class.
- After the presentation, an open house will discuss all the examples to find out the correct list items.

Factz Funda

A counter is a sub-class of the dictionary. It is used to keep the count of the elements in an iterable in the form of an unordered dictionary where the key represents the element in the iterable and value represents the count of that element in the iterable.

4.1.1 Advantages of using Collection

- ❖ Collections allow programmers to group multiple items into a common group/set.
- ❖ A collection is resizable and can grow.
- ❖ Grouping of items makes it possible to identify the items easily and perform different operations on them like retrieving and modifying data.
- ❖ Collection increases the performance of the program
- ❖ Collection reduces the effort to maintain because every user knows Collection API classes.
- ❖ Collection increases productivity and reduces operational time.

Activity 4.2

- ▣ Participate in the activity on "**Algorithm for a perfect square**". Work in pairs.
- ▣ Each pair will learn and prepare/write how to write an algorithm for finding whether the given number is a perfect square or not.
- ▣ Before starting, consider the following questions:

  How quickly can we determine whether a number is a perfect square?

  And, if a number is a perfect square, how can we find out its square root?

  Can we write the steps for finding the same for any given large number?

Let us try with a few examples and identify the repeatable steps in the process.

Example 1: Is 49 a perfect square?

To solve this problem, we can use the following algorithm:

Suppose in the following algorithm, "n" is the input number (49 in this case)

The desired output is true when the number is a perfect square and false when it is not a perfect square.

```
begin
        for num :=1, num <= n, increase num by 1;
        if n is divisible by num, and n / num = num, then
        return true
done
return false
end
```

Can we think of ways to improve this algorithm?

Now, look at the following optimised algorithm:

1. Say the number is n
2. Start a loop from 1 to n/2
3. During iteration for every integer 'i', calculate x=i*i
4. Now, with this 'x,' there are three possibilities:
   a. If x==n, then n is a perfect square, return true.
   b. If x>n, then x has crossed the n, which is not a perfect square. Return false.
   c. If the above steps a or b are not true, then continue.

We have noticed that the number of times we multiply and compare is reduced significantly in the modified algorithm. This is how we can use an optimized algorithm to find the square of numbers.

Factz Funda

On modifying collections while traversing, may create problems like unexpected Results and concurrency problems.

4.2 ARRAYS

An array is employed/used to store a collection of data. An array is also defined as a collection of variables of the same type. Thus, an array is a collection of similar data type variables. Arrays do not support different data types in the same Collection. For example, we can make an 'Array of Integers' as well as another 'Array of Strings .'But we cannot make an Array having Integer and Strings in the same Collection. In the real world, we can consider books in a library to be the example of arrays where all the shelves have a common data type (read – book) in them.

An array is a data structure that can store a fixed-size collection of elements of the same data type. Python doesn't have an explicit array data structure because we can do the same things with the List.

The 'List' contains a collection of items and it supports add/update/delete/search operations. That's why there is not much use of a separate data structure in Python to support arrays.

Factz Funda

All elements of an array are given an index number that starts from 0. This is called the 'Array Index'.

Consider an Array with variables of Integer Data Type stored in it.

This array can be declared in following format:

arr = [5,10,15, 20, 25, 30];

Using the above syntax, we can deduce that an array named "arr" is declared with data type as integer, i.e., this array can only hold integer values. We have initialized this array with six values, i.e., 5, 10, 15, 20, 25, 30.

Below is the diagram that displays how data and indexes are structured in such an Array:

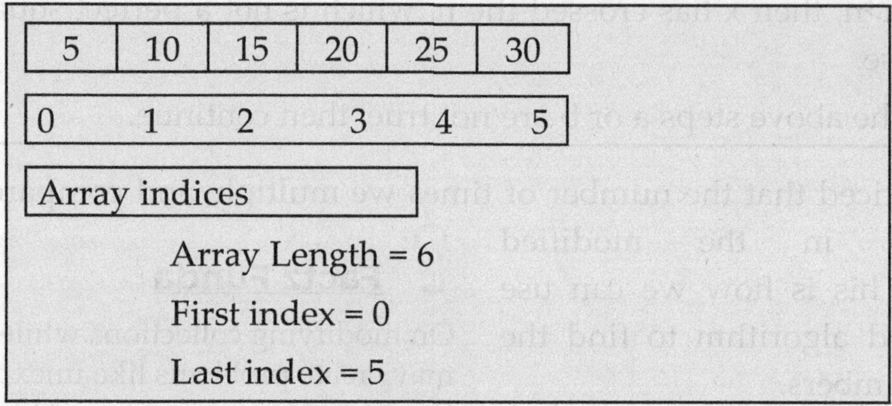

Figure 4. 2

Now, let us try to implement a similar example using Arcade MakeCode Platform. Let us now follow below step by step procedure to replicate this output on our screen:

Step 1: Create a new project in Arcade MakeCode. Click on the "Variables" link from Toolbox and click on "make a variable ."Create a variable "a" and click on the "Ok" button.

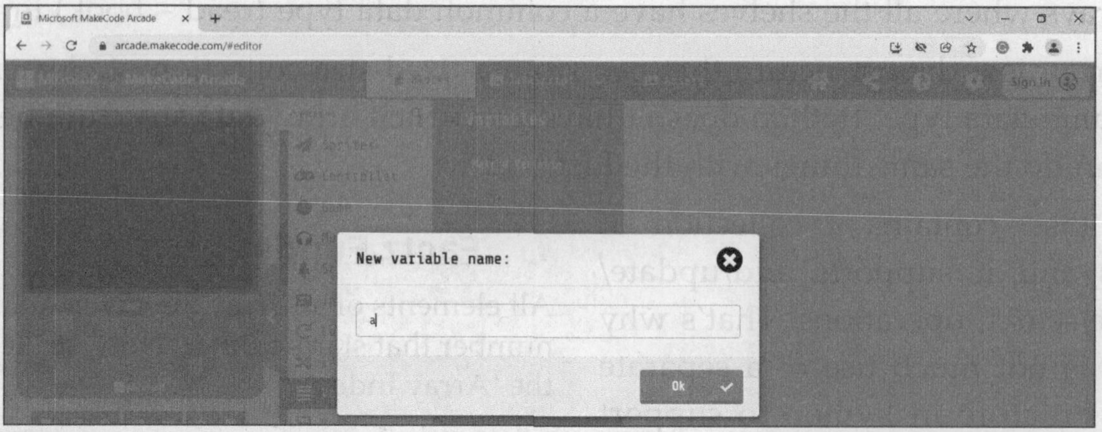

Figure 4.3

Step 2: From the Toolbox, click on the link "Arrays ."From the sub list, drag and drop blocks of "set list to" to the play area.

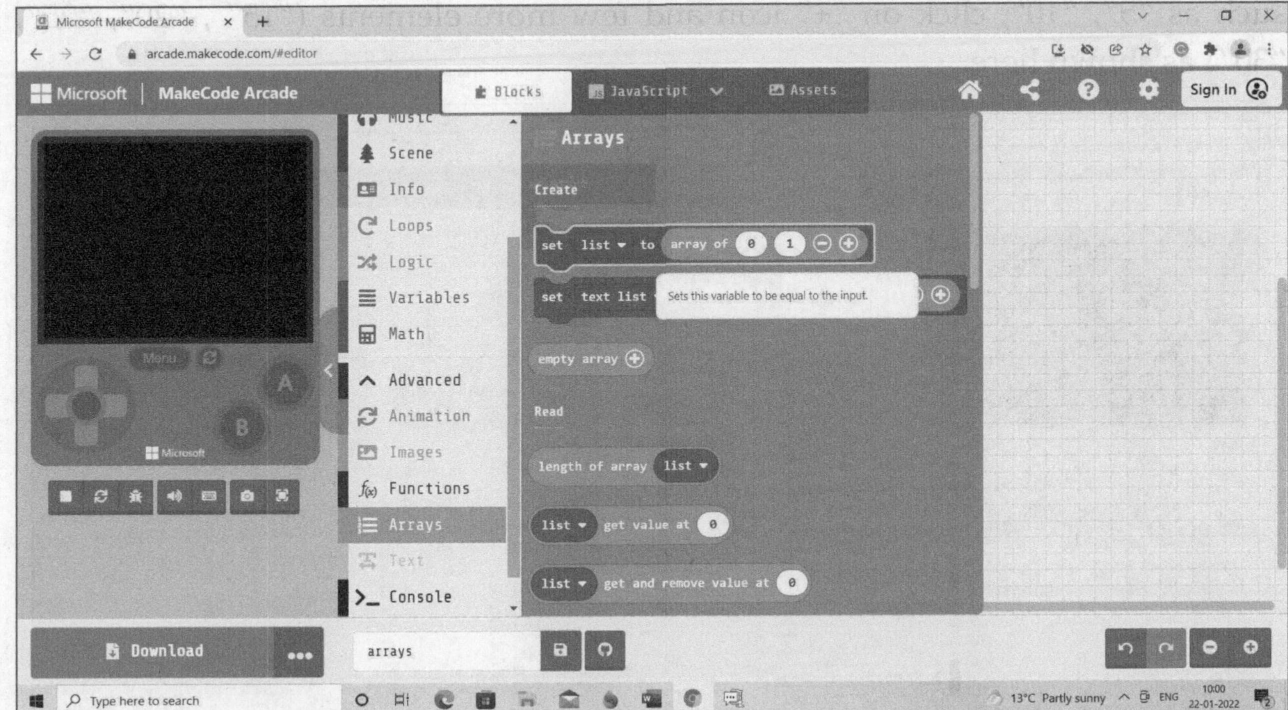

Figure 4.4

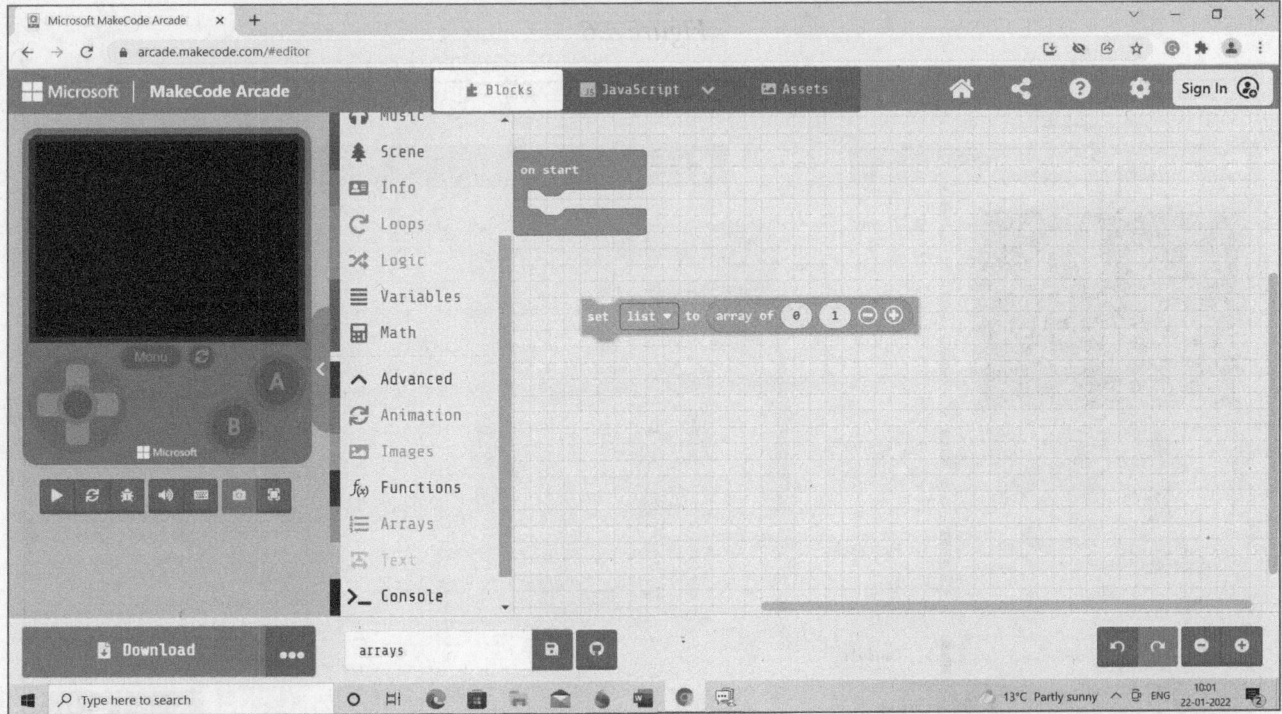

Figure 4.5

Step 3: In the set block, click on the drop-down which says "List" and select variable "a" that we had earlier created. In the next text boxes, rewrite values such as "5", "10", click on "+" icon and few more elements ("15" , "20", "25", "30") as shown here.

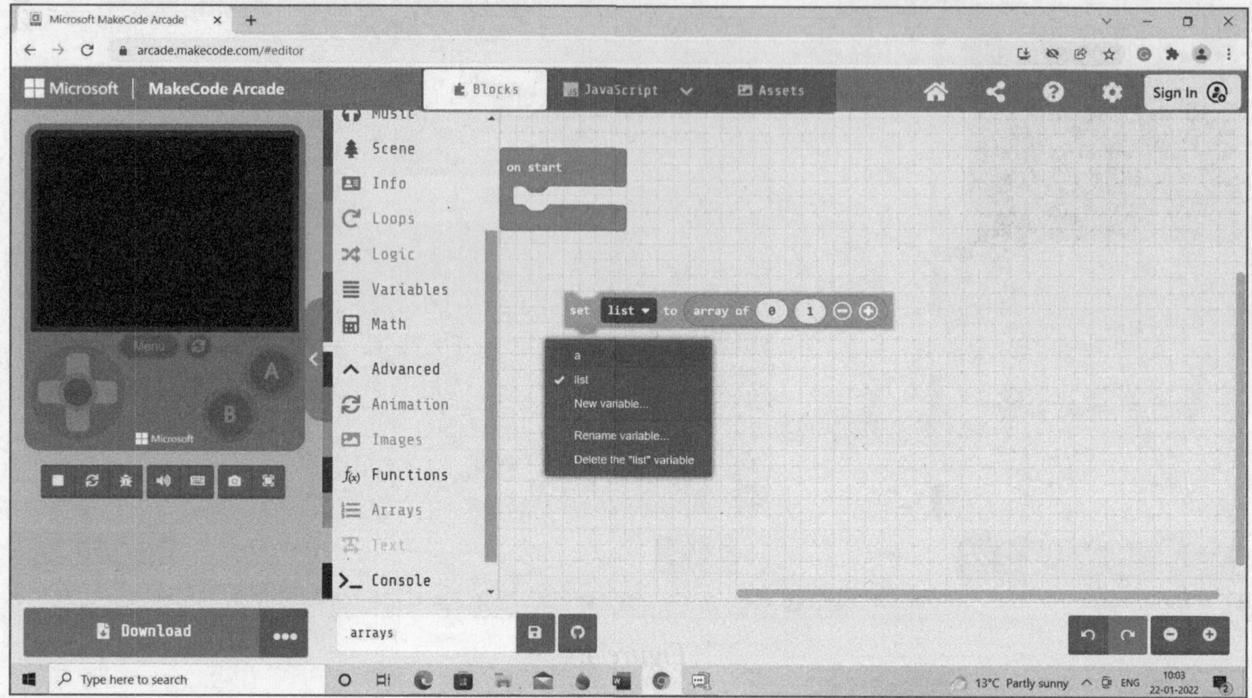

Figure 4.6

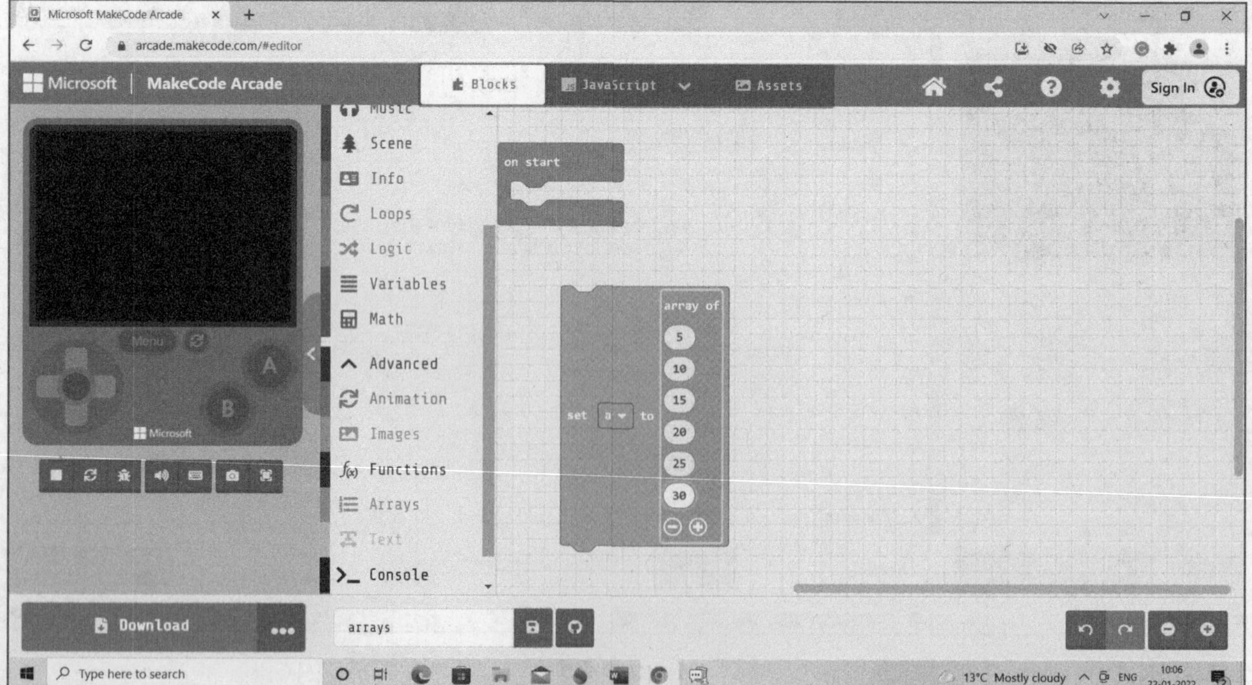

Figure 4.7

Step 4: Attach the "Set" block that we had created into "On start " block, as shown here.

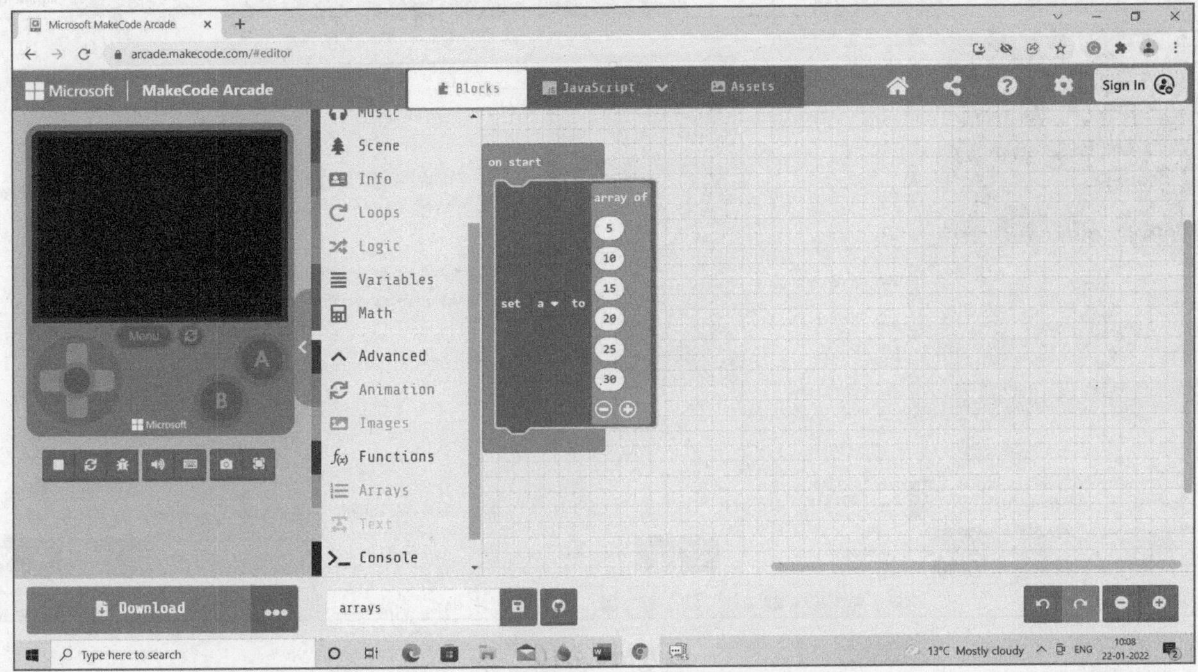

Figure 4.8

Step 5: Click on the "arrays" link from Toolbox. Drag and drop the "Length of array" block to the play area. In the "Length of Array" block, select "a" in the drop-down, which has a default value of "list".

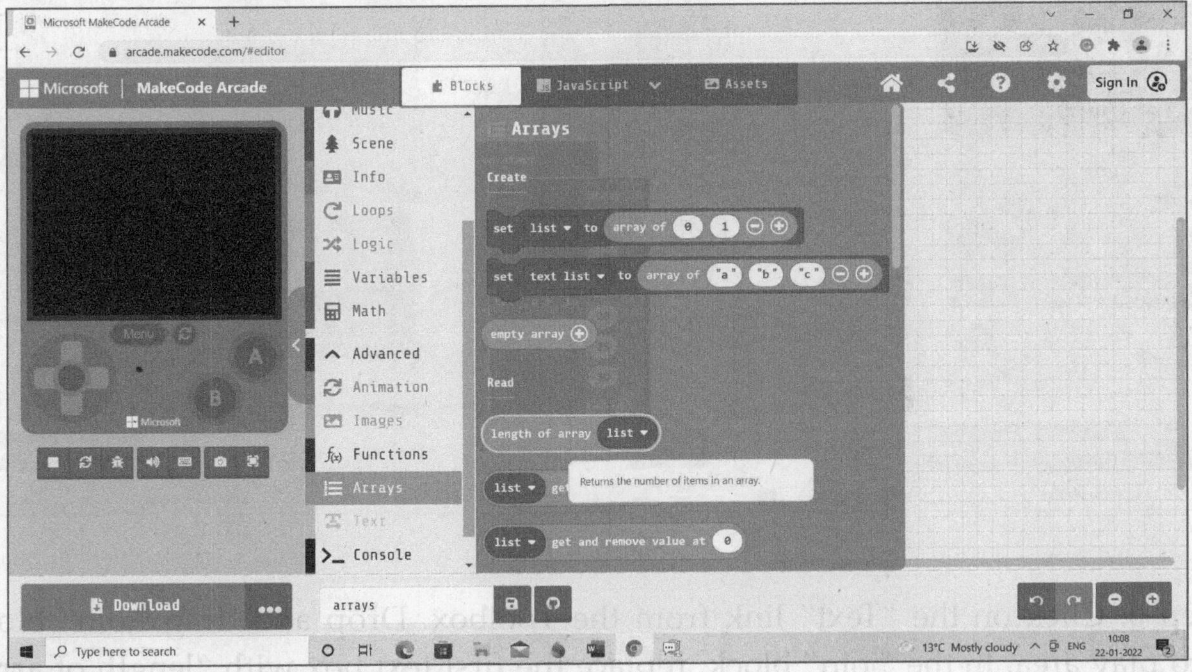

Figure 4.9

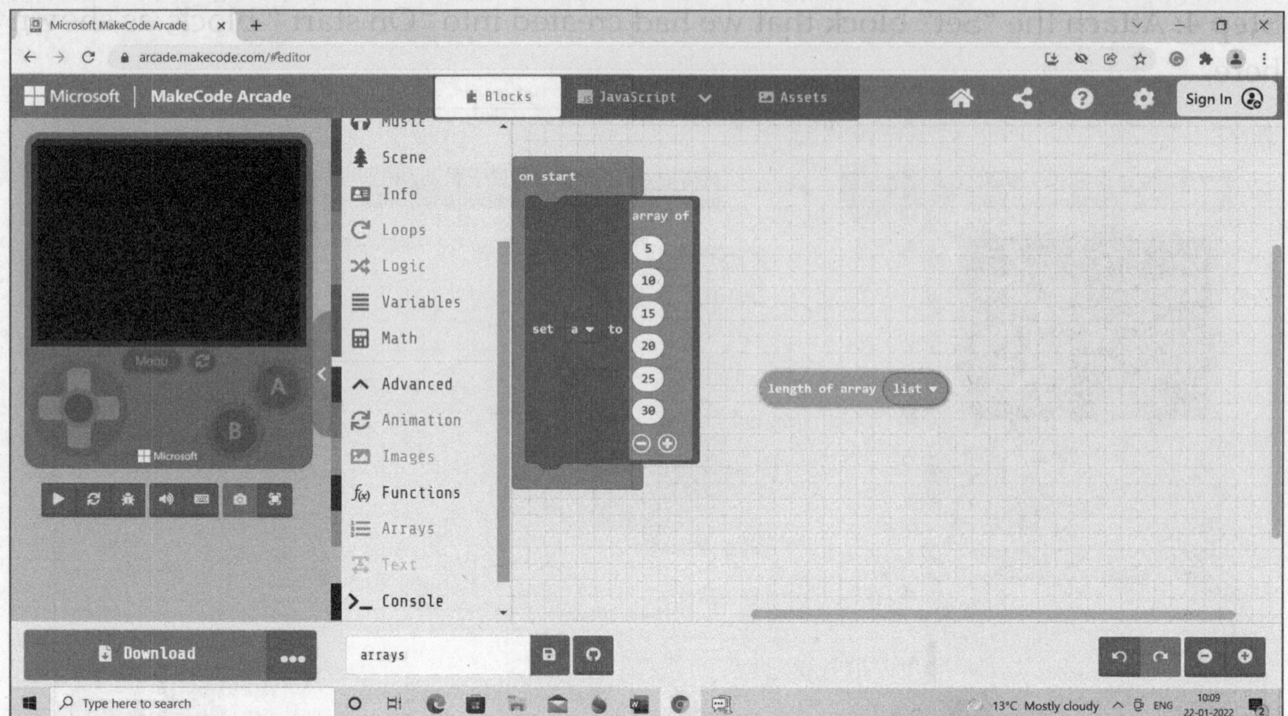

Figure 4.10

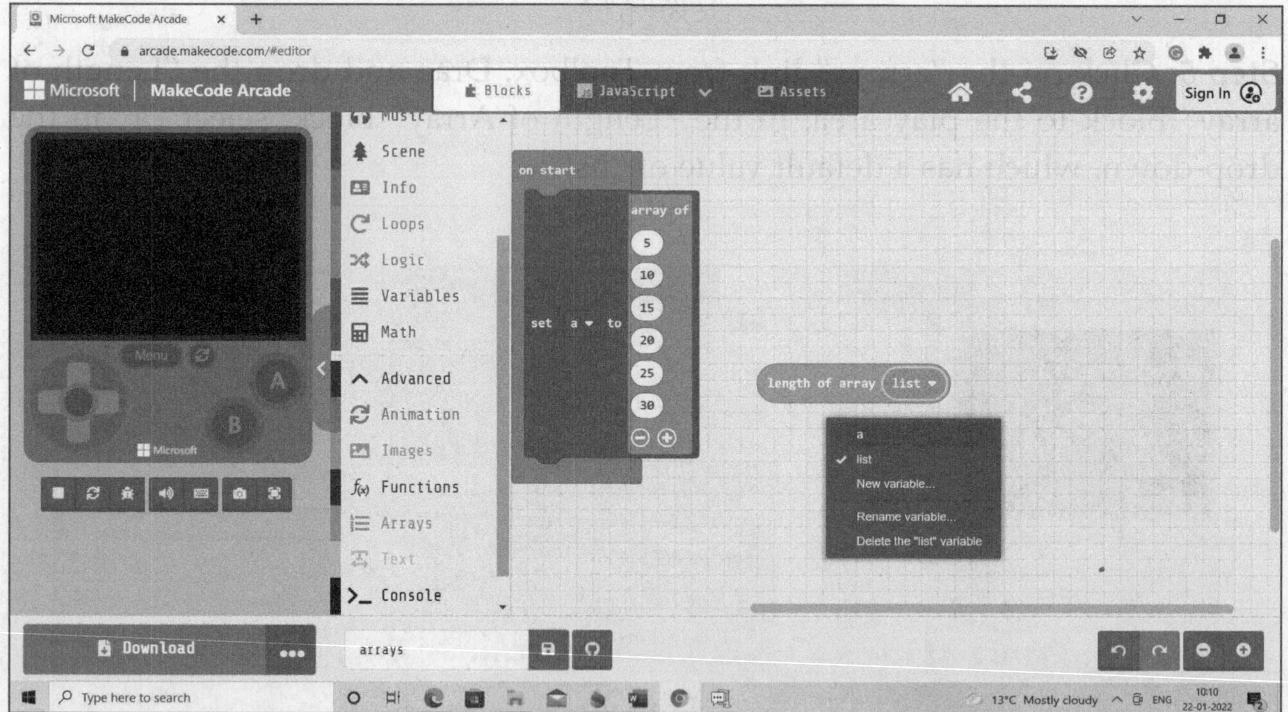

Figure 4.11

Step 6: Click on the "Text" link from the Toolbox. Drop and drag "join" block into play area. In the "join" block, replace the first text box with "length of array is" and fix "length of array" block second text box as shown here.

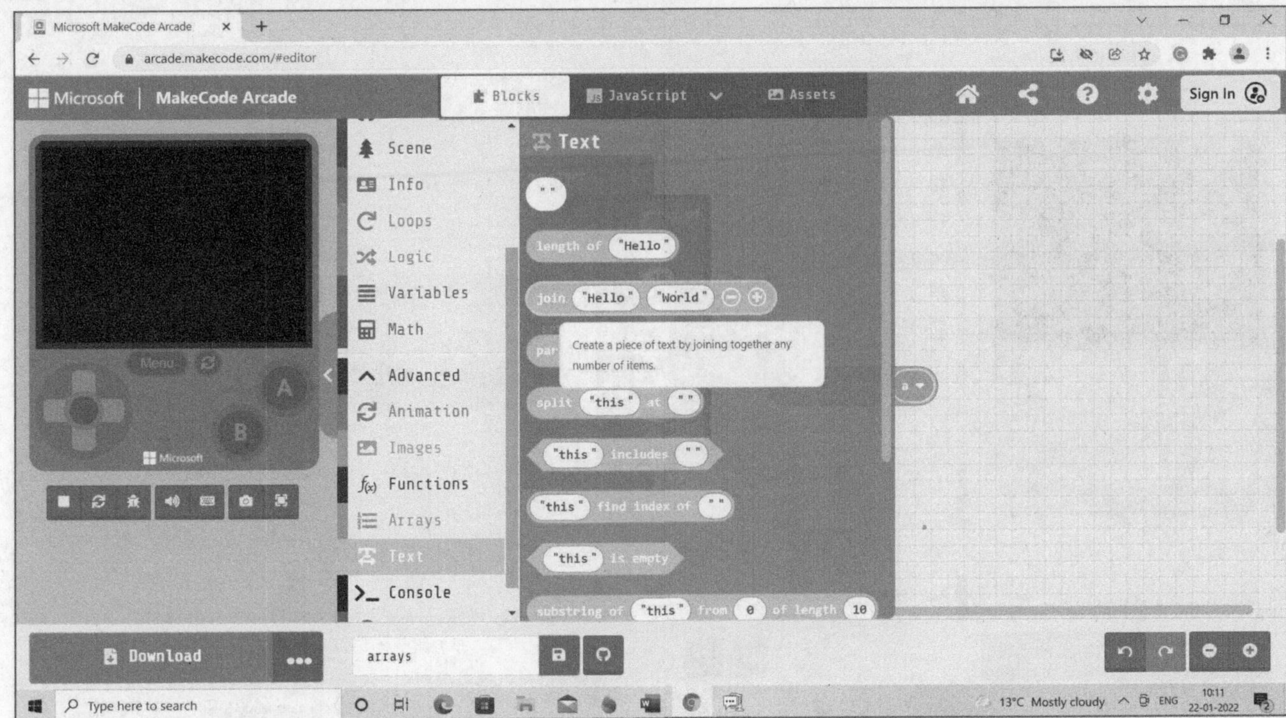

Figure 4.12

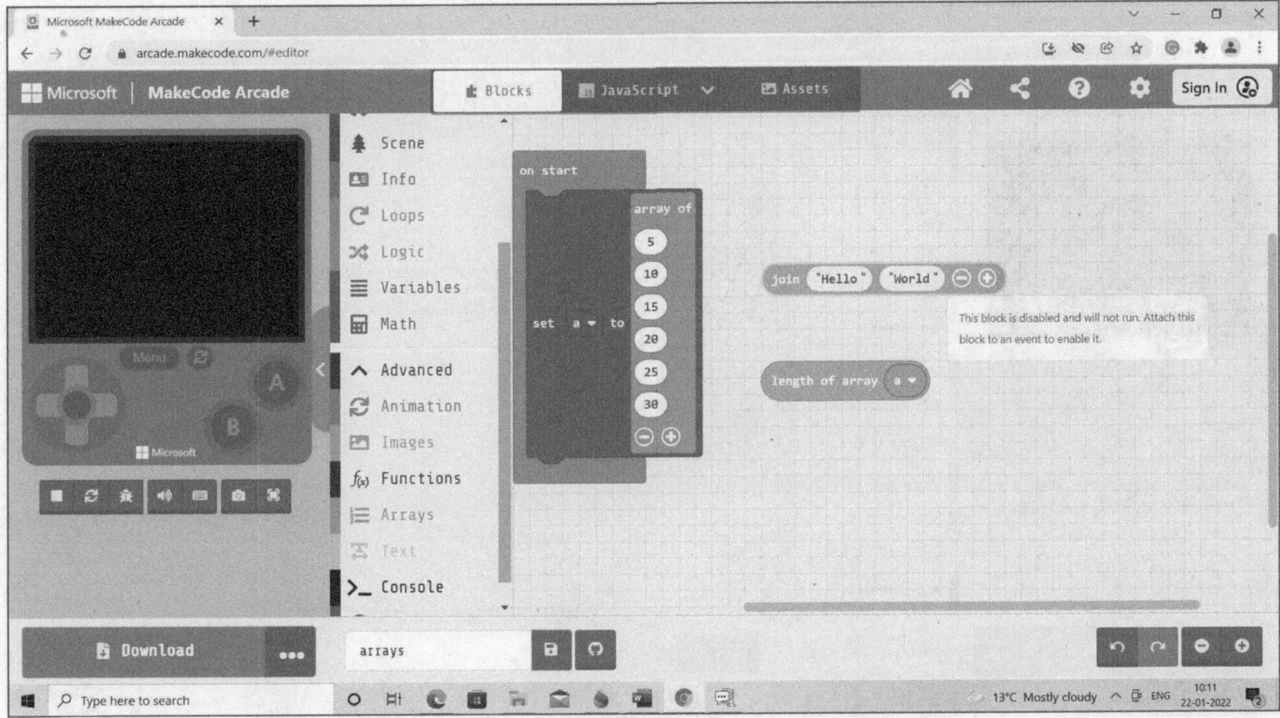

Figure 4.13

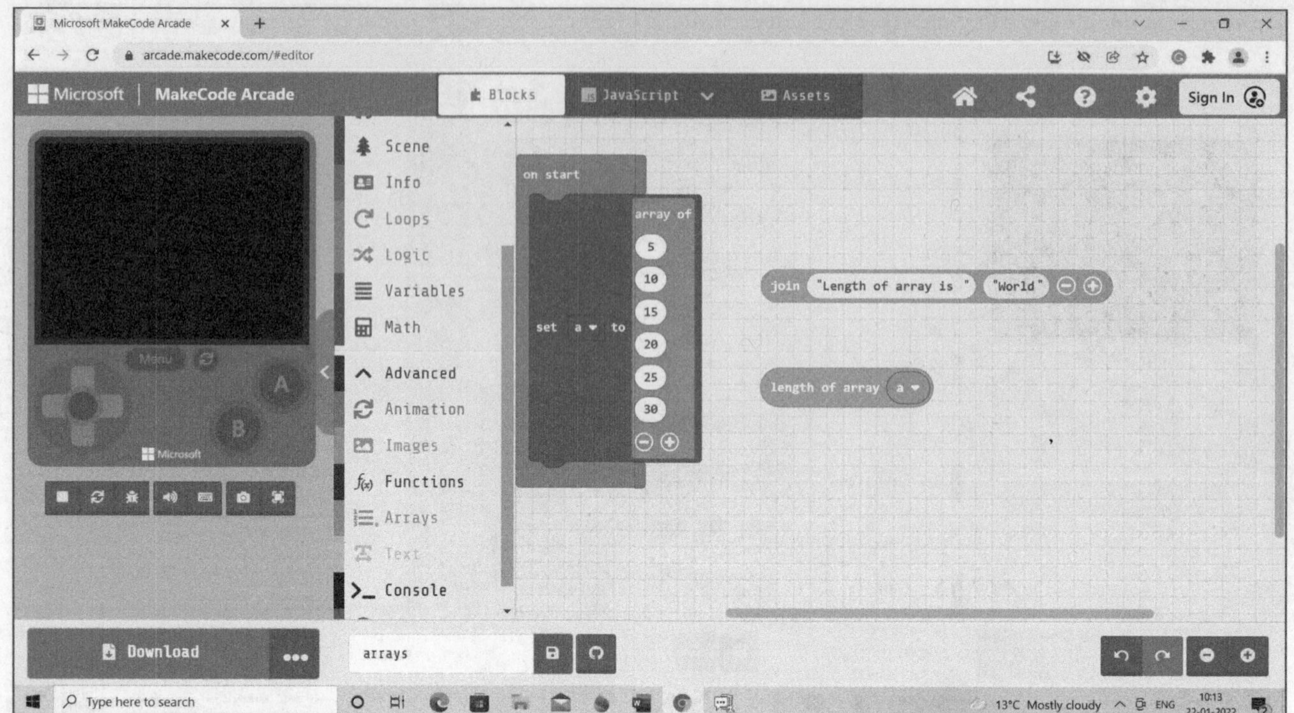

Figure 4.14

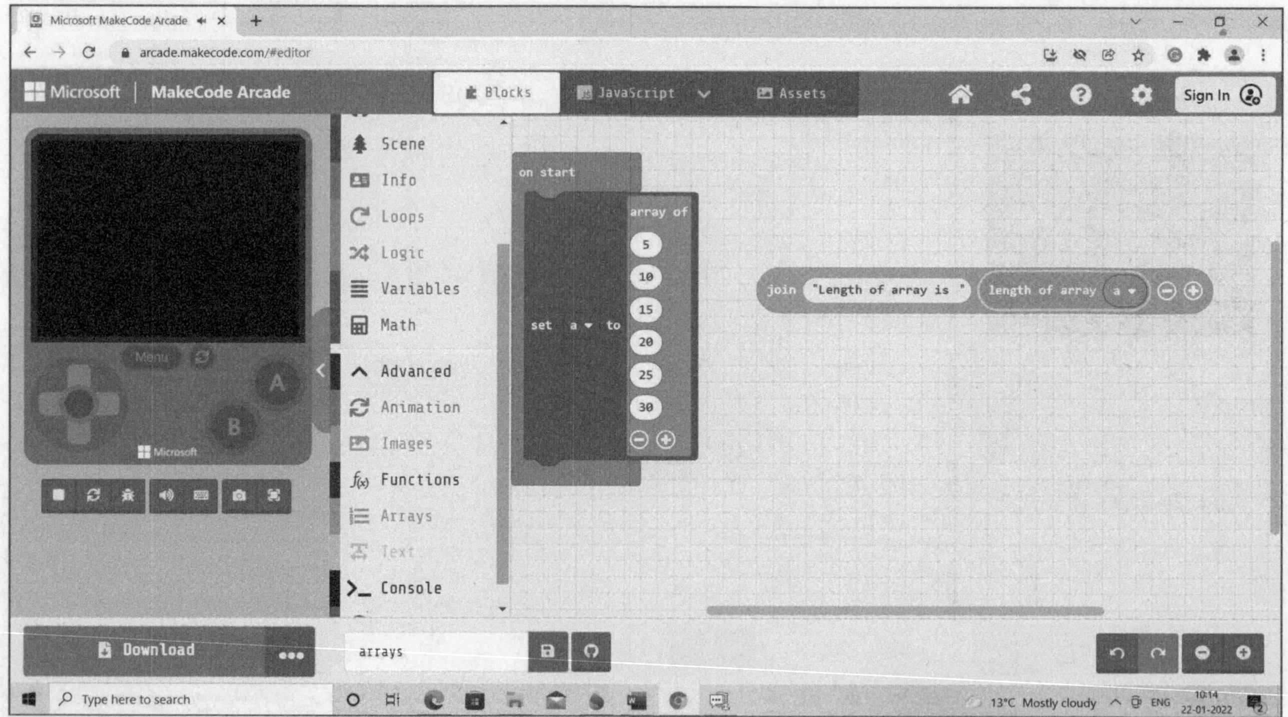

Figure 4.15

Step 7: Click on "Game" link from the Toolbox and drag and drop "splash" block in the play area. Now, append "join" block that we had created into "splash" block and place "splash " block below "set" block on "On start' block as shown here. Finally, click on green play button at the bottom of the page. It will display an output "array length is 6" on the console.

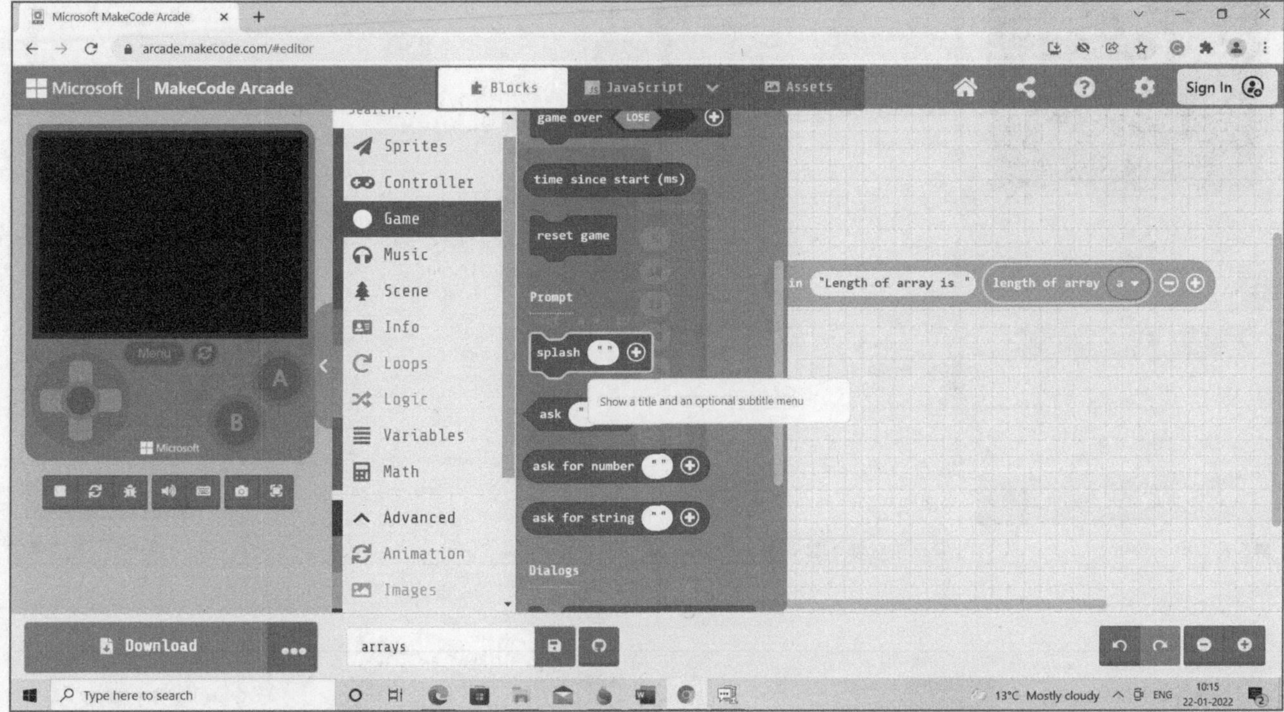

Figure 4.16

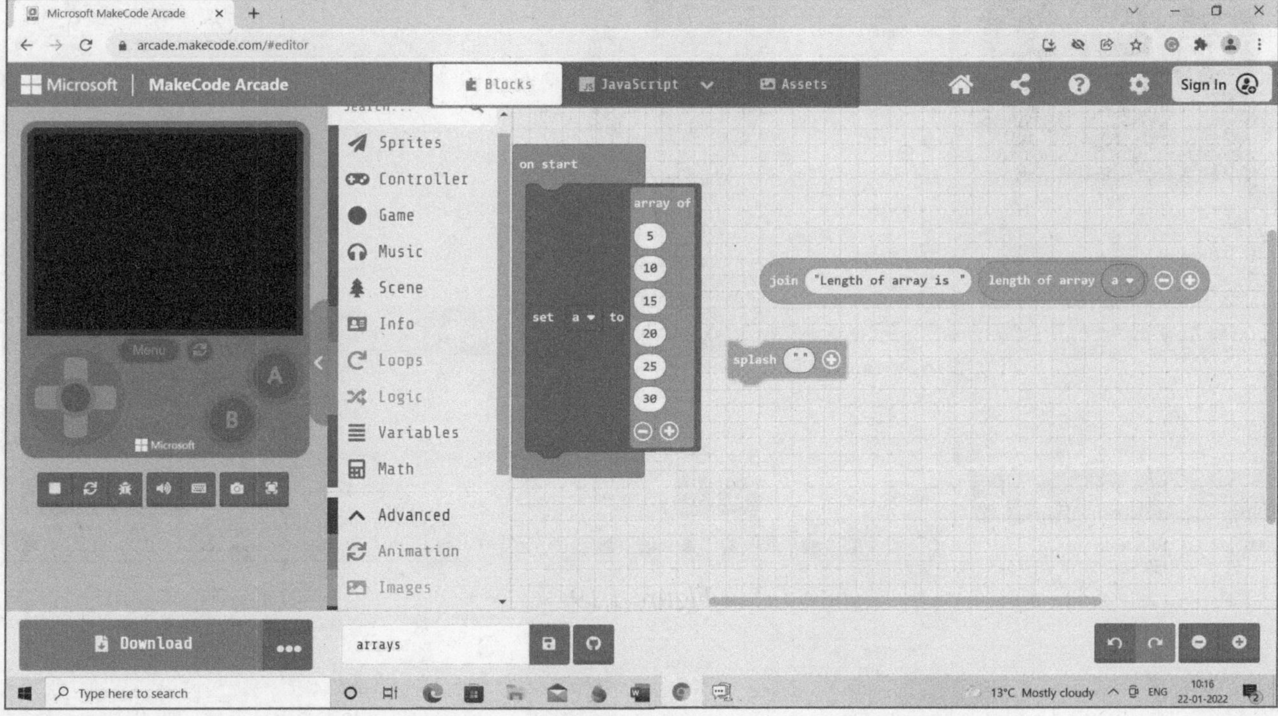

Figure 4.17

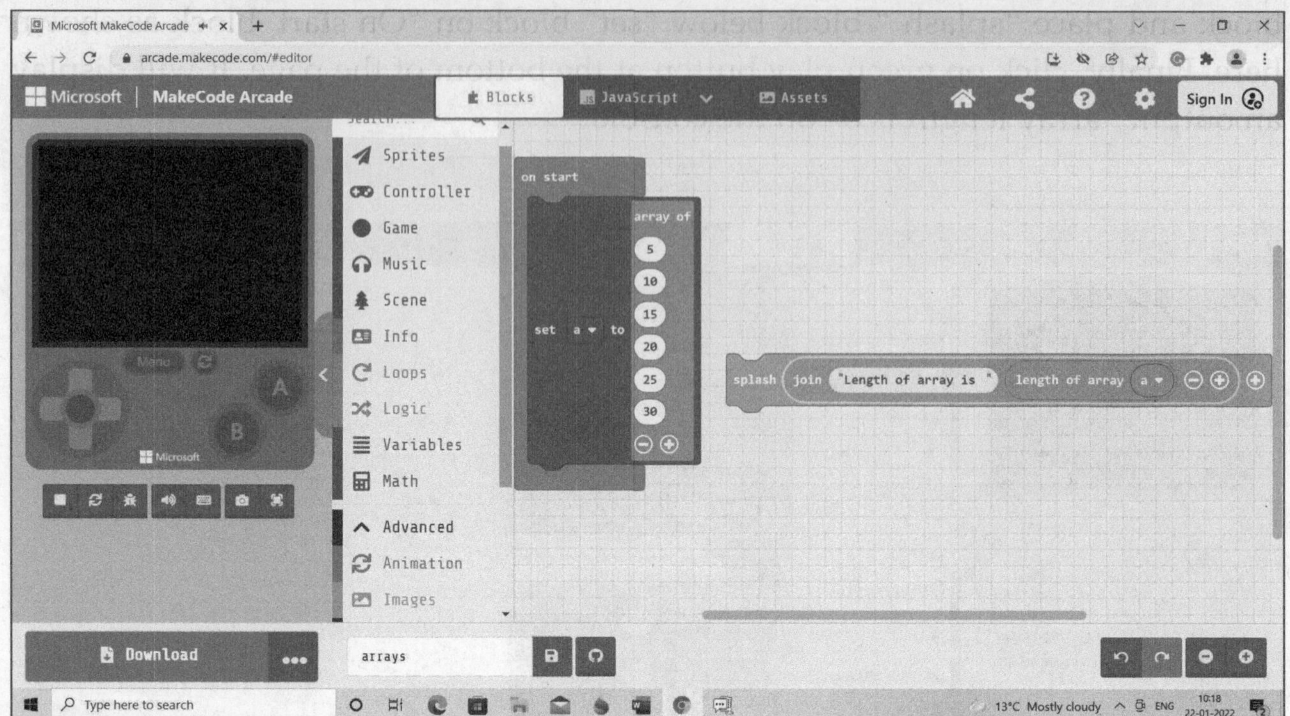

Figure 4.18

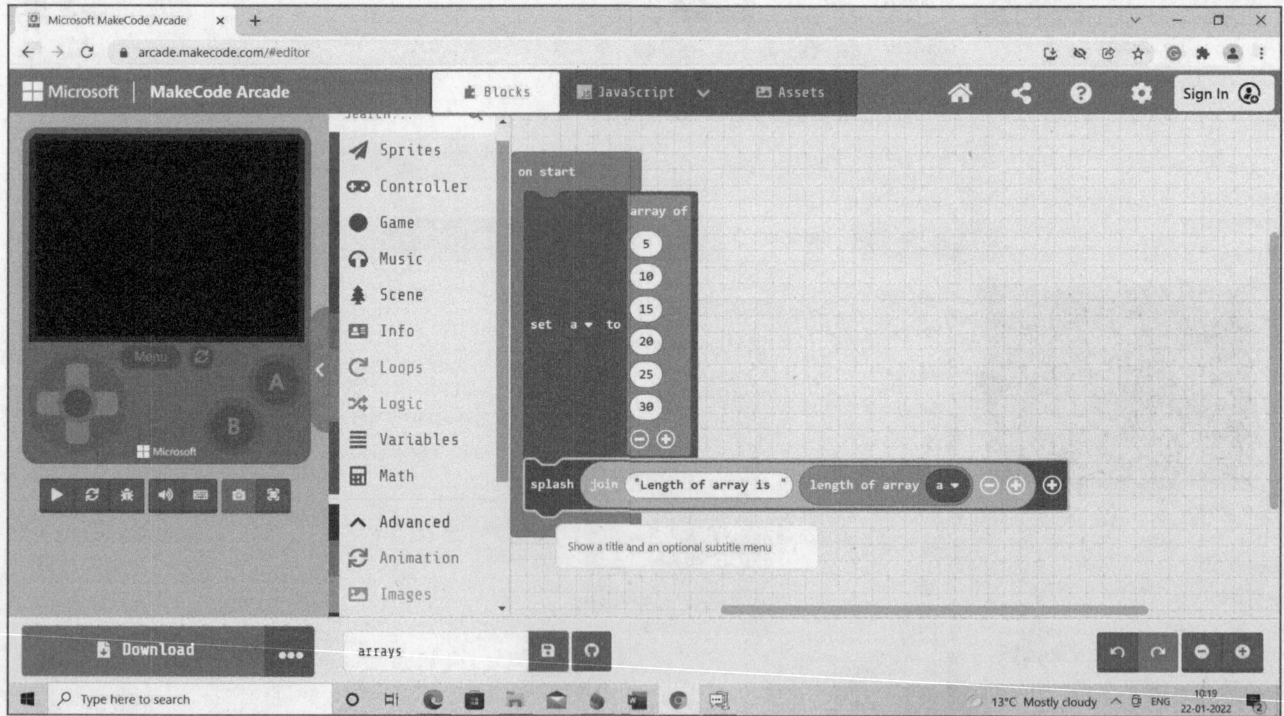

Figure 4.19

The final output will be displayed as follows:

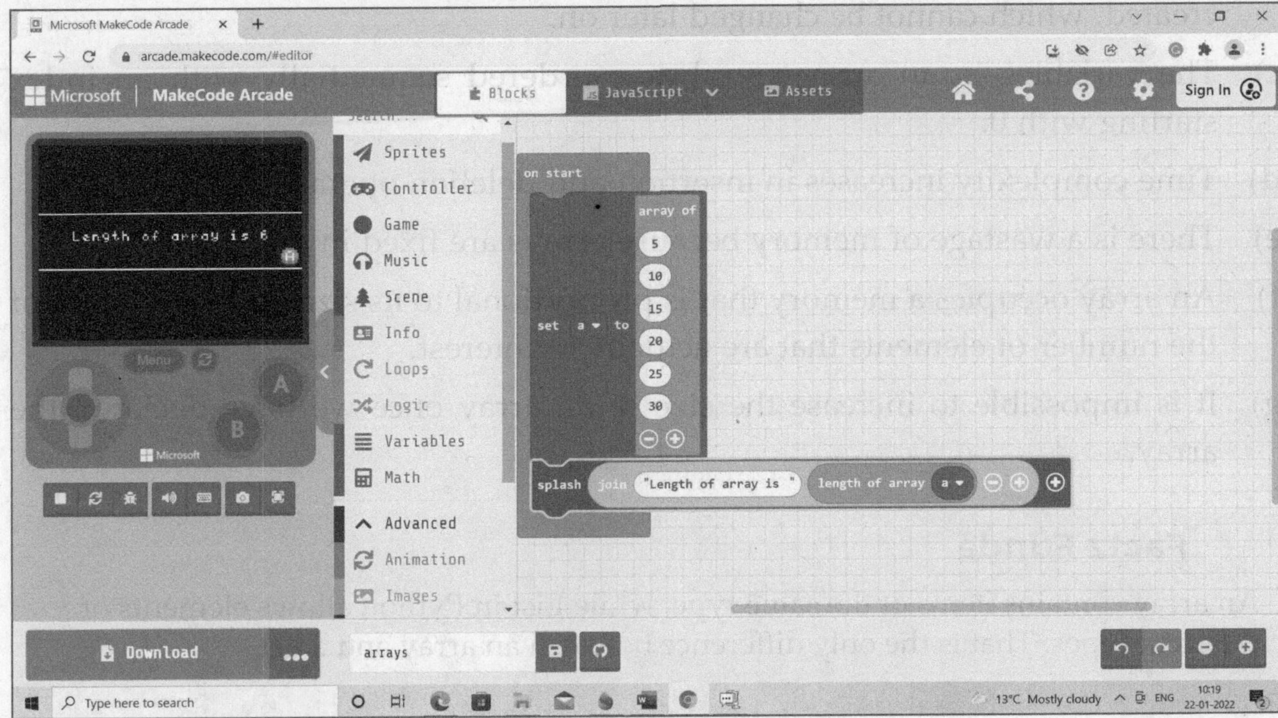

Figure 4.20

4.2.1 Advantages of Arrays

Arrays have the following advantages:

a) Arrays improve the readability of code by using a single variable for a large set of data.

b) Arrays are a collection of similar types of data.

c) When we want to store the marks of all students, it will be easy to store them in an array; otherwise, we have to store marks in different locations, which is difficult to memorize.

d) Only the first index of an array is to be remembered.

e) An array is used to implement other data structures like linked lists, stack, queue, trees, graph etc.

f) A 2-Dimensional array is used to represent a matrix.

4.2.2 Limitation of Arrays

The limitations of the array in the data structure are as follows:

a) Variables with same data types only can be stored in an Array.

b) The dimension of an array is fixed/determined the moment the array is created, which cannot be changed later on.

c) The variables in an array are always ordered sequentially with an index starting with 0.

d) Time complexity increases in insertion and deletion operations.

e) There is a wastage of memory because arrays are fixed in size.

f) An array occupies a memory that is proportional to its size, independently of the number of elements that are actually of interest.

g) It is impossible to increase the size of an array once we have declared the array.

Factz Funda

An array contains items of the same type, while List in Python allows elements of different types. That is the only difference between an array and a list.

4.3 EXAMPLES OF ARRAYS USING ARCADE MAKECODE PLATFORM

Example 1: Printing the first element of the array

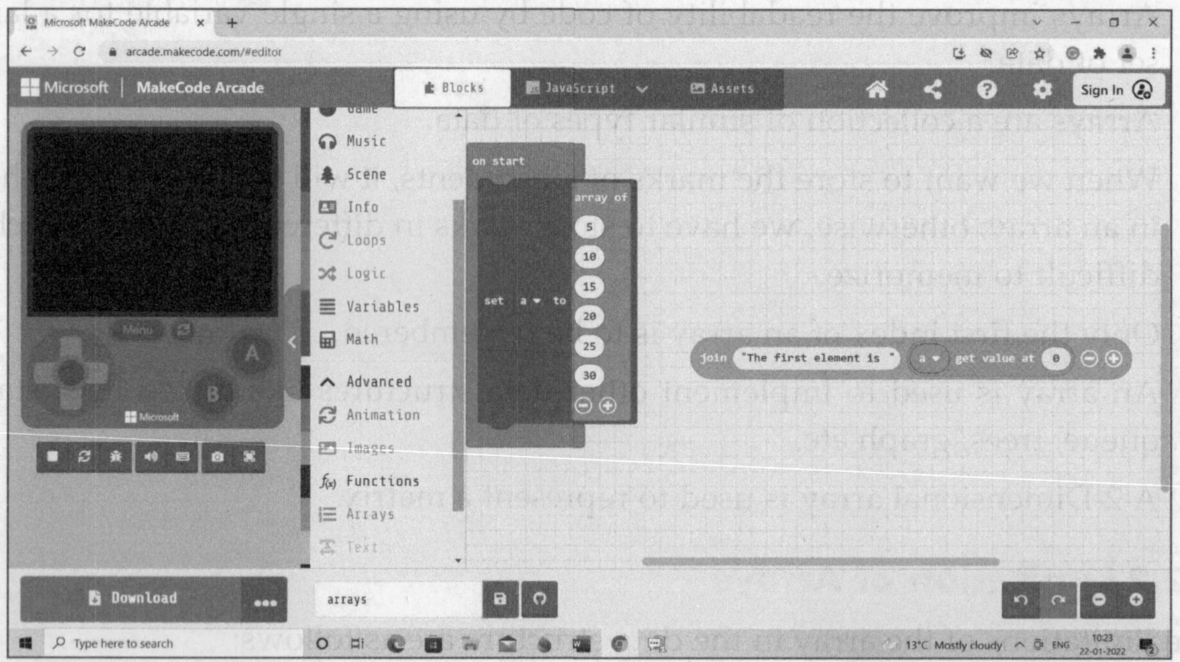

Figure 4.21

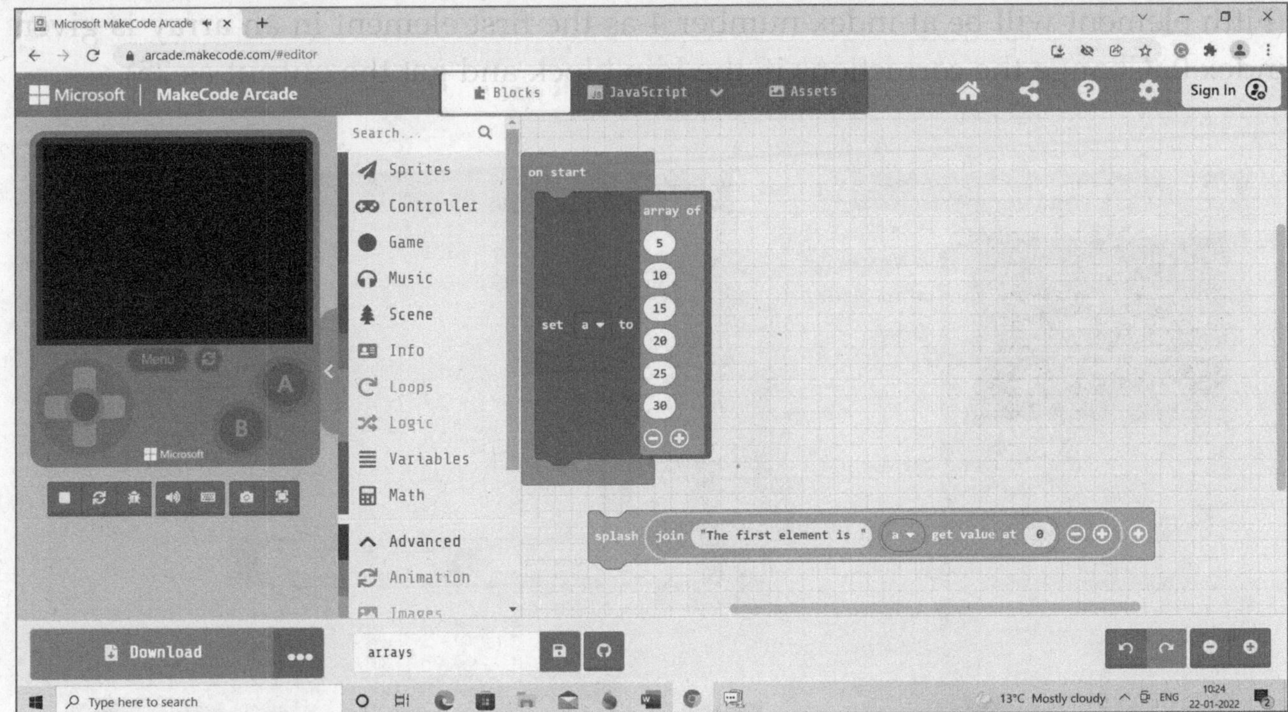

Figure 4.22

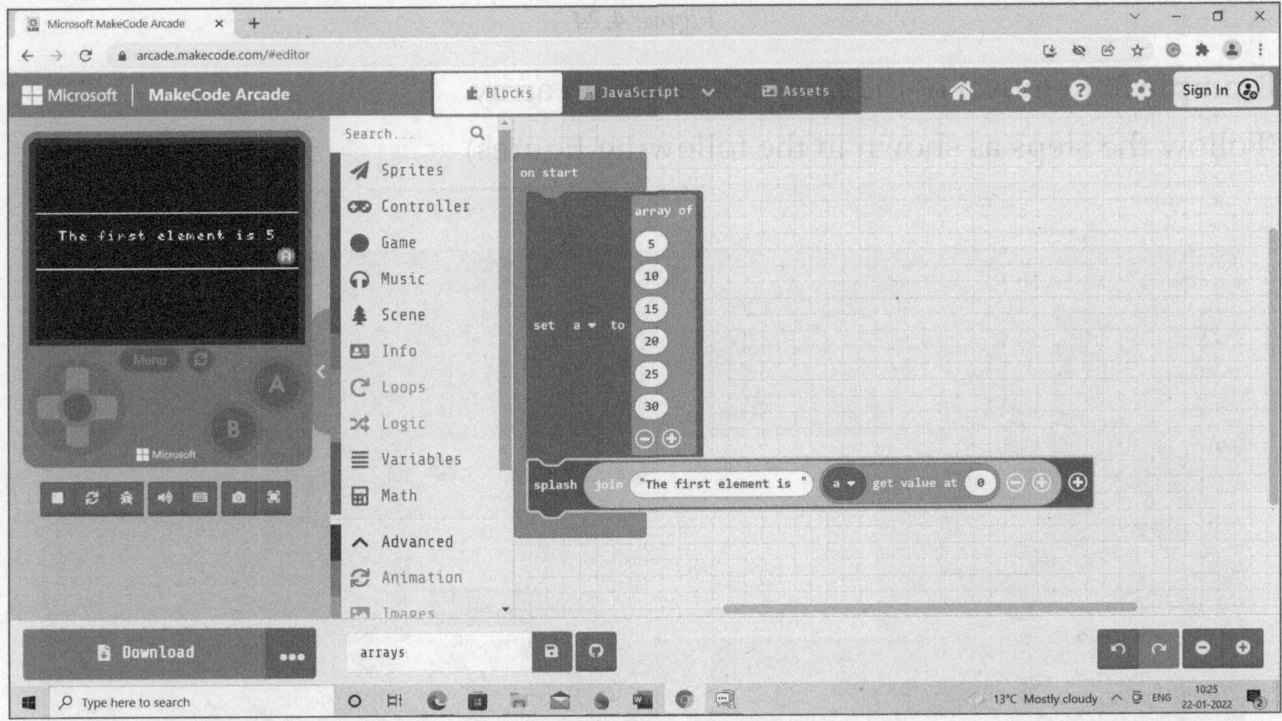

Figure 4.23

Example 2: Printing the fifth element of the array

(Fifth element will be at index number 4 as the first element in an array is given index 0. Change the corrections in the Join block and get the output as 25)

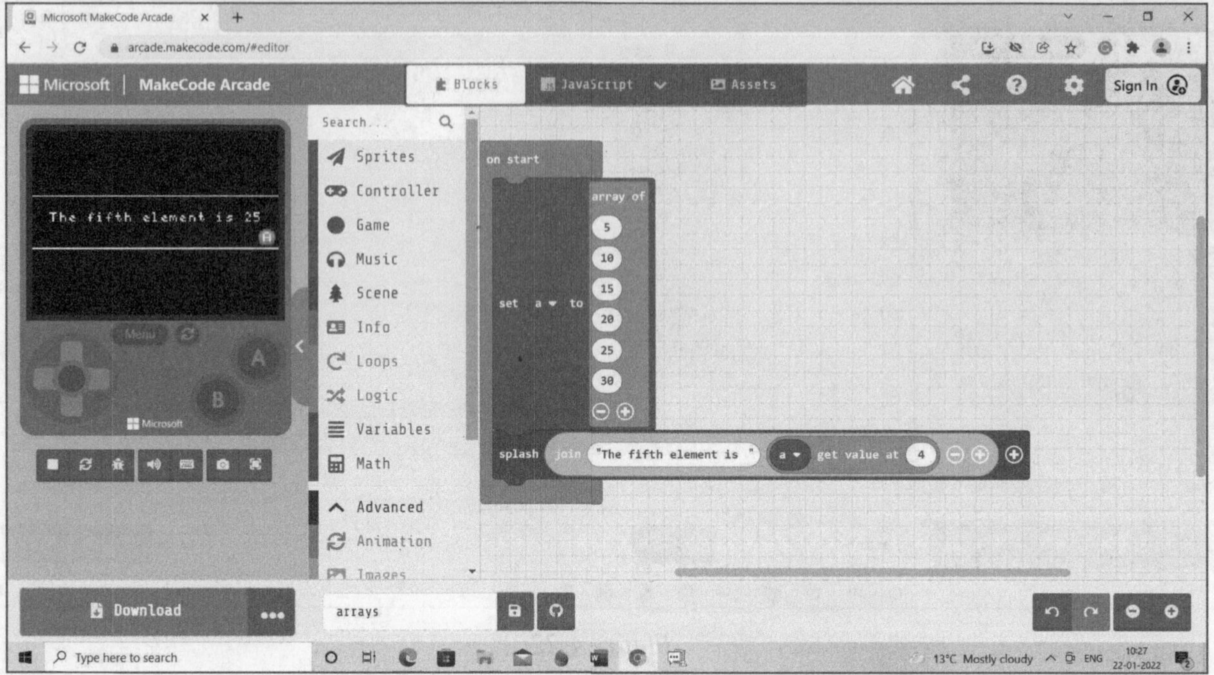

Figure 4.24

Example 3: Removal of the first element in an array

(Follow the steps as shown in the following figures)

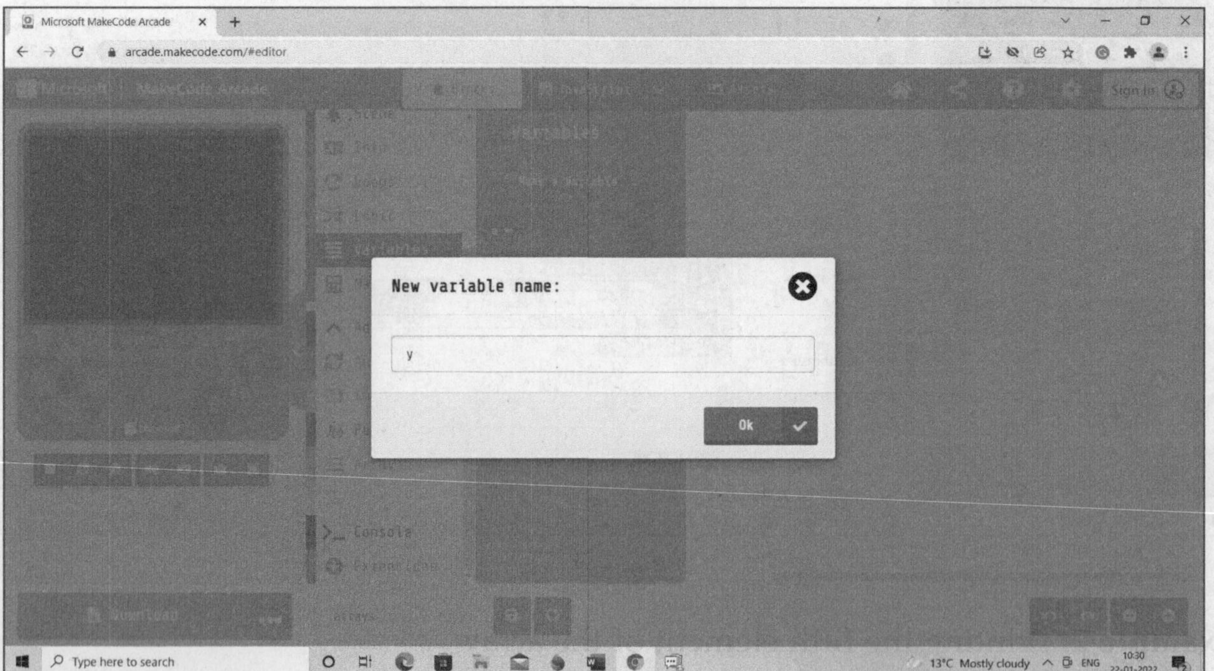

Figure 4.25

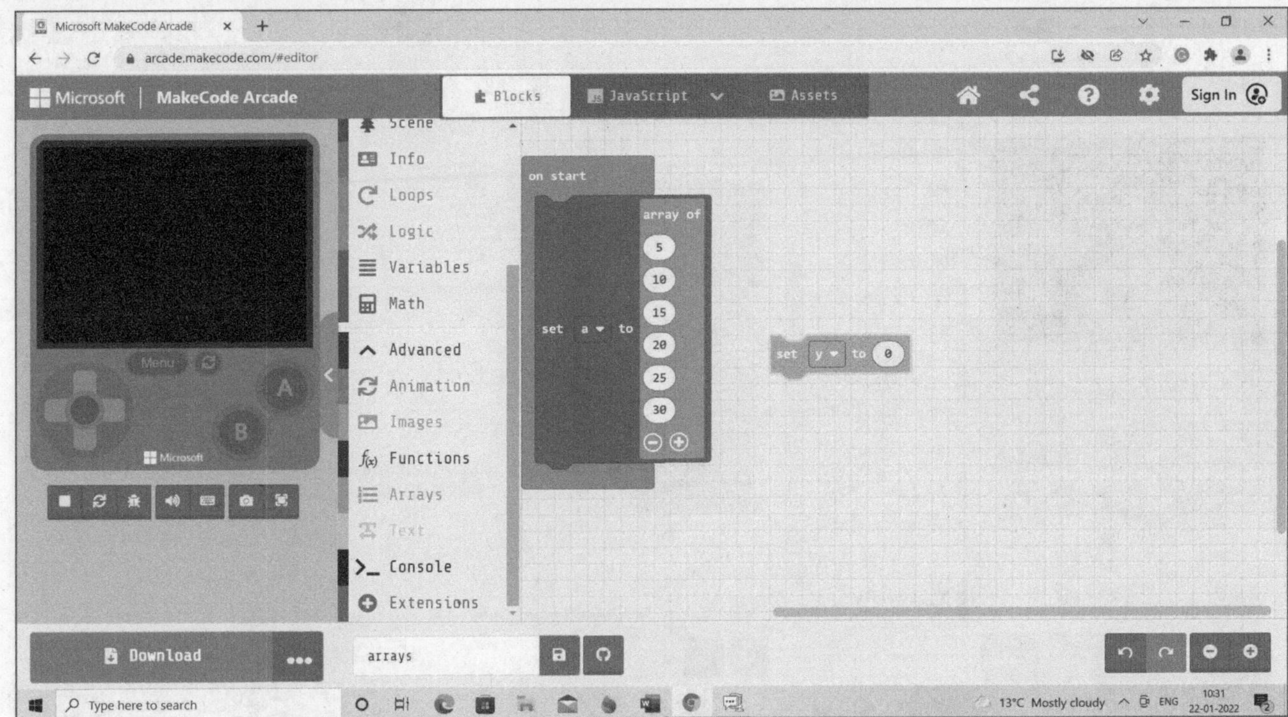

Figure 4.26

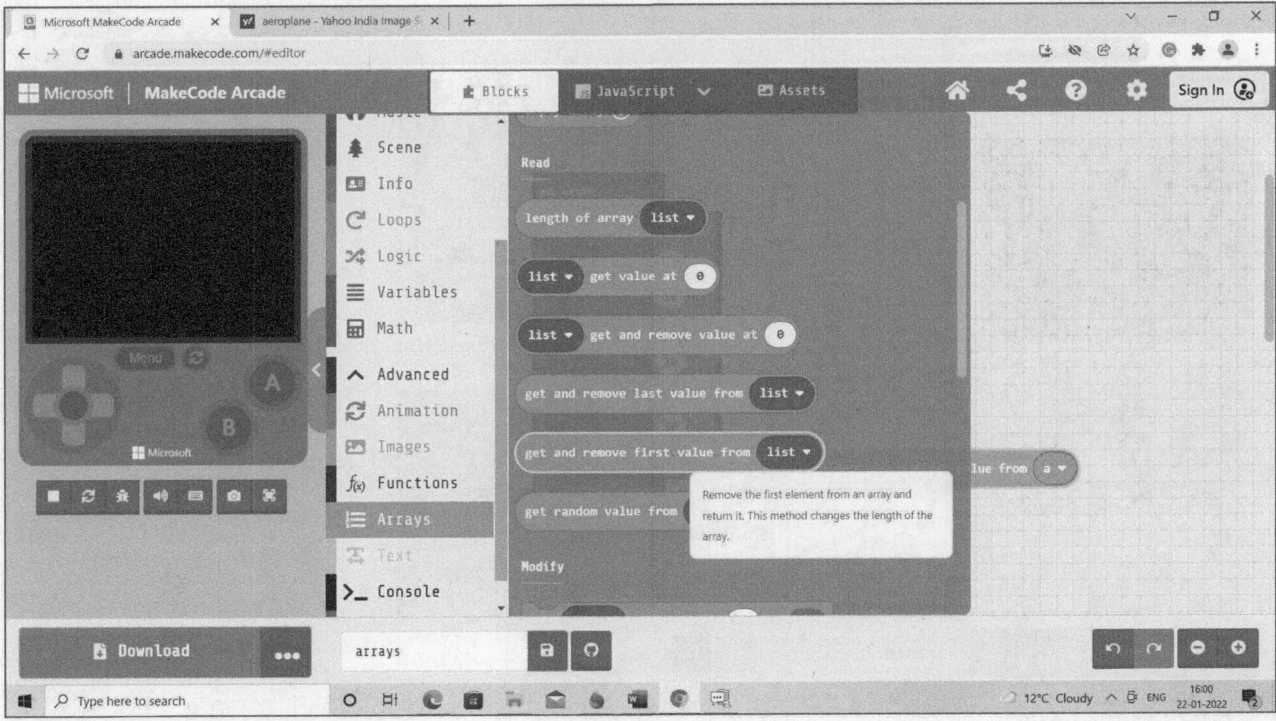

Figure 4.27

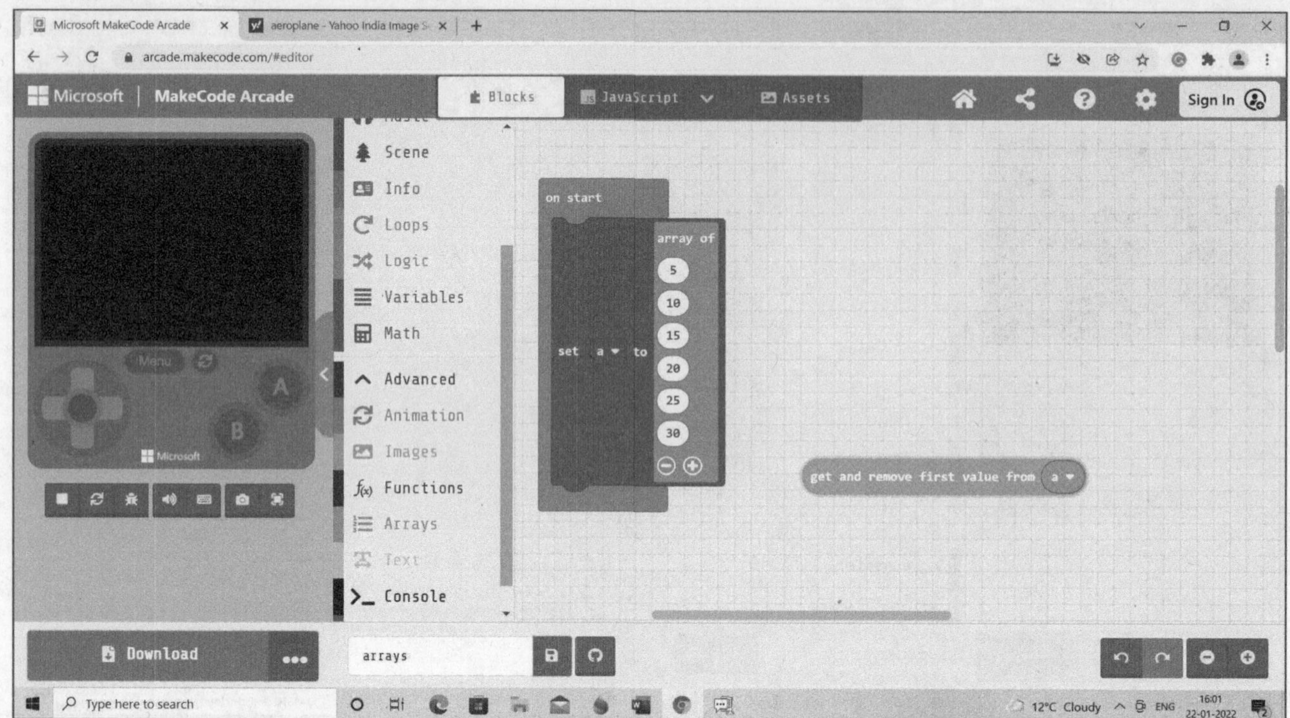

Figure 4.28

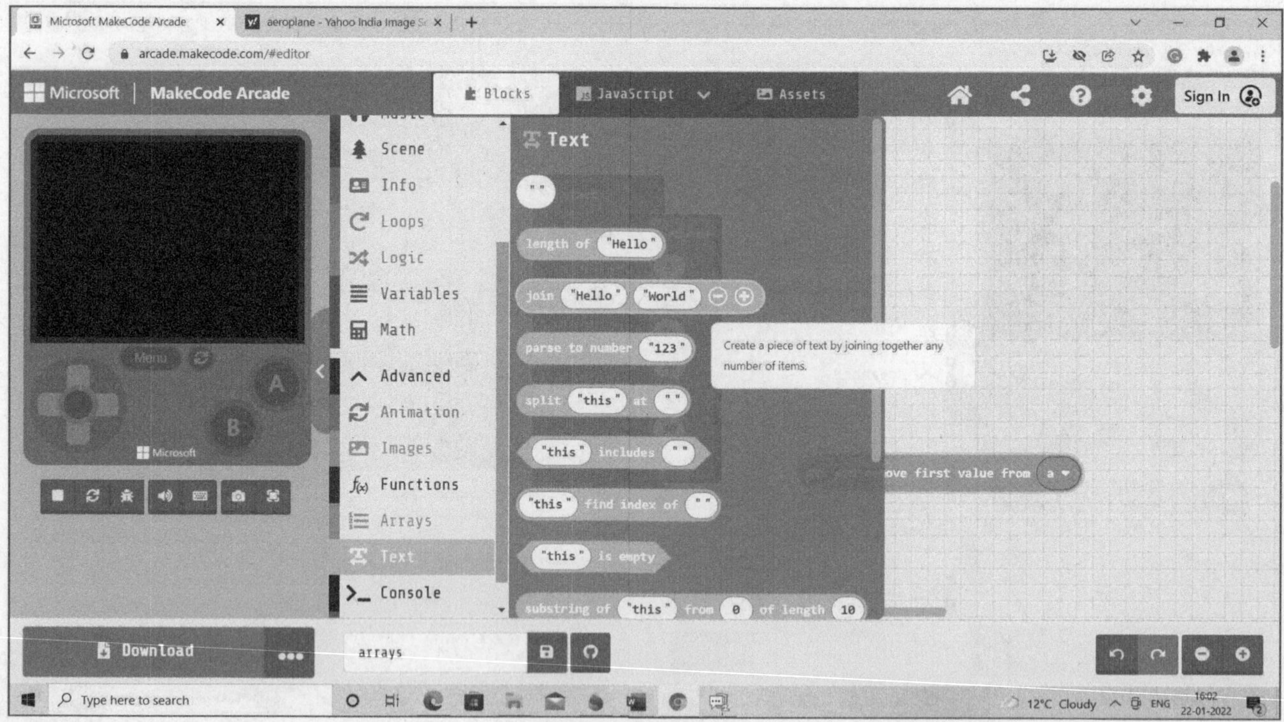

Figure 4.29

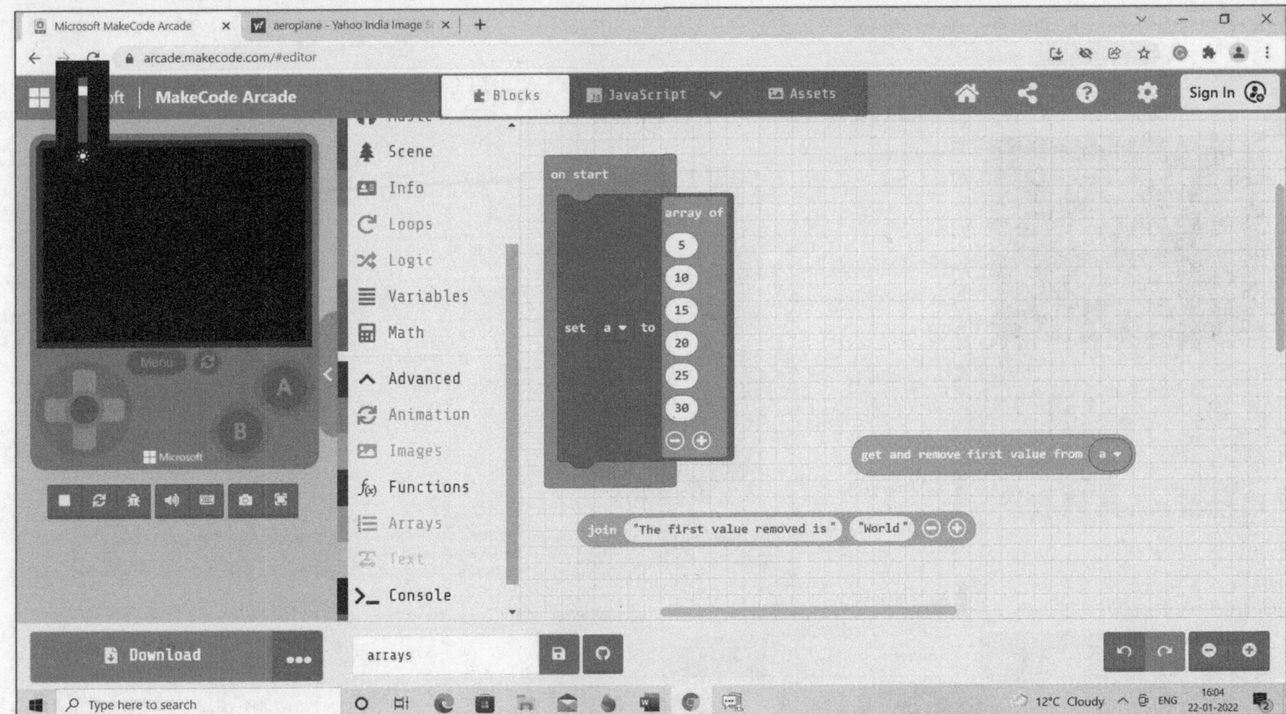

Figure 4.30

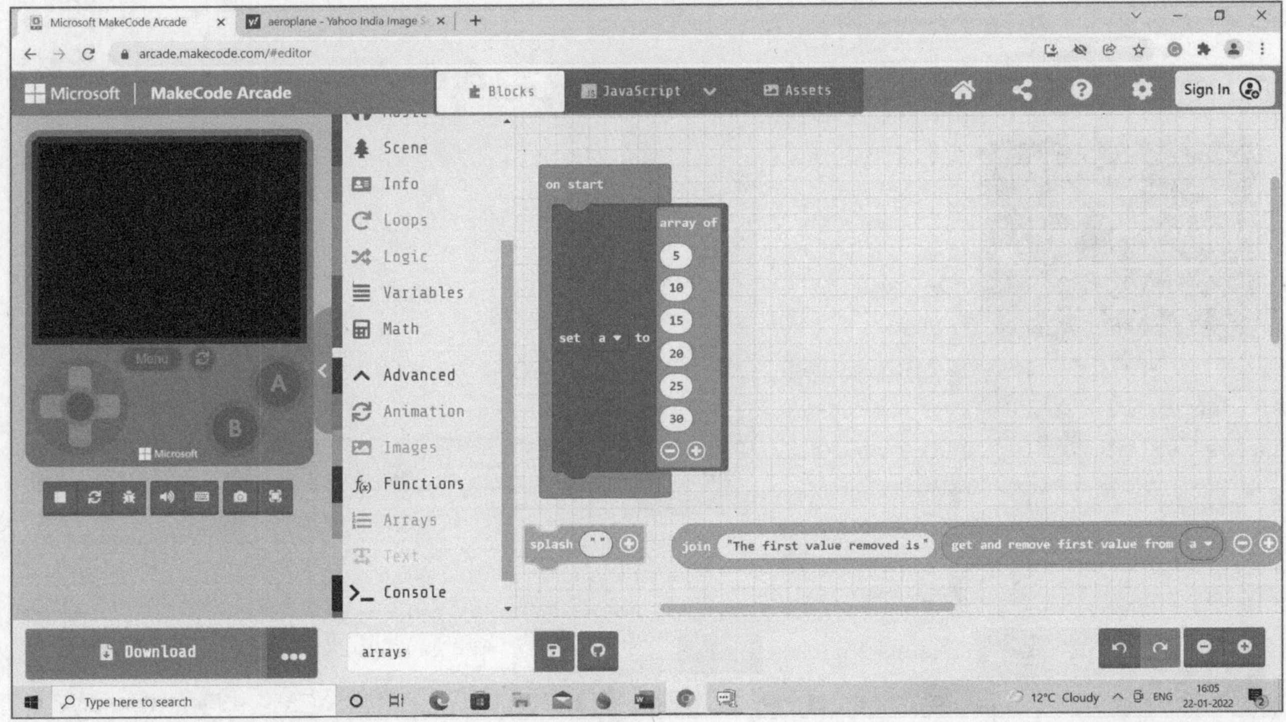

Figure 4.31

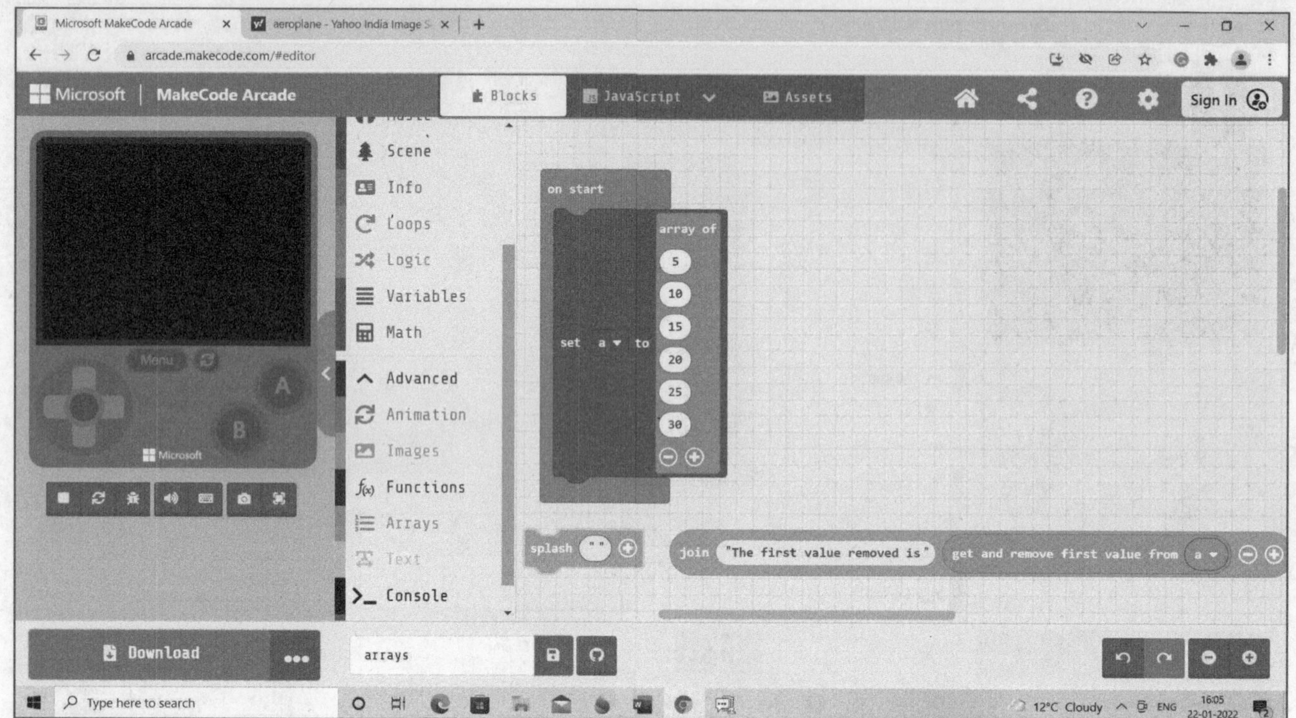

Figure 4.32

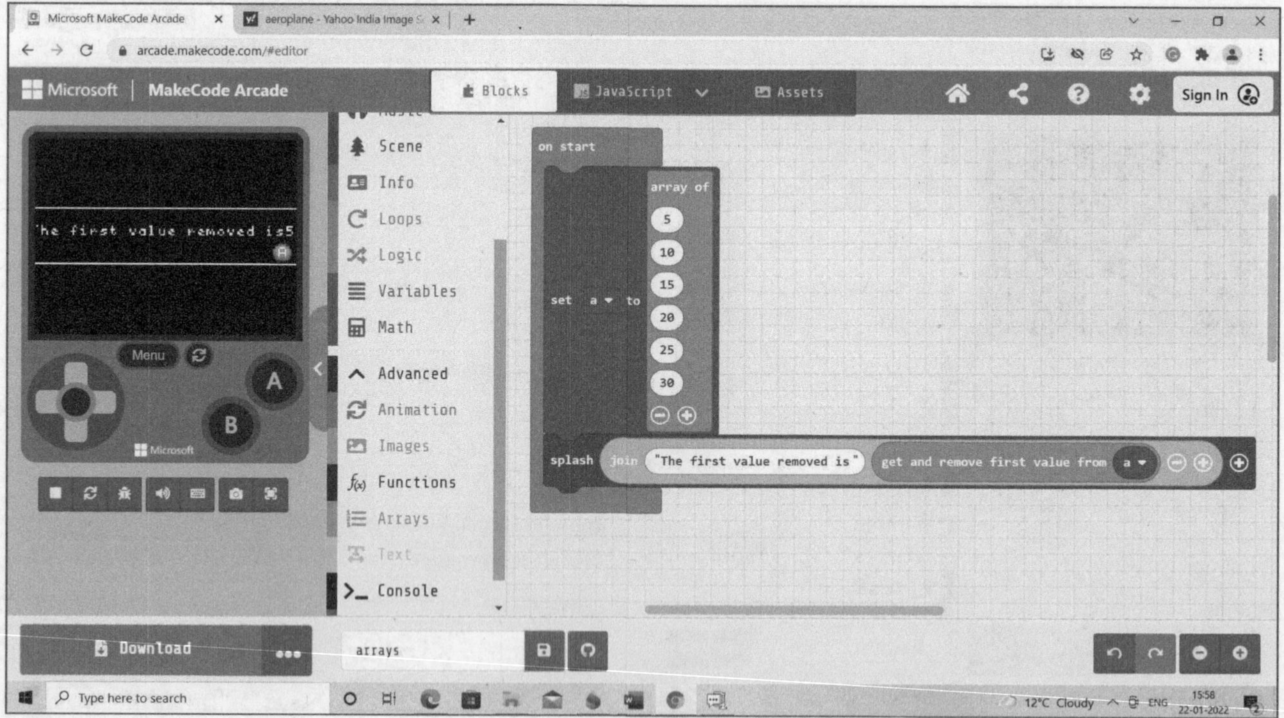

Figure 4.33

Example 4: Printing/ displaying the length of array.

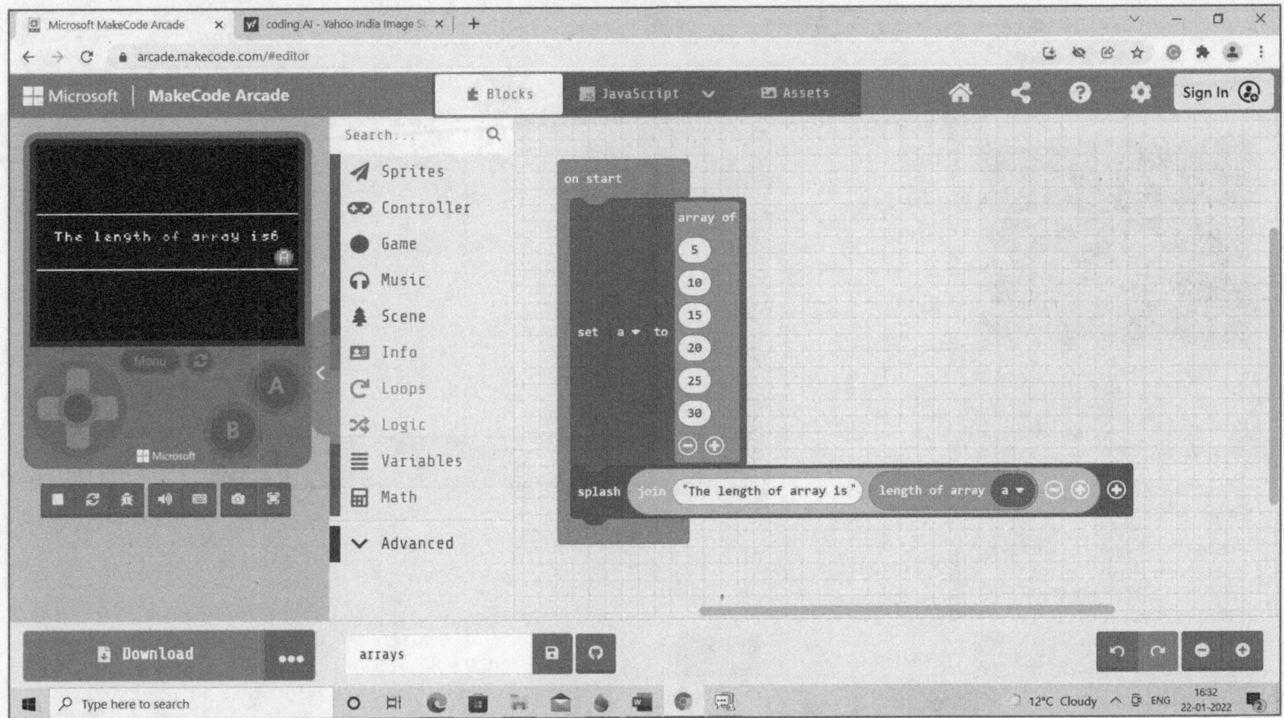

Figure 4.34

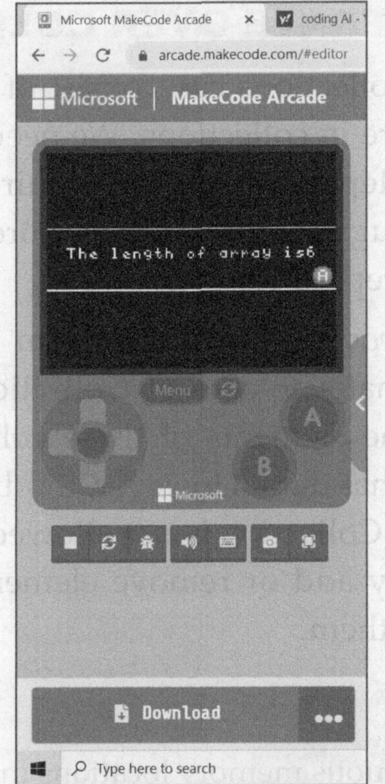

Figure 4.35

Example 5: Get and display random values in an array

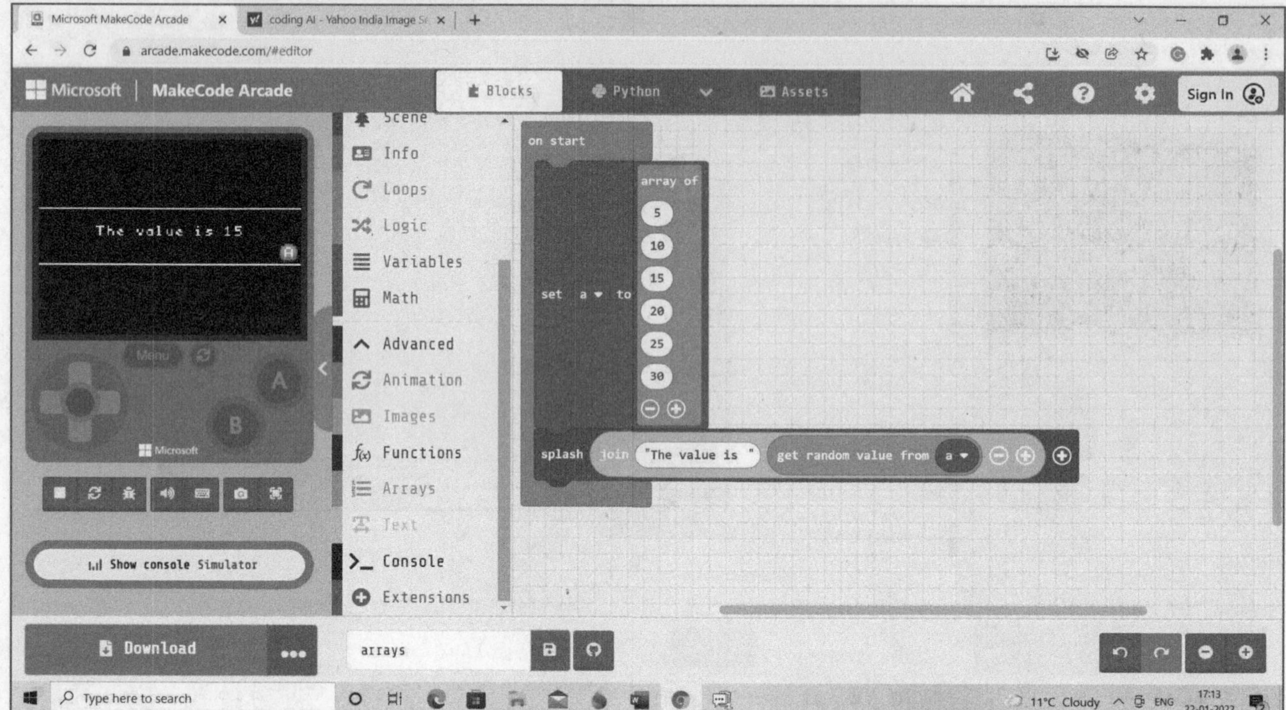

Figure 4.36

4.4 HOW CAN WE ITERATE OVER COLLECTIONS?

Now, we understand that collections can consist of lists, sets, or maps. There is a lot of data that we can store in collections. We need to use this data or perform modifications on this data depending on the requirements of a program. To do this, we need to iterate through the data that is stored in these collections. Now, we will understand the concept of Iterator.

The iterators are used to provide users a uniform way of accessing collections in a sequential manner. Whatever type of Collection we are using, we always need to traverse through the elements of these collections to fetch the data or make any modifications to that data. However, modifying a collection's elements while iterating through that Collection is not allowed and exhibits an error in the program. We cannot directly add or remove elements during iterating through the Collection that includes them.

Factz Funda

All arrays consist of contiguous memory locations in which the lowest address corresponds to the first element, and the highest address to the last element.

4.5 MODIFYING COLLECTIONS

Till now, we have a clear understanding of what collections are and how do we store data in collections and iterate over the data. Now, we will discuss how we modify this data that is stored in the Collection.

Coding/Programming provides multiple ways of modifying the data stored in collections. Every Collection cannot be modified, and there is a limitation on what can be modified in a collection. As we have read above, modifying a collection's elements while iterating through that Collection is not allowed and throws an error in the program. We cannot directly add or remove elements while iterating through the Collection that includes them.Table 4.1 enlists important points about collections.

Table 4.1 Important features of collections

a) Collections that do not support modification operations (such as add, remove and clear) are known as "unmodifiable". Collections that are not unmodifiable are modifiable.

b) There are some collections that give a guarantee that no change in the Collection object will be visible. These are called immutable. Collections that are not immutable are mutable.

c) Lists assuring that their size remains constant even though the elements can change, are known as fixed size. Lists that are not fixed-size are referred to as variable-size.

d) We cannot iterate or modify a Collection that is null.

Now, we will understand the modifications that we can do on collections.

4.5.1 Adding Elements During Iteration

To add elements while iterating a list, set or map, keep the new elements in a temporary list, set, or map and add them to the original after finishing iterating the Collection.

4.5.2 Removing Elements During Iteration

To remove elements from a list, we can create a new list, then insert the elements we wish to keep. Or, add the elements we wish to remove to a different list and remove them after finishing iterating the Collection.

Coding Quiz

1. An array is:
   (a) A group of elements of the same data type
   (b) A type of Collection that contains more than one element
   (c) A type of Collection in which elements are stored in memory in continuous or contiguous locations
   (d) All of the above
2. What is the starting index of an array?
   (a) -1 (b) 0
   (c) 1 (d) 2
3. Which one is an incorrect array?
   (a) Arr[] = [2 ,3 ,4] (b) Arr[] = ['a' , 'b' ,'c' 'd', 'e']
   (c) Arr[] = [1, 'd', 'h', 6] (d) Arr[] = [5.0 , 7.4, 9.7 , 3.4]
4. Collections in programming can consist of:
   (a) Lists, (b) Sets,
   (c) Maps (d) Any of the above
5. Which of the following statements is a correct statement about Arrays?
   (a) An array address is the address of the first element of the array itself.
   (b) Array size must be declared if not initialised immediately.
   (c) Array size is defined as the sum of sizes of all elements of an array.
   (d) All of the above
6. Which of the following is a disadvantage of arrays?
   (a) Variables with the same data types only can be stored in an Array.
   (b) Arrays improve the readability of code by using a single variable for a large set of data.
   (c) Arrays are a collection of similar types of data.
   (d) Only the first index of an array is to be remembered.

ANSWERS
1. (d) 2. (b) 3. (c) 4. (d) 5. (d) 6. (a)

SUMMARY

- In programming, a collection is a class that is used to represent a group/set of similar data type items as a single unit.
- Some Collection classes of Java are Vector, Stack, and Array.
- A counter is a sub-class of the dictionary that is used to keep the count of the elements during iteration.
- Collections allow programmers to group multiple items into a common group/set. A collection is resizable and can grow.
- Collection increases the performance of the program.
- Collection increases productivity and reduces operational time.
- On modifying collections while traversing, it may create problems like, unexpected Results and concurrency problems.
- An array is defined as a collection of variables of the same type.
- An array is a collection of similar data type variables, and hence, arrays do not support different data types in the same Collection.
- A 'List' contains a collection of items and it supports add/update/delete/search operations.
- An array contains items of the same type, while List in Python allows elements of different types.
- Arrays improve the readability of code by using a single variable for a large set of data.
- The variables in an array are always ordered sequentially with an index starting with 0.
- Time complexity increases in insertion and deletion operations.
- There is a wastage of memory because arrays are fixed in size.
- An array occupies a memory that is proportional to its size, independently of the number of elements that are actually of interest.
- It is impossible to increase the size of the array once you have declared the array.
- The iterators are used to provide users with a uniform way of accessing collections in a sequential manner.
- Every Collection cannot be modified, and there is a limitation on what can be modified in a collection.
- Collections that do not support modification operations (such as add, remove and clear) are known as "unmodifiable."
- Collections that are not unmodifiable, are modifiable.

- There are some collections that give a guarantee that no change in the Collection object will be visible. These are called immutable.
- Collections that are not immutable, are mutable.
- Lists assuring that their size remains constant even though the elements can change known as fixed size.
- To add elements while iterating a list, set, or map, keep the new elements in a temporary list, set, or map and add them to the original after finishing iterating the Collection.
- To remove elements from a list, we can create a new list, then insert the elements we wish to keep. Or, the elements we wish to remove to a different list and remove them after finishing iterating the Collection.
- All arrays consist of contiguous memory locations.

PRACTICE TIME

(A) True/False Type Questions

1. In programming, a collection is a class that is used to represent a group/set of similar data type items as a single unit.
2. An array is employed/used to store a collection of data.
3. A counter is a sub-class of the dictionary that is used to keep the count of the elements during iteration.
4. Collections do not allow programmers to group multiple items into a common group/set.
5. Grouping of items makes it possible to identify the items easily and perform different operations on them like retrieving and modifying data.
6. Collection decreases the performance of the program.
7. Python doesn't have an explicit array data structure because we can perform the same things with the List.
8. The 'List' contains a collection of items and it supports add/ update/ delete/ search operations.
9. Collection decreases productivity and reduces operational time.
10. On modifying collections while traversing, it may create problems like unexpected Results and concurrency problems.

ANSWERS							
1. T	2. T	3. T	4. F	5. T	6. F (increases)	7. T	8. T
9. F (increases)	10. T						

(B) Fill in the Blanks

1. A ____________ is resizable and can grow.
2. Some collection classes of ____________ are Vector, Stack, Hashtable, and Array.
3. Collection ____________ effort to maintain because every user knows Collection API classes.
4. An array contains items of the same type, while Python allows elements of different types.
5. A 2-Dimensional array is used to represent a ____________.
6. ____________ with the same data types can be stored in an Array.
7. There is a wastage of memory because arrays are fixed in ____________.
8. Collections that do not support modification operations (such as add, remove and clear) are known as ____________.
9. There are some collections that give a guarantee that no change in the Collection object will be visible, and these are called ____________.
10. All ____________ consist of contiguous memory locations.

ANSWERS					
1. Collection	2. Java	3. reduces	4. List	5. matrix	6.Variables
7. size	8. unmodifiable	9. immutable	10. arrays		

(C) Very Short Answers Questions

1. Define an Array.
2. What are collections?
3. What is an array index?
4. What do you mean by a List?

(D) Short Answer Questions

1. Write two real-life collections which work like Arrays.
2. How can we iterate over collections?
3. What are the different types of modifications that we can perform on collections?
4. Do collections allow backward traversing of data? Justify your answer.

(E) High Order Thinking Skill Questions (HOTS)

1. Why is there not much use of a separate data structure in Python to support arrays?
2. What is the only difference between an array and a list?
3. Draw a flowchart for the optimized algorithm for finding the square of numbers.
4. Write a program to create an array of prime numbers from 40 to 80.

(F) Projects

Problem Statement: 'Create an exercise in Arcade MakeCode to create and Arrays of even numbers from 1 to 20 and then iterate over each element of this Array.'

5 Hello World with Code

Structure

In this chapter, you will learn:

- The basics of a programming language.
- Different types of programming languages.
- The use of syntax.
- Variables and data types.

INTRODUCTION

Artificial intelligence is nowadays regarded as the future technology of the world. We can see so many AI-Based applications around us that are used by a large number of people daily. The programming/coding of such types of devices needs a programming language. If we wish to develop an AI application, then we have to know a programming language. The different programming languages, like Lisp, Prolog, C++, Java, and Python, can be used for developing applications of AI. Python has become a widely used computer programming language nowadays.

AI has not only revolutionised information technology, but it has attracted the scientists to apply it in all other fields also. Many new things are being prepared by using the latest advances in every aspect of AI including machine learning, data mining, fuzzy logic, etc.

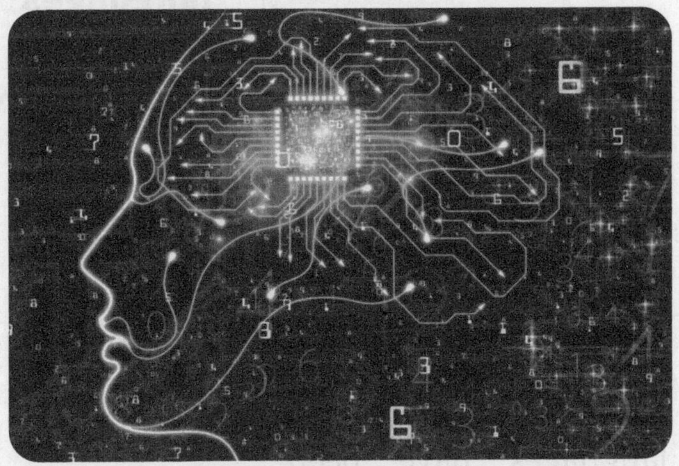

Figure 5.1

Source: https://morioh.com/p/2e5867121898

In this chapter, we will learn about programming languages and some fundamentals of coding.

Learning Objectives:

At the end of this chapter, you will be able to:

- Explain high and low-level programming languages.
- Understand the use of syntax.
- Explain variables and data types.
- Perform a fun activity to create a Calculator in Arcade.

5.1 PROGRAMMING LANGUAGE

A computer program may be defined as a set of instructions that are given to a computer to execute. A programming language is defined as a tool we use to write instructions for computers to follow. Therefore, a programming language is a computer language that is used by programmers (developers) to communicate with computers. We need a programming language since computers cannot understand the languages humans speak (natural language). Computers can only understand binary strings of 1s and 0s.

A programming language is chiefly used to develop desktop applications, websites, and mobile applications. It is a set of instructions written in a programming language (C, C++, Java, Python) to perform a specific task.

It is interesting to note that the very earliest computers were programmed by changing ones and zeros manually by alternating the circuit and the wiring. But nowadays, all modern programming languages are made up of a series of syntax and symbols that act as a bridge to allow humans to translate their thoughts into instructions so that computers can understand them..

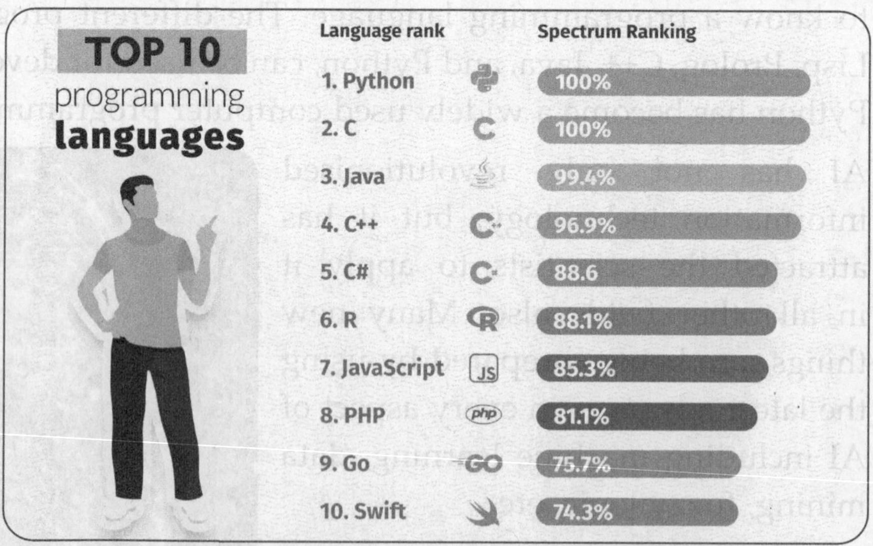

Figure 5.2 Some Programming languages

Source: https://qawerk.com/blogs/how-to-quickly-choose-open-source-tools-for-automated-testing-of-web-and-mobile-applications/

A good number of programming languages have been created since now, and more are being created every year but the most popular programming languages are Python, JavaScript, Java, and C++.

5.2 LOW LEVEL AND HIGH-LEVEL PROGRAMMING LANGUAGES

Programming languages are broadly classified into two categories: high-level languages and low-level languages. Both types of languages have their own applications, so it is important to understand the difference between the two types of languages.

(a) Low-Level Languages: A low-level programming language is the programming language that is made to be easily understood by the computer. These languages include machine code (or Object code) and assembly language (ASM), both of which instruct computer hardware components to carry out instructions directly. The main advantage of assembly language is that it requires less memory and less execution time to execute a program. But, low-level programming languages are difficult to learn, and they are time-consuming to code.

Factz Funda

Machine language is easier to read due to its display in binary or hexadecimal form (base 16 form). It does not require any translator to convert the programs.

(b) High-Level Languages: A high-level programming language is made to help human programmers communicate easily to the computer. A high-level programming language is easy to read, write, and maintain. High-level programming language mainly includes Python, Java, JavaScript, PHP, C#, C++, Objective C, Cobol, Perl, Pascal, LISP, FORTRAN, and Swift programming language. These languages are usually compiled or converted into low-level programming languages so that they can be executed directly. Grace Hopper, sometimes called "Amazing Grace," invented the concept of a compiler.

5.3 PYTHON

Python is an object-oriented programming language, and it was created by Guido Rossum in 1989. It is ideally designed for rapid prototyping of complex applications. It has interfaces to many OS systems and libraries and is extensible to C or C++. Many companies like NASA, Google, YouTube, BitTorrent, etc., use the Python programming language. Python is a case-sensitive language in which 'A' and 'a' are different and do not have the same meaning.

Python programming is widely used in Artificial Intelligence, Natural Language Programming, Neural Networks, Data Science, and other advanced fields of Computer Science. Python had a deep focus on code readability. Some of the applications are enlisted in Table 5.1.

Table 5.1 Applications of Python

a) Web and Internet Development
b) Desktop GUI Applications
c) Software Development
d) Build Artificial Intelligence algorithms
e) Business Applications
f) 3D Graphics
g) Database Access
h) Programs: various scientific programs such as statistical models

Factz Funda

The selection sort algorithm sorts an array by finding the minimum element (considering ascending order) from the unsorted part and swapping it.

5.3.1 Advantages of Python

- Python is Interpreted. Python is processed at runtime by the interpreter. The user does not need to compile the program before executing it.
- Python language is easy to read, easy to understand, and easy to write.
- Python integrates with other programming languages like C, C++, and Java.
- Python is Object-Oriented. Python supports Object-Oriented style or technique programming that encapsulates code within objects.
- Python executes code line-by-line, and hence, it is easy for the programmer to find the error and debug it in the code.
- Python is platform-independent. It means that the user can write code once and run it on any other platform.

5.3.2 Disadvantages of Python

- Python is not found suitable for developing mobile applications and games.

- Python works with the interpreter. That's why it is slower than some other programming languages like C and C++.

Activity 5.2

- Participate in this individual activity on "**Sorting the list**" to learn the concept of Selection Sort.

Aim: Suppose we have a list of unsorted numbers and want to sort the list in such a way that the smallest number is on top of the list and the largest number is at the bottom.

Process: We start with finding the smallest number from the list. Once we find this number, we want to put it at the top of the list. However, if you put this number on the top of the list, where should the number which currently is on the top of the list be shifted to? We do not have any additional space here.

Hence, once we spot the smallest number from the list, we swap/replace it with the number which was present at the top position in the unsorted list.

Now, the first row from our list is sorted. We will sort the second row now. We will repeat a similar technique here.

We will find the smallest number from the remaining unsorted list and swap it with the number in the second row. We will repeat the process till we reach the last row from the list. When you are done with the last element from the list, you can look back and check that all the numbers from the list are now sorted, and our list is now ordered in ascending order.

This method of sorting in programming is called "Selection Sort."

The algorithm for Selection Sort is as stated below:

Step 1: Set MIN to location 0 (zero).

Step 2: Search the element with minimum value in the list.

Step 3: Swap with element at location MIN.

Step 4: Increment MIN to point to the next element.

Step 5: Repeat until the list is sorted.

Let us now sort the below array in ascending order using selection sort algorithm:

Array = {3, 2, 11, 7}

Step 1: For i = 0

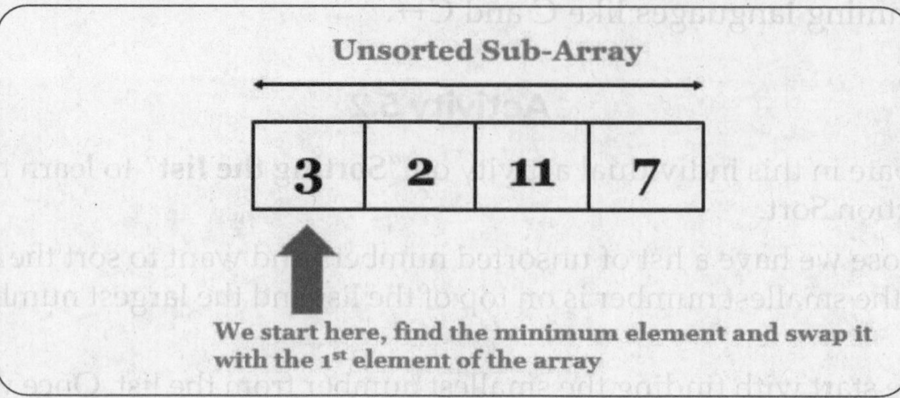

Figure 5.3

Step 2: For i = 1

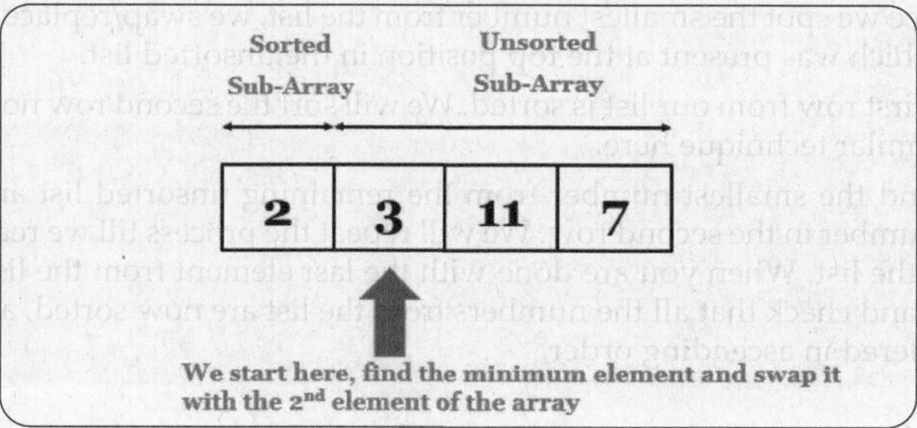

Figure 5.4

Step 3: For i = 2

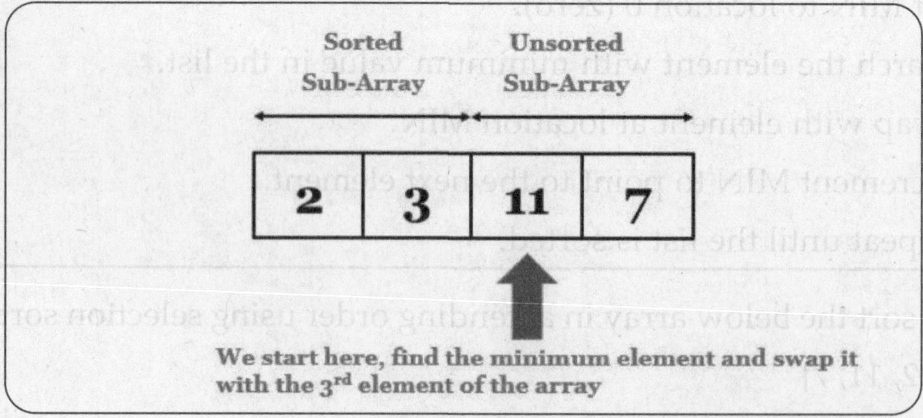

Figure 5.5

Step 4: For i = 3

The loop gets terminated as "i" becomes 2. The final state of the array after the loop is terminated looks like below:

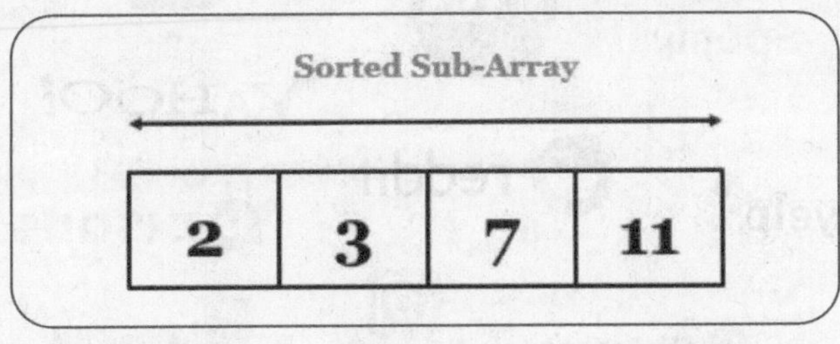

Figure 5.6

Factz Funda

In selection sort, the smallest value among the given unsorted elements of the array is selected in every step/pass and inserted to its appropriate position into the array. It is also the simplest algorithm.

5.4 GETTING USED TO SYNTAX

The syntax of a language explains the form of a valid program without provuding any information about the meaning of the program and/ the results of executing that program. The meaning given to a combination of symbols is handled by semantics.

The syntax of a computer language is the set of rules to define the combinations of symbols. Syntax is necessary to understand the meaning or semantics of a language.

Python is an, easy-to-learn programming language used to build a variety of applications. Python is used in web development, game development, and the development of desktop-based applications. Python is also widely used for data science, machine learning, and artificial intelligence.

It is interesting to know that the world's most famous websites like Google, YouTube, Instagram, etc., use Python.

Factz Funda

When the syntax of a programming language is not followed, then the code will not be understood by a compiler or interpreter.

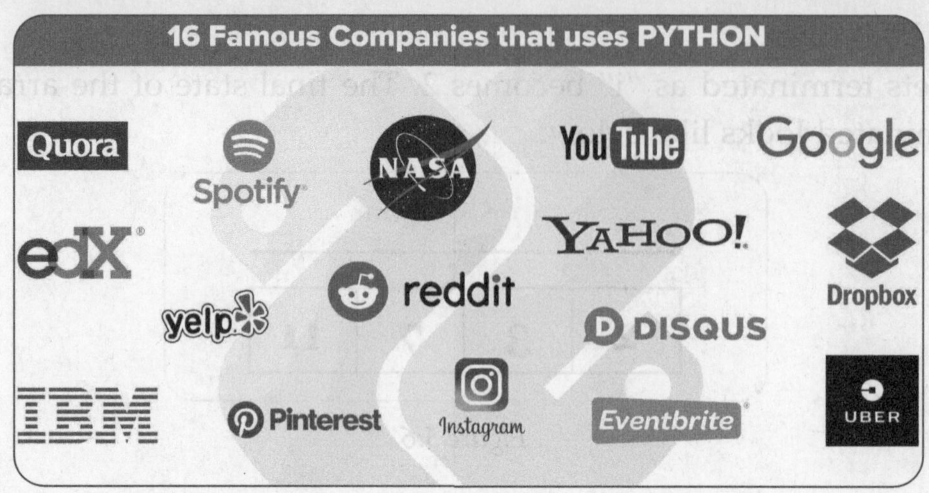

Figure 5.7

Source: https://www.codingdojo.com/blog/why-you-should-learn-python

Now let us get started with some basic Python syntax.

5.5 VARIABLES AND DATA TYPES IN PROGRAMMING

Variables are used by programmers to store values. Variables are useful for several purposes like counting how many times an event occurs, saving inputs from users, and performing complex calculations.

5.5.1 Variables

A variable is a named location that is used to store data in the memory of the computer. Whenever a variable is created, Python assigns a spot to it so that its value can be stored till the program runs. We can store lots of different types of information in a variable. For example, we can store a number, text, or a list of items. We can also change the value assigned to a variable while the program is running.

It is like that variable as a container that holds data that can be changed later throughout programming. For example,

```
x = 35
y = 91
```

These declarations make sure that the program reserves memory for two variables with the names x and y. The variable names stand for the memory location. It's like the two shoeboxes. These shoeboxes are labeled with x and y, and the corresponding values are stored in the shoeboxes. Like the two shoeboxes, the memory is empty as well at the beginning.

5.5.2 Datatypes

In any programming language, a variable can only store a value that is in a format. The various formats are called data types. Python has several in-built data types.

Every value in Python has a datatype. As everything is an object in Python programming, data types are actually classes, and variables are instances (object) of these classes. There are various data types in Python. Some of the important data types are mentioned in Table 5.2.

Table 5.2 Data types in Python

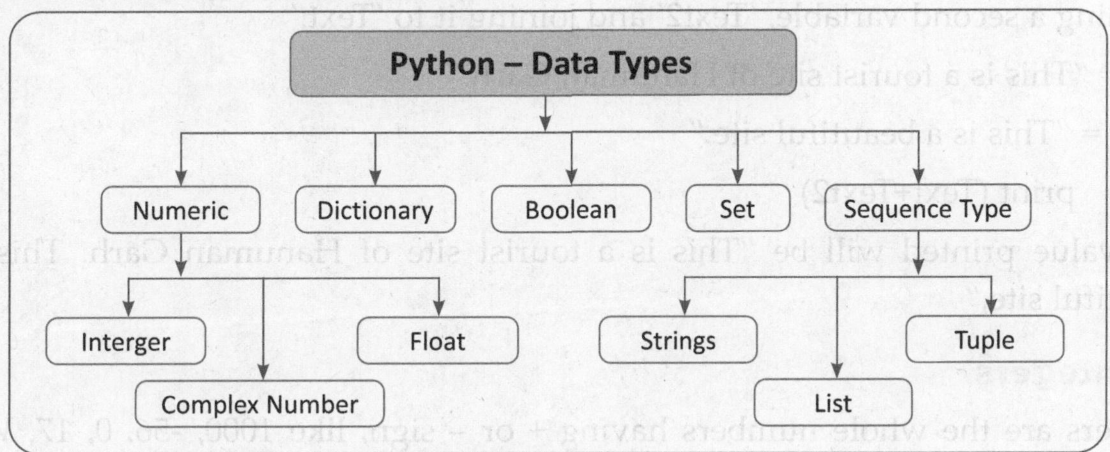

Figure 5.8

(a) Strings

In Python, a string is defined as a sequence of characters enclosed in either single, double, or triple quotes.

The characters can be alphabets of any language or symbols. Strings are also called str in short. You can perform many different operations on strings. You can access each character in a string using its position in the string.

A string is defined as an ordered sequence of letters/characters. Strings are enclosed in single quotes (' ') or double (" "). The quotes are not part of any string, but they only tell the computer where the string begins and ends. They can have any character or sign, including space in them.

Thus, strings in Python are identified as a contiguous set of characters represented in the quotation marks. Subsets or a part of strings can be taken using the slice operator([] and [:]) with indexes starting at 0 at the beginning of the string. The plus (+) sign is the string concatenation operator, and the asterisk (*) is the repetition operator.

We can also join two or more strings together to create a longer string. To concatenate strings, we use a + symbol between the two strings.

Let's look at the syntax for these operations.

Defining a variable 'Text' and setting its value.

```
Text = "This is a tourist site of Hanuman Garh."
```

Accessing the first letter of the 'Next' variable. The value printed will be N.

```
print(Text[0])
```

Defining a second variable, 'Text2' and joining it to 'Text.'

```
Text = "This is a tourist site of Hanuman Garh."
Text2 = "This is a beautiful site."
    print (Text+Text2)
```

The value printed will be "This is a tourist site of Hanuman Garh. This is a beautiful site."

(b) Integers

Integers are the whole numbers having + or – sign, like 1000, -56, 0, 17. While writing a large integer value, don't use commas to separate digits. Also, integers should not have leading zeros.

In Python, integer variables are used to store whole numbers, which can be positive or negative. Quotation marks should not be used while defining integers. Moreover, integer variables are treated like numbers for all mathematical operations.

Examples:

```
x = 5
y = 9
z = -12
```

(c) Floats

Float () is a built-in Python function that converts a number or a string to a float value and returns the result. When it fails for any invalid input, then an appropriate exception occurs. Numbers with fractions or decimal points are called floating-point numbers. A floating-point number will consist of a sign (+,-) sequence of decimals digits and a dot, like 0.0, -21.9, 0.98333328, 15.2963, etc. These numbers may also be used to represent a number in engineering/ scientific notation.

-3.0×10^{5} will be represented as -3.0e5

$4.3X10^{-6}$ will be 4.3e-6

If you need to store decimal numbers in Python, you should use float variables as integer variables ignore the decimal part of a number. When we combine a float variable and an integer variable in a mathematical calculation, the resulting answer will always be a float.

We can do several arithmetic operations with floats and integers. Let us see some common operations with floats and integers.

- Addition
- Subtraction
- Multiplication
- Division
- Modulus (Remainder)

Now that we will understand the syntax for performing different Mathematical operations on integers and floats in our Program:

Performing Addition of Integers and Floats

```
x = 15
y = 26
sum = x + y
```

Performing Subtraction of Integers and Floats

```
x = 71
y = 24
subtraction = x - y
```

Performing Multiplication of Integers and Floats

```
x = 61
y = 22
multiplication = x * y
```

Performing Division of Integers and Floats

```
x = 32
y = 8
division = x / y
```

Performing Modulus of Integers and Floats

```
x = 76
y = 7
modulus = x % y
```

Now that we are familiar with various arithmetic operations, we will use them in activity 5.3.

Project Time

Project 5.1

Aim: Making a Calculator.

Process: To understand the arithmetic operations better, we will now perform this activity by using Arcade MakeCode editor.

Open the link https://arcade.makecode.com/, and you will get the home page. Click on 'New Project' and fill the Project's name as "Calculator."

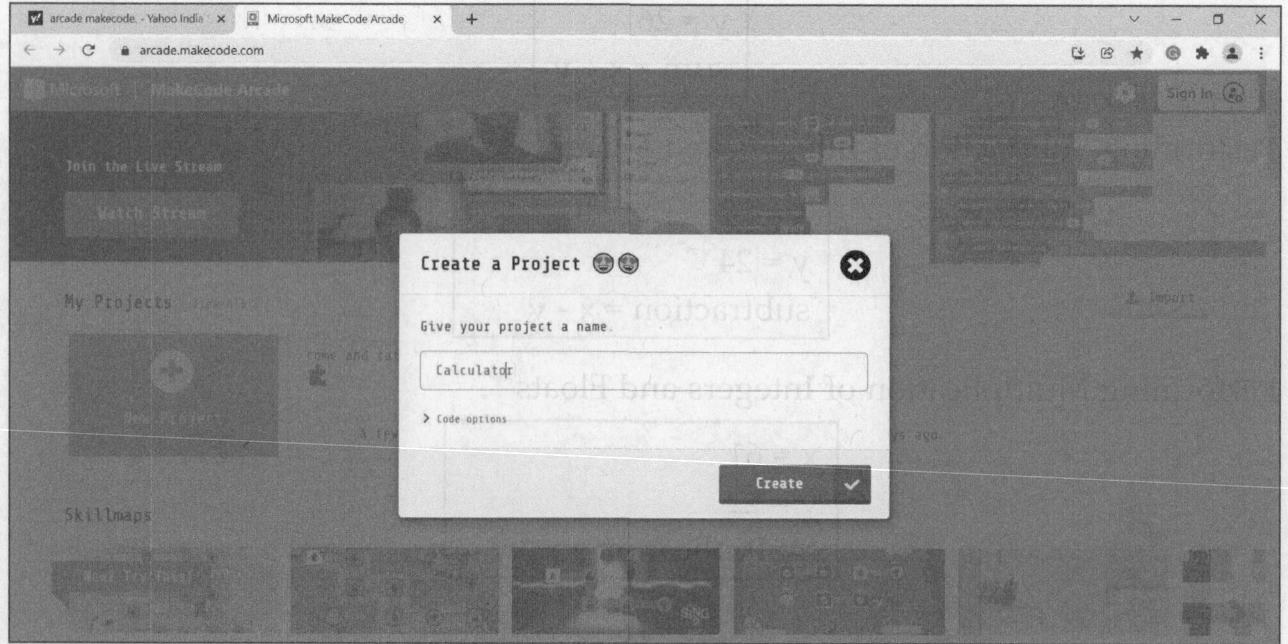

Figure 5.9

On clicking the "Create" button, you will get the following page:

Figure 5.10

Now, follow the following steps:

Step 1: Now, in Arcade MakeCode Editor, click on the "Variables" link from the toolbox and then click on the "Make a Variable" link.

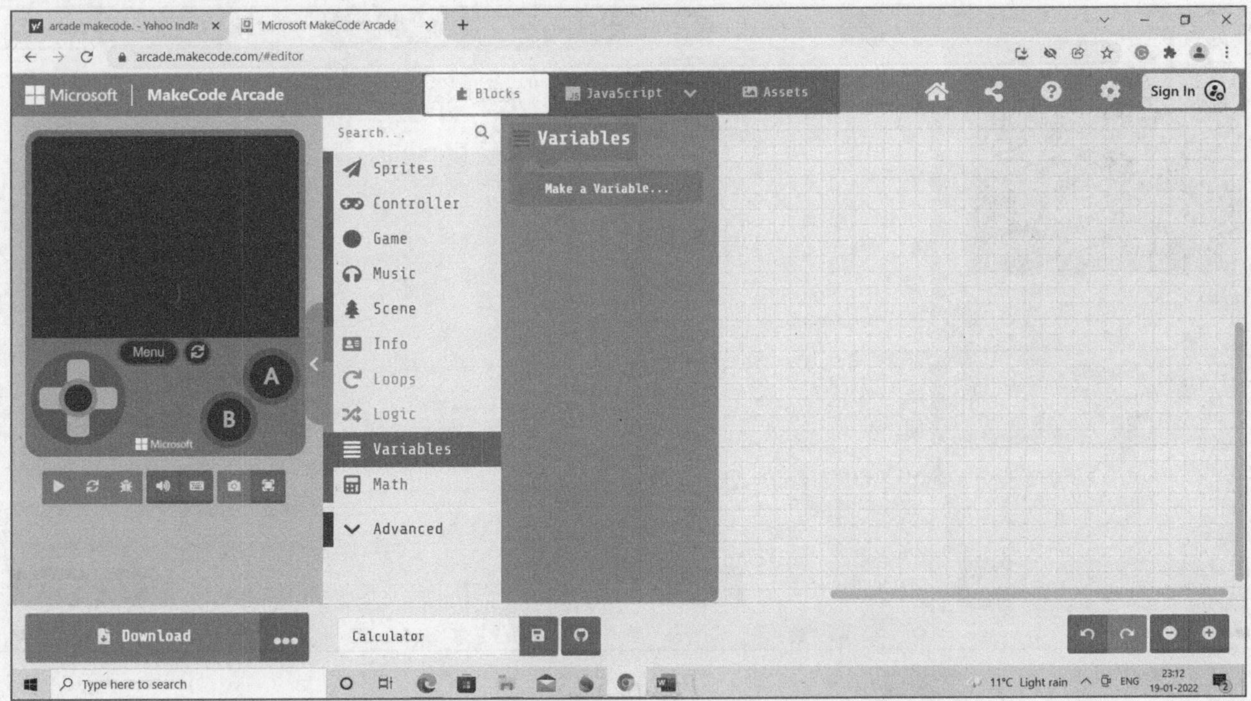

Figure 5.11

Step 2: Make a variable "a" and set its value to "30". Similarly, create another variable "b" and set its value to "9" as shown here.

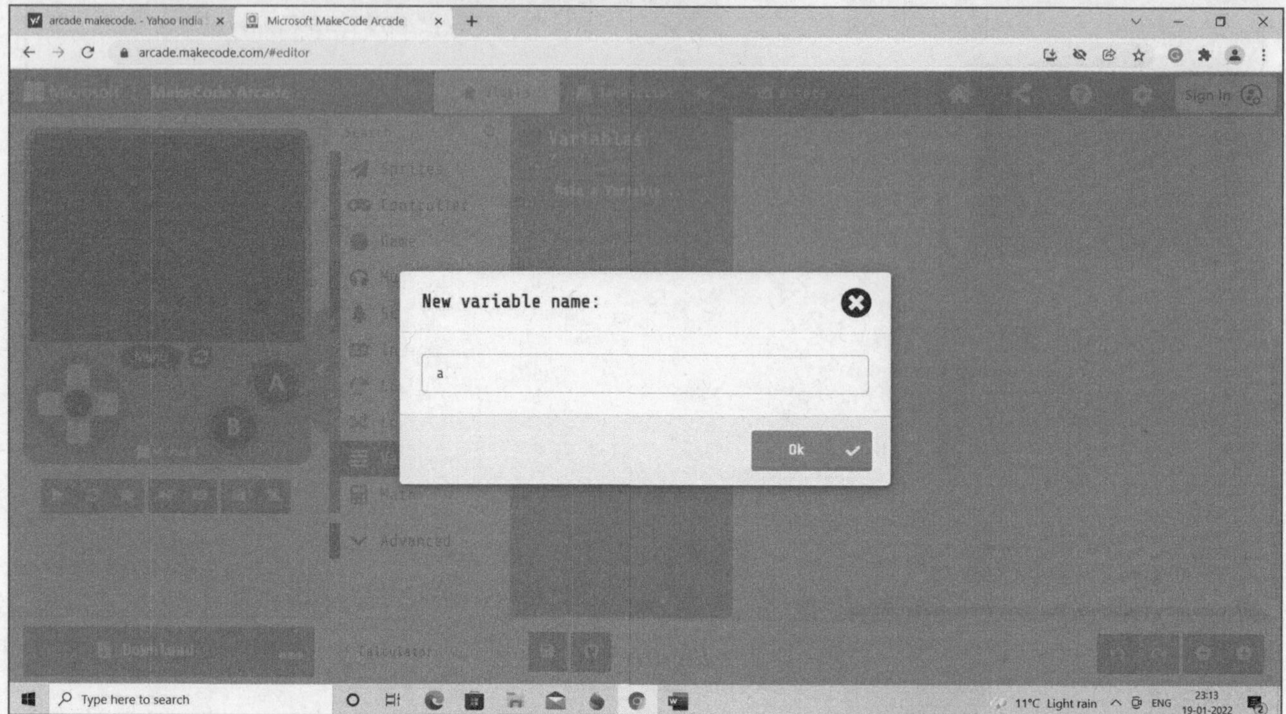

Figure 5.12

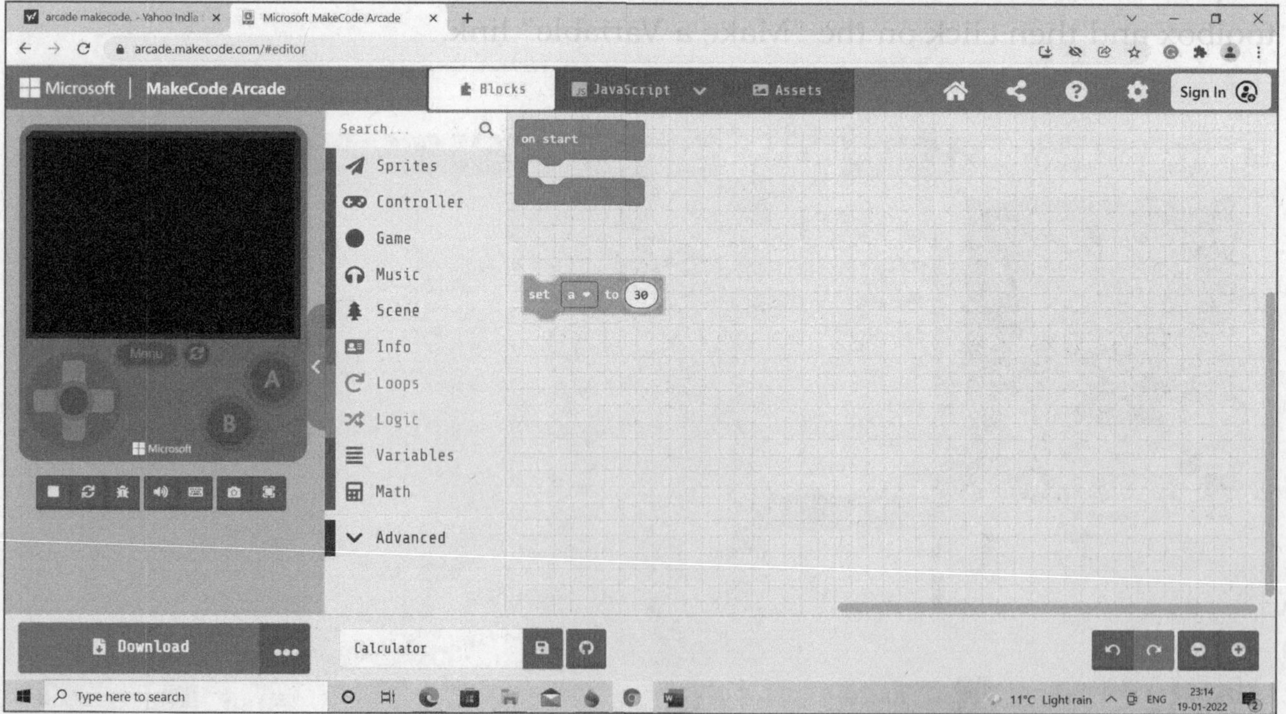

Figure 5.13

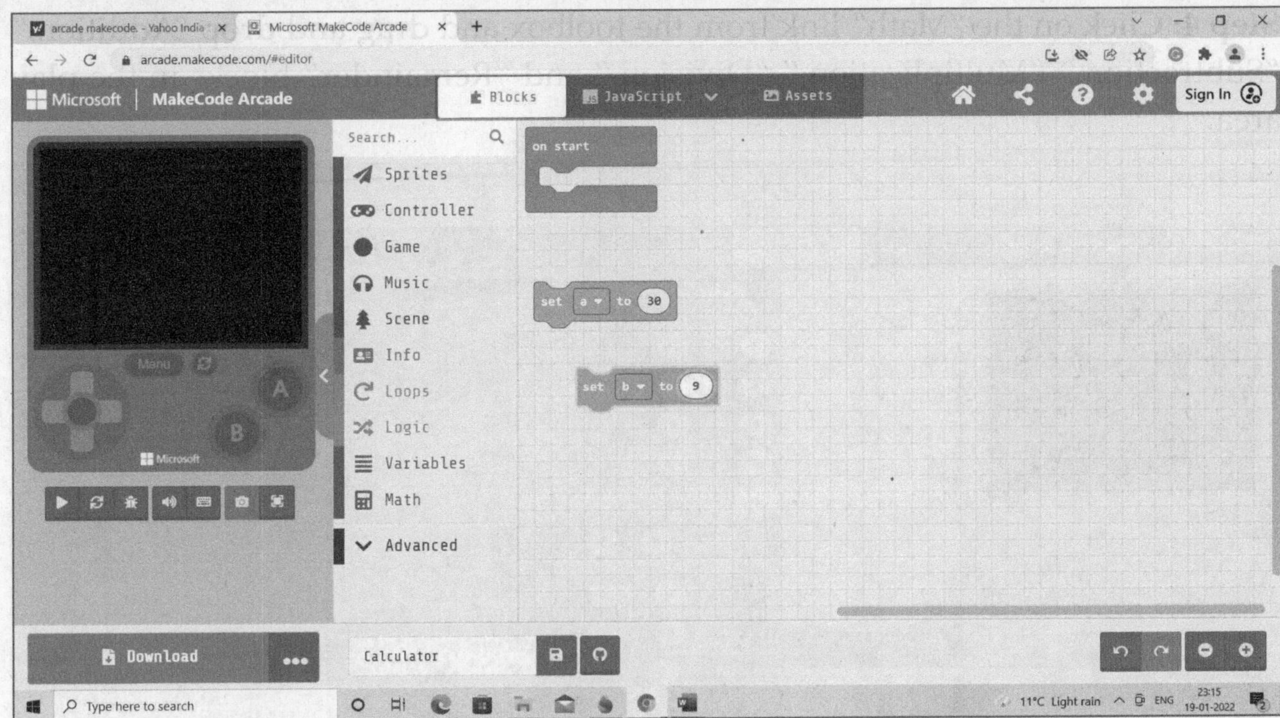

Figure 5.14

Step 3: Now, drag and drop blocks of both the variables in the "On start" block.

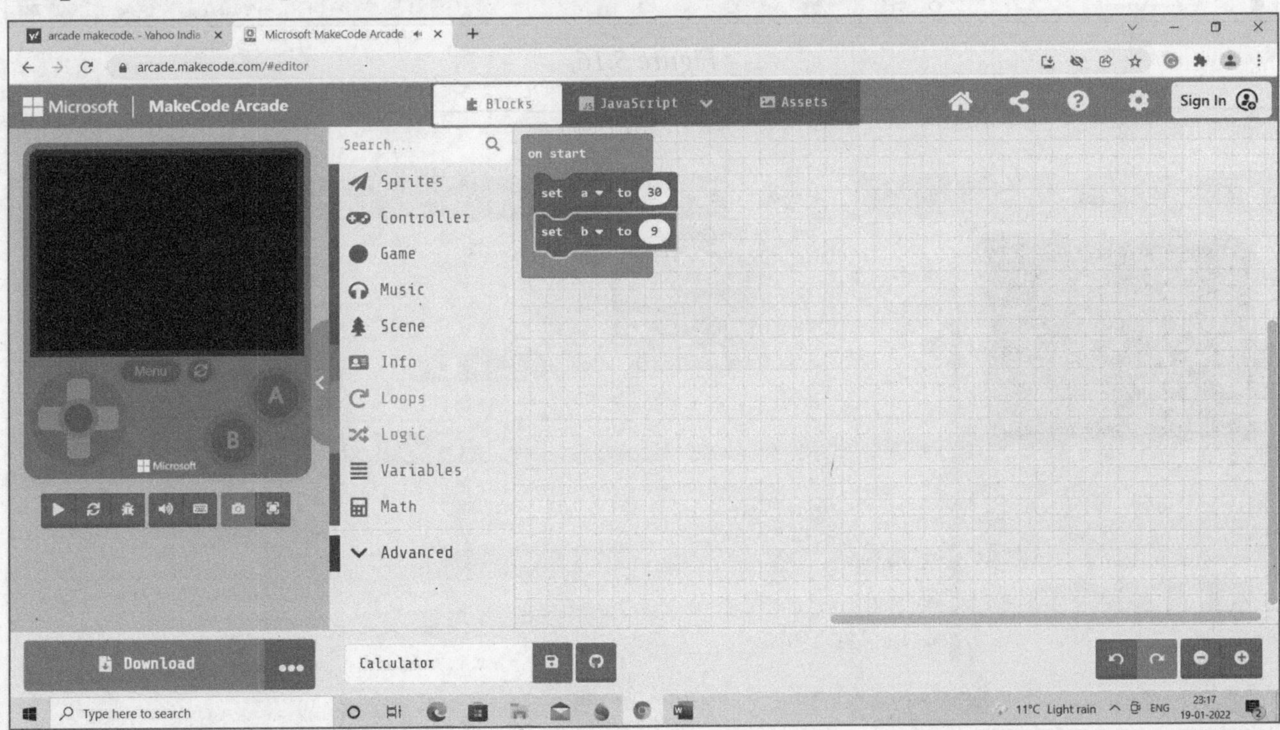

Figure 5.15

Step 4: Click on the "Math" link from the toolbox and drag and drop "Addition," "Subtraction," "Multiplication," "Division," and "Remainder" blocks in the play area.

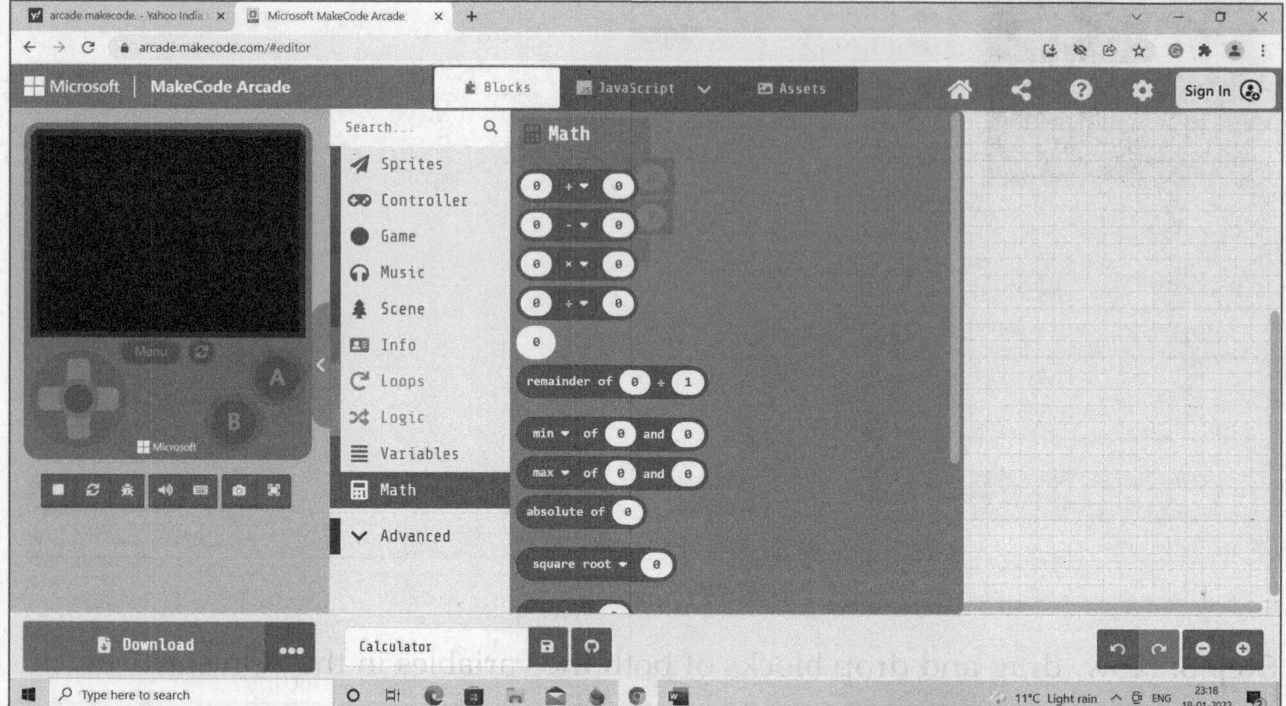

Figure 5.16,

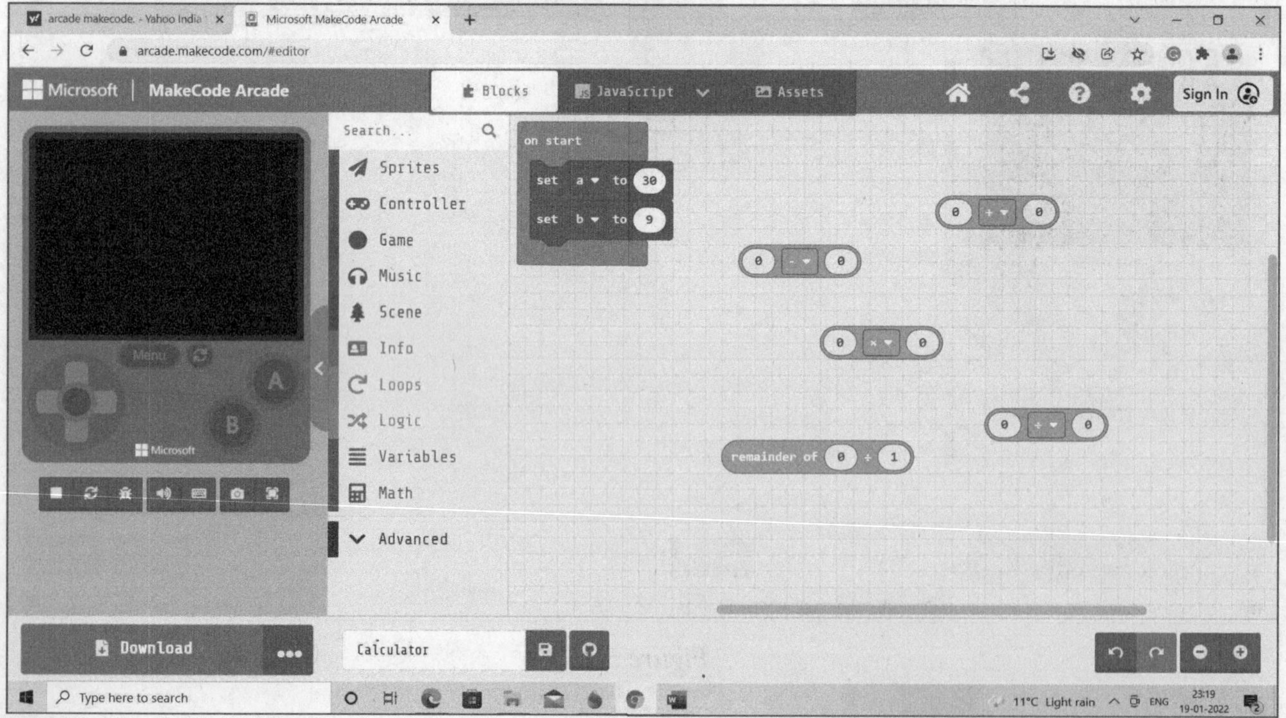

Figure 5.17

Step 5: Now, fix variables "a" and "b" in all the mathematical blocks placed in the play area.

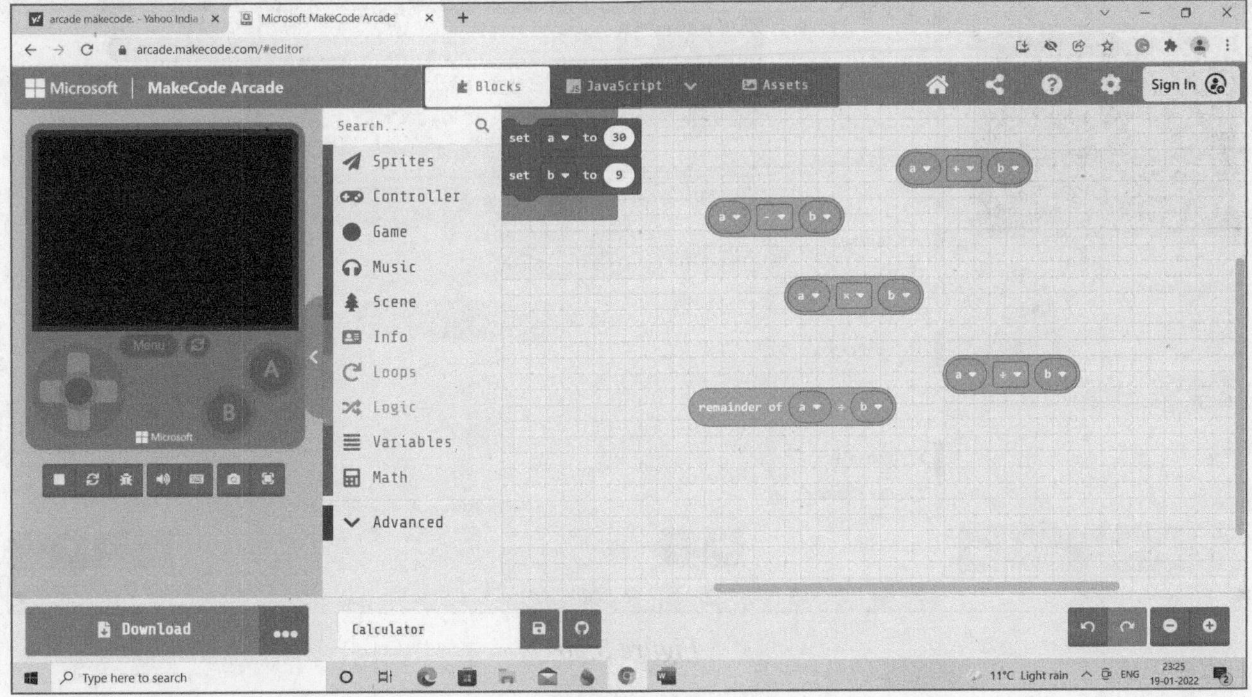

Figure 5.18

Step 6: Click on Advance to get "Text" link from the toolbox and then drag and drop the "Join" block to the play area.

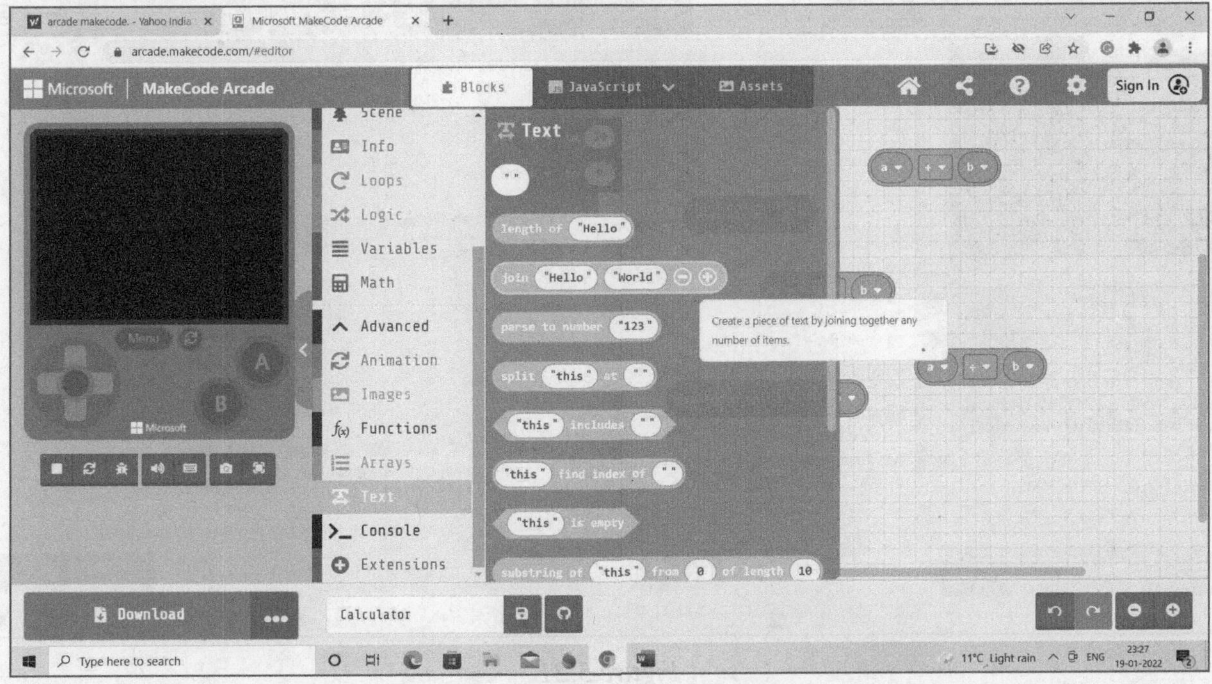

Figure 5.19

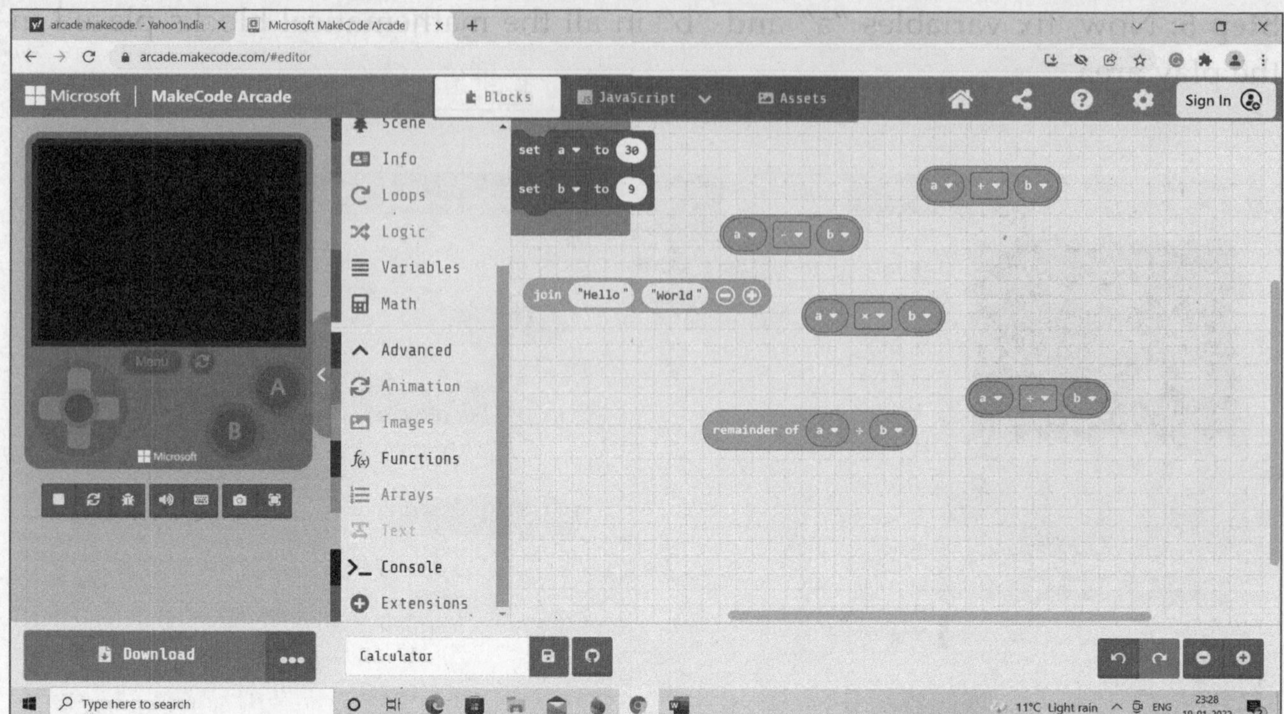

Figure 5.20

Step 7: In the "Join" block, rename the first text box to "Addition is" and attach the 'addition' block in the second text box as shown here.

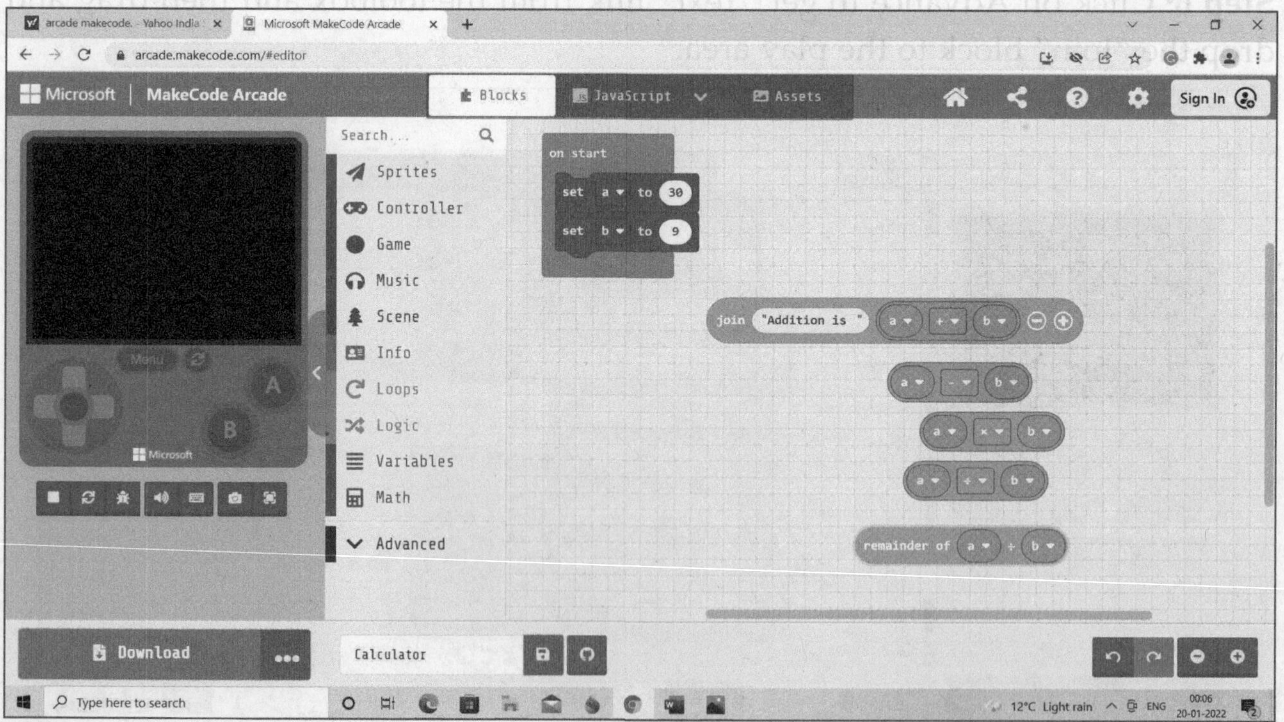

Figure 5.21

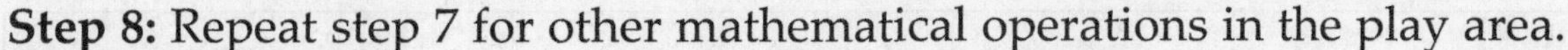

Step 8: Repeat step 7 for other mathematical operations in the play area.

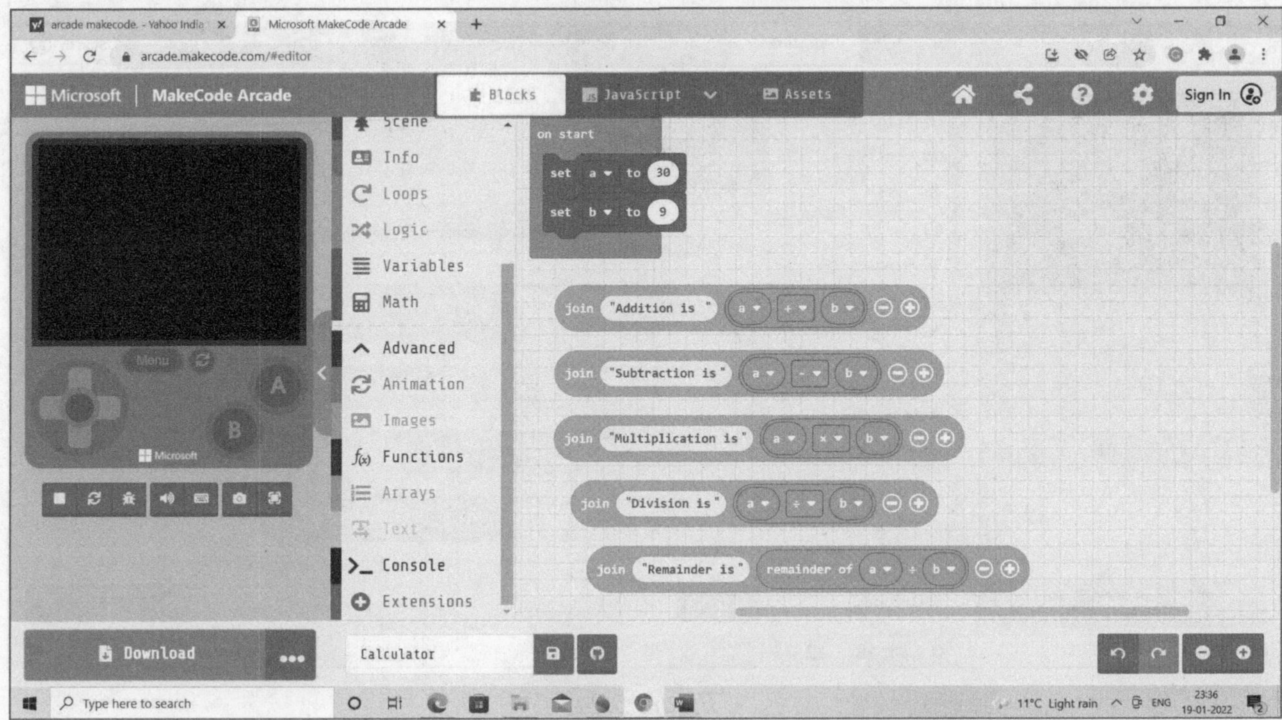

Figure 5.22

Step 9: Click on "Game" link from the toolbox and drag and drop the "Splash" block in the play area.

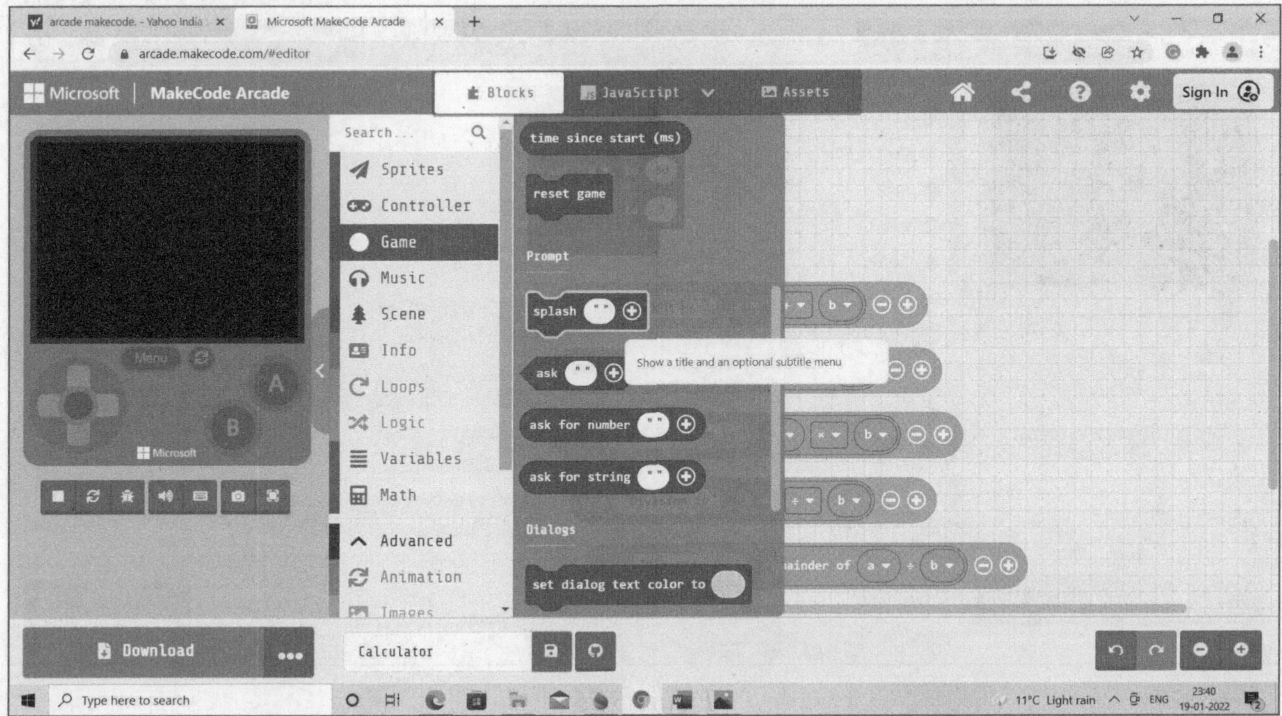

Figure 5.23

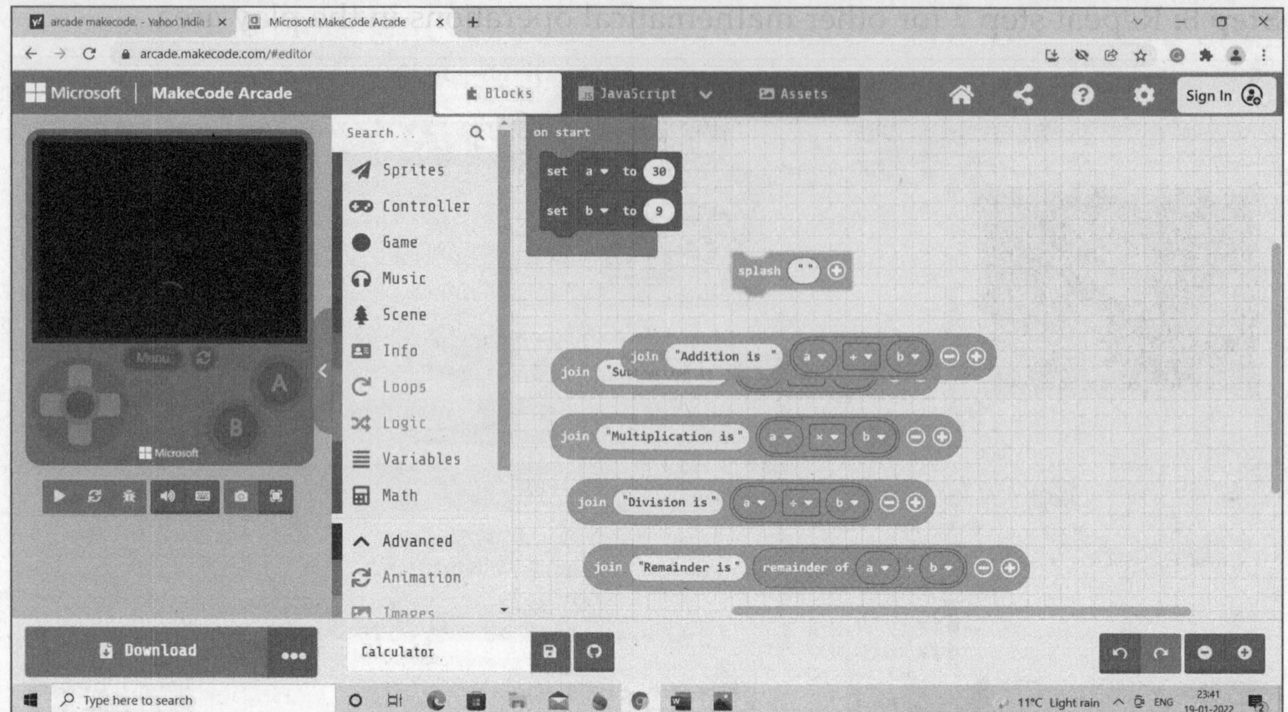

Figure 5.24

Step 10: Now, attach the 'Addition' block in the Splash block. Later, fix this block to the "On start" block as shown here.

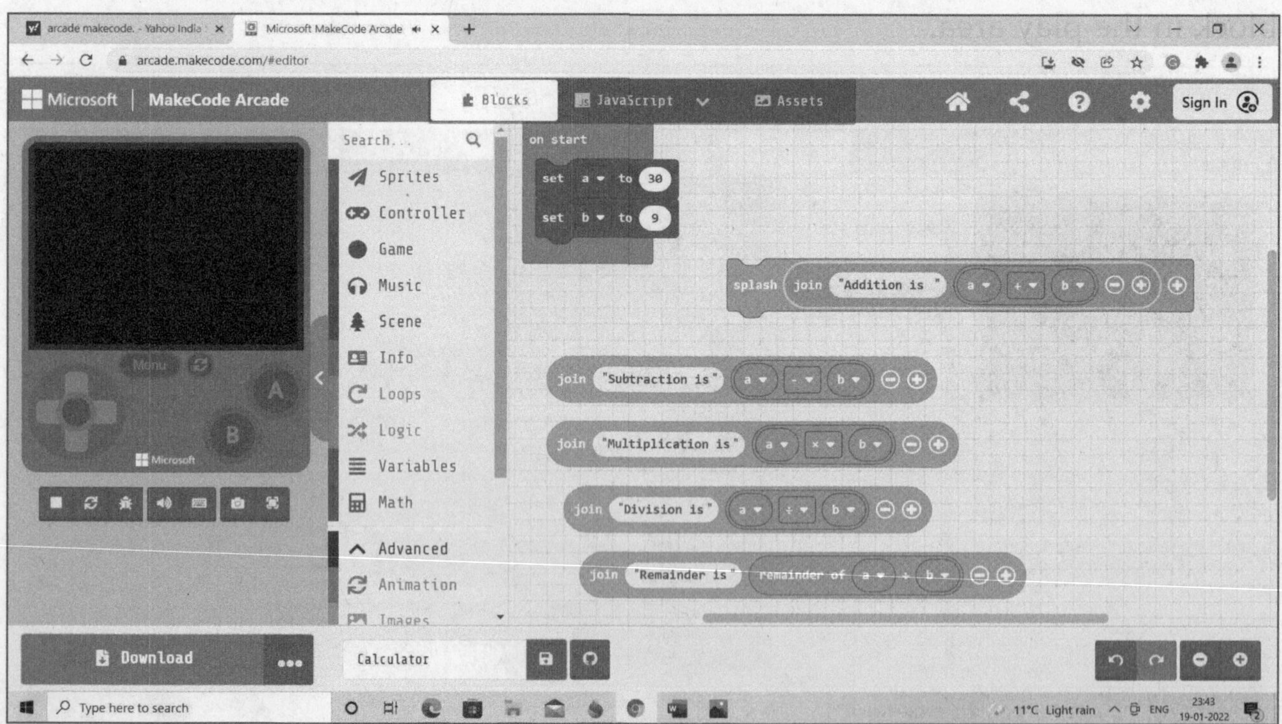

Figure 5.25

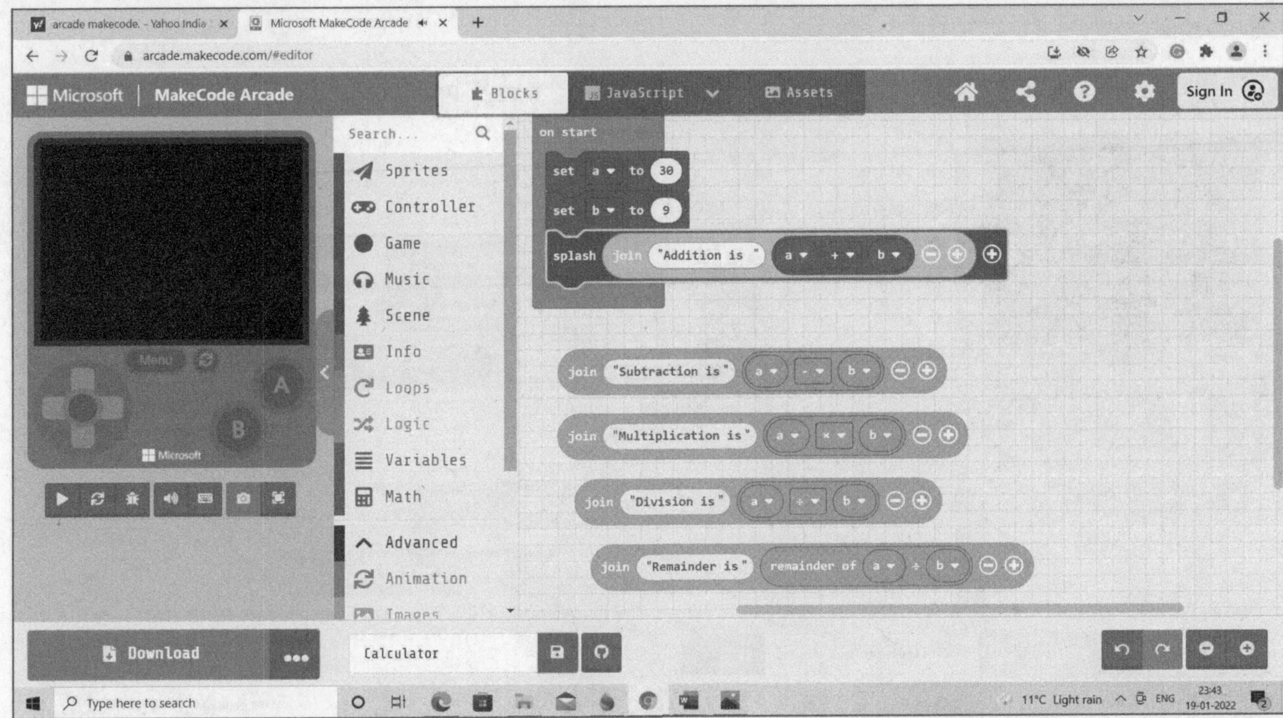

Figure 5.26

Step 11: Now, repeat step 10 for the rest of the mathematical operations as shown here.

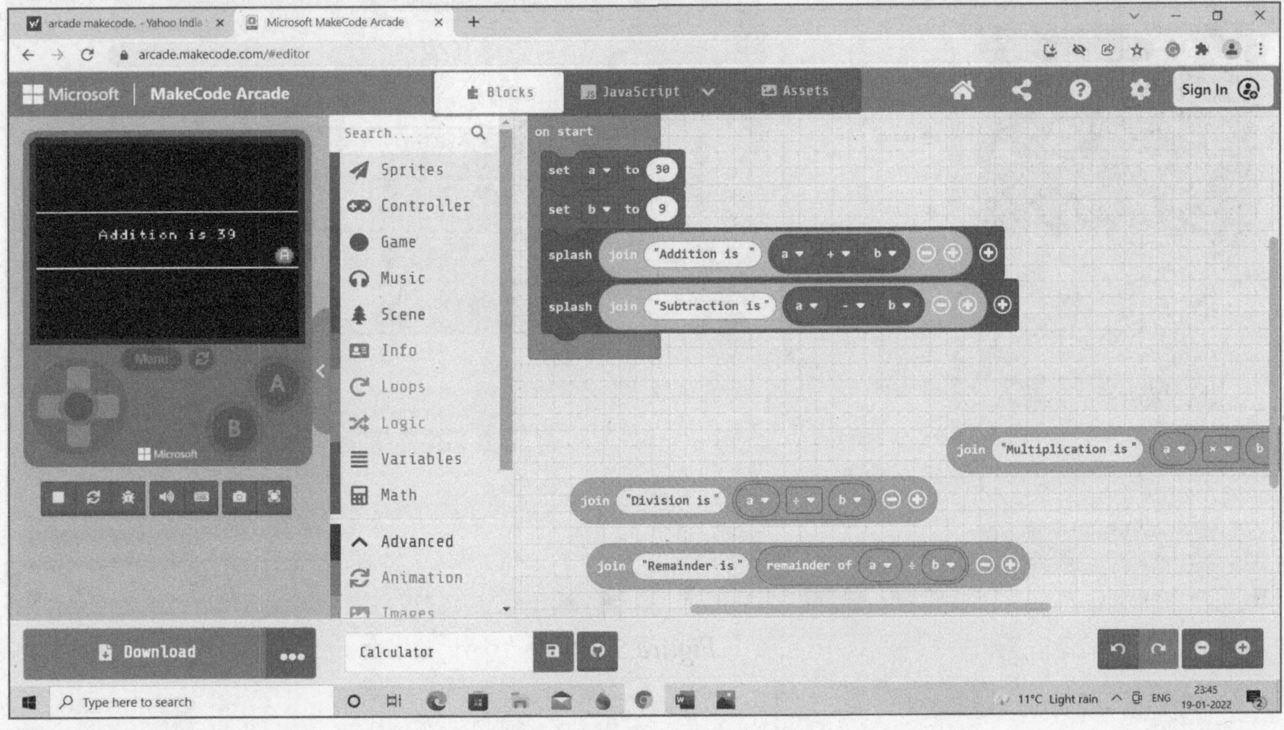

Figure 5.27

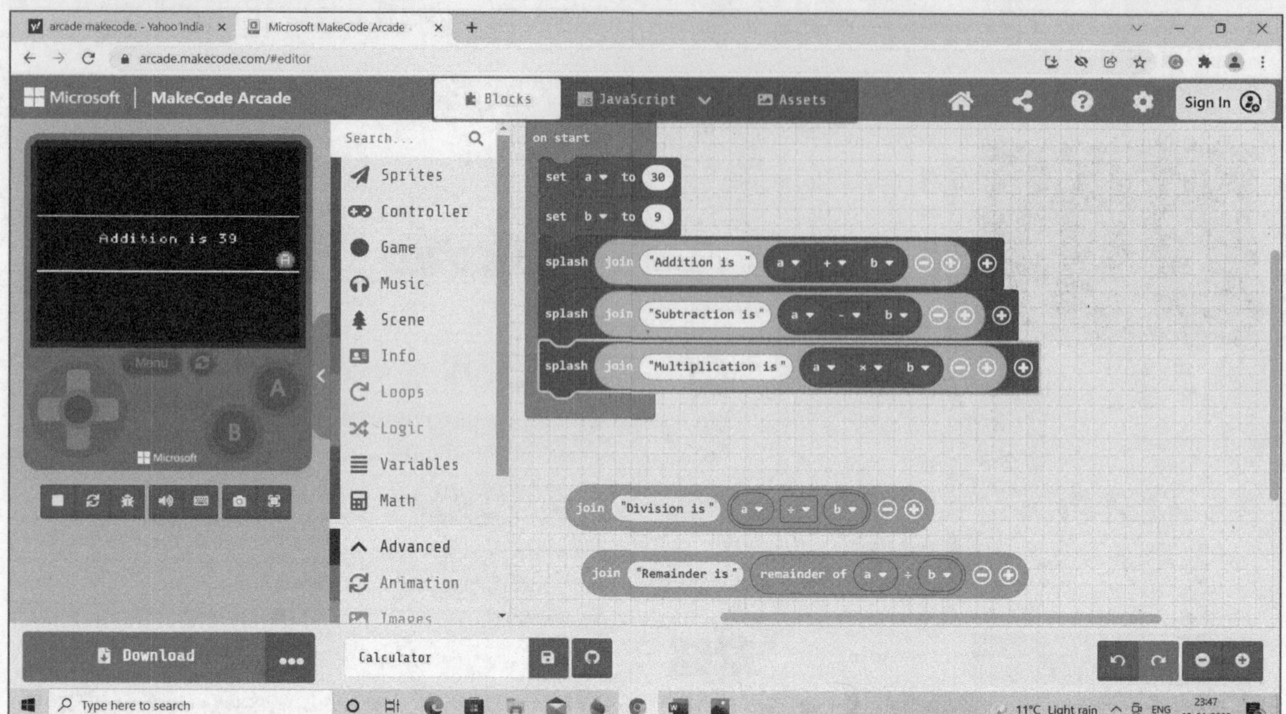

Figure 5.28

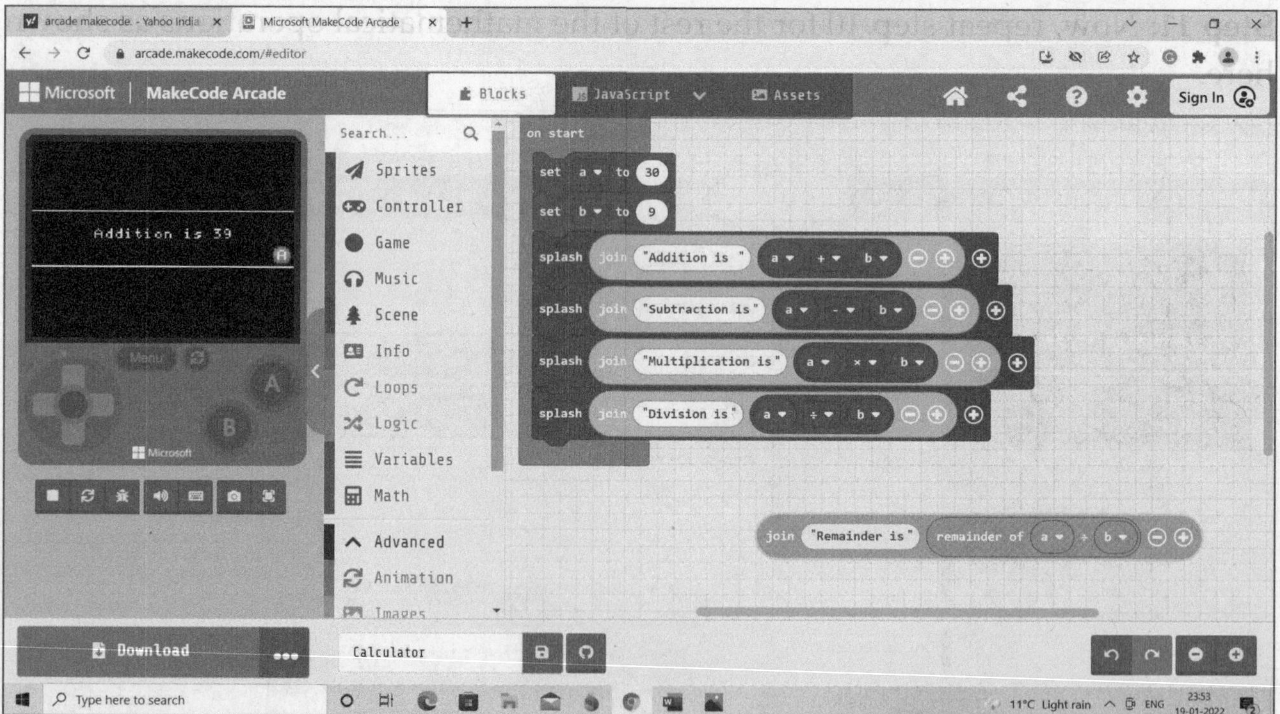

Figure 5.29

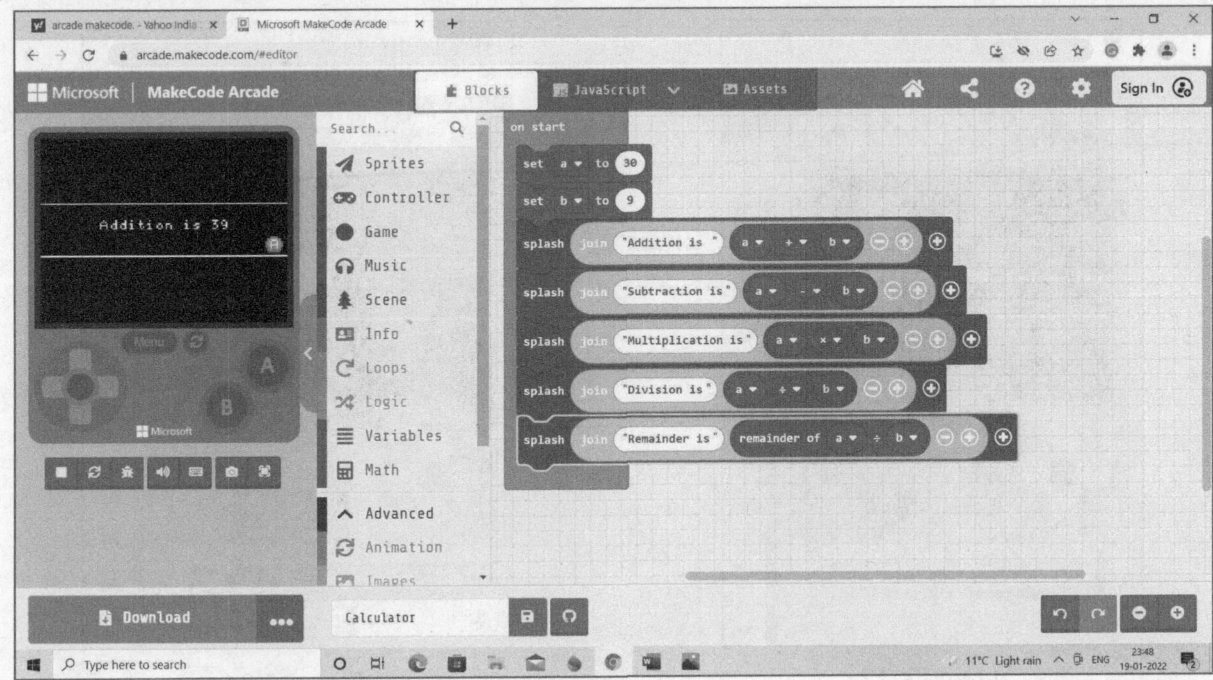
Figure 5.30

The addition of two variables is shown in the display area as 39. If we want to see the subtraction of two variables, click the "A" button below the display area, and the subtraction of two variables will be displayed in the display area. Similarly, on clicking "A" again, you will get multiplication of two variables; on clicking "A" again, you will get division output of two variables, and on clicking "A" once again, you will get remainder.

Figure 5.31

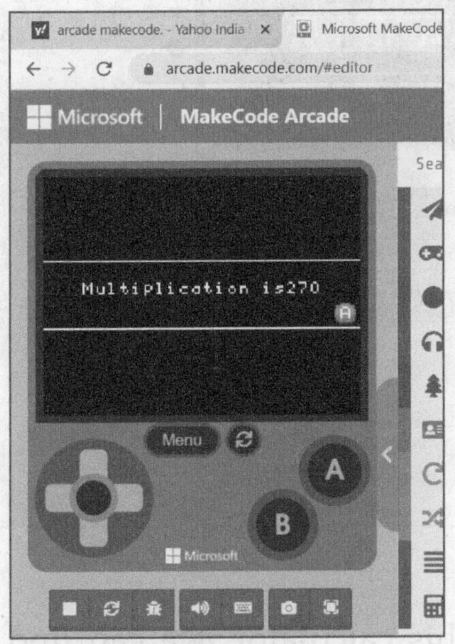

Figure 5.32

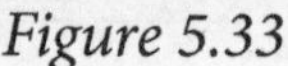

Figure 5.33

Figure 5.34

When we change the values of two variables (a=678, b=65), then the 'Addition' value will be changed to 743 as follows: (other mathematical operations for the changed variables may be seen after clicking the "A" button)

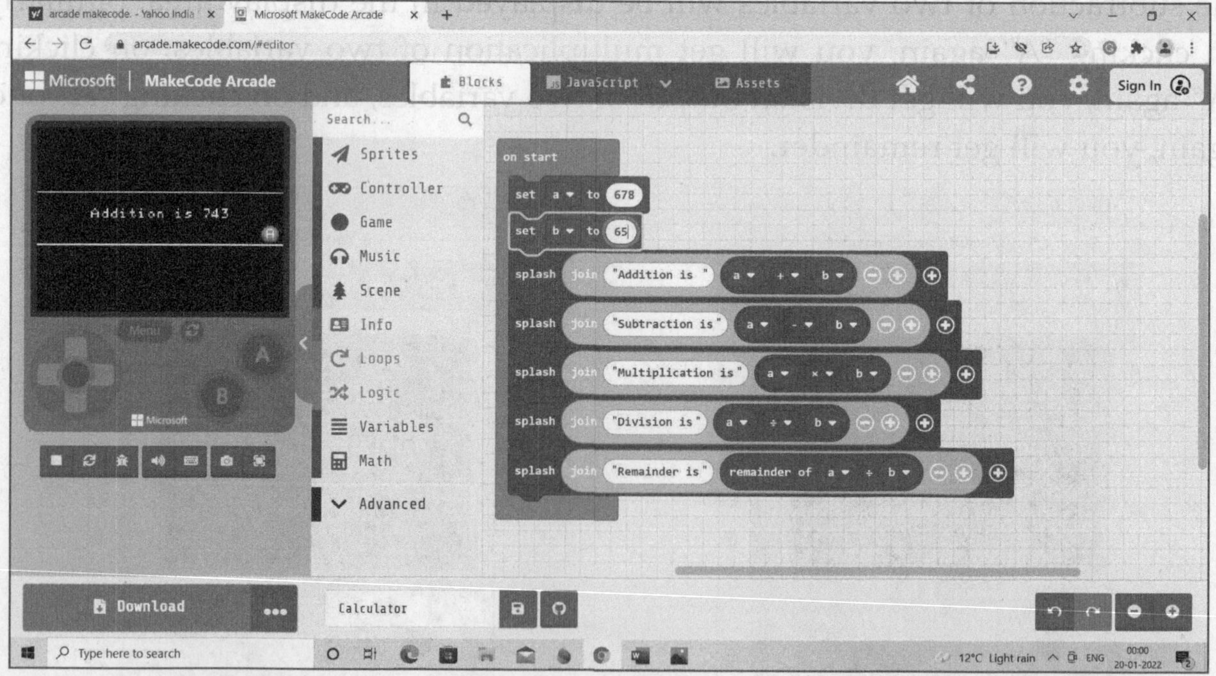

Figure 5.35

With this calculator, we can find out the mathematical operations by changing the values of two variables. Variables may be integers or floats.

For Your Information...

The above code for making the calculator in Python language will be as follows:

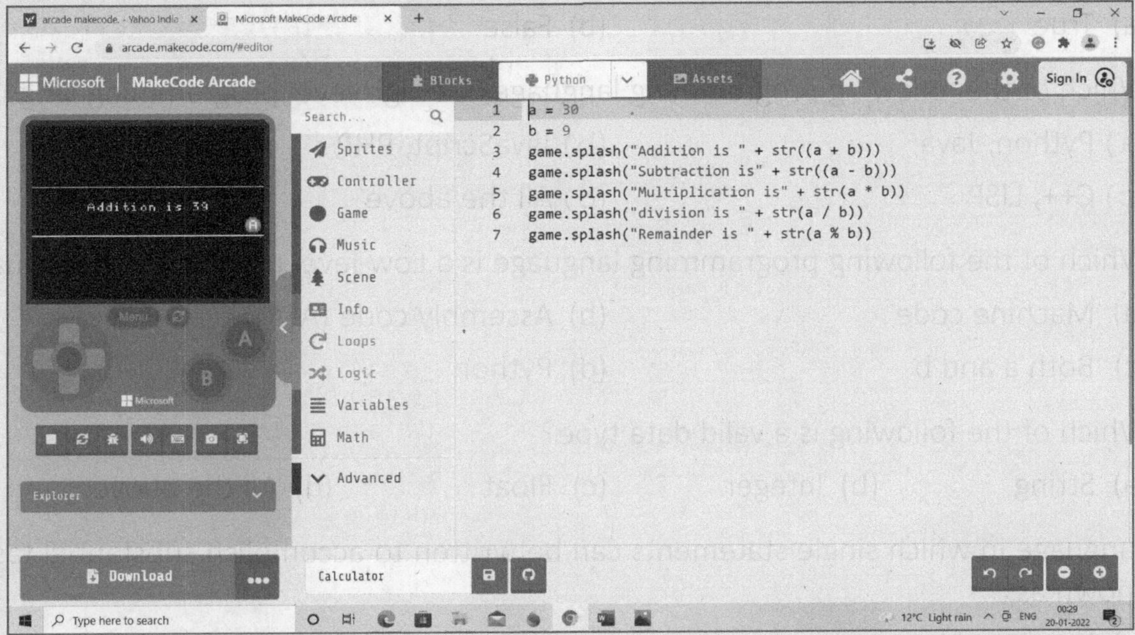

Figure 5.36

And the same code in Javascript will be as follows:

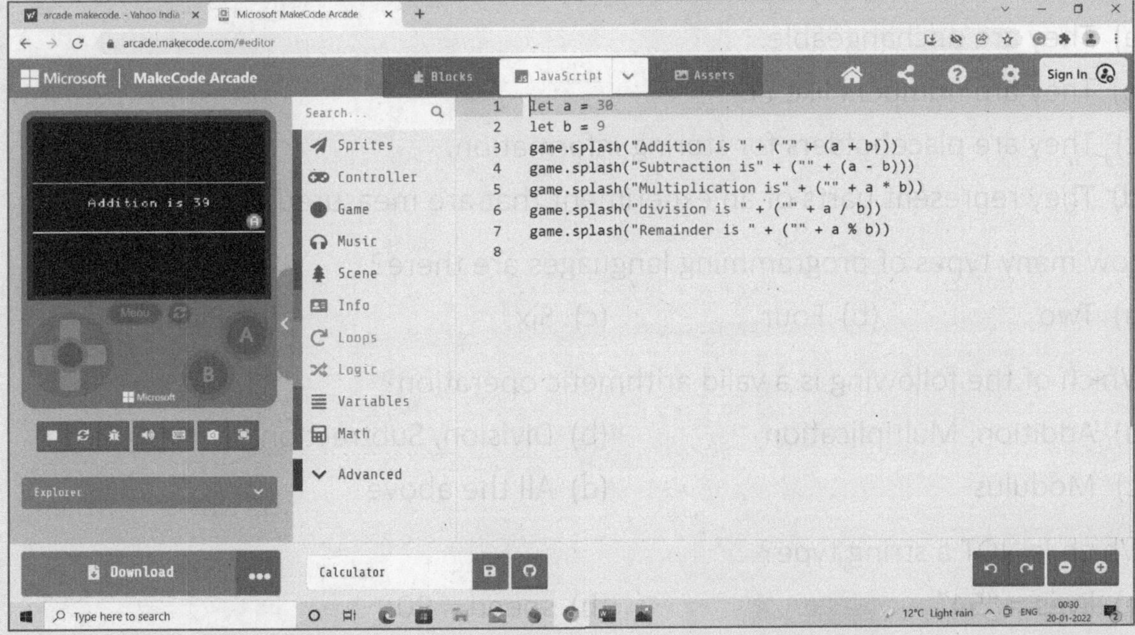

Figure 5.37

You will study the details of these coding languages in higher classes.

1. Low-level languages are not user-friendly.
   (a) True (b) False
2. Which of the following programming language is a high-level programming language?
   (a) Python, Java, (b) JavaScript, PHP,
   (c) C++, LISP (d) All the above
3. Which of the following programming language is a Low-level programming language?
   (a) Machine code (b) Assembly code (ASM)
   (c) Both a and b (d) Python
4. Which of the following is a valid data type?
   (a) String (b) Integer (c) Float (d) All the above
5. Language in which single statements can be written to accomplish substantial tasks is known as:
   (a) Low-Level Language (b) High-Level Language
   (c) Machine Language (d) Natural Language
6. In computer science, what are variables?
   (a) They are unchangeable.
   (b) They are numbers like Pi.
   (c) They are placeholders for storing information.
   (d) They represent parts of an experiment that are measured or tested.
7. How many types of programming languages are there?
   (a) Two (b) Four (c) Six (d) Eight
8. Which of the following is a valid arithmetic operation?
   (a) Addition, Multiplication (b) Division, Subtraction
   (c) Modulus (d) All the above
9. Which is NOT a string type?
   (a) lives = "54" (b) speed = 90
   (c) character = "Mrs." (d) vehicle = "Car"

10. Name the translator which is used to convert codes of assembly language into machine language.
    (a) Compiler (b) Assembler (c) Attempter (d) Debugger

ANSWERS									
1. (a)	2. (d)	3. (c)	4. (d)	5. (b)	6. (c)	7. (a)	8. (d)	9. (b)	10. (a)

SUMMARY

- A computer program may be defined as a set of instructions that are given to a computer to execute.
- A programming language is defined as a tool we use to write instructions for computers to follow.
- The different programming languages, like Lisp, Prolog, C++, Java, and Python, can be used for developing applications of AI.
- Python has become a widely used computer programming language nowadays.
- A programming language is a computer language that is used by programmers (developers) to communicate with computers.
- A programming language is a set of instructions written in any specific language (C, C++, Java, Python) to perform a specific task. A programming language is mainly used to develop desktop applications, websites, and mobile applications.
- Programming languages are broadly classified into two categories: high-level languages and low-level languages.
- A low-level programming language is a programming language that is made to be easily understood by the computer.
- Low-level programming languages include machine code (or Object code) and assembly language (ASM).
- The main advantage of assembly language is that it requires less memory and less execution time to execute a program.
- Low-level programming languages are difficult to learn, and they are time-consuming to code.
- Machine language/Machine code does not require a translator to convert the programs.
- A high-level programming language is made to help human programmers communicate easily to the computer.
- A high-level language is easy to read, write, and maintain.

- High-level programming language mainly includes Python, Java, JavaScript, PHP, C#, C++, Objective C, Cobol, Perl, Pascal, LISP, FORTRAN, etc.
- Python is an object-oriented programming language, and it was created by Guido Rossum in 1989.
- Python is a case-sensitive language that has interfaces to many OS systems and libraries and is extensible to C or C++.
- Syntax of a computer language is the set of rules to define the combinations of symbols.
- In any programming language, a variable can only store a value that is in a format. The various formats are called data types.
- Everything is regarded as an object in Python programming, and data types are actually classes, whereas variables are instances (object) of these classes.
- Integers are the whole numbers having + or – sign, like 1000,-56, 0, 17.
- When we combine a float variable and an integer variable in a mathematical calculation, the resulting answer will always be a float.
- We can do several arithmetic operations with floats and integers like addition, subtraction, multiplication, division, and modulus (Remainder).

PRACTICE TIME

(A) True/False Type Questions

1. If we wish to develop an AI application, then we have to know a programming language.
2. The different programming languages, like Lisp, Prolog, C++, Java, and Python, can be used for developing applications of AI.
3. Python is a low-level programming language.
4. A computer program is defined as a set of instructions that are given to a computer to execute.
5. The most popular programming languages include Java, Python,JavaScript, and C++.
6. Programming languages are broadly classified into two categories: high-level languages and low-level languages.
7. A high-level programming language is a programming language that is made to be easily understood by the computer.
8. Low-level programming languages include machine code (or Object code) and assembly language (ASM).

9. The main advantage of assembly language is that it requires less memory and less execution time to execute a program.

10. Low-level programming languages are easy to learn, and they are time-consuming to code.

ANSWERS					
1. T	2. T	3. F (High-level programming language)	4. T	5. T	6. T
7. F (Low-level)	8. T	9. T	10. F (difficult to learn)		

(B) Fill in the blanks

1. A ____________ language is defined as a tool we use to write instructions for computers to follow.

2. ____________ are used by programmers to store values.

3. ____________ is a case-sensitive language and has interfaces to many OS systems and libraries, and is extensible to C or C++.

4. ____________ are the whole numbers having + or – sign, like 1000, -56, 0, 17.

5. In any programming language, a variable can only store a value that is in a format. These various formats are called ____________.

6. ____________ is a built-in Python function that converts a number or a string to a float value and returns the result.

7. The main advantage of a ____________-level language is that it is easy to read, write, and maintain.

8. ____________ does not require any translator to convert the programs.

9. ____________-level programming language includes Python, Java, JavaScript, PHP, C#, C++, Objective C, Cobol, Perl, Pascal, LISP, FORTRAN, etc.

10. In ____________, the smallest value among the given unsorted elements of the array is selected in every step/pass and inserted to its appropriate position into the array.

ANSWERS			
1. programming	2. Variables	3. Python	4. Integers
5. data types	6. Float	7. high	
8. Machine language/Machine code		9. High	10. selection sort

(C) Very Short Answers Questions

1. Define variables.

2. Enlist two high-level programming languages.

3. Name a low-level programming language.
4. What do you mean by syntax?
5. Define float.

(D) Short Answer Questions

1. Why are variables used in programming?
2. Name different Mathematical Operations that we can perform on variables in Python.
3. Differentiate between High Level and Low-Level Languages in Computers.
4. Explain different data types used in Python.
5. Mention six important programming languages and classify them into high-level programming languages and low-level programming languages.

(E) High Order Thinking Skill Questions (HOTS)

1. Draw a flowchart to explain the flow of selection sort technique in programming.
2. Write an algorithm to sort the below list in descending order using Selection Sort Technique: [20, 12, 74, 67, 27].

(F) Projects

Problem Statement: Create a program in Arcade to perform Modulus operation on two variables.

REFERENCES / FURTHER READINGS

- Microsoft MakeCode Arcade: https://arcade.makecode.com
- Microsoft MakeCode for Minecraft: https://minecraft.makecode.com
- Minecraft Computer Science Subject Kit: https://education.minecraft.net/class-resources/computer-science-subject-kit
- Code of Ethics: https://www.acm.org/code-of-ethics
- CSPathsala: https://cspathshala.org
- https://www.piqsels.com/en/public-domain-photo-sphsw/download

Annexure 1
Coding Terminology

Abstraction: A simplified representation of something more complex.

Accessibility: The design of products, devices, services, or environments taking into consideration the ability for all users to access, including people who experience disabilities or those who are limited by older or slower technology.

Algorithm: A set of instructions that are followed to solve a problem.

Arithmetic operators: Operators that are essential in almost every application, especially in games.

Assignment operators: Operators that combine variable assignments with arithmetic operators.

Augmented reality (AR): An interactive experience where digital objects are placed in a real-world environment in real time.

Binary alphabet: The two options used in your binary code.

Binary numbers: A computer's way to represent information using only 1's and 0's.

Bit: The individual 1's and 0's in binary are called bits.

Block-based programming language: Any programming language that lets users create programs by manipulating "blocks" or graphical programming elements, rather than writing code using text.

Blockly: The visual programming language used in Code.org's online learning system for K-5 students.

Bug: An error in a program that prevents the program from running as expected.

Byte: The most common fundamental unit of digital data. A single byte is 8 bits-worth of data.

C++: A low-level versatile programming language.

Camel case: A system in which the first word of the name of a variable is lowercase and each new word after that is capitalized.

Code: The language that programmers create and use to tell a computer what to do.

Coding languages: Languages that computer can understand.

Coding: A set of instructions for computers to follow to complete a task.

Command: An instruction for the computer. Many commands put together make up algorithms and computer programs.

Computational thinking: Modifying a problem in such a way that it can be modeled or solved using a computer or machine.

Computer program: A group of instructions given to a computer to be processed.

Conditional statements: Statements that evaluate to true or false. Conditional statements run only under certain conditions.

Crowdsourcing: Getting help from a large group of people to finish something faster.

Cyberbullying: Doing something on the internet, usually again and again, to make another personal feel angry, sad, or scared.

Data: Information. Often, quantities, characters, or symbols that are the inputs and outputs of computer programs.

Debugging: Finding and fixing problems in an algorithm or program.

Decompose: Break a problem down into smaller pieces.

Digital citizen: Someone who acts safely, responsibly, and respectfully online.

Digital footprint: The information about someone on the Internet.

Double-click: Press the mouse button very quickly two times.

Drag: Click the mouse button and hold as the user move the mouse pointer to a new location.

Drop: Release the mouse button to "let go" of an item that the user was dragging.

Else statements: The statements are used to do something else when the condition in the if statement isn't true.

For loops: Loops that allow you to run a block of code repeatedly to run a block of code for a set number of times.

Function call: The piece of code that you add to a program to indicate that the program should run the code inside a function at a certain time.

Function: A block of code that can be referenced by name to run the code it contains.

If statement: A statement that runs a block of code based on whether or not a condition is true.

Input: A way to give information to a computer.

Integrated Development Environment: A software where you type your code and run your programs for making coding simpler.

Internet: A group of computers and servers that are connected to each other.

IP address: A number assigned to any item that is connected to the Internet.

Iteration: A repetitive action or command typically created with programming loops.

Java: A powerful multi-platform programming language.

Linux: An open-source operating system designed to run on multiple types of devices, like laptops, phones, tablets, robots, and many others.

Loop: The action of doing something over and over again. Loops check a condition and then run a code block.

Online: Connected to the Internet.

Output: A way to get information out of a computer.

Packets: Small chunks of information that have been carefully formed from larger chunks of information.

Parameter: An extra piece of information passed to a function to customize it for a specific need.

Pattern matching: Finding similarities between things.

Pixel: Short for "picture element", the fundamental unit of a digital image, typically a tiny square or dot that contains a single point of colour of a larger image.

Program: An algorithm that has been coded into something that can be run by a machine.

Programming: The art of creating a program.

Run program: Cause the computer to execute the commands you've written in your program.

Search engine: A program that searches for and identifies items in a database that correspond to keywords or characters specified by the user, used especially for finding particular sites on the World Wide Web.

Servers: Computers that exist only to provide things to others.

Toolbox: The tall grey bar in the middle section of any online learning system that contains all of the commands the user can use to write the program.

URL (universal resource locator): An easy-to-remember address for calling a web page .

Username: A name you make up so that you can see or do things on a website, sometimes called a "screen name."

Variable: A placeholder for a piece of information that can change.

***Virtual* Reality:** An interactive experience where digital objects creates a completely artificial environment

Website: A collection of interlinked web pages on the World Wide Web.

While loop: A loop that continues to repeat while a condition is true.

Wi-Fi: A wireless method of sending information using radio waves.

Workspace: The white area on the right side of any online learning system where the user drag and drop commands to build the program.

Annexure 2
Some World Famous Coder

Dennis MacAlistair Ritchie,
Creator of "C" programming language and co-creator of the UNIX operating system

Linus Torvlds,
The chief architect of the Linux kernel

Alan Cooper,
Developer of Visual Basics

Alan Kay,
Developer OOP (Object-Oriented Programming)

Bjarne Stroustrup,
Developer of C++

Brendan Eich,
Developer of Java Script

Tim Berners-Lee,
Creator of World Wide Web (www)

Brian Kernighan,
The co-creator and developer of UNIX and co-author of the AWK and AMPL programming languages.

Guido van Rossum,
Creator of Python Language

John Backus,
Inventor of Fortran

James Gosling,
Developer of Java

Robin Milner,
Inventor of Machine Learning